W9-CTP-411

Praise for *Guide to Western Canada* . . .

"Whether you are planning a visit to Vancouver, Victoria, Calgary, Edmonton, Regina, Saskatoon, or Winnipeg or an adventure to a remote region, this guide is one to take along."
                                        —*Unique & Exotic Travel Report*

"Provides all the insight a traveler unfamiliar with Western Canada needs to know to plan an unforgettable trip."
                                        —*The Blade,* Toledo, Ohio

"A pleasantly written, straightforward manual."
                                        —*Booklist ALA*

"There are few, if any, aspects of travel to Western Canada that are not covered in this guide. This, combined with its reasonable price, is likely to make it the standard guide to travel in Western Canada."
                                        —*American Reference Book Association*

"A thorough work . . . for the traveler. History, geography, and ecology, as well as the more expected travel guide information such as hotels, etc., are included."
                                        —*KLIATT Paperback Book Guides*

Help Us Keep This Guide Up to Date

Every effort has been made by the author and editors to make this guide as accurate and useful as possible. However, many things can change after a guide is published—establishments close, phone numbers change, hiking trails are rerouted, facilities come under new management, etc.

We would love to hear from you concerning your experiences with this guide and how you feel it could be made better and be kept up to date. While we may not be able to respond to all comments and suggestions, we'll take them to heart and we'll also make certain to share them with the author. Please send your comments and suggestions to the following address:

The Globe Pequot Press
Reader Response/Editorial Department
P.O. Box 833
Old Saybrook, CT 06475

Or you may e-mail us at:

editorial@globe-pequot.com

Thanks for your input, and happy travels!

Guide to
Western Canada
Fifth Edition

by
Frederick Pratson

edited by
Raymond Chatelin

Old Saybrook, Connecticut

Although the authors have received and used information and photographs from many different sources, *this guide is not an official publication of any company, association, or government agency mentioned or described herein.* This guide has been independently researched and written by the authors and independently produced and marketed by the publisher. Within this guide, reference is made to a number of attractions, rides, systems, components, entities, products, fictional and animal characters, processes, and the like that are protected by copyrights and trademarks, both registered and pending, used by particular companies, attractions, and entertainments that own them. No attempt has been made by the authors and the publisher of this guide to infringe these and other copyrights and trademarks. Every effort has been made to present this trademarked and copyrighted material in those contexts to which they legally and properly belong and to no other.

Every effort has been made to make the material contained in this guide current and accurate. The authors and the publisher are responsible neither for inadvertent errors or material that becomes obsolete due to circumstances beyond their control nor for changes made by others that are either unknown or not communicated to the authors and publisher before publication.

Copyright © 1987, 1990 by Frederick Pratson
Copyright © 1993, 1996, 1998 by The Globe Pequot Press

Library of Congress Cataloging-in-Publication Data
Pratson, Frederick John.
    Guide to western Canada/by Frederick Pratson; edited by Raymond Chatelin.—5th ed.
        p.   cm.
    Includes index.
    ISBN 0-7627-0182-X
    1. Canada, Western—Guidebooks.   I. Chatelin, Raymond. II. Title.
F1060.4.P74   1998
917.1204'3—dc21   97-49599
                                                                              CIP

Photographs courtesy of the tourism services of Alberta, British Columbia, Manitoba, the Northwest Territories, Saskatchewan, and the Yukon and of the federal tourism-promotion department of the government of Canada.

Photo page 199 © Mel Buschert, courtesy Calgary Convention and Visitors Bureau.

Manufactured in the United States of America
Fifth Edition/First Printing

Contents

How to Use This Guide vi

1. The Special Allure of Western Canada 1
2. General Information 14
3. Canada for Non-Canadians 36
4. Touring Spectacular British Columbia 53
5. Vancouver: Camelot by the Pacific 92
6. Victoria: England by the Pacific 141
7. Touring Alberta and the Canadian Rockies 184
8. Touring Saskatchewan 242
9. Touring Manitoba 278
10. Exploring the Yukon and
    the Northwest Territories 303

Index 336

Maps

Western Canada 2–3
British Columbia 56
Metro Vancouver 102
Downtown Vancouver 103
Metro Victoria 150
Alberta 186
Metro Calgary 201
Metro Edmonton 233
Saskatchewan 243
Manitoba 279
Metro Winnipeg 290
The Yukon and the Northwest Territories 304

How to Use This Guide

Chapter 1 of this guide tells why Western Canada is a special region of North America for visitors. It provides some basic information on history, geography, weather, and other general aspects of the region that will help you better appreciate Western Canada.

Chapter 2 provides general information for all travelers to Western Canada—the nuts and bolts of how to get there, sources of information, and so on. Chapter 3 will orient non-Canadians to Canada in historical terms as well as to practical concerns such as customs regulations.

Chapters 4 through 10 describe touring the four provinces and two territories of Western Canada, focusing on major cities and what they offer and on the national parks of this region. A great deal of specific information in these chapters concerns attractions, accommodations, dining, transportation, sports, shopping, and entertainment. If you require more precise information than is contained in this guide, refer to the lists of provincial government tourism agencies and how to contact them; most have toll-free telephone numbers. Although this guide is perhaps a bit more comprehensive than others, it is not an encyclopedia for travelers. All the listed provincial government tourism agencies will provide the information you need free of charge, either over the phone or through the mail. They will also send you maps and brochures free of charge. If you use this guide in conjunction with material provided by these agencies, you will have all the information you need.

This guide has been designed for easy use both while you are planning your trip and while you are en route. It is also a handy source of good ideas for future vacations in Western Canada. For those who have visited this part of Canada before or for Canadians living in other parts of Canada, some information may seem familiar. For others living outside the country or who have not experienced this wonderful part of the world, it will be fresh and, we hope, intriguing. The region is so vast that you cannot visit it all on one trip, unless you have unlimited time, and its allure is so powerful that you will want to come back many times.

CHAPTER 1

The Special Allure of Western Canada

To say that Western Canada is one of the most magnificent regions in North America is not a trite superlative but an understatement. Within this vast region are some of the highest mountains on the North American continent; sprawling glaciers and giant trees; scores of wild rivers and thousands of unnamed lakes; seacoasts, richly described in Indian legend; sprawling prairies thick with golden wheat; and the mysterious Arctic region, itself inhabited by the "first people" of the Western Hemisphere. One will also find cosmopolitan cities offering the best of both the modern world and quaint towns that bespeak bygone times and values; major expositions and international sports events, ethnic festivals, and authentic rodeos; and magnificent resorts and charming inns. In Western Canada you can go helicopter skiing, white-water rafting, and trail riding; play golf surrounded by the Rocky Mountains; canoe, sailboard, hunt, and fish; photograph the beauty all around you; hike or camp; ride on top of a glacier; attend plays, operas, and symphonies; stay at some of the finest hotels in the world and dine at superior gourmet restaurants; see unusual exhibits of art and science; and thrill to the sight of orcas (killer whales), eagles, bears, moose, caribou, elk, and mountain sheep. Western Canada is an untamed wilderness that also offers the utmost in human civilization.

Although many travelers might have some knowledge of Western Canada, if only through brushes with it in geography lessons, it

ALASKA

YUKON

NORTHWEST
TERRITORIES
(WESTERN
ARCTIC)

Kluane
National Park

Whitehorse
Marsh Lake

Nahanni
National Park

Muncho Lake
Provincial Park

BRITISH
COLUMBIA

AL

Pacific Ocean

W.A.C. Bennett Dam

Inside Passage

Rocky Mounta
Parks

N

Monashees
and Selkirks

Lake Lou

Calgary

Fraser and
Thompson Canyons

Vancouver

Pacific Rim
National Park

Victoria

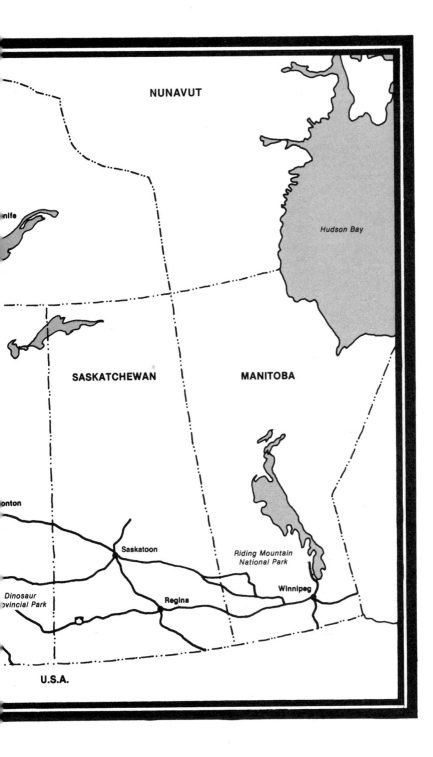

NUNAVUT

Hudson Bay

nife

SASKATCHEWAN

MANITOBA

onton

Saskatoon

Riding Mountain
National Park

Dinosaur
ovincial Park

Regina

Winnipeg

U.S.A.

was not until 1986, with the promotion of the Expo in Vancouver, that people began to consider it a prime destination for their vacations. Expo, with its barrage of television and print advertising from Canadian tourism agencies, brought people to Western Canada in large numbers. When they returned home, raving about their fabulous Western Canada experiences, a growing trend was set in motion. Today the great crowds brought into the region by the World's Fair in Vancouver have thinned out and there is a calmer pace to all aspects of travel in Western Canada. The best of the region remains. Its natural attributes are as awesome as ever. Its cities, such as Vancouver and Calgary, are even better and more exciting than before. And the proud people of Western Canada, representing every ethnic and racial group on earth, are eager to make new friends—warmly welcoming you and your family to their promised land.

Geography

Western Canada forms its southern border with the United States at the forty-ninth parallel. The southeastern section of Vancouver Island, facing the Pacific Ocean, with the capital city of Victoria at its tip, dips below the forty-ninth parallel and nears the forty-eighth. This section of Vancouver Island is in the area of the Strait of Juan de Fuca and the San Juan Islands, and it is pointed toward Seattle, Washington. Along the forty-ninth parallel, from west to east, are the provinces of British Columbia, Alberta, Saskatchewan, and Manitoba. South of the border, from west to east, are the states of Washington, Idaho, Montana, North Dakota, and Minnesota. To the north of British Columbia is the Yukon Territory, which borders eastern Alaska and the western Northwest Territories. The Yukon also has a small coast along Mackenzie Bay, which is part of the Beaufort Sea and thence the Arctic Ocean. The Northwest Territories span much of northern Canada, from the Yukon to Davis Strait, which separates Canada from Greenland.

Looking at the impressive, varied topography of Western Canada, from west to east, the Pacific coastline of British Columbia is indented with long fjords and broken into hundreds of islands, the largest of which are Vancouver Island and the Queen Charlotte Islands. Queen Charlotte Strait and the Strait of Georgia separate Vancouver Island from mainland British Columbia. Most of the people in the province live in the extreme southwestern part of

British Columbia. The Fraser River, a great waterway of Canada, flows through the province and empties into the Strait of Georgia at the city of Vancouver. British Columbia is essentially a province of mountain ranges: Vancouver Island Ranges, Coast Mountains, Columbia Mountains, Monashee Mountains, Selkirk Mountains, Purcell Mountains, and Rocky Mountains. The Japan Current helps to create a mild climate along the Pacific coast. The Coast Mountains trap most of the storms moving east, and a great deal of rain is dumped along the coast, creating extremely lush forests of giant trees and a relatively long growing season. As a result, this area supports thriving lumber, agricultural, and allied industries, with much of the product exported to other countries, particularly those on the Pacific Rim. Fisheries, especially those that catch and process salmon, are also vital to the economic life of the province. Just east of the Coast Mountains, however, the landscape is very arid, almost similar to that of the southwestern United States. This region is also one of the most productive agricultural areas in the province because of intensive irrigation.

North central British Columbia is a rugged plateau with many lakes and dense forests. The cordillera (system of mountain ranges) continues through much of the Yukon and through Alaska. Mount Logan (19,850 feet/5,955 meters) in the Yukon is Canada's highest mountain. The famous goldfields of the Klondike are also in the Yukon; mining is a principal economic activity in both the Yukon and British Columbia. The western section of the Northwest Territories is primarily tundra with many lakes, such as Great Bear Lake and Great Slave Lake, two of the largest in North America. The Mackenzie River, running north from Great Slave Lake to Beaufort Sea, is one of Canada's most important and longest waterways.

The border between British Columbia and Alberta is formed by the impressive Rocky Mountains. Here, too, is the Great (Continental) Divide, where rivers and streams on the west side flow toward the Pacific and those on the east side flow toward the Atlantic and Hudson Bay. Recreation (national parks, resorts, skiing, trail riding, and hiking), mining, ranching, and forestry are the chief economic activities in the Rockies. The Rockies form only the western edge of Alberta; the rest of the province is flat or rolling terrain, known as the Interior Plains, also as the Prairies of Canada.

The Interior Plains/Prairies stretch across the rest of western Canada—Saskatchewan and Manitoba—to the Ontario border. Much of the land is devoted to growing wheat and other grains and to raising beef cattle. Alberta has large deposits of oil, oil-bearing materials (tar sands), and natural gas. Because of its high volume of petroleum production, this province is often referred to as the Texas of Canada. Saskatchewan is one of the world's leading producers of potash, used as fertilizer in agriculture.

Located in the interior of Manitoba is Lake Winnipeg, almost 2,000 square miles (5,200 square kilometers) larger than Lake Ontario. The northeastern portion of this province also has shoreline on Hudson Bay, the largest inland sea in the Western Hemisphere. The Churchill River, a favorite haunt of naturalists and explorers, flows through northeastern Manitoba into Hudson Bay, where there is a major polar bear population.

Northern Alberta, Saskatchewan, and Manitoba are primarily wilderness areas of countless lakes, which are attractive to the serious angler. All the principal cities, towns, and transportation routes in these three provinces are located in the south, where the land is more suited to agriculture and the winter climate is less severe.

History

In 1885, two significant events took place in Western Canada—the completion of the country's transcontinental railroad, and the Battle of Batoche. On November 7 of that year, at Craigellachie—within the rugged Monashee Mountains region and near the Eagle River—the last spike of the Canadian Pacific Railroad was driven into place. Canada was at last linked, from coast to coast, by a modern transportation system that would greatly increase the human settlement and economic progress of this vast area of North America. The completion of this railroad was one of the great accomplishments of the nineteenth century—in its time similar in complexity, effort, and investment to that required to land people on the moon in our own time.

Prior to the completion of the railroad, Canada was a confederation of seven provinces: Ontario, Quebec, New Brunswick, Nova Scotia, Prince Edward Island, Manitoba, and British Columbia. British Columbia joined the confederation with the strict stipulation that it be connected to the rest of the country by rail; otherwise, it might choose to remain a colony of Great Britain, join the United States, or become independent. At that time, Canada was fortunate to have had Sir John A. Macdonald as its first prime minister under the British North America Act, the instrument that created confederation. Macdonald goaded Parliament into moving ahead with the railroad in order to keep British Columbia in confederation and, as a result, forge a new country.

Building the railroad used the sweat and muscle of thousands of workers. The hazards of harsh weather, rugged terrain, bad food, and poor medical care killed or injured many of them. Great numbers of men from China were brought in to work as coolies at this task. In addition to the other hardships, the Chinese had to endure bigotry, lower wages, poorer working conditions than their co-workers enjoyed, and cruel separations from their families.

While the line was being built, the railroad ran out of money, but thanks to Lord Revelstoke, head of Barings, London's prestigious investment-banking firm, the necessary funds were provided. Both a small town and a mountain are named in honor of Lord Revelstoke, near the spot where the last spike was hammered down.

The settlement and economic development of Western Canada then began in earnest, and Canada as such evolved from fractious coastal enclaves into what would become the second-largest nation in the world. Once the means of transcontinental transportation were set in place, tens of thousands of settlers—native-born North Americans; immigrants from Britain, eastern Europe, Germany, Scandinavia, and other countries; and canny investors—headed west. Small towns, such as Winnipeg, and police garrison posts, such as Calgary, rapidly became cities of consequence. Alberta and Saskatchewan became provinces in confederation, joining the seven others in 1905. Victoria and Vancouver emerged as major cities on the Pacific coast.

Also in 1885, at Batoche, 55 miles (88 kilometers) northeast of the city of Saskatoon in Saskatchewan, the last decisive battle of the Northwest Rebellion (also known as the Riel, Red River, or Métis Rebellion) took place. Louis Riel was the leader of the Red River (Manitoba) Métis, people of mixed French and Amerindian blood whose lands were taken from them by speculators and settlers. Riel, one of the most charismatic figures in Canadian history, wanted his people to have permanent ownership rights to lands of their own and to preserve their culture. He and his people fought—establishing a provisional government that led to the creation of Manitoba as a province of Canada in 1869.

The downfall of Riel began at Duck Lake, Saskatchewan, where a member of the Northwest Mounted Police was killed. This murder caused concern in Eastern Canada, and the federal government sent troops to subdue Riel. The Métis concluded that they would get no justice and, using what we now term guerrilla tactics, fought a series of battles against professional soldiers. The Métis made their last stand at Batoche. Because they were well dug in, the battle lasted for four long days. Riel, however, had no alternative but surrender. After surrendering he was taken to Regina, where he was put on trial, found guilty, and hanged. Although his execution pacified an agitated public in the East, it also became part of the folklore of Canada. Many people believed, and continue to believe, that Louis Riel was murdered by a Canadian justice system that preferred expediency to truth. With the defeat of the Métis and the death of Riel, the broad, fertile lands of Manitoba and Saskatchewan were now open to all comers. The newcomers were the winners, and the losers were, as in the United States, those of Amerindian and mixed blood.

The history of Canada was also shaped by a number of other important events. In 1670 the Hudson's Bay Company was founded in London, where it continues to have a headquarters. Its purpose as a trading company was not to develop a nation in the political sense but to use its leverage to make as much money as possible for British investors through the North American fur trade. In time, because of its strategically located trading posts throughout the North and West, Hudson's Bay controlled much of the territory of what is Canada today. Hudson's Bay hired tough, canny Scots to operate these far-flung outposts, and they made their deals with the native peoples, trappers, and mountain men. Some Montreal Scots, seeing no need to share hard-earned proceeds with a far-off gentry, started a trading company of their own, the North West Company. For many decades, these two companies were in savage competition for turf, product, and profit. Their enterprises ranged from the Arctic to what are now the states of Washington and Oregon. Eventually, Hudson's Bay won, absorbing the operations of the North West Company, not unlike today's corporate mergers and leveraged buyouts. In 1868, however, Britain's Parliament made Hudson's Bay turn over its immense holdings of territory to the relatively new government of Canada, although the company continued with its business dealings throughout much of these lands. Today, Hudson's Bay Company is familiar to all Canadians, and to visitors, as a chain of excellent department stores known as the Bay. Yet, if you travel to the remote reaches of northern Canada, you will likely make a stop for supplies at a Hudson's Bay Company trading post, because they are often the only source for hundreds of miles. At these trading posts, one can experience a bit of the atmosphere and heritage of the seventeenth century.

To adventuresome souls in the nineteenth century, the big news coming out of Western Canada was not the creation of a railroad but the discovery of gold—and gold fever became the great contagious disease of that age. The coast of British Columbia and the interior regions of the Yukon were flooded by thousands of men with wild dreams of fabulous wealth. The sandbars of the lower Fraser River and the Klondike region became famous and have been immortalized in folklore. Some of the thousands who came would strike it rich by finding gold. Some would become rich by bilking those who sought gold. Many, however, would lose their shirts and their health in the quest. Still others, wearing ragged clothes with pockets empty of cash, would die on the trails, in the mines, and at the panning streams. These risk takers, whether successful or not, infused Western Canada with a bullish spirit that anything is possible with a lot of pluck—in contrast to the East, where proper establishment credentials counted for more than the magic of individual potential and achievement. Much of this individualistic, entrepreneurial spirit still exists in Western Canada and motivates its people, be they progeny of several generations or the most recent immigrant.

Western Canada is different from the western United States in a fundamental way: It was not as wild in the gun-shooting, Indian-chasing sense. Law and order came to Western Canada in the form of tough, disciplined men wearing the red tunics and blue pants of the Northwest Mounted Police—the world-famous and legendary Mounties, established in 1874. This glowing legend generally contains more truth than falsehood. The Mounties came to Western Canada as the federal government's strong arm and to provide assistance to provincial and territorial governments that had few if any law-enforcement services of their own. The Mounties protected the rights of both Indians and white settlers in a fair and just manner, not every time, but often enough to win respect.

After the battle of the Little Bighorn, thousands of U.S. Indians, including Sitting Bull, knowing that their victory was a prelude to attack by U.S. soldiers, moved across the border into lower Alberta, seeking refuge ensured by a shield of compassion and resolve provided by the Mounties. One Mountie legend says that a Mountie

always gets his man. In case after case, the Mounties have pursued lawbreakers, often under extremely harsh conditions of weather and terrain, refusing to give up the chase until the fugitive has been captured—preferably alive. Their record in this regard isn't perfect, but it and the quality of the men and women themselves has been good enough to serve as a deterrent to crime. Today's Mounties are officially known as the Royal Canadian Mounted Police, or RCMP. Their major training center is at Regina, Saskatchewan.

The early history of Western Canada is replete with the immortal names of important explorers. Some historians speculate that Sir Francis Drake could have seen the coast of British Columbia from his ship in the sixteenth century, but they are sure that Captain James Cook landed on what would be later called Vancouver Island in 1778. Captain George Vancouver, from whom the island and the chief city of the province derive their name, mapped the British Columbia coast from 1792 to 1794 to strengthen British claims to this North American territory. Around the same time, in 1793, Sir Alexander Mackenzie, a Scot working for the North West Company, reached the Pacific after crossing much of the continent. He accomplished this amazing feat, including extremely difficult crossings of the Rockies and other mountain ranges of British Columbia, about thirteen years before Lewis and Clark stood at the shores of the Pacific. Mackenzie was also the explorer of the 1,120-mile-long (1,792-kilometer) river bearing his name that runs north, through the Northwest Territories and near eastern Alaska, from Great Slave Lake to Mackenzie Bay and Beaufort Sea above the Arctic Circle. Western Canada also saw countless trading company explorers, trappers, mountain people, French Jesuit priests, and others who were keen on adventure and on staking territorial claims for their patrons. Much of the northern portion of Western Canada remains unexplored today.

The human history of Canada began thousands of years ago, when nomadic, tribal peoples crossed the then-existing land bridge between what is now Siberia and Alaska. No one knows for sure what climatic changes and food shortages caused this migration, but enough people did come over to spread throughout the Western Hemisphere. Some created impressive civilizations, such as those in Mexico, Peru, Ecuador, and Western Canada. Today the

◀ **The Royal Canadian Mounted Police have a long history of distinguished public service. The Mounties opened and secured Western Canada.**

many descendants of these ancient peoples continue to live and develop their cultures in Western Canada—the Inuit (Eskimos, as most people call them) in the Arctic areas (the Northwest Territories); the coastal tribes of British Columbia (also inland tribes), the Yukon, and Alaska; and the plains tribes of Alberta, Saskatchewan, and Manitoba. The land that was new, strange, and amazing to white explorers and settlers was a familiar and long-standing home to these native peoples. Despite frequent contention among themselves, they lived in harmony with this magnificent nature, taking from it only what they needed, occasionally a little more, but never exploiting out of avarice what they considered a gift from God. These "first people's" sons and daughters who today live in Western Canada continue to pursue the same pragmatic and spiritual values of their ancestors. The perception of human existence gained through their eyes can be one of the most rewarding experiences of your trip to Western Canada.

The Great Cities of Western Canada

It is hard to believe that just over a hundred years ago the great cities of Western Canada—Vancouver, Victoria, Calgary, Edmonton, Saskatoon, Regina, Winnipeg—were little more than trading posts, frontier police garrisons, or logging towns. When you see their gleaming, impressive skylines today, all the marks of a progressive, contemporary society are there. You see commercial and industrial activities of all kinds, a wide variety of cultural and entertainment attractions, fine universities and medical centers, and wonderful hotels and restaurants. You see, too, a broad diversity of people representing just about all ethnic, racial, and religious groups inhabiting this planet. In the cities of Eastern Canada, great emphasis is placed on the two founding cultures—French and British. In Western Canadian cities, however, the second most important culture, after English, might be Ukrainian or Chinese.

Although Western Canadian cities can't boast of long, dramatic histories, except in the case of Amerindian tribes, a dynamic "We can do it!" spirit is here that is often lacking in more established areas. These cities have had their boom-and-bust times, particularly in the commodities they produce and ship—oil, minerals, lumber, fish, and grain. Regardless, they have always bounced back bigger and better than before.

The quality of urban life the people here have created and continue to refine is the envy of cities centuries old. Here, there is always a sense of anticipation, of becoming, of something new around the bend. On a more mundane but nonetheless important level, Western Canadian cities are kept as clean as cities can be. The crime rates are also low enough that most people are not afraid of the risk.

These cities are on the threshold of the great Canadian wilderness, where a person can travel hundreds of miles over a rugged, magnificent landscape and meet hardly another soul. After you've visited some of the great cities of Western Canada and toured their countryside, you won't return home wondering when you'll be back for another visit. You will, most likely, be planning to return to stay for good.

CHAPTER 2

General Information

Free Information for Travelers

The following provincial and territorial tourism agencies will supply you with free information, maps, and brochures. For the quickest response, use toll-free (800) telephone numbers, accessible throughout the continental United States and Canada.

BRITISH COLUMBIA
Ministry of Tourism and Provincial Secretary
Parliament Buildings
Victoria, British Columbia
Canada V8V 1X4
Toll free (800) 663–6000

ALBERTA
Travel Alberta
10025 Jasper Avenue
Edmonton, Alberta
Canada T5J 3Z3
Toll free (800) 661–8888

SASKATCHEWAN
Tourism Saskatchewan
1919 Saskatchewan Drive
Regina, Saskatchewan
Canada S4P 3V7
Toll free (800) 667–7191

MANITOBA
Travel Manitoba
155 Carlton Street
Winnipeg, Manitoba
Canada R3C 3H8
Toll free (800) 665–0040

YUKON
Tourism Yukon
P.O. Box 2703
Whitehorse, Yukon
Canada Y1A 2C6
(403) 667–5340

NORTHWEST TERRITORIES
Northwest Territories Tourism
Box 1320
Yellowknife, Northwest Territories
Canada X1A 2L9
Toll free (800) 661–0788

NUNAVUT TOURISM
P.O. Box 1450
Iqaluit, Northwest Territories
Canada X0A 0H0
Toll free (800) 491–7910

VIA RAIL CANADA (coast-to-coast rail travel)
Toll free (800) 561–8630

Free tourism information about Western Canada can also be obtained by contacting Canadian consulates general in the United States.

ATLANTA
1175 Peachtree Street, NE
Suite 1700
Atlanta, GA 30361–6205
(404) 532–2000

BOSTON
Three Copley Place, Suite 400
Boston, MA 02116
(617) 262–3760

BUFFALO
1 Marine Midland Center, Suite 3000
Buffalo, NY 14203–2884
(716) 858–9500

CHICAGO
180 North Stetson Avenue, Twenty-fourth Floor
Chicago, IL 60601
(312) 616–1860

DALLAS
750 North St. Paul Street, Suite 1700
Dallas, TX 75201
(214) 922–9806

DETROIT
600 Renaissance Center, Suite 1100
Detroit, MI 48243
(313) 567–2340

LOS ANGELES
California Plaza
500 South Hope, Ninth Floor
Los Angeles, CA 90071–2627
(213) 346–2700

MIAMI
200 South Biscayne Boulevard, Suite 1600
Miami, FL 33131
(305) 579–1600

MINNEAPOLIS
701 Fourth Avenue South
Minneapolis, MN 55415
(612) 332–7486

NEW YORK CITY
Exxon Building
1251 Avenue of the Americas
New York, NY 10020
(212) 596–1600

SAN JUAN
107 Cereipo Street, Alt. de Santa Maria, Guaynabo
San Juan, PR 00969
(787) 790–2210
Fax: (787) 790–2205

SEATTLE
412 Plaza 600 Building
Sixth and Stewart Avenue
Seattle, WA 98101
(206) 443–1777

WASHINGTON, D.C.
Canadian Embassy
501 Pennsylvania Avenue NW
Washington, DC 20001
(202) 682–1740

Calculating Costs

For North Americans, Canada continues to be a good travel/vacation value because one doesn't have to spend as much to get there and stay as one does for other international destinations. Visitors from the United States and from other countries with high-value currencies (e.g., Japan and Germany) have the incentive of a currency exchange rate in their favor. At this writing, the worth of the U.S. dollar is more than 30 percent above that of the Canadian dollar (the actual exchange rate varies from day to day).

Rather than publishing specific prices that are subject to quixotic change, this guide uses a scale of relative prices to indicate costs for accommodations and restaurant meals: *expensive, moderate,* and *inexpensive.*

Accommodations

An *expensive* double room in Vancouver, Victoria, Calgary, or Edmonton is likely to cost $125 and up a night in Canadian dollars. Even when booking a room at a deluxe hotel, ask about special discounts, such as weekend packages. Some hotels may offer discounted rates for children, seniors, and salespeople. Special rates are usually unavailable during peak vacation periods, but if you don't ask, you won't save.

Accommodations rated *moderate* cost $60 to $125 a night in Canadian dollars. It is important to know that the quality of a moderately priced accommodation in a smaller city or town in Western Canada may be equal to (if not better than) that of some *expensive* places in the large metropolitan areas.

An accommodation rated *inexpensive* costs less than $60 a night in Canadian dollars.

Restaurants

Prices for restaurant meals are about the same throughout Western Canada, with the exception of remote areas and communities in the Yukon and the Northwest Territories, where expensive transportation raises the price of goods. This means that a simple meal costs about the same in Winnipeg as it does in Vancouver, but a similar meal tends to cost more in Yellowknife and Whitehorse.

An *expensive* meal for two at a top restaurant in a big city can cost $75 and up. A *moderate* dinner for two can range from $30 to $75. An *inexpensive* meal costs less than $30 in Canadian dollars.

Although the restaurants designated *expensive* in this guide generally offer excellent ingredients, preparation, ambience, and service, those marked *moderate* and *inexpensive* have been selected with regard to their high quality and value to customers as well. This guide's emphasis is on diversity—presenting a wide choice of dining opportunities. Not every meal has to be a memorable culinary experience. Many times it's more satisfying to have a region's version of honest home cooking when you're far away from your own hearth.

Most resorts in Western Canada offer meal plans: the Modified American Plan (MAP), consisting of breakfast and dinner daily, and the Full American Plan (FAP), offering three meals daily. Regardless of your food plan, you are expected to leave a tip, signed on your bill and charged to your account. Cocktails and wines are also extra charges.

If you want to save money when staying at a big-city hotel, avoid making frequent use of room service. Have breakfast at a nearby coffee shop or diner, where meals are served faster and cost less. Also consider bringing to your room a deli sandwich, pizza, or carton of chicken wings.

Attractions

Admission to many of the attractions described in this book is *free*. Others are designated *admission is charged* or *donations are ac-*

cepted. Major attractions usually have several price categories—adults, children, seniors, groups, and so forth. During the peak summer vacation season, from the end of June to Canada's Labour Day (first Monday in September), most attractions are open from 10:00 A.M. to 5:30 P.M. Some major attractions (amusement parks, historical villages, fairs, expositions) extend their hours into the evening during the peak season. Each attraction has its own method of operation. Sometimes when a historic home or local museum is closed on a Sunday or Monday, for example, the staff members might open it up for you. Don't be too shy to inquire if your curiosity is aroused about a place. Local communities are proud of their heritage and want to share it with interested visitors from distant places.

Food and Lodging in Western Canada

Accommodations

Accommodations in Western Canada—hotels, motels, resorts, bed-and-breakfast places, hunting or fishing camps, farm and country houses, inns, tourist homes, and so on—are comparable in quality and diversity to those in the United States and in any other highly developed, industrialized country. You'll find that accommodation standards—housekeeping, safety, amenities—are exceptionally high in Canada.

Both the federal and the provincial governments have done a fine job in providing roadside and park camping areas. Many of these include power hookups, safe drinking water, toilet and bathing facilities, fireplaces, picnic tables, and various recreational offerings.

Canada offers country home/farm vacations (including bed-and-breakfast places). Here you enjoy the best in Canadian rural life, including superb home-cooked meals, for a reasonable cost. The hosts even invite you to take part in the chores.

From May to August, most Canadian universities and other schools welcome overnight guests. For a nominal charge, you can have a room on campus; some offer a private bath, cafeteria services, and recreational facilities. Such arrangements constitute a bargain that can make travel budgets stretch further. Contact the various tourism promotion agencies listed at the beginning of this section for more information.

Dining

In Western Canada you can eat every kind of food, from mass-produced hamburgers to the finest in gourmet cuisine. I recommend that you try the many regional foods, such as fresh salmon in British Columbia and ranch-raised beef in Alberta. Most familiar fruits and vegetables are grown in abundance in Western Canada. Decent wines are being developed in British Columbia, and they are worth a try. Bread making is a high art; after all, the grain-producing provinces of Alberta, Saskatchewan, and Manitoba are the breadbaskets of Canada. Ethnic restaurants abound—here's your chance to sample the best of Ukrainian, Japanese, Portuguese, Chinese, Greek, and Italian foods. Prices for meals at restaurants in Western Canada are about the same as in the United States.

Tipping

A service charge is not automatically added to bills in Canada. It is customary, however, to give a tip of 15 percent of the total amount on a bill, excluding sales tax, to the people who serve you. Excellent service in a restaurant, for example, warrants an additional 5 percent or more. Taxi drivers receive a 10 to 15 percent tip of the meter's total. People who handle your bags receive $1.00 per piece of luggage. Don't forget the person who tidies your room, makes your bed, and cleans the bath; $1.00 to $2.00 a night shows appreciation for his or her efforts. And note, as part of the tipping bottom line, that indifferent or poor service warrants the usual—an empty plate.

Alcohol and Drug Laws

The legal drinking age in British Columbia, Saskatchewan, the Northwest Territories, and the Yukon is nineteen; in Alberta and Manitoba, eighteen.

Bottled liquor is sold through stores operated by the provincial governments. Selling hours vary from province to province. Liquor can also be purchased in licensed restaurants and bars. Hours for sale at these establishments also vary.

Canada has strict drug laws, sharp enforcement, and tough penalties. It would be prudent to abstain while in the country.

The dream of most skiers is to take on the magnificent downhill slopes of ➤ the Canadian Rockies.

Provincial Sales Taxes

All Canadian provinces, except for Alberta, the Northwest Territories, and the Yukon, have a sales tax applied to purchases of most goods, food in restaurants, and accommodations. In some provinces a sales tax refund is available when the goods you buy are taken out of the country. You should inquire about sales tax rebates when you make purchases.

Canada also has a national Goods and Services Tax (GST) that is currently 7 percent. It is applied on all sales of hard goods and of services in addition to provincial sales taxes. Tax rebates are available when purchases total more than $100. Pick up a rebate form at the nearest Travel InfoCentre, or telephone (800) 668–4748 (613–991–3346 from outside Canada) for further details.

Weather

The best time for most vacation travel in Western Canada is during the warm-weather months—from mid-May to the end of September. July and August are the peak summer months. Spring and fall, in terms of seasonal transitions, are relatively short periods, except for coastal British Columbia, where the weather is mild throughout much of the year. The mountain regions, of course, get snow early, and some peaks are white year-round. June can be a tricky month in the high mountains—at Banff, for instance, where one day it can be shirtsleeves warm and the next a surprise snowstorm can drop a few inches. In winter the mountains offer some of the best skiing in the world. The prairies region of Alberta, Saskatchewan, and Manitoba is like a corridor down from the Arctic, whence high winds and cruel temperatures flow. During the summer, however, it can get hot enough to fry eggs on the Trans-Canada Highway. During the late fall and winter along British Columbia's coast, a great deal of rain falls, and people wonder if they'll ever see the sun again; it's much like the weather in Seattle. But the heavy rains help to grow the lush forests and profusion of lovely flowers, some blossoming through winter. Very little snow falls along the southern coast, and what does quickly melts. Overall, during the primary months of vacation travel, the weather throughout Western Canada is nearly perfect.

As to how you should dress for the weather, tailor your

wardrobe to the season and the kinds of outdoor activities you'll want to do. A windbreaker, warm sweater, and basic rain gear should be standard, even in summer. In case you forget something, all these items can be purchased virtually anywhere in Canada. There are some good values in English and Scottish woolens, in just about every form of clothing (weavings, patterns, colors) you want. Unless you are going up to the Arctic reaches of the Northwest Territories, the clothing you bring should be no different from what you would take if you were going to northern California, Oregon, Washington, or the coast of Maine.

Time Zones

Western Canada is divided into three time zones: Central Standard Time (Manitoba, Saskatchewan), Mountain Standard Time (northwest Saskatchewan, Alberta, eastern British Columbia), and Pacific Standard Time (British Columbia and Yukon); the Northwest Territories span all these time zones, plus Eastern Standard Time and Atlantic Standard Time. There is a one-hour difference between time zones (e.g., 12:00 noon Mountain Standard Time in Calgary is 11:00 A.M. Pacific Standard Time in Vancouver).

Telephone Area Codes

Telephone area codes for Western Canada are as follows:

Alberta	403
British Columbia	604, 250
Manitoba	204
Northwest Territories (Yellowknife)	867
Saskatchewan	306
Yukon (Whitehorse)	867

Toll-free 800 numbers are in common use throughout Canada, and you should use them, if possible, before making a toll call. Some establishments don't offer toll-free numbers, but enough do to make your effort worthwhile. This book lists toll-free numbers wherever possible.

How to Get to Western Canada

Your Travel Agent

Travel anywhere these days has become so complicated and costly that even the most sophisticated traveler needs help to get through the maze of details and figures. For such assistance, you need go no farther than your local travel agent. He or she can book your accommodations, meal plans, transportation, tours, rental cars, and many other aspects of your trip; everything will be arranged to fit the budget you specify. In addition, your travel agent will give advice based on his or her own familiarity with popular places and special programs in Western Canada.

Your local travel agent delivers a tremendous amount of service at no extra cost to you, though you may be charged for special services. Travel agents receive a commission from the hotels and transportation companies, but you pay the same rates as when you book yourself. Some of the best travel agents belong to the American Society of Travel Agents (ASTA); look for the ASTA symbol when you select your agent. Not all travel agents, however, are as we would like them to be—top-notch professionals who place the well-being and satisfaction of their clients first. Ask your friends and business associates for recommendations. Don't be timid about shopping around until you get the best for your needs. After all, it's your hard-earned money and your hard-earned vacation.

Discount Fares

Travelers over sixty-five years of age are eligible to receive discounts on air, rail, and bus fares in some provinces. You must show proof of age when tickets are purchased. Those between the ages of thirteen and twenty-one can also travel by air at reduced rates by providing proof of age (birth certificate or driver's license). Discounts are offered for children under the age of thirteen. Get full details on these money-saving arrangements from your local travel agent or the transportation company's ticket clerk.

Package Tours, Cruises, and Vacations

Through your local travel agent, you can book many different kinds of package tours and vacations to Western Canada—for example, bus tours of every kind, fly-and-drive packages, ski and resort packages, big-city tours, hunting and fishing packages, railroad and cruise packages. Many escorted tours include accommodations, meals, sightseeing, transportation, tour managers and guides, entertainment, and special events.

For example, Maupintour, 1515 St. Andrews Drive, Lawrence, KS 66044, (913) 843–1211, is one of the blue-chip companies in this business in terms of quality services and customer satisfaction. Maupintour offers packages to the Canadian Rockies, the resorts of Banff, Jasper, and Lake Louise, and the cities of Vancouver, Victoria, and Calgary; train packages across Canada; cruises through the Inside Passage along the coasts of British Columbia and Alaska; and special Christmas and New Year's tours of the Canadian Rockies.

Major Canadian Transportation Companies

Air Canada (check local listings or call the 800 operator for the toll-free number) is the national airline of Canada. Air Canada's regularly scheduled flights provide service to most urban centers in the country and direct flights to Canadian destinations from several U.S. cities. This carrier also works with a number of leading package-tour operators, providing travelers with a wide variety of package tours to Western Canada—touring, skiing, big-city holidays, and so on.

Canadian Airlines, a merging of Canadian Pacific and Pacific Western airlines (check local listings or contact your travel agent), provides regularly scheduled service to Western Canada destinations from most centers in Canada and the United States. This carrier also offers vacation packages to British Columbia.

Canada 3000 (ask your travel agent for details) is a charter airline that provides high-quality group travel and vacation packages.

VIA Rail (call 800–561–8630), the national rail service of Canada, provides regularly scheduled passenger rail service throughout much of Canada, including one of the world's great rail trips—from Halifax, Nova Scotia, on the Atlantic to Vancouver, British Columbia, on the Pacific. Departures for Western Canada are from most major cities—Halifax, Quebec, Montreal, Ottawa, Toronto, Winnipeg, Calgary, Vancouver. Sleeping accommodations and dining cars are on board. Western Canada package tours are also available.

Direct Flights to Western Canada Cities from U.S. Cities

Vancouver is served by direct flights from these U.S. cities: Chicago, Dallas, Denver, Honolulu, Los Angeles, Minneapolis, New York, Phoenix, Portland, Reno, San Diego, San Jose, and Seattle.

Calgary has direct service from Boise, Chicago, Dallas, Denver, Houston, Las Vegas, Los Angeles, New York City, Palm Springs, Phoenix, San Diego, and San Francisco.

Edmonton is directly served from Chicago, Dallas, Denver, Houston, Las Vegas, Miami, Minneapolis, Phoenix, San Francisco, and Seattle.

Winnipeg can be reached directly from Chicago, Denver, Fort Lauderdale, Los Angeles, Miami, Minneapolis, New York, Phoenix, San Francisco, Seattle, and Tampa.

Travelers from other U.S. locations can reach any Western Canada destination through connecting flights. For the convenience of many eastern-seaboard U.S. travelers, Western Canada flight connections are made through airports in Toronto or Montreal. Ask your travel agent for details. The recent Canada/USA Open Skies Treaty means that more airlines are flying between the two countries. Check with your travel agent for specifics.

Airport Services

Major airports providing international services in Western Canada are in Vancouver, Victoria, Calgary, Edmonton, Regina, and Winnipeg. These airports provide foreign exchange, lockers, telephones, duty-free shops, bars, restaurants, newsstands, bookstores, drugstores, and various other shops and services. Hotels and motels are conveniently located near all international airports.

These airports also offer ground transportation to city centers by bus, taxi, or limousine. The major car-rental companies have facilities at the airports as well.

All these terminals have special facilities for the handicapped, including ramps, washrooms, and automatic doors.

Primary Gateways to Western Canada from the United States and Eastern Canada by Car

You can enter Western Canada through the following gateways: From Eastern Canada, eastern United States (New York, Pennsylvania, New Jersey, New England, Washington, D.C.), Toronto, or other Ontario cities: via the Trans-Canada Highway, through the gateway of Winnipeg, Manitoba. The Trans-Canada Highway runs across the country, from sea to sea, essentially east/west, connecting most of the major cities.

From Detroit, Cleveland, other midwestern, mid-Atlantic, or southern U.S. cities: via Interstate 75 to Sault Sainte Marie, to the Trans-Canada, thence to Winnipeg.

From Chicago, Saint Paul/Minneapolis, other midwestern, or southern U.S. cities: via Interstate 94 to Fargo, North Dakota, then Interstate 29 to Manitoba Highway 75, to Winnipeg.

From U.S. cities in the Rocky Mountain and southwestern states: to Interstate 15, which runs north/south through Montana, to Alberta Highway 4 leading to Lethbridge, thence to Highway 2 to Calgary and Edmonton.

From U.S. cities in California and the Pacific Northwest: to Vancouver via Interstate 5; to British Columbia, Highway 99; also from Port Angeles on Washington's Olympic peninsula to Victoria, British Columbia, via ferry.

There are a number of other access routes into Western Canada from the United States. Consult your atlas to find the routing and entry points most convenient for you.

Road Distances to Western Canada from Selected North American Cities

The following list gives driving distances from major North American cities to various destinations in Western Canada. For example, traveling from east to west, the distance from Winnipeg (the gateway to Western Canada for those coming into the region from the east) to Regina is 571 kilometers (km)/343 miles (mi); to Calgary, 1,336 km/802 mi; to Edmonton, 1,357 km/814 mi; to Vancouver, 2,232 km/1,339 mi; and to Victoria, 2,337 km/1,402 mi.

Canada

Toronto, Ontario, to Winnipeg = 2,099 km/1,259 mi
Ottawa, Ontario, to Winnipeg = 2,218 km/1,331 mi
Montreal, Quebec, to Winnipeg = 2,408 km/1,445 mi
Quebec City, Quebec, to Winnipeg = 2,678 km/1,607 mi
Halifax, Nova Scotia, to Winnipeg = 3,656 km/2,199 mi

United States

Fairbanks, Alaska, to Edmonton = 1,840 mi/2,962 km
Fairbanks, Alaska, to Vancouver = 2,207 mi/3,553 km
Los Angeles, California, to Vancouver = 1,437 mi/2,314 km
San Francisco, California, to Vancouver = 1,013 mi/1,631 km
Seattle, Washington, to Vancouver = 144 mi/232 km
Washington, D.C., to Winnipeg = 1,641 mi/2,642 km
Chicago, Illinois, to Winnipeg = 895 mi/1,441 km
Saint Paul/Minneapolis, Minnesota, to Winnipeg = 436 mi/702 km
Detroit, Michigan, to Winnipeg = 1,182 mi/1,903 km
Philadelphia, Pennsylvania, to Winnipeg = 1,630 mi/2,624 km
New York, New York, to Winnipeg = 1,854 mi/2,985 km
Boston, Massachusetts, to Winnipeg = 1,835 mi/2,954 km

Services and Safety Tips

Rules of the Road for Safe Driving

Everyone in your vehicle should wear seat belts when driving in Canada. Strict seat-belt laws are in effect throughout Canada, with the exception of Alberta, the Yukon, and the Northwest Territories.

U.S. drivers should remember that maximum speed limits in Canada are posted in kilometers per hour (km/h). Distances are also given in kilometers (e.g., Vancouver 1,244 km; 771 mi). One hundred km/h equals 60 miles per hour, the maximum speed on many major highways.

Studded tires are permitted without seasonal limitation in Saskatchewan, the Northwest Territories, and the Yukon, but only during the winter in the other provinces.

Use of radar-detection devices is illegal in Alberta, Manitoba, the Northwest Territories, the Yukon, and in some of the eastern provinces. If you are driving across the country, pack the device away in a suitcase.

Emergencies

In an emergency, simply dial 0 on the telephone and ask the operator for the police, who have been specially trained to handle all types of emergencies. In major cities dial 911 for emergencies.

◀ Traveling the Alaska Highway in a camper rig.

If someone has an urgent need to get in touch with you but does not know where or how, he or she should contact the RCMP (Royal Canadian Mounted Police) in the area where you are traveling (leave your itinerary with a friend or relative back home). Several times each day, many of the CBC (Canadian Broadcasting Company) radio outlets broadcast the names of individuals traveling in their areas of Canada, requesting them to contact the nearest RCMP office for an emergency message. This excellent service should be used only for genuine emergencies.

Auto Clubs

The Canadian Automobile Association (CAA) extends full services to the American Automobile Association (AAA), Alliance Internationale de Tourisme (AIT), Federation Internationale de l'Automobile (FIA), Federation of Interamerican Touring and Automobile Clubs (FITAC), and Commonwealth Motoring Conference (CMC). These services, obtainable upon presentation of your membership card, include travel information, itineraries, maps, tour books, information on road and weather conditions, accommodation reservations, and emergency road and travel agency services.

Bear and Forest Fire Safety

The rugged mountain and wilderness areas of Western Canada, in British Columbia and Alberta, are home to North America's kings of beasts—the bears. This is their natural and legitimate place; you are merely a guest in their territory. Grizzly and black bears are most common, and many have been spoiled by well-meaning humans with handouts of food. Forget about how cute your teddy bear is back home—here you're dealing with dynamite that can maim and kill. You can assume that these magnificent animals, especially mothers with cubs, are always unpredictable and very dangerous. Most people never come close enough to a bear to fear an attack. Nevertheless, when you are hiking, make enough noise on the trail so that bears will avoid you. Never get between a mother and her cub. When you spot a bear, keep a safe distance between you and it—the bear is considerably faster than you and is about as powerful an animal as exists. Resist moving in closer for a better camera shot.

When camping, keep your area clean. This means wrapping all food items in airtight packages and placing the supply caches away from your tent. Clean up all traces and scents of food that can attract bears. Avoid bringing any food, such as a sandwich or snack, into your tent before going to sleep. If you have problems with a bear, make a report to the nearest wildlife officer. When entering a national or provincial park, be sure to get the latest information on bear sightings and advice on what to do should you have a problem.

The forests of Western Canada are among the great riches of the continent. Enjoy them and protect them from destruction by fire. Be careful in the use of matches and lighting instruments. Make sure that anything that was burning (match, campfire) is out cold. Do not dispose of your smoking material until you are certain it is no longer burning. Build your campfires on hard, clear ground and away from vegetation, leaves, pine needles, and other materials that can accidentally catch fire and spread flames throughout the forest. When entering a national or provincial park, be sure to get current information on fire regulations, use of wood, and safe campfire locations.

Safe Driving on Gravel Roads

Throughout most of your travels in Western Canada, if you are driving you will find that the hard-surface roads are well engineered and constructed for various terrain and climatic conditions, with escape roads for runaways and plenty of scenic overlooks and rest areas. Roads are well maintained during periods of bad weather, such as snow and ice, and directional, warning, and destination signs are well placed and easy to read. Service stations, restaurants, and accommodations are along most routes. If, however, you plan to do some off-the-main-highway exploring, which will usually place you on gravel roads, the following safe-driving tips will make your touring adventure more secure and enjoyable.

Gravel sections of the Alaska Highway (most of the Alaska Highway is now paved) and major roads in northern British Columbia, Alberta, the Yukon, and the Northwest Territories are generally safe and well maintained. They are paved with loose gravel because of harsh climatic conditions during certain times of the year. The rapid deterioration of asphalt or concrete surfaces during severe weather (freezing and thawing), for example, causes road hazards and difficult maintenance; gravel surfaces, by contrast, provide better, safer traction in snow, ice, and mud. Further, be careful of slippery road conditions after heavy rains or thaws. A four-wheel-drive vehicle is ideal for north-country driving. Studded tires are recommended for ice and hard-packed snow.

Make sure your vehicle is in top mechanical condition. Repair shops are scarce on long stretches of road, and bills for work performed are high. Take some spare parts and tools with you—a spare tire in prime condition, a fan belt, spark plugs, wrenches, and so on. Take a container of extra gas, a jug of coolant, some extra motor oil, and plenty of windshield washer fluid.

Protect your gas tank from being punctured by loose gravel by fastening a rubber mat to the surface that faces the road. Protect your headlights from rocks by attaching plastic shields and your radiator from swarms of bugs by using an appropriate screen. Most of this auto equipment can be bought at your local supply store or at stores in Western Canada. Many garages located near major gravel roads can help equip your vehicle.

Take the following personal gear in the event that you get stranded for a while: sleeping bags, warm coats, sweaters, hats and mittens, insect repellent, basic pots and pans, drinking water, enough food for a couple of days, fuel and fire-making tools, first-aid materials, emergency flares, and, if possible, a citizens band radio. If you have to spend a night off the road, the best bet is to sleep in your vehicle. Doing so will save your skin from insects and your hide from bears. Be alert to animals suddenly getting in your way on the road. Hitting an elk at 60 miles per hour is not much different from smashing into a brick wall.

Keep a good distance between your vehicle and the one in front—a strategy that will help keep rocks from spinning up and cracking your windshield. Anticipate that you may very well have bits and pieces of gravel hitting the glass and metal of your vehicle when trucks and cars, which travel at high speeds on these roads, pass you. Most travelers get through their journey without any damage occurring, but don't be surprised if it happens. It's part of the way of travel in these areas, and your insurance policy should help set things right again when you're back home. During dry periods, moving cars and trucks send up thick plumes of dust—another reason to keep a healthy distance between you and the next car. Keep your headlights on at all times—whether it's dusty or not—while traveling the gravel roads. Keep your windshield washer filled with fluid and use it frequently. When being overtaken by a truck, pull over to the shoulder and let it pass, but don't stop—keep moving.

Don't let your gas tank go below half full. Top it off at frequent intervals. Know how far it is to the next gas station, and don't let yourself come up short.

Don't drive when tired. Take plenty of rest stops and enjoy the scenery. Share the wheel with your partner. Be alert at all times. Do, though, enjoy the country you're passing through—it's among the great adventures of a lifetime.

Free Culture on the Road

One of the best treats while touring Western Canada by auto is tuning into a CBC (Canadian Broadcasting Company) radio station. A federal government–operated network, CBC provides some of the finest news, discussion, cultural, and entertainment programming in the English- and French-speaking worlds. Its broadcasts of classical music are outstanding in variety and amount.

Marina Services

Full marina services are available for travelers sailing their private boats into British Columbia ports. During the peak summer season, however, available moorages are hard to get, particularly in or near the popular cities of Victoria and Vancouver. Yachting is a primary recreational activity along the British Columbia coast, and many people can afford it. For information on reserving moorages in ports you want to visit, contact British Columbia's Ministry of Tourism (see page 14).

Gasoline

Gasoline is plentiful throughout Western Canada. Canada uses the metric system and gasoline is measured in liters.

Hunting and Fishing Regulations

Hunting is regulated by federal, provincial, and territorial laws. You must obtain a license from that province or territory in which you plan to hunt. A federal permit for hunting migratory game birds is required for such species, and available at most Canadian post offices. Many of Canada's provincial parks, reserves, and adjacent areas prohibit entry with any type of weapon. The Northwest Territories requires an export permit for all unprocessed wildlife that is taken out.

Fishing is also regulated by law. You must obtain a nonresident license for the province in which you wish to try your luck.

In British Columbia, you need a license for tidal-waters sport

fishing. Also, in British Columbia you cannot export salmon or other game fish beyond the possession limit without obtaining written authorization from a fishery officer. No more than forty kilograms gross weight of canned salmon, taken by sport fishing, can be exported from the province in any year.

A special fishing permit is needed in all national parks and can be obtained at any national park site for a nominal fee; these permits are valid throughout Canada.

Non-Canadian fishing guides cannot work in Canada without approval from the Canada Employment and Immigration Commission, and such approval must be obtained *before* you come to Canada (contact your nearest Canadian consulate; see pages 15–17).

For more information on parks, reserves, hunting and fishing laws, licenses, and wildlife conditions, contact provincial and territorial tourism agencies (see pages 14–17).

◀The culture of Canada is as varied as its landscape.

Canada for Non-Canadians

The Canadian Nation

Canadians are governed by a parliamentary form of democracy, in contrast to the republican form in the United States. Elizabeth II, Queen of the United Kingdom, is also Queen of Canada. The Governor-General, a noteworthy Canadian citizen appointed by the prime minister and approved by the Queen, is her representative. When the queen is not present in the country, the governor-general acts as the symbolic chief of state. The Prime Minister, who is also a member of Parliament and the leader of the political party having a majority of members in Parliament, is the chief executive officer of Canada. Unlike the U.S. system, which separates the executive and legislative branches, the Canadian political system combines both, similar to the United Kingdom's method. There are five major political parties in Canada: the Progressive Conservative party, the Reform party, the Quebec-based Bloc Quebecois, the New Democratic party (NDP), and the Liberal party. All members of a prime minister's cabinet must be elected members of Parliament—another difference from the U.S. system, in which a president's cabinet members are appointed and cannot hold elective office. Ottawa, in the province of Ontario—between Toronto and Montreal—is Canada's federal capital.

Canada is a member of the United Nations, NATO, and the Commonwealth of Nations. Because of its generosity to people in need everywhere around the globe and its reasonable position on

The pioneers traversed Western Canada in covered wagons. You can do ➤ the same with a lot more fun and without the hardship.

many key international issues, Canada is one of the most respected nations in the world.

The following are the provinces of Canada and their capitals (provinces are similar in concept to states but possess far more powers for self-governance): Newfoundland/Labrador (St. John's), Prince Edward Island (Charlottetown), Nova Scotia (Halifax), New Brunswick (Fredericton), Quebec (Quebec City), Ontario (Toronto), Manitoba (Winnipeg), Saskatchewan (Regina), Alberta (Edmonton), and British Columbia (Victoria). Canada also has two vast land areas in the north that are awaiting designation as provinces: the Yukon Territory (Whitehorse) and the Northwest Territories (Yellowknife). On the provincial level, the Queen of Canada is represented by Lieutenant Governors-General, whose functions are chiefly ceremonial. These officials are outstanding citizens of their respective provinces. When the Queen and members of the royal family visit the provinces of Canada, the Lieutenant Governors-General are their chief hosts. Political power in the provinces lies with the legislative assemblies and with the premiers who hold dominant power both in the executive and legislative branches and within the majority political party. The operational form of government here is similar to what it is on the federal level.

Canada has a population of more than thirty million. Close to two-thirds of Canadians reside in the provinces of Ontario and Quebec, and about three-fourths of all Canadians live within a hundred miles of the U.S. border. (Most of the important urban centers of Canada are near the border.) About 30 percent of all Canadians are French; more than 40 percent are of British stock (English, Irish, Scottish, Welsh); and the remainder are of various groups, among them Ukrainians, Poles, Japanese, Germans, Italians, Chinese, West Indians, and Greeks. Unlike the United States, which thinks of itself as a "melting pot" in which groups are assimilated into the dominant Anglo-Saxon culture, Canada considers itself a "cultural mosaic" whose citizens can be equally proud of their ethnic and Canadian heritages. This concept of a cultural mosaic has become institutionalized in most aspects of Canadian life and is the official cultural policy of every level of government throughout the country. Although a majority of Canadians are Christians of various denominations, the country is also home to large concentrations of Jews, Muslims, and numerous other religious groups.

Canadians enjoy one of the highest standards of living in the world. For example, through government subsidies, low-cost medical care is available to all citizens. Moreover, through government subsidization the cost of higher education is considerably lower in Canada than in the United States.

In April 1982, Canadians witnessed a historic event when Elizabeth II, queen of Canada, sat before a crowded assembly of the House of Commons and Senate of the Parliament of Canada in Ottawa and presided over the proclamation of the Constitution Act of 1982. This great moment in history marked a number of significant changes in Canada's constitution and is a milestone in this country's political evolution. With the proclamation of the Constitution Act, Canada repatriated from the British Parliament its constitution and shed an outmoded vestige of its colonial past.

Entry into Canada

Canada Customs clears foreign visitors for entry into Canada. Its checkpoints are located on all highways that cross the border between the United States and Canada and at international airports and seaports. The French word for customs is *douane*, and it is part of the official bilingual signature of this vital federal department. You will find the people of Canada Customs to be courteous and professional. They try hard to make your entry into Canada a most pleasant start to your trip. They are, however, masters of their craft—among the best of their kind in the world—and it is highly inadvisable to attempt to slip illegal drugs and undeclared goods past their keen senses. Many travelers have tried, much to their regret.

Citizens or permanent residents of the United States do not require passports or visas and can usually cross the U.S.–Canadian border without difficulty or delay. It is strongly recommended, however, that you carry some form of valid personal identification, such as proof of residence and citizenship (birth certificate or other document that provides legal evidence). Naturalized U.S. citizens should carry their naturalization certificate or other evidence of citizenship. Permanent residents who are not citizens should carry their alien registration receipt card. Persons under the age of eighteen who travel to Canada without an adult must have a letter of permission from a parent or guardian. U.S. citizens can also enter Canada from third countries without a passport or visa.

All other persons—with the exception of U.S. citizens or legal residents, citizens of France residing on the islands of Saint Pierre and Miquelon, and residents of Greenland—require a valid passport, visa, or other acceptable travel document to gain entry into Canada. If you are entering Canada from the United States, make sure that your travel documents are acceptable to the U.S. Immigration Service before you leave the United States so that you won't have trouble reentering.

Employment and Study

If you want to study in Canada—and thousands of non-Canadians do so every year—you must obtain a student authorization before coming to Canada. Your own school or Canadian studies program should be able to help you with this kind of red tape. You will also need an authorization for working in Canada. Employment authorizations are usually not issued if qualified Canadians or permanent residents are available for the kind of work you are seeking. Those who are being transferred by their companies to positions in Canadian offices and operations should seek the assistance of their human resources (personnel) departments. Another good source of information about employment or study in Canada is your nearest Canadian consulate general (see pages 15–17).

Clearing Canada Customs
By Car

The entry of vehicles and trailers into Canada for touring purposes, for periods of up to twelve months, is generally a quick, routine matter that does not require the payment of duty. Motor vehicle registration forms should be carried, as should a copy of the contract if you are driving a rented vehicle. If you are driving a vehicle registered to someone else, you must carry that person's authorization to use the vehicle. All national driver's licenses, as well as the International Driver's Permit, are valid in Canada.

By Private Aircraft

Visiting aviators should plan to land at an airport that provides customs clearance. You must report to Canada Customs immediately and complete all documentation. In emergencies, you can land at other fields, but then you must, as soon as possible, report your arrival to the nearest regional customs office or the nearest detachment of the RCMP (Royal Canadian Mounted Police). For more details on flying your own plane to Canada, contact your nearest Canadian consulate general (see pages 15–17).

By Private Boat

If you're planning to come to Canada on your own boat, contact the regional Canada Customs office nearest to where you intend to enter Canadian waters for a list of ports of entry that provide customs facilities and their hours of operation. When you arrive, you should immediately report to customs and complete all documentation. If you have an emergency, report your arrival, as soon as possible, to the nearest regional customs office or to the local detachment of the RCMP (Royal Canadian Mounted Police).

For Personal Exemptions

Everything you bring into Canada must be declared and is subject to inspection by Canada Customs. The following are common-sense rules and should present no real burden to the average traveler.

Tobacco. If you are sixteen years of age or older, you can bring in duty free fifty cigars, 200 cigarettes, and two pounds of processed tobacco.

Alcoholic beverages. You can bring into Canada duty free forty ounces of liquor or wine or twenty-four cans or bottles of beer or ale. You must be at least nineteen years of age in British Columbia, the Northwest Territories, Saskatchewan, and the Yukon; at least eighteen, in Alberta and Manitoba.

Gifts. You can bring in duty-free gifts for friends and relatives provided that the value of each gift does not exceed $100 (Canadian) and that the item is not tobacco, liquor, advertising material, or any good that does not qualify as a gift under customs definitions. You must declare currency exceeding $5,000 Canadian. Contact your nearest Canadian consulate (see pages 15–17) if you have any questions.

Business equipment and materials. Printed materials, commercial samples, blueprints, charts, audiovisual materials, convention and exhibit displays, and the like brought into Canada may be subject to the full rate of duty and tax or a portion thereof, or they may be duty and tax free. Canada wants business travel to be as easy and convenient as possible. Contact the Commercial and Trade Division at your nearest Canadian consulate general for answers and information (see pages 15–17). This is what Canada Customs says about its system regarding business and convention visitors: "We have taken steps to simplify customs and excise requirements and to reduce border-crossing formalities."

Pets. Canada is a pet-loving nation. You can bring your dogs and cats into Canada provided that each animal has a certificate from a licensed veterinarian confirming vaccination against rabies within the preceding thirty-six months. Puppies and kittens under three months and seeing eye dogs accompanied by their owners can enter Canada without certification or restriction.

Pet birds, songbirds, and birds of the parrot family can be brought into Canada provided that the owner accompanies the birds and declares on arrival that they have been in his or her possession during the preceding ninety days and have not been in contact with other birds during that period. There is a limit of two birds per family.

Pet monkeys, other small pet mammals, fish, and most reptiles can come into Canada without restriction. Pet foxes, skunks, raccoons, and ferrets, however, can come into Canada without health certification or a Canadian import permit only when they are accompanied by the owner. Turtles and tortoises require an import permit before admission.

Livestock, horses, wild or domestic fowl, and commercial shipments of animals, including all species of birds, are subject to veterinary health inspection upon arrival in Canada.

Endangered species. The importation of endangered species of animals, plants, and their products is restricted and may require the prior issuance of an import permit. This restriction also applies to certain animal skins and to mounted animals and trophies.

Plants, fruits, and vegetables. Houseplants can be brought into Canada without phytosanitary (plant health) certification when carried as personal items. All other plants require phytosanitary certification, which is issued by your nearest office of the U.S. Department of Agriculture. Visitors from other countries should contact their national agricultural agency.

You can bring most fruits and vegetables into Canada; however, there are restrictions regarding certain types, and these stipulations change from time to time. Contact your nearest Canadian consulate general for current information (see pages 15–17).

Food for two days' personal use can be brought into Canada.

Recreational boats and vehicles. You can bring in your boats, motors, trailers, snowmobiles, and other types of recreational vehicles duty and tax free under a temporary entry permit, issued by Canada Customs when you arrive, on the condition that such vehicles are for personal use only and will be taken out of the country at the end of your visit.

Recreational equipment. You can bring in the following items duty and tax free provided that they are for your personal use only: fishing tackle; camping, golf, tennis, scuba, and skiing equipment; radios, television sets, and typewriters; camera equipment with a reasonable amount of film; and other recreational or hobby items.

Radio communication equipment. Radio equipment that has a power output of 100 milliwatts or less, operating in the 26.97/27.7 megahertz band or on the carrier frequencies of 49.830, 49.845, 49.860, 49.875, or 49.890 megahertz, may be operated in Canada without licensing.

Visitors to Canada are permitted to operate aircraft, ship, amateur, and citizens-band radio stations provided that such stations are properly licensed by the government of the United States or by the government of the nation from which you originate.

The following stations, which must have a U.S. license, require a Canadian permit for operation in Canada: citizens-band radio-telephone stations and radio-telephone stations in vehicles that move back and forth across the international border or that are operated through a common carrier to connect with the telephone system. Permits can be obtained by writing the Director General, Radio Regulatory Branch, Department of Communications, Ottawa, Ontario K1A 0C8. Visitors must carry their Canadian permit and national license at all times.

Nonresident household goods. A nonresident of Canada who purchases, constructs, owns, or leases for at least three years a seasonal residence (not a mobile home or other movable residence) may qualify for the duty- and tax-free entry of furniture and household goods.

Firearms. Firearms having no legitimate sporting or recreational use (e.g., handguns) are not permitted entry into Canada. Canada has strong handgun laws, and they are enforced to the limit. Don't even try to bring such a weapon into the country. If you are traveling through Canada to get to Alaska, you must ship your prohibited or restricted weapons by commercial carrier; you cannot bring them in with you. If you are discovered in possession of a restricted weapon, it can be legally taken away from you.

If you plan to bring in a handgun for a shooting competition, you must obtain a permit in advance from a local Canadian registrar of firearms.

Long guns—those used for hunting and competition shooting—can be brought into Canada and used without a permit by visitors sixteen years of age and older. Nonresident hunters may bring in 200 rounds of ammunition (per person) duty free. Nonresident sharpshooters competing in meets recognized by the Amateur Trap Shooting Association, the Shooting Federation of Canada, the Dominion of Canada Rifle Association, or the National Skeet Shooting Association may bring in 1,000 rounds of ammunition (per person) as personal baggage. For more information contact your nearest Canadian consulate general (see pages 15–17) and your hunting/shooting organization, such as the National Rifle Association in the United States.

Firearms in British Columbia. A nonresident carrying a firearm in British Columbia, while not on an arterial (main) or secondary highway, must have either a British Columbia firearms license or a hunting license.

Explosives, ammunition, fireworks, and pyrotechnics. Blasting explosives and detonators, propellant explosives and ammunition, and all types of fireworks and pyrotechnic devices are prohibited from being brought into Canada without an official permit.

The Canada–U.S. Free Trade Agreement eliminates duties on most goods over a period of ten years. Contact your nearest Canadian consulate (see pages 15–17) for information on specific items.

Reentry into the United States

U.S. citizens and residents must satisfy U.S. Immigration authorities as to their right to return to the United States. You can do this by presenting some form of identification or proof of citizenship. (Preferable is your passport or a copy of your birth certificate; driver's licenses are generally not good forms of identification at border crossings.)

Make a list of all the Canadian purchases that you plan to take across the border, keeping sales slips ready for inspection. Pack these purchases separately for easy inspection. Don't hide anything—the authorities will find it.

You can take out of and bring into the United States up to $10,000 in U.S. currency. You must report amounts above this limit to U.S. Customs.

Items of cultural, historical, or scientific value to the heritage of Canada that are more than fifty years old (e.g., antique furniture and paintings) cannot be taken out of the country without official permission.

You can bring plants of Canadian origin into the United States provided that you have obtained a phytosanitary certificate from the Plant Products and Quarantine Division, Agriculture Canada. Offices are located in major urban centers throughout Canada.

Exemptions

By staying in Canada for at least forty-eight hours, you can bring into the United States up to $400 (U.S. dollars) of purchases duty free.

Regardless of age, every member of your family, is entitled to this exemption. Members of the same family can pool their exemptions into a larger duty-free total. For example, if five of you are traveling together and Mother falls in love with a $2,000 designer gown in Vancouver, she can bring it back home duty free because your family has five $400 exemptions that total a $2,000 one. All duty-free purchases must accompany you back across the border.

You can also bring home duty free one hundred cigars, as long as they have not been made in Cuba; 200 duty-free cigarettes; and one liter of liquor (the minimum age to bring in alcohol is twenty-one).

Duty-free gifts can be sent from Canada to friends and relatives in the United States if the value of each gift does not exceed $50. The package should be marked UNSOLICITED GIFT.

Your Health while Traveling

Unexpected health problems may happen on a trip. You may need the services of a doctor, for example, or even a stay in a hospital. The best way financially to protect yourself and members of your family is to make sure your health insurance plan provides the coverage you might need while traveling—adequate to pay for the costs of treatment. Although Canadians are protected by the health care system administered by their province, the benefits therein are not available to nonresidents. Daily rates for hospital care vary from hospital to hospital and from province to province. Charges for adult inpatient care can start at $800 per day; charges for children in specialized hospitals can be even higher. Some provinces impose a surcharge of up to 30 percent on care for nonresidents. Before you come to Canada, seek advice on your present health care benefits and ascertain what additional coverage you might need; to obtain such information, contact your organization's human resources (personnel) department, your auto club, or your insurance or travel agent. Also be sure to bring copies of your prescriptions in the event that they need to be renewed by a Canadian doctor.

Special Auto Insurance Identification

All provinces in Canada require motorists to produce evidence of financial responsibility in case of an accident. The minimum liability insurance requirement in Canada is $200,000 (in the Northwest Territories, $50,000). U.S. motorists are advised to obtain from their insurance agents a Canadian Nonresident Interprovincial Liability Insurance Card, which is issued free of charge. If you have an accident in Canada and don't have this card, your vehicle can be impounded and other serious legal action can be taken against you. *Don't leave home without it.*

Canadian Holidays

Many services—banks, government offices, factories, business offices, and so on—are closed during the national and provincial holidays listed here. Places of accommodation, many restaurants, and some services, however, are open for the convenience of travelers.

National Holidays
New Year's Day
Good Friday
Easter Monday
Victoria Day, third Monday in May
Canada Day (formerly Dominion Day), July 1
Labour Day, first Monday in September

Thanksgiving Day, second Monday in October
Remembrance Day (memorial for Canadian men and women who
    served in the military), November 11
Christmas Day, December 25
Boxing Day, December 26

Provincial Holidays
Alberta
Heritage Day, first Monday in August
British Columbia
British Columbia Day, first Monday in August
Manitoba, Saskatchewan, Northwest Territories
Civic Holiday, first Monday in August
Yukon
Discovery Day, third Monday in August

The Metric System

All measurements in Canada follow the metric system, which is commonplace in most countries outside the United States.

Temperature is given in degrees Celsius (C); gas is sold by the liter, groceries by grams and kilograms; and road speeds are posted in kilometers per hour.

If you are not already familiar with the metric system, the following measurements will be helpful during your travels in Canada:

Speed
15 miles per hour = approximately 24 kilometers (km) per hour
30 miles per hour = approximately 48 kilometers (km) per hour
50 miles per hour = approximately 80 kilometers (km) per hour
60 miles per hour = approximately 96 kilometers (km) per hour

Length
1 inch = 2.54 centimeters (cm)
1 foot = 0.3 meters (m) or 30 centimeters (cm)
1 yard = 0.9 meters (m) or 90 centimeters (cm)
1 mile = 1.6 kilometers (km) or 1,600 meters (m)

Mass
1 ounce = 28 grams (g)
1 pound = 0.45 kilograms (kg) or 450 grams (g)

Volume

1 fluid ounce = 28 milliliters (ml)
1 Imperial pint = 0.57 liters (l) or 570 milliliters (ml)
1 Imperial quart = 1.14 liters (l) or 1,140 milliliters (ml)
1 Imperial gallon = 4.5 liters (l) or 4,500 milliliters (ml)

When buying gasoline in Canada, remember that the Imperial gallon is close to one liter larger than the U.S. gallon. The Imperial gallon will at first seem to cost more, but the price tends to equal out in the total purchase price.

Temperature

86°F = approximately 30°C (a hot summer day)
68°F = approximately 20°C (room temperature)
32°F = approximately 0°C (water freezes)
–6°F = approximately minus 20°C

The following is a formula for temperature conversion; it may, however, be useful only to mathematicians:

To convert Celsius to Fahrenheit $(C \times 9/5) + 32 = F$
To convert Fahrenheit to Celsius $(F-32) \times 5/9 = C$

Money Matters

The Canadian System

The monetary system of Canada, like that of the United States, is based on dollars and cents. The denominations of coins and paper bills is the same. In addition, each denomination of Canadian paper money is of a different color, which makes it easier to tell a $5.00 bill from a $10.00 bill. The $1.00 denomination is a coin known as the "Loonie." It is called as such because of the loon featured on the coin's face. Canada also has a $2.00 coin.

More Value for Your Travel Dollars

The value of the Canadian dollar has averaged between $.25 and $.40 *below* the U.S. dollar, depending on prevailing market values. While the West German mark, the British pound, and the Japanese yen have risen in value against the U.S. dollar (at this writing), the value of the Canadian dollar has remained substantially lower than that of the U.S. dollar. For every U.S. dollar that is converted to Canadian, an exchange advantage of from 25 to 30 percent is realized (sometimes more and sometimes less, depending on fluctuations in world currency markets). For example, a traveler converting $100 in U.S. money with a 15 percent exchange rate should receive $115 in Canadian money. Although some goods and services cost more in Canada, you should be able to stretch your U.S. travel/vacation money further in Canada than in many other popular destinations around the world—perhaps even to splurge on a few pleasures that otherwise might not be possible.

Where to Convert to Canadian Money

U.S. currency, including major traveler's checks and credit cards, is widely accepted throughout Canada for the purchase of goods and services. Some places will even give you a better exchange rate just to get your business. The canny traveler will keep a sharp eye out for these establishments.

It's a good idea to convert some of your money into Canadian currency at your hometown bank (about $100 for initial expenses, such as cabs, tips, and fast food). The larger U.S. banks usually handle Canadian currency. You can also buy traveler's checks in Canadian denominations before you leave on your trip. Both your local banks and traveler's check–issuing companies must give you the benefit of the prevailing exchange rate.

Canadian banks are usually the best places in which to convert your money to Canadian currency (that is, if you want to get the best rate of exchange). Places of accommodation are not good sources, unless they use a more favorable exchange rate as a promotion to attract your business. The only advantage to converting your money at a hotel is that its cash department keeps longer hours than banks, and it is open on weekends and holidays. Canadian banking hours are usually from 10:00 A.M. to 4:00 P.M. Monday through Friday. Almost all banks have extended hours of operation (set by individual banks) on certain days of the week, such as Saturday.

Automatic Teller Machines (ATMs)

Need cash? Various Automatic Teller Machines (ATMs) are located in most cities in British Columbia, Alberta, Saskatchewan, and Manitoba. Consult your bank card company to find out which ATMs in the Western Canada provinces will provide the instant-cash services you might need.

Many ATMs will make cash advances on major credit cards as

49

well; be sure that before leaving home, you inquire at your credit card company about the availability of this option in Canada.

Credit Cards

All major national and international credit cards (such as American Express, Visa, and MasterCard) are widely accepted throughout Canada. Major credit cards are necessary for renting automobiles and are used as a form of identification when checking into places of accommodation. In hotels, restaurants, shops, and other business establishments, be sure to check beforehand that your card will be accepted.

Postal and Telecommunications Services

Canadian postage stamps must be used on all mail sent from Canadian locations. First-class letters sent from Canada to a U.S. address must have a first-class Canadian stamp. First-class letters sent from the United States to a Canadian address carry a U.S. stamp (ask your post office for the current rate). Goods and Services Tax (GST) is added to the price.

Electricity and Water

Travelers from the United States can use their electric appliances— shavers, hair dryers and curlers, irons, and so on—as they would at home. Special adapters are not needed.

Drinking water throughout Western Canada is safe to use from the tap.

Business Hours

Business hours in Canada are similar to those in the United States. Most offices are in full operation by 9:00 A.M., and work for most people usually ends by 5:00 P.M.; executive lunches are as long as needed. Most stores are open from 10:00 A.M. to 6:00 P.M., and late-hour drugstores and newsstands can be found in most large cities. The hourly routine of everyday life is not very different in Canada from what it is in the United States.

◄ Put on stout hiking boots and what you need on your back and experience the wonder of the Canadian Rockies by being close to the boundless land and sky.

CHAPTER 4

Touring Spectacular British Columbia

British Columbia in Brief

British Columbia is Canada's third-largest province, after Quebec and Ontario. It is also the third most populous, with more than three million inhabitants. More than 90 percent of its people speak English as their first language. Most British Columbians are of British stock—English, Scottish, Welsh, Irish—and this is Canada's most British province, not just in name but in attitudes and lifestyle, although a burgeoning Chinese population is gaining in clout, especially in Vancouver and Victoria. British Columbia also contains large populations whose ethnic roots are Germanic, Scandinavian, Slavic, and Asian. In fact, almost all the world's ethnic, racial, and religious groups are represented in British Columbian society. The vast majority of British Columbians reside in the southern part of the province, close to the U.S.–Canadian border along the forty-ninth parallel.

The capital of British Columbia (the province is known most typically in Canada as *B.C.*) is Victoria, named in honor of the "Great Queen" and empress of what was once a significant empire. Victoria is located on the southern tip of Vancouver Island, well below the forty-ninth parallel. The largest city in British Columbia is Vancouver, third in economic importance after Toronto and

◀ **Fine dining is available throughout Western Canada.**

Montreal. Other large B.C. cities are Prince George, Kamloops, Kelowna, Nanaimo, and Penticton.

B.C. entered the Canadian Confederation in 1871, about four years after Upper Canada, Lower Canada, Nova Scotia, and New Brunswick came together in a united country. British Columbia has always felt itself far removed from the centers of economic and political power represented by Toronto, Ottawa, and Montreal. The linking of B.C. with the rest of Canada through the transcontinental railroad in the nineteenth century ended some of this isolation, as did the Trans-Canada Highway and the advent of transcontinental air travel.

In recent years, B.C. has turned its attention toward the thriving nations of the Pacific Rim, and its future growth and prosperity will depend increasingly on the Far East, especially Japan, Taiwan, Singapore, and South Korea. The province also has a close affinity with the nearby states of Alaska, Washington, Oregon, and California, and the majority of American tourists who visit B.C. come from these states. The actual borders of British Columbia are the Yukon and Northwest Territories to the north; Alberta to the east; the states of Montana, Idaho, and Washington to the south; and the Pacific Ocean to the west.

The climate along the Pacific coast throughout the year is mild: dry and sunny during the summer, rainy and foggy during the winter. Coastal areas receive little if any snow during the winter, except in the high mountains. It is not unusual to see delicate, colorful flowers blooming in Victoria throughout the winter. On Vancouver Island one can see many trees that are hundreds of years old and that have grown to incredible heights. The heavy rainfall here has created lush vegetation, such as giant ferns and thick moss. From the Coastal Mountains to the Rockies on its far eastern border, British Columbia is rippled with mountain range after mountain range. All these ranges and valleys are thickly forested, except for the southern part of the Okanagan region, where the terrain is desertlike, similar in many respects to that of Arizona or New Mexico. The north central interior flattens out into a rolling plateau. Throughout the interior are countless lakes, rivers, streams, waterfalls, and glaciers. Some of the great national parks of Canada, such as Yoho, Glacier, and Kootenay, are in eastern British Columbia. Near the Alberta border is Mount Robson, the highest point in the

◄ **One of the many B.C. ferries that leave from Horseshoe Bay near Vancouver.**

BRITISH COLUMBIA

97

Dawson Cr.

97

16

Prince
George

5

Campbell
River

Powell River

1

Kamloops

Kelowna

Cranbrook

Port
Alberni

Nanaimo

Vancouver

Richmond

1 VICTORIA

N

Canadian Rockies (Mount Fairweather, however, at 4,663 m/15,300 ft, is the highest in the province). In contrast to the coast, which is either sunny or rainy, the climate of the interior is more typical of North America, with four distinct seasons.

A substantial part of British Columbia's economy is based on developing and processing natural resources—lumber, minerals, food (cattle, fruits and vegetables, and, of course, fish). Travelers to British Columbia dine on such treats as Pacific salmon and province-grown fruits and vegetables of almost every kind. In the 1800s, the province was a center for the fur-trading operations of the Hudson's Bay Company and for the discovery of gold in the Northwest. The city of Vancouver today is an important North American business center, with banking, investment ventures, motion picture and television production, tourism, and insurance leading the way. Like Switzerland and the Cayman Islands, the banking regulations are structured in a way that stimulates foreign investment.

British Columbians enjoy an exceptionally high standard of living. There is affluence as well as a high level of culture. The educational system is superb, particularly the major universities, such as the University of British Columbia, Victoria, and Simon Fraser. The same can be said for the quality of health care, which is heavily subsidized by the government and available to all. British Columbians are law-abiding, civilized people, and the amount of crime and violence is very low in comparison with that in the United States.

Tourism is the second most important economic sector, and its infrastructure—accommodations, restaurants, shops, parks, transportation, attractions, entertainment—is generally excellent in all parts of the province, especially in the prime vacation areas: Vancouver, Victoria, Whistler, the Okanagan, and the Rockies.

No other province in Canada has such a diverse range of magnificent scenery that is largely accessible to most visitors. In the end, it is this glorious spectacle of nature that one remembers the most about British Columbia. B.C.'s motto—concerning its beauty and quest for excellence—is therefore most apt: *Splendor Sine Occasu* ("splendor without diminishment").

Tourism British Columbia

For free information (maps, brochures, etc.) and touring advice, contact:

Ministry of Tourism and Provincial Secretary
Parliament Buildings
Victoria, British Columbia V8V 1X4
or call toll free in North America (800) 663–6000

Regional Tourist Associations

The following regional tourist associations will be happy to provide you with information on all-seasons sports, attractions, culture, dining, and accommodations in their areas:

Vancouver Island, (250) 382–3551
Southwestern B.C. (Vancouver metro area), (604) 739–9011
Okanagan-Similkameen, (250) 860–5999
Kootenay Country, (250) 352–1656
B.C. Rockies, (250) 427–4838
High Country, (250) 828–4656
Cariboo-Chilcotin, (250) 392–2226
North by Northwest, (250) 847–5227
Peace River/Alaska Highway, (250) 785–2544

Touring British Columbia

Note: See chapter 5 for information on the city of Vancouver and its environs, the Whistler resort area, and the Gulf Islands; see chapter 6 for information on the city of Victoria, Vancouver Island, the Inside Passage, and trips from Prince Rupert to Prince George.

The Sunshine Coast

Exploring British Columbia's Sunshine Coast brings you into a magnificent area of islands, mountains, and sea, all within close proximity to the city of Vancouver. You can take a one-day trip here or undertake a major touring adventure. Because of its great beauty and relative closeness to Vancouver, the Sunshine Coast is home to writers, craftspeople, and those who wish to live a more independent life a bit removed from the hassles of civilization. In addition to touring, this region offers sport fishing, camping, hiking, canoeing, wild bird and animal photography, beach walking, heritage museums, Canadian cultural displays, fishing and sightseeing charters, horseback riding, golf, tennis, and local festivals.

It's easy to get to the Sunshine Coast. Take Highway 99 north to the ferry terminal at Horseshoe Bay. From here, take a B.C. ferry (in Vancouver, call 604–685–1027 for information or 604–669–1211 for recorded information twenty-four hours a day; in Victoria, call 250–656–0757) across Horseshoe Bay, passing between Bowen and Gambier islands, to Langdale, the beginning of the Sunshine Coast tour. From Langdale, follow Highway 101 up the coast to Gibsons, Sechelt, Secret Cove, Madeira Park, Pender Harbour, Irvines Landing, Garden Bay, and Earls Cove. At Earls Cove, take another ferry across Jervis Inlet to Saltery Bay, Lang Bay, and Powell River. The ferries running from Powell River can take you across the Strait of Georgia to Comox on Vancouver Island. From Comox, head north to Port Hardy and the Inside Passage trip on the B.C. ferry; head south to Qualicum Beach, which will take you to Highway 4 and thence to the west coast of the island, facing the open Pacific, and the Pacific Rim National Park; or go farther south to the city of Victoria (see chapter 6). At Powell River, take the ferry to Texada Island, or stay on the mainland and keep driving north on Highway 101 to the end of the road at Lund (the communities north of Lund to Prince Rupert are served by ferries and airplanes).

Accommodations and attractions on the Sunshine Coast are varied. At **Gibsons,** visit the Elphinstone Pioneer Museum and the Captain Vancouver Cairn, or stroll along the sea walk. Sea Cavalcade and jazz festivals take place in July.

Sunshine Lodge is 4 km (2.4 mi) west of ferry terminal, (604) 886–3321. Moderate.

Bonniebrook Lodge, 1532 Ocean Beach Esplanade, (604) 886–2887, is a romantic inn with the charm of yesteryear. Steps from the beach, it offers ocean views and a restaurant with fine dining. Moderate.

While in **Sechelt,** visit the Sunshine Coast Arts Centre, featuring paintings, graphics, sculpture, and crafts by local area artists; open Wednesday to Sunday; (604) 885–5412. There is a Sunshine Coast Golf Course in this town.

Driftwood Inn, on Highway 101, (604) 885–5811, has a restaurant and a swimming beach. Moderate.

In **Halfmoon Bay, Lord Jim's Resort** offers a dining room, scuba diving, and a heated pool, (604) 885–7038. Moderate.

Sundowner Inn is a bed-and-breakfast at a historic site in **Garden Bay,** (604) 883–9676. Moderate.

In **Powell River,** visit Willington Beach, Valentine Mountain lookout, the archaeological display, and the salmon hatchery.

There are canoe circle routes from here and a ferry to Texada Island. Try the Powell River Golf Course.

Beach Gardens Resort Hotel, on Highway 101, (604) 485–6267, has a restaurant and landscaped grounds; the rooms offer views of water and mountains. Moderate to expensive.

Lund Hotel, on Highway 101 in **Lund,** (604) 483–3187, has a dining room. Inexpensive.

Metro Vancouver to Lake Louise, Alberta, via the Trans-Canada Highway 1

The Trans-Canada Highway 1 goes across lower British Columbia and over some of the most varied topography in North America. Beginning your trip in Vancouver, travel through the sprawling eastern suburbs of the city: Burnaby, Port Coquitlam, New Westminster, and Surrey. From the Langley area to the town of Hope, you'll be paralleling the Fraser River as you move through the Fraser Valley. The Fraser Valley is broad, flat, rich agricultural land, with many fruit, vegetable, grain, and livestock farms and pretty communities that serve them. The Fraser River along this stretch meanders toward its delta in a leisurely fashion and empties into the Strait of Georgia just below Vancouver city center.

As you travel east, the valley narrows, with the walls of mountains pulling closer to the road. The road begins climbing, and the Fraser River flows through rock gorges in angry torrents. At Hope there is a junction of the Trans-Canada and the Crowsnest Highway 3. The Crowsnest dips south and then moves east, hugging the U.S.–Canadian border (see page 76) for a description of this route to Banff, Alberta). From Hope, the Trans-Canada goes north until it reaches Cache Creek. Here you move away from the eastern slopes of the Coast Mountains, on the western side of which are thick forests and much rain in the winter months, and enter a more arid, almost desertlike region to the south. The Trans-Canada and Highway 97 meet at Cache Creek. Highway 97 takes you north through the Cariboo-Chilcotin region and eventually to the Alaska Highway, which leads to the Yukon, the Northwest Territories, and the state of Alaska.

At the city of Kamloops, the Trans-Canada heads in an easterly direction toward the Canadian Rockies, Lake Louise, and Banff. Along the way you will cross several mountain ranges, such as the Monashee, the Selkirks, the Purcells, and the Great Divide at the Canadian Rockies themselves. Kamloops is the gateway to the Okanagan region, one of the province's prime four-season vacation areas. The Okanagan is also famous for its many fruit orchards, vineyards, and wineries. Once you pass the Okanagan Valley and begin moving toward Revelstoke, the topography becomes alpine, with high, snow-capped mountains; lush forests; long lakes; and such attractions as Rogers Pass and Glacier National Park.

The distance between Vancouver and Banff, Alberta, is 858 km (515 mi). The drive along the Trans-Canada is not only the most direct road route between these two points but also one of the most scenic and interesting drives in Canada. There are plenty of accommodations, restaurants, parks, recreational opportunities, and gas/repair stations along the way.

As you head east out of Vancouver, via Highway 1A, you may want to take a side trip to **New Westminster** to see these interesting attractions:

Westminster Quay and Public Market, on the waterfront at the foot of Eighth Street. This is the heart of New Westminster's waterfront redevelopment. Open daily with shops, dining, walkway along the Fraser River. The Inn at Westminster Quay is an exciting concept: It is built on pillars and reaches out over the river.

Museum of the Royal Westminster Regiment, The Armoury, 530 Queen's Avenue; call (604) 526–5116 for hours and visiting information. Displays of the regiment's history from 1863.

Samson V Maritime Museum, on the waterfront between Eighth and Tenth streets; call (604) 522–6894 for hours and visiting information.

Beyond New Westminster are several small, historical communities, including Fort Langely and Abbotsford.

Fort Langley National Historic Park (site of the birthplace of British Columbia), is reached via Highway 10, off the Trans-Canada, about 75 km (45 mi) from Vancouver city center; call (250) 888–4424. Open daily except Christmas Day, Boxing Day, and New Year's Day. Admission charged. A restored Hudson's Bay Company post, with one building dating back to 1840. All buildings are furnished in the mid-nineteenth-century period, and costumed inhabitants are engaged in the crafts and chores of the fur-trading pioneers and those who worked provisioning the company's Columbia District.

Abbotsford is famous for its **International Air Show,** held annually in early August at the airport on Highway 401; call (604) 852–8511 for information. For accommodations, try the following, which have dining rooms and other amenities:

Holiday Inn Express Abbotsford, 2073 Clearbrook Road, (604) 859–6211. Moderate.

Best Western Bakerview Motor Inn, 1821 Sumas Road, (604) 859–1341. Moderate.

Best Western Regency Inn and Conference Centre, 32110 Marshall Road, (604) 853–3111; (800) 771–3077. Full amenities, including Jacuzzis, fitness center, conference facilities, free movie channel, two indoor pools. Moderate.

In the **Mission/Hatzic** area, via Highways 11 North to 7 East, Westminster Abbey, a community of Benedictine monks, provides a place of natural beauty for rest and prayer; call (604) 826–8975 for visiting hours.

Take the Lougheed Highway (Highway 7) east from Mission City and you'll come to Morris Valley Road. There you'll find **Rowena's Inn On The River** (604) 796–0234; (800) 661–5108. This grand private estate is one of the most spectacular inns in the province, with guest cottages on the property to supplement the in-house rooms. Set on 160 acres, the private estate-turned inn is luxurious and includes a 70-foot swimming pool. Expensive.

Harrison Hot Springs Resort Area can be reached via the Trans-Canada to Bridal Falls, then north across the Fraser to Highway 7 (the Sasquatch Highway); turn left on 7 and then right on 9 North. Harrison Hot Springs is on Lake Harrison. It is in the deep woods of this area that the human/ape creature known as Sasquatch (Big Foot) is supposed to roam. So far, no one has been able to get near it, although some have taken photos of a strange being purported to be Sasquatch; perhaps it is better for both the creature and us that Sasquatch remain a mystery. Within this popular vacation area are hot springs for bathing, golf courses, and the Sasquatch Provincial Park, with hiking trails and camping. Accommodations include the following:

Harrison Hot Springs Hotel, (604) 796–2244; (800) 663–2266. Lake/mountain setting, golf, pools, boating, tennis, restaurant for fine dining, dancing, and entertainment. Expensive.

Harrison Village Motel, (604) 796–2616. Overlooking lake, some rooms with patios; heated pool. Moderate.

Campgrounds; call the Chamber of Commerce, (604) 796–3425, for information.

Mountain range follows mountain range in British Columbia, each one ▶ ahead seemingly more splendid than the one most recently passed.

Originally a Hudson's Bay Company post, **Hope** was laid out by royal engineers in 1858. Later, gold seekers came here to find fortunes in the sandbars of the Fraser River. The Dewdney Trail, the first pack trail, was opened here in 1860. In 1965 the side of a mountain (a hundred-million-ton slide of mud, rock, and snow) broke away and crashed down on many homes in an area near town; the people, homes, and autos remain buried in a common grave under the rubble from the mountain. Also near Hope is the Hell's Canyon Airtram (see below); a doll museum and minigolf are in the area. The Crowsnest Highway 3 joins the Trans-Canada at Hope.

All accommodations have dining rooms and other amenities:

Quality Inn, 350 Hope/Princeton Highway, (604) 869–9951. Moderate.

Maple Leaf Motor Inn, 377 Hope/Princeton Highway, (604) 869–7107. Moderate.

Skagit Motel, 655 Third Avenue, (604) 869–5220. Moderate.

Yale was once known as Fort Yale, in its Hudson's Bay Company days. St. John the Divine, located here, is B.C.'s oldest Anglican church. Visit the Pioneer Cemetery, Spirit Cave Hiking Trail, the National Monument to Chinese Pioneers (those who helped build the transcontinental railroad), and the Cariboo Wagon Road National Monument. During August the Fraser River Barrel Race takes place.

Hell's Canyon Airtram, on the Trans-Canada, is just northeast of Yale, (250) 867–9277. Open April to October. Admission is charged. A pair of twenty-five–passenger airtrams takes you high above the Fraser Canyon, through which the mighty Fraser River surges. This facility also has floral gardens, landscaped grounds, a gift shop featuring British Columbian jade items, and a restaurant serving grilled salmon and salmon chowder.

Cache Creek, at the junction of the Trans-Canada and Highway 97, is the gateway to the Cariboo-Chilcotin region and on the route to the Alaska Highway (see page 84 for accommodations).

Kamloops, with a population of about 73,000, is one of the province's largest cities and is strategically located at the junction of three major highways and two railways. Just four hours east of Vancouver, along the Coquihalla Highway (longer along scenic Fraser Canyon/Thompson Valley routes of the Trans-Canada Highway), it's the entryway into Jasper National Park in Alberta along Highway 5 and 16 (Yellowhead) and into southern Alberta and Banff (along Highway 1, the Trans-Canada). The route to Jasper eventually takes you past Mount Robson, the highest point in the Rockies (3,954 m/ 12,972 ft) and through Yellowhead Pass (1,146 m/3,717 ft), for which the highway is named.

The city, known as the tournament capital of British Columbia, attracts sporting events from around the country, and its golf courses are among the finest in the province. The Kamloops Wildlife Park allows visitors to see native animals in their natural settings; and the Secwepemc Native Heritage Park provides insight into the culture of the Schuswap people. Sitting at the confluence of the north and south arms of Thompson River, the city combines a sense of city living with rustic country charm. Nearby Sun Peaks Resort at Tod Mountain, with fifty-six runs, has developed into one of the province's major ski destinations.

Attractions in Kamloops include the following:

Kamloops Museum and Archives, 207 Seymour Street, (250) 828–3576. Closed Mondays and holidays. Free. Displays of local history, Amerindian cultures, fur trade, ranching, and railroading.

Kamloops Waterslide and R.V. Park, east of city center on the Trans-Canada, (250) 573–3789. Admission is charged. Six water slides, minigolf, hot tubs, a children's playground, and facilities for recreational vehicles (RVs).

Kamloops Wildlife Park, east of city center on the Trans-Canada, (250) 573–3242. Admission is charged. Displays of live wild animals, minitrain rides, and a nature trail.

All accommodations have restaurants and other amenities:

The Place Inn, on the Trans-Canada, (250) 374–5911. Moderate to expensive.

The Dome Motor Inn, 555 West Columbia Street, (250) 374–0358. Moderate.

Panorama Inn, 610 West Columbia Street, (250) 374–1515. Expensive.

Hospitality Inn, 500 West Columbia Street, (250) 374–4164. Moderate.

Sandman Inn, 550 Columbia Street at Sixth Avenue, (250) 374–1218. Moderate.

Coast Canadian Inn, 339 St. Paul Street and Third Avenue, (250) 372–5201. Moderate to expensive.

Riverland Motel, 1530 River Street, (250) 374–1530. Inexpensive to moderate.

Rider's Motor Inn, 1759 Trans-Canada, east of the city, (250) 374–2144. Moderate.

Courtesy Inn Motel, 1773 Trans-Canada, east of the city, (250) 372–8533. Moderate.

Highway 97 South joins the Trans-Canada at Kamloops. It leads to one of British Columbia's top vacation areas: the **Okanagan/Similkameen** region, frequented by travelers from the west coast of the province, Americans from south of the border, and those from Alberta who want to relax and have fun in an environment different from their own.

Whether you are traveling east or west along the Trans-Canada (or on the Crowsnest Highway 3 to the south), you will probably want to take a side trip through the Okanagan/Similkameen region, even for a day or two. Okanagan Lake, a long stretch of warm water, is perfect for swimming, sailboarding, boating, fishing, and waterskiing. It even has its own resident monster—affectionately called Ogopogo—that is supposed to be a cousin of "Nessie" in Scotland's Loch Ness.

This is a prime fruit-producing area, and you'll find stands selling freshly picked crops throughout the region. Accommodations, from bed-and-breakfasts to deluxe resorts, are plentiful, and the golf is excellent, as are tennis, trail riding, skiing, and just about any other sports activity you enjoy. Be sure to visit the vineyards and their wineries, many of which offer free samples at the end of tours.

The key vacation cities in the Okanagan are Vernon, Kelowna, and Penticton. Smaller communities, such as Enderby, Armstrong, Westbank, Peachland, Summerland, Keremeos, and Osoyoos (see page 77), though a bit quieter, also offer most of the vacation features and attractions of the three main cities.

Okanagan Festivals

Highland Games, Penticton, mid-July
Peach Festival, Penticton, end of July to end of August
Square Dancers Jamboree, Penticton, early August to mid-August
Iron Man Canada, Penticton, August
Air Fair, Penticton, August
Okanagan Wine Festival, throughout the region, end of September
    into early October

Wineries in the Okanagan

In addition to being one of British Columbia's leading vacation regions, the Okanagan is the province's wine-producing country. Botanist G. W. Henry was the first to plant grapevines in B.C. in

1899. In 1926, J. W. Hughes, a Kelowna rose grower, planted the first vineyard in the Okanagan on the same site that Father Charles Pandosy planted the region's first apple orchard in 1862. Both men knew that the soil and climate were suitable for fruit growing and that the growing season was long (five and a half months), considering the region's northern location. Dr. Eugene Rittich, a Hungarian with extensive experience in wine making in France, Germany, and Austria, came into the Okanagan in the early 1930s, and the region's involvement in this most enjoyable industry began because of his know-how and efforts.

Today the Okanagan has more than a dozen wineries producing a wide variety of wines. Some are excellent, though others have a ways to go in terms of their acceptance by connoisseurs. What is impressive is that through scientific research and advanced agriculture, Okanagan wines are improving and might one day challenge some of the best from France and California. If you are in the region from late September to mid-October, be sure to attend the Okanagan Wine Festival, featuring various events and the tasting of the region's best wines; call (800) 663–5052 for more information. You can also discover the wines of the Okanagan by taking the Wine Roads Vineyard Tour (250) 496–5600; or toll-free in B.C., (888) 717–9463. Leisurely half-day tours take you to a selection of vineyards between Penticton and Kelowna. The wineries listed below welcome visitors.

Calona Wines, 1125 Richter Street in Kelowna. Tours from the end of May to the end of October; (250) 762–9144.

Casabello Wines, 2210 Main Street in Penticton. Call for hours, (250) 492–0621.

Cedar Creek Winery, off Highway 97, south of Kelowna. Tours from May to end of October; (250) 764–8866.

Claremont Estate Winery and Vineyards, off Highway 97 in Peachland. Tours end of May to Labour Day; (250) 767–2992.

Gray Monk Estate Cellars, Camp Road in Okanagan Centre. Tours May to end of October; (250) 766–3168.

Okanagan Vineyards, RR 1, Road 11 in West Oliver. Tours April to September; (250) 498–6663.

Sumac Ridge Estate Winery, Highway 97 North. Tours end of May to Canadian Thanksgiving; (250) 494–0451.

A prominent vacation center in northern Okanagan, **Vernon** offers every kind of water sport, as well as fine entertainment, culture, accommodations, dining, and shopping. Three lakes and five mountains are close by—and so are golf, skiing at Silver Star Mountain, hot springs bathing, hunting, and trail riding. This is a friendly and relaxing place to stop during your travels across the province. Attractions in Vernon include the following:

Vernon Museum, 3009 Thirty-second Avenue at the Civic Centre, (250) 542–3142. Open Monday through Saturday. Free. Exhibits on the lifestyle of the early settlers and on the paddle-wheel boats that sailed on the lake.

O'Keefe Ranch, on Highway 97, (250) 542–7868. Open mid-May to Canadian Thanksgiving. Admission charged. Established in 1867, this ranch, consisting of about 20,000 acres, was once the biggest cattle empire in the Okanagan. You can visit the ranch buildings and see the mansion and furnishings of the O'Keefe family as well as St. Ann's Church.

Topham Brown Art Gallery, 3009 Thirty-second Avenue in the Civic Centre; call (250) 545–3173 for hours and fees. Exhibitions by local artists and traveling shows.

Accommodations are varied. Below are some possibilities to consider:

Village Green Inn, junction of Highway 97 and Silver Star Road, (250) 542–3321. Excellent accommodations and dining, indoor and outdoor pools, championship tennis courts; near lake, beaches, golf courses, and skiing. Moderate.

Best Western Vernon Lodge, 3914 Thirty-second Street, (250) 545–3385. Indoor pool, dining room, nightclub. Moderate.

Best Western Villager Motor Inn, 5121 Twenty-sixth Street, (250) 549–2224. Moderate.

Vernon Sandman Inn, 4201 Thirty-second Street, (250) 542–4325. Indoor pool, dining room. Moderate.

Swiss Hotel Silver Lode Inn, at Silver Star Mountain Ski Area, (250) 549–5105. At base of lifts; Swiss-style dining room, sauna, and swimming pool. Moderate to expensive.

Vance Creek Hotel, at Silver Star Mountain Ski Area, (250) 549–5191. At base of lifts; dining room, lounge, rooftop hot tubs. Moderate to expensive.

Kelowna is in the middle of the Okanagan vacation region. It boasts thirty-one parks, with nine of them on Okanagan Lake. Hot Sands Beach, for example, perfect for sunbathing and swimming, is right in city center. Kelowna's cultural life includes the Okanagan Symphony and the Sunshine Theatre for live drama and comedy. Knox Mountain offers hiking and terrific views of the city and surrounding landscape. There are excellent accommodations, restaurants, and shops in Kelowna. It prides itself on treating vacationers well—and it succeeds.

Listed below are some of the main attractions in Kelowna:

Father Pandosy Mission, Benvoulin Road, (250) 860–8369. Founded in 1859, this mission was the first permanent white settlement in the Okanagan Valley. There are several restored log buildings and displays of equipment.

Okanagan Butterfly World, 1190 Stevens Road, (250) 769–4408. Tropical butterflies flying free in the gardens. All stages of the butterfly's life are exhibited.

Guisachan Heritage Park, 1060 Cameron Avenue. Part of one of Kelowna's earliest ranches, and the one-time home of Lord Aberdeen, Governor-General of Canada, 1893–98. There are a perennial garden and a restaurant.

Kasugai Gardens. Tucked behind Bennett on Queen Street, this Japanese garden is complete with a boulder-ringed pond, waterfall, and stone garden. Kasugai, in Japan, is Kelowna's sister city.

Centennial Museum, 470 Queensway Avenue. Call (250) 763–2417. Open daily during the summer. Free. Displays about local history include a Chinese house and store, McDougal's Trading Post, a 1910 street scene, the first Kelowna radio station, and the interior of a Salish Amerindian home.

Accommodations abound. Here are several suggestions:

Lake Okanagan Resort, on the lake near Kelowna, (250) 769–3511; (800) 663–3273. This is one of the finest resort hotels in central British Columbia. It has been awarded the AAA four-diamond award for excellence. The resort is located on more than 300 acres and includes a mile of shoreline on the lake. Excellent rooms and dining facilities, seven championship tennis courts, par-3 golf, swimming, horseback riding, and hiking. Moderate to expensive.

Coast Capri Hotel, 1171 Harvey Avenue, (250) 860–6060. Modern hotel, nicely appointed rooms; suites available. Swimming pool, restaurants, grills, and lounges. Convenient to all recreational attractions in the area. Moderate to expensive.

Stay 'n Save Motor Inn, 1140 Harvey Avenue, (250) 862–8888; (800) 663–0298. Family restaurant, pool, sauna, opposite shopping mall, nonsmoking units, housekeeping units. Inexpensive to moderate.

Holiday Inn Express, 2429 Highway 97 North, (250) 763–0500; (800) 465–0200. Indoor pool, complimentary breakfast buffet, near golf and family attractions. Moderate to expensive.

Grand Okangan Lakefront Resort, 1310 Water Street, (250) 763–4500; (800) 465–4651. Heated pools, all amenities, fourteen meeting rooms, located on the lakeshore in downtown Kelowna. Moderate to expensive.

Super 8 Motel, 2592 Highway 97 North, (250) 762–8222. Seasonal outdoor heated pool, year-round hot tub, family plan, off-season rates. Inexpensive to moderate.

Sandman Hotel Kelowna, 2130 Harvey Avenue, (250) 860–6409. Centrally located, twenty-four-hour family restaurant, senior-citizen discount, sports bar. Inexpensive to moderate.

Safari Motor Inn, 1651 Powick Road, (250) 860–8122. Moderate.

Big White Mountain Ski Area Central Reservations, (250) 765–8888. For booking hotel rooms and condo units at this popular ski area.

Das Hofbrauhaus, in the Big White Mountain Ski Area, (250) 879–8687. Condos, fireplaces, dining room, deli, entertainment, indoor pool. Moderate to expensive.

Between Kelowna and Penticton, on Highway 97, is the community of **Peachland.** When passing through, stop and visit the **Peachland Museum** at 5890 Beach Avenue, (250) 767–3441; open June through August. Call for hours and fees. The museum is housed in the former Peachland Baptist Church, a unique, eight-sided wood structure built in 1910. Its collection tells about some of the first orchards in the Okanagan, which were planted in this area.

Penticton, on Lake Okanagan, is encircled by mountains, and located nearby are many beaches, orchards, and vineyards. You might call it Eden, and for those who stay awhile, it is. What could be better than attending the Peach Festival, sailing on the lake, dining on schnitzel at Karl's restaurant, or playing golf on lush fairways? All vacation amenities are here. Some of Penticton's attractions are listed below:

The Okanagan Summer School of the Arts offers classes in music, the visual arts, drama, dance, creative writing, and voice; call (250) 493–0390 for information.

Tin Whistle Brewery, 954 W. Echkhardt Avenue, (250) 770–1112. You can taste three types of British ale here plus a special Peaches and Cream brew that's available only May through September.

Art Gallery of the South Okanagan, 11 Ellis Street at Front Street, next to the Delta resort; call (250) 493–2928 for hours and fees. Changing exhibitions of painting, photography, pottery, and drawings. World's first art gallery operating on passive solar energy. **Dominion Radio Astrophysical Observatory,** Whitelake Road off Highway 97, (250) 497–5321. Open Monday to Friday. Free. A visitor center has displays on the scientific work being conducted at this facility. There are both radio and optical telescopes, and astronomers are on hand to explain their science.

Reg Atkinson Museum, 785 Main Street, (250) 492–6025. Open Monday through Saturday. Free. Collection of Salish and local archaeological artifacts, natural history specimens, the Braun collection of mounted animals, military memorabilia, and pioneer tools.

Okanagan Game Farm, on Highway 97. Open daily; (250) 497–5405. Admission is charged. A wide variety of North American and African animals (zebras, cougars, grizzly bears, timber wolves) roaming 560 acres overlooking Skaha Lake.

For accommodations and dining in the Penticton area, try the following:

Clarion Lakeside Resort, 21 Lakeshore Drive, (250) 493–8221. One of the premier resorts in the Okanagan, the Delta Lakeside fronts on Okanagan Lake and has its own sandy beach for sunbathing and swimming. The spacious rooms have balconies; there are fine restaurants, saunas, a health club, an indoor pool, and tennis courts. Arrangements for skiing, snowmobiling, skating, ice sailing, and trail riding can be made through the hotel. Expensive.

Best Western Inn at Penticton, 3180 Skaha Lake Road, (250) 493–0311. Near beach; indoor and outdoor pools, restaurant. Moderate.

Sandman Hotel Penticton, 939 Burnaby Avenue, (250) 493–7151. Moderate.

Penticton Travelodge, 950 Westminster Avenue, (250) 492–0225. Moderate.

The Rochester Resort, 970 Lakeshore Drive, (250) 493–1128. Moderate.

Spanish Villa, 890 Lakeshore Drive, (250) 492–2922. Moderate.

Bowmont Motel, 80 Riverside Drive, (250) 492–0112. Moderate.

Ramada Courtyard Inn, 1050 Eckhardt Avenue West, (250) 492–8926; (800) 665–4966. Near convention center, shopping, and airport. Adjacent to golf course. Laundry, kitchenettes. Inexpensive to moderate.

Penticton Inn and Conference Centre, 333 Main, (250)

492–3600; (800) 665–2221. City center, all amenities, licensed restaurant, ski and golf packages. Moderate to expensive.

Black Sea Motel and Restaurant, 970 Lakeshore Drive, (250) 492–5722. Opposite sandy beach and Okanagan Lake, near golf, arena, and convention center; allows pets. Inexpensive.

Black Forest Motel, 707 Westminster Street, (250) 492–0028. Moderate.

Apex Alpine Ski Resort, c/o 160–1636 Main Street, (250) 493–3200. Moderate to expensive condominium units.

After a time in the Okanagan, if you wish to continue east on the Trans-Canada, follow Highway 97 to 97A North, which connects with the Trans-Canada at **Revelstoke.** (If you are traveling west, take 97 North to the Trans-Canada and Kamloops, or if you want to take the Crowsnest Highway 3 East [see page 76], follow 97 South.)

Situated on the source waters of the Columbia River and between the Selkirk and Monashee mountains, Revelstoke was named in honor of Lord Revelstoke, head of a British bank that helped to finance the transcontinental railroad at a critical time in its development. In the late 1800s the town became the mountain divisional center for the Canadian Pacific Railroad (CPR), and it continues to function as an important transportation and supply center for its mountain region. While in Revelstoke, visit the following:

Revelstoke Art Gallery, 315 West First Street, (250) 837–3067. Open June to September; call for hours. Free. Works by local and regional artists and traveling shows.

Revelstoke Museum, 315 West First Street, (250) 837–3067. Call for hours. Free. Displays of the history and development of the town, focusing on the railroad, mining, lumbering, and riverboats.

All of the following accommodations have restaurants and other amenities.

Three Valley Gap Motor Inn, 19 km (11.4 mi) west of town, (250) 837–2109. Moderate.

Sandman Inn, off the Trans-Canada, (250) 837–5271. Moderate.

Best Western Wayside Inn, 1901 Laforme Boulevard, (250) 837–6161. Moderate.

Swiss Chalet Motel, 1101 Victoria Road, (250) 837–4650. Inexpensive to moderate.

Other attractions in the area include **Nakusp Hot Springs** on Highway 23 south from the Trans-Canada at Revelstoke, (250) 265–3689, which offers natural hot springs bathing 44°C (105° to 112°F); waterskiing; helicopter skiing; and golf.

Access to **Mount Revelstoke National Park** is off the Trans-Canada in the Revelstoke area. The 263-square-mile park is located on the western slope of the Selkirk Mountains. There are wonderful views of mountain peaks, glaciers, alpine meadows, and lakes. Hiking trails (65 km/40 mi of them), such as Skunk Cabbage, Giant Cedars, and Mountain Meadows, take you into the interior of the park. A road off the Trans-Canada goes to Mount Revelstoke and its alpine meadows. Also in this area is Balsam Lake. From Mount Revelstoke a hiking trail, along which the natural beauty of the wilderness is both poetic and awesome, goes farther into the park to Eva Lake. Campgrounds are located at Mountain Creek, Loop Brook, and Illecillewaet. The interpretive or information center is at Rogers Pass. For more information, contact Superintendent, Mount Revelstoke and Glacier National Parks, Box 350, Revelstoke, British Columbia V0E 2S0; (250) 837–5155.

Glacier National Park (same address and telephone number as Mount Revelstoke National Park, described above) can be reached from the Trans-Canada. The community of Rogers Pass is at the center of the park. There are more than a hundred glaciers in this national park, as well as dense stands of hemlock and cedar. During the winter and thawing seasons, this is avalanche country, and the frequent plunge of millions of tons of ice and snow down the slopes made the Rogers Pass area one of the most difficult obstacles to overcome in the building of the transcontinental railroad and the Trans-Canada Highway. Today howitzers are used to break up the snow and prevent avalanches from becoming a danger to travelers. Guided hikes begin at the Illecillewaet Campground and move through diverse ecological zones. If you are interested in hiking on the glaciers themselves, check for full details with your local mountaineering club or with the Sierra Club branch in your area. Among the trails in Glacier National Park (140 km/93 mi of them) are Trestle, Loop, Meeting of the Waters, and Abandoned Rails. There are campgrounds in the park.

In 1881, A. B. Rogers, an employee of the CPR, found a pass through the Selkirk Range (later named in his honor) so that one of the final links in the transcontinental railroad could be built. The railroad was put through **Rogers Pass** (elevation 1,323 m/4,302 ft) at great effort and expense in 1885 and 1886. As the area was subject to frequent avalanches, the 8-km (4.8-mi) Connaught Tunnel was built in 1916 to protect lives and the passage of trains. The Trans-Canada Highway came through here in 1962.

Avalanches are still a problem, but an excellent safety program protects travelers moving through this area.

Rogers Pass Information Centre is on the Trans-Canada, (250) 837–6274. Open July to Labour Day; call for times during rest of year. Free. This information center, operated by Parks Canada, is located at the top of Rogers Pass. It provides information on the building and operation of the transcontinental railroad through this rugged part of the country and on the natural history of the area—glaciers, avalanches, caves, alpine meadows, and wildlife— and shows a movie on the secrets of the Nakimu Cave System. The center is well worth the stop to understand the magnificent landscape you are passing through.

For accommodations, try the **Best Western Glacier Park Lodge,** off the Trans-Canada, (250) 837–2126. Great location; dining room and lounge. Moderate.

The town of **Golden,** on the Trans-Canada between the Selkirk Mountains and Glacier National Park and the Rockies and Yoho National Park, was once known as Kicking Horse Flats. You'll find golf, hunting, fishing, wild-river rafting, hiking, and access to some of the top national parks in Canada here. The **Golden Rim Motor Inn,** off the Trans-Canada, (250) 344–2216, has saunas, an indoor pool, and a dining room. Moderate.

The main access to **Yoho National Park** is off the Trans-Canada Highway, and the park's office is in the community of Field. Yoho and Kootenay are "Siamese twin" parks in that they join each other at the B.C.–Alberta border. Yoho, the northern park, runs along the spine of the Canadian Rockies, and Kootenay is the southern park. There's no mistaking that you are in high mountain country here, with a landscape of deep forests, icy glaciers, wild rivers, pure lakes, and an abundance of wildlife. Within its shale area— particularly Burgess, now a World Heritage site—are fossils from prehistory. They're protected and not for collecting, but you can see the remains of ancient creatures by hiking into the shale zone.

Among the many features of the park are the Spiral Tunnels Viewpoint, Kicking Horse Pass, Kicking Horse River, Lake O'Hara (the Alpine Club of Canada has a shelter here), Emerald Lake, Takakkaw Falls, Yoho River, Twin Falls, Laughing Falls, Point Lace Falls, Angel's Staircase Falls, Yoho Glacier, Hamilton Falls and Lake, and Natural Bridge. There are numerous hiking trails (360 km/ 225 mi of them), such as the Deer Lodge Trail and the Avalanche Trail, and the following campgrounds: Kicking Horse, Hoodo

Creek, Chancellor Peak, Takakkaw Falls, and Lake O'Hara. Trout fishing is allowed in Yoho, but you have to get a permit from park authorities; canoeing is possible on Lake O'Hara and Emerald Lake; and you can go trail riding from a stable at Emerald Lake. For more information, contact Superintendent, Yoho National Park, Box 99, Field, British Columbia V0A 1G0; (250) 343–6324.

In addition to its impressively high mountains, **Kootenay National Park** is famous for its wild rivers, glaciers, canyons, and hot springs. Access is from many points along the Banff-Windermere Highway 93 and from the Trans-Canada and Highway 95. The southern end of the park, Radium Hot Springs, is slightly more arid than the northern part at Vermilion Pass (Lake Louise and Banff can be reached from here). These dual climate zones make for diverse vegetation and animal and bird life. Kootenay is a naturalist's paradise, and when the naturalist gets through trekking and observing, there are natural hot springs to soak away fatigue and reestablish a more complete tranquility. The many hiking trails (200 km/125 mi of them), such as Marble Canyon, Paint Pots, Fireweed, Valley View, and Juniper, lead throughout the park. Paint Pots is a bed of ocher that was used in long-past days by the local native peoples. A suspension bridge, reached via the Paint Pots Trail, crosses the powerful Vermilion River.

The hot springs at Radium (noted on page 83) are world famous, and people come from all over North America and many foreign countries to seek a cure for what ails them. A soak in these hot mineral waters is the perfect ending to a long day's drive or hours spent on nearby ski slopes.

Camping with facilities for recreational vehicles is at Redstreak, off Highway 95 near the Trans-Canada; McLeod Meadows, to the north of Radium Hot Springs; and Marble Canyon. Kootenay also offers fishing (permit required) and canoeing on the Kootenay and Vermilion rivers.

For more information, contact Superintendent, Kootenay National Park, Box 220, Radium Hot Springs, British Columbia V0A 1M0; (250) 347–9615.

Highly recommended for accommodations in this area is **Emerald Lake Lodge,** near Field, off the Trans-Canada, about thirty minutes from Lake Louise, Alberta; (403) 343–6321. This is a historic, chalet-type lodge in Yoho National Park. For more than eighty-five years it has been popular with sophisticated travelers seeking tranquility, and it has been recently restored and renovated to contemporary standards. The outstanding setting takes advantage of the essential beauty of the Canadian Rockies. Within the Emerald Lake area you can hunt for fossils or go canoeing, fishing, trail riding, cross-country skiing, or dogsledding. Nearby are Lake O'Hara, Takakkaw Falls, and Yoho Glacier. The main lodge has a dining room and an 1890s Yukon saloon. Entertainers (singers, musicians, dancers, comics) are brought in from Banff. Expensive.

The Canadian Rockies: The B.C.–Alberta Border. The Trans-Canada Highway crosses the **Continental Divide** and enters the province of Alberta through **Kicking Horse Pass** (1,647 m/5,402 ft). Just a few miles past the border, near the Trans-Canada, is Lake Louise. If you head north on Highway 93, you'll reach Jasper (connecting with the Yellowhead Highway 16 East to Edmonton). Highway 93 South leads to Banff and Calgary.

Metro Vancouver to Banff, Alberta, via the Crowsnest Highway 3

The Crowsnest Highway 3 (and Rocky Mountain Trench Highway 93/95 East in the Kootenay region) takes you through or near towns with familiar- and odd-sounding names alike: Princeton, Osoyoos, Greenwood, Trail, Castlegar, Creston, Yahk, Kitchener, Cranbrook, Wasa, Skookumchuck, Fairmont Hot Springs, Invermere, and Radium Hot Springs. You travel over several mountain ranges, through thickly forested valleys, arid ones, and those lush with fruit orchards, until you come to the Kootenays and the Canadian Rockies. View after view of gorgeous alpine scenery and fields of wild mountain flowers are breathtaking. All along the way are museums, historical sites, and places for swimming, fishing, camping, boating, skiing, tennis, hiking, trail riding, wild river rafting, and golf. The accommodations in the towns are fine; some of the resorts are as outstanding as those you'll find anywhere in the world. Although there are few gourmet restaurants as such, most places serve good, honest cooking—both North American and ethnic cuisines—that will satisfy travelers' appetites. If you've previously traveled across B.C. along the Trans-Canada, you'll find this southern route a nice change and see new aspects of this beautiful province. U.S. travelers coming from eastern Washington, Idaho, and western Montana will also find this an enjoyable route to Vancouver.

Osoyoos is the southern gateway to the Okanagan vacation region. In architecture and style, Osoyoos reminds one of a town in Arizona or New Mexico—in fact, it's called the Spanish capital of

Canada. Although the hills around the town are almost desertlike, the land in the valley is irrigated to support extensive orchards and vegetable crops. In July the folks here hold a **Cherry Festival** to honor the fruit they grow in such abundance. Just to the south of town is **Osoyoos Lake,** a perfect place for swimming, sunbathing, boating, fishing, and windsurfing. The **Osoyoos Museum,** (250) 495–6723, welcomes visitors who want to learn about the history of this pleasant community. Osoyoos is just a stone's throw from the B.C.–Washington border, and U.S. travelers can enter the province via U.S. Highway 97.

The following accommodations have restaurants and other amenities:

Desert Motor Inn, on Highway 3, (250) 495–6525. Moderate.

Holiday Sunspree Resort, Highway 3, (250) 495–7223; (800) 216–6246. A new waterfront complex that opened in May 1997 that has all the amenities plus golf packages, a marina, and boat rentals. Moderate to expensive.

Grand Forks is right on the B.C.–Washington border, and U.S. highways 21 and 395 give access to the province at this point. Within the town are a local history museum, a Doukhobor museum (see page 78), and an art gallery. **Grand Forks Motor Inn,** in town, (250) 442–2127, has a restaurant and a pool. Moderate.

Both gold and copper were discovered in the **Trail** area in the late 1800s. Today the primary economic activity is smelting minerals (zinc, lead, and silver) from the region's mines. U.S. travelers coming from Washington can take Washington Highway 25 to B.C. Highway 22. In the city are the Birchbank eighteen-hole golf course, Beaver Creek Provincial Park, Wright Public Pool, Gyro Park, and Seven Mile Dam. Other attractions include the following:

City of Trail Museum, in City Hall. Open weekdays from June through August. Free. Exhibits of local history.

Rossland Historical Museum, in **Rossland.** Open from mid-May to mid-October, (250) 362–7722. Admission is charged. Displays on the geological history of the area. Le Roi Gold Mine underground tour here. Home of B.C. Ski Hall of Fame.

Also in the Rossland area are the **King George VI Provincial Park** and **Red Mountain Ski Area.**

The following accommodations have restaurants and other amenities:

Ram's Head Inn, Red Mountain Road, (250) 362–9577. In a forest setting 3 km (2 mi) from Rossland on Highway 3B. Fireside lounge, at the base of Red Mountain Ski Area. Moderate.

Uplander Hotel, 1919 Columbia Avenue, (250) 362–7375. Family restaurant, cable TV, dining room, lounge, and conference facilities. Just five minutes from Red Mountain ski facilities.

Castlegar is well worth the side trip on Highway 22 North from Trail. The Doukhobors, a unique community of people who live here, came from the steppes of czarist Russia, where they were persecuted for their strong religious beliefs. They were pacifists and refused to serve in the military; they lived in a highly structured communal society; they were vegetarians; and their religious practices were simple and basic in comparison with those of the Byzantine Russian Orthodox.

The writer Tolstoy and the North American Society of Friends (the Quakers, whom the Doukhobors resemble in attitudes and religious practices) helped the Doukhobors leave Russia and settle in Canada. They originally settled in Alberta and Saskatchewan, carving out farms on the prairies. Because of disputes with the provincial governments, they had to move on again and, at last, found refuge in south central British Columbia. The Doukhobors are famous for their choirs, which have performed to enthusiastic audiences throughout Canada, the United States, and other countries. Visit the Zuckerberg Island Heritage Park, the Kootenay Indian Pit House, the Russian Chapel House, the Doukhobor Bridge, and Verigin's Tomb. Peter Lordly Verigin was the Doukhobor spiritual leader who brought them to Canada. Castlegar is also the gateway to the Arrow Lakes—reached via Highway 6—with great opportunities for fishing, swimming, camping, hiking, and sunbathing. While in Castlegar, be sure to see the following:

Doukhobor Historical Museum, across from Castlegar Airport. Open May through September; (250) 365–6622. Admission is charged. Buildings show the communal character and lifestyle of the Doukhobors and tell of their history in Russia and Canada. Sample Russian culinary specialties, such as borscht and perogie, at the Doukhobor Restaurant, where all dishes are vegetarian.

West Kootenay National Exhibition Centre, next to the Doukhobor Museum. Open daily; (250) 365–3337; Free. One of twenty-three National Exhibition Centres in Canada. Exhibits from local and international cultures.

The following inns have restaurants and other amenities:

Sandman Hotel, 1944 Columbia Avenue, (250) 365–8444. Moderate.

Best Western Fireside Motor Inn, 1810 Eighth Avenue, (250) 365–2128. Moderate.

Creston, on the Kootenay River on Highway 3, is famous for its fruit orchards and fields (strawberries, raspberries, cherries, apricots, peaches, plums, pears, and most kinds of apples). A visit here in the spring, when the blossoms are out, or in the summer, when apples are ripening, is a memorable experience in human-cultivated beauty set against a backdrop of magnificent nature. There's a golf course in town.

If you have extra time for exploring, take Highway 3A North to the **Kootenay Lake** area, where there are several golf and fishing resorts. At Kootenay Bay you can take a ferry to Balfour and then Highway 3A to the hot springs at **Ainsworth.** This area can also be visited by taking Highway 3A North from Castlegar to Nelson or Highway 6 to Nelson and then Highway 3A. U.S. citizens coming to Creston from Idaho should take U.S. Highway 95 to Idaho Highway 1 to the border and then B.C. Highway 21 to Creston.

The annual **Blossom Festival** is held in May. Other attractions in Creston include the following:

Creston Valley Museum, off Highway 3, (250) 428–9262. Call for hours. Admission is charged. Housed in the old Stone House; depicts the town's agricultural heritage.

Creston Valley Wildlife Management Area, outside the downtown district. Open throughout the year. Free. Seventeen thousand acres of lakes, streams, and marshes supporting a wide variety of wildlife; guided walks, canoe trips, films, talks, gift shop, and snack bar. For campgrounds, call (250) 428–3260.

Wayside Garden and Aboretum, on Highway 3. Open May to October, (250) 428–2062. Admission is charged. Beautiful floral displays: rose garden, rhododendron dell, water lily and fish ponds, perennial borders, rock garden and lily beds, teahouse, and gift shop.

Recommended accommodations are as follows:

Skimmerhorn Inn, on Highway 3, (250) 428–4009. Moderate.

The Hacienda Inn, in town, (250) 428–2224, has a dining room. Inexpensive to moderate.

City Centre Motel, in town, (250) 428–2257. Moderate.

Downtowner Motor Inn, 1218 Canyon Road, (250) 428–2238. Seniors discount, golf packages, adjacent to licensed restaurants, conference rooms, complimentary in-room coffee.

U.S. travelers entering British Columbia in the **Cranbrook** region can take Montana Highway 93 or Idaho Highway 95. Both these highways come into the city of Cranbrook and continue north through the eastern part of the province to Banff, Alberta; the Trans-Canada; and Lake Louise. If you are headed for Banff and then Calgary, leave the Crowsnest Highway at Cranbrook and continue on Highway 93/95 North.

Cranbrook was developed in the late 1800s when the railroad serving this region selected it over Fort Steele as the terminal point. Today Cranbrook serves as one of the major commercial and transportation centers for the lower Kootenay region. There are fine accommodations, restaurants, shops, and services in this city.

Don't miss **Sam Steele Days** in June, and if you're interested in the railroads, visit **Cranbrook Railway Museum** in downtown Cranbrook, (250) 489–3918. It's open daily throughout the summer and has limited hours in the winter. Admission is free. The museum has restored luxury railway cars—1920s vintage—and a caboose for children to explore.

All of the following accommodations have restaurants and other amenities:

Sandman Inn, 405 Cranbrook Street, (250) 426–4236. Moderate.

Heritage Estate Motel, 362 South Van Horne Street, (250) 426–3862. Inexpensive.

Town and Country Motor Inn, 600 Cranbrook Street, (250) 426–6683. Moderate.

Inn of the South, 803 Cranbrook Street, (250) 489–4301. Moderate.

Best Western Coach House Motor Inn, 1417 Cranbrook Street, (250) 426–7236, (800) 528–1234. Moderate.

From Cranbrook, the Crowsnest Highway 3 continues east to the Alberta border, where, at Pincher Creek, Alberta, it forms a junction with Highway 6. By heading south on 6 you come to Waterton Lakes National Park (see page 212). Just below Waterton—actually, adjoining it—is Glacier National Park in Montana. Between Cranbrook and the Alberta border is the Fernie Ski Area, and just past the town of Sparwood, you go through Crowsnest Pass (elevation 1,396 m/4,533 ft) at the border of the two provinces.

This region of British Columbia (between Cranbrook and the Alberta border) has numerous resort areas offering everything from skiing and white-water rafting to horseback riding and golf. While you're in the area, be sure to visit the following:

Fort Steele Historic Park, 13 km (7 mi) north of Cranbrook on Rocky Mountain Trench Highway 93/95; (250) 489–3351. Open daily. Free. Fort Steele is the main historical attraction in the Kootenay region and should not be missed. A canny fellow by the name of John Galbraith—no relation to the famous economist—saw the potential of this site as settlers, miners, and merchants began moving in, and he started a ferry line. Then there came disputes between the whites and local natives. In 1887, Superintendent Samuel B. Steele and seventy-five North West Mounted Police (D Division) arrived aboard Galbraith's Ferry to establish law and order, and here they built the first NWMP post in British Columbia. Fort Steele, on the bank of the Kootenay River, became a transportation, commercial, and social center for this area. In 1898, however, after the B.C. Southern Railway chose Cranbrook as its divisional point, Fort Steele declined into oblivion. It was brought back to life as a historical park, and today you can stroll Fort Steele's streets and visit its buildings as they were in the 1800s. You can step into the millinery shop; the blacksmith shop; Bleasdell's drugstore; Dr. Watt's office; the Kershaw family store; Coventry's opera house; the Presbyterian, Anglican, and Roman Catholic churches; the Windsor Hotel; and numerous private residences from the Victorian period. Vaudeville shows are performed at the Wild Horse Theatre. There are also a Tea Room for snacks and an interesting museum of local lore.

The city of **Kimberley,** a highly recommended side trip via Highway 95A that is tucked away in the Purcell Mountains, is Bavaria in Canada. Its architecture is a mix of southern German, Austrian, Swiss, and English Tudor. Der Platz (town center) in downtown draws people to shops, restaurants serving schnitzel, outdoor cafés, and the sight of Happy Hans jumping out from what the people here say is the world's largest cuckoo clock. There are outdoor band concerts and strolling musicians. Residents wearing lederhosen and dirndls are a common sight during the summer.

One of Kimberley's main attractions is **Trickle Creek,** an eighteen-hole, par-71 Canadian Professional Golfers Association (CPGA) golf course set in the midst of magnificent scenery. The **Alpine Slide,** a 2,700-foot thrilling run down the side of a mountain, is in operation from July to Labour Day. Kimberley's annual festivals include the **International Old-time Accordion Festival** in July. The **Bavaria City Mining Railway** gives rides from the end of June until Labour Day. Be sure to visit the **Kimberley Heritage Museum,** located above the public library in the Platz, and the **Comico Gardens** with its flowers and plantings.

The following accommodations are highly recommended:

Top of the World Ranch, off Highway 93/95, north of Fort Steele, (250) 426–6306. Top of the World is a family-owned ranch high in the Canadian Rockies (Kootenay region). It takes guests year-round and offers the authentic western ranch experience: trail rides, camp fires, hearty home-cooked food, comfortable accommodations, the panorama of changing seasons, the sight of wild animals and birds, the glory of the mountains, barbecues, fishing, and the knowledge that you have escaped civilization and are enjoying it. Moderate.

Fairmont Hot Springs Resort, in Fairmont Hot Springs on Highway 93/95; (250) 345–6311. The largest natural mineral hot pools in Canada are at Fairmont Hot Springs Resort, which has been a favorite with families since 1922. In addition to swimming and hot springs bathing, it features two championship eighteen-hole golf courses, deluxe hotel and villas, and excellent facilities for camping at its RV park. Its natural hot springs pools have a clear, odorless water with temperatures of 35° to 45°C (90° to 106°F).

The resort also offers tennis, racquetball, squash, trail riding, hiking, and helicopter sightseeing; a game room for children; and canoeing, fishing, and windsurfing on nearby Columbia Lake. In the winter, it operates its own ski center with 10-mile runs (see page 90). The resort is located at the base of the Kootenay section of the Canadian Rockies, and the alpine and lake scenery is fantastic. Fairmont, considered one of Canada's top family resorts, is worth a visit or a prolonged stay. Reservations are essential during peak summer and winter seasons. Moderate to expensive.

Invermere, a small resort community, is at the northern end of Windermere Lake, which flows into Columbia Lake, the source of the mighty Columbia River. The lakes in this area are good for swimming, canoeing, fishing, and windsurfing. There are a number of places with accommodations (such as the Fairmont and Panorama resorts), restaurants, and stores in this scenic area. Be sure to visit the following:

Windermere Valley Pioneer Museum, in town, (250) 342–9769. Open June through August. Admission is charged. Museum in old railroad station; pioneer log cabins, old schoolhouse; copy of the journal of David Thompson (an early explorer, fur trader, surveyor, and mapmaker who helped establish the border between Canada and the United States); pleasant park setting.

Food and lodging are available at the following:

Panorama Resort, in the Invermere area; (250) 342–6941. Panorama is one of Canada's finest alpine resorts. It's actually a self-contained village of deluxe hotel and inn rooms and condos. Grocery, liquor, sports equipment, and gift shops are within the Panorama complex. The resort offers trail rides, wild-river rafting trips, guided treks through the rugged wilderness, tennis, and winter sports (see page 90). Golf is nearby and so is swimming in Columbia Lake. In late August the resort is the host site for the **Annual Scottish Gathering.** Moderate to expensive.

Radium Hot Springs, at the junction of Highways 93 and 95, bordering Kootenay National Park (250–347–9331), is one of the world's famous hot springs. Before the coming of the whites, Amerindians sought to cure their ills in these baths (40°C/102°F). So did Winston Churchill during one of his trips to Canada. Thousands of people believe that these odorless, clear waters heal, and many have indeed experienced relief. The Aquacourt accommodates both bathers and swimmers; it is open to all, every day of the year, with summer hours from 8:30 A.M. to 11:00 P.M. At the Radium Hot Springs Resort an eighteen-hole golf course and facilities for squash, racquetball, and tennis are available. Also within the area are water slides, wild-river rafting trips, hiking trails (some reached by helicopter), and trail rides. Other places to visit are the nearby Bugaboo Ski Area and Our Lady of Peace Shrine.

White Water Trips, Glacier Raft Company, (250) 344–6521, provides thrilling wild-river raft trips on the Vermilion and Kootenay rivers; horseback trips through Yoho National Park, the Continental Divide, and Top of the World Provincial Park; and other trips on the Alberta side of the Rockies.

Accommodations in the area are listed below:

Radium Hot Springs Golf Resort (see above); (250) 347–9311. Moderate to expensive.

Motel Bavaria, (250) 347–9915. Moderate.

Alpen Motel, (250) 347–9823. Moderate.

Crystal Springs Motel, Radium Boulevard, (250) 347–9759. Moderate.

Mount Assiniboine Lodge, in Mount Assiniboine Provincial Park, bordering Kootenay and Banff national parks; (403) 678–2883. Access by hiking trail, helicopter, or cross-country skiing. Log lodge overlooks Magog Lake. Reservations essential. Expensive.

The Canadian Rockies: The B.C.–Alberta border. If you are heading for the Canadian Rockies in Alberta, take Highway 93 East through Kootenay National Park, which crosses the Great Divide at Vermilion Pass (1,639 m/5,367 ft) and enters Banff National Park. The highway joins the Trans-Canada in Alberta just south of Lake Louise. Highway 95 splits off from 93 and continues north until it joins the Trans-Canada at Golden, B.C. From here, you can head east, entering Alberta through Kicking Horse Pass, just a few miles north of Lake Louise or south of Jasper National Park.

Metro Vancouver to the Yukon and Alaska, via Highway 97: The Cowboy and Gold Fever Country of the Cariboo

Cache Creek, at the junction of the Trans-Canada and Highway 97 North, might be a good place to stop for the night if you have come up nonstop from Vancouver and intend to go north on Highway 97. The following accommodations have restaurants and other amenities:

Sandman Inn, (250) 457–6284. Moderate.

Cache Creek Motor Inn, (250) 457–6224. Moderate.

The old gold town of **Clinton** is 40 km (25 mi) beyond Cache Creek. Here, there's the pleasant feeling that not much has changed. In town, real-life Dr. Frank Cambell's office has a sign outside that dates from the 1800s. It reads: BONES SET, BLOOD LET, HOLES PATCHED, BABIES HATCHED.

Fifty miles west of Clinton, set at the base of Mount Bowman, is the spectacular **Echo Valley Ranch Resort,** (250) 459–2386; (800) 253–8831. Combining the rolling grazing lands of the Cariboo with down-home luxury, the resort offers an 8,500-square-foot log ranch house with six themed bedrooms, two private cabins, and a honeymoon cabin. Horse rides, pack trips, white-water rafting, native feast, and teepee accommodation. Moderate to expensive.

In the 1860s, this part of British Columbia—near **100 Mile House**—attracted persons in quest of furs and gold. The 100 Mile House is a hundred miles from the town of Lillooet, which is at "mile 0" on the Cariboo Wagon Road. In the 1930s, Lord Martin Cecil came into the area to manage his father's ranch. This is prime western ranchland for the raising of cattle. Lumbering, mining, and tourism are also major industries.

For fun and adventure, try the following:

The Great Cariboo Ride Society, (250) 395–4096. A nine-day horseback trek across the Fraser Plateau to Gang Ranch; great meals; fishing and dips in waterfalls.

Annual Festivals
Western Days, May
South Cariboo Square Dance Jamboree, June
Great Cariboo Ride, August

Accommodations include the following:
Red Coach Inn, in the village, (250) 395–2266. Moderate.
Imperial Motel, in the village, (250) 395–2471. Moderate.
Best Western 108 Resort, 108 Ranch, (250) 791–5211. Moderate to expensive resort with eighteen-hole golf course.
The Hills Health and Guest Ranch, Highway 97, (250) 791–5225. Moderate to expensive with a new lodge.

Williams Lake is named after Chief William of the Sugar Cane Reserve. Its Indian name is Colunetza, which means "gathering place of the lordly ones." Williams Lake serves the many cattle ranches in the area. Lumbering and mining are also important economic activities. While in town visit the Bullion Gold Mine, see the downtown murals, and tour the Gibralter mines.

The Williams Lake Golf and Tennis Club, (250) 392–6026, has an eighteen-hole golf course, three tennis courts, and a restaurant.

All of the following accommodations have restaurants and other amenities:
Sandman Inn, 664 Oliver Street, (250) 392–6557. Moderate.
Fraser Inn, 285 Donald Road, (250) 398–7055. Moderate.

From Williams Lake, take Highway 20 to **Bella Coola** on the coast, a long journey of 465 km (279 mi). The first fourth of the way, up to **Hanceville,** is paved road, and the rest of the way is gravel. If your vehicle is in good condition and prepared for some rough spots, this trip could be a nice adventure from the interior of the province to the coast. The scenery along the way is beautiful. You pass through several small towns and **Tweedsmuir Park**. You can camp and enjoy the wilderness along the way. If you are bringing along a canoe, all the better. Be careful not to stir up a grizzly en route. The paved road picks up again at the western end of Tweedsmuir Park and takes you to Bella Coola, which is at the Labouchere, Dean, and Burke channels, just east of the Inside Passage (see page 177). There are accommodations, supplies, gas, and food in the villages and in Bella Coola. Midsummer is a good time for this trip, and it is best not to travel under a tight schedule.

In the old days, **Quesnel,** on Highway 97, was a supply center and steamboat landing for the gold-mining town of Bakersville, which is now a historic park. Today Quesnel continues as a transportation center for the local mining and lumbering industries. Both natural gas and oil potential have been found here, and Quesnel may be important to our future as a source of energy.

Barkerville Historic Park, at the end of Highway 26 East, is 82 km (49 mi) from Quesnel. Open daily, (250) 994–3332. Free. A restored village, it dates from the gold rush period in the late 1800s. During the summer, there are stage shows and demonstrations of how people lived and worked in those days. The buildings include a blacksmith shop, saloon, miner's cabin, churches, Chinese herbal shop, general store, and many more. Barkerville does a good job of telling its story. Although it takes some extra time to get there, a visit is well worthwhile.

The Alexander Mackenzie Heritage Trail, between Quesnel in Cariboo's interior and Bella Coola on the coast, is a demanding but immensely satisfying hiking trek through beautiful and historic country; for more information call Heritage Properties Branch in Victoria, (250) 387–1619, or write Alexander Mackenzie Trail Association, P.O. Box 425, Kelowna, British Columbia V1Y 7P1.

For accommodations, try the following:

Cascade Inn, 383 St. Laurent Avenue, (250) 992–5575. Moderate.

Talisman Inn, 753 Front Street, (250) 922–7247. Moderate.

As you travel north from Quesnel, you'll pass through Prince George (described on page 182), the next major city along Highway 97. From here, you can take a few routes. If you are still headed for the Alaska Highway, continue on Highway 97 North until you come to Chetwynd. At the junction, take Highway 29 North, which reconnects with Highway 97 just above the town of Fort St. John. This loop will save you a great deal of time and mileage. Once you commit yourself to the Alaska Highway going north, your only other option (should you decide to turn south) is to take Highway 37 (above Watson Lake in the Yukon) to Prince Rupert; otherwise, you have to backtrack until you reach Prince George.

The Yellowhead Highway 16 bisects Highway 97 in Prince George, and at this point, if you wish to turn east, take the Yellowhead to Jasper and then to Edmonton. From Jasper you can go south on Highway 93 through Jasper National Park and to the Trans-Canada to Lake Louise, Banff, and Calgary. Near the British Columbian border, the Yellowhead passes through Mount Robson Provincial Park, where Mount Robson, the highest point in the Canadian Rockies, and Mount Terry Fox, named in honor of the brave Canadian cross-country runner, are located.

On the banks of the Peace River, once a link in a chain of fur-trading posts, **Fort St. John** became in recent times a center for exploring and developing oil and natural gas in this part of the province. Attractions here include a monument to Alexander Mackenzie, the North Peace Museum of local history, and the North Peace Art Gallery.

The following accommodations have restaurants and other amenities:

Cedar Lodge Motor Inn, 9824 Ninety-ninth Avenue, (250) 785–8107; (800) 661–2210. Full amenities, free airport pickup. Inexpensive to moderate.

Alexander Mackenzie Inn, 9223 One-hundreth Street, (250) 785–8364; (800) 663–8313. Indoor pool, sports lounge. Inexpensive to moderate.

In 1800 the North West Company established a trading post in **Fort Nelson** (408 km/246 mi north of Fort St. John), and the Hudson's Bay Company took over in 1865. Exploration for oil and natural gas has improved the economy here. Lumbering is a principal activity.

Accommodations are available at the **Coachhouse Inn,** 4711 Fiftieth Avenue, (250) 774–3911. Dining room and lounge. Moderate.

To the B.C.–Yukon border: The distance between Fort St. John and the Yukon border is 940 km (564 mi). The only community of any size en route is Fort Nelson, which is about halfway, although there are some small villages. Your best bet is to make sure, while you are in Fort St. John, that your vehicle is fit for the trip—the town is a good place for getting supplies, gas, and whatever else you need. The Alaska Highway going through B.C. is paved, except for a stretch just before the Yukon border. Take advantage of the accommodations and hot meals available in Fort Nelson. It's a good stopping point if you're there in the afternoon; night driving can be hazardous because of the wild animals that cross the road. Of course, you can camp almost anywhere. Two provincial parks with facilities—Muncho Lake and Stone Mountain—are located on the highway north of Fort Nelson. After you enter the Yukon, the first town of any size is Watson Lake, where there are accommodations, food, and auto and other services.

Winter Sports in British Columbia

British Columbia has more opportunities for enjoying winter sports than any other of the provinces in Western Canada (Alberta comes in a close second, with its Rocky Mountain area). Within B.C. you can ski downhill or cross-country, be dropped off on virgin powder from helicopters or Snow-Cats, or go ice-skating, snowshoeing, ice climbing, or fishing. The province's infrastructure of resorts, hotels, restaurants, transportation system, après-ski activities, shops, and ski schools is among the best on the continent. If you haven't yet enjoyed winter in B.C., you've got a cornucopia of treats and thrills waiting for you.

Downhill Skiing

Mount Washington, in the Courtney area of Vancouver Island, (250) 338–1386. Twenty downhill runs; lodges and condos; ski school; après-ski dining and entertainment; by-the-week packages; equipment rentals.

Grouse, in North Vancouver, a few minutes from city center (see page 120), (604) 984–0661. All runs are lit until 11:00 P.M.; Bavarian beer garden; snow-making; Canadian Ski Instructor's Alliance (CSIA) ski school; 1,110-m (3,641-ft) summit; close to city accommodations and restaurants.

Whistler/Blackcomb, one of the top ski resort areas in Western Canada; more than sixty marked runs for every level of expertise (see page 110 for more details); call (604) 932–4222 or (800) 944–7853 for information on packages and hotel reservations.

Hemlock Valley, in Hemlock Valley, two hours from Vancouver city center via Highway 7, (604) 797–4411. Five hundred acres of skiing terrain; Winter Carnival; helicopter skiing; Hemlock Inn; ski school; night skiing.

Apex Alpine, in the Okanagan region (Penticton area), (250) 493–2880; (800) 387–2739. Thirty-six runs—2,000-foot vertical drop; ski school; ice rink; hot tubs; condos.

Big White Ski Resort, in the Okanagan region (Kelowna area), (250) 765–8888; (800) 663–2772. Forty-one runs—1,900-foot vertical drop; ski packages; ski school day-care facility.

Silver Star Mountain Resort, in the Okanagan region (Vernon area), (250) 542–0224; (800) 663–4431. Thirty-two runs; new accommodations; equipment rentals; ski school.

Sun Peaks Resort, in the Okanagan region (Kamloops area), (250) 578–7222; (800) 663–2838. 3,100-foot vertical drop; forty-six runs; ski school. Several new mountain-top hotels have been constructed in the past two years.

Big White near Kelowna. ➤

White Water, in the southeastern corner of the province, the Selkirk Range of the Canadian Rockies, (250) 354–4944. Eighteen runs; helicopter skiing on virgin powder; accommodations in Nelson.

Red Mountain, in the Castlegar area, (250) 362–7700. 2,800-foot vertical drop; powdery alpine meadows; hot racing slopes; ski school; equipment rentals; helicopter skiing.

Panorama Resort, located south of the Bugaboos, (250) 342–6941; (800) 663–2929. 3,800-foot vertical drop; cross-country trails; helicopter skiing; luxury accommodations; outdoor hot tubs.

Fairmont Hot Springs, in the heart of the Canadian Rockies, (250) 345–6311. Runs for all levels of expertise; cross-country trails; excellent accommodations; ski packages.

Kimberley Resort, which in the Rockies is called Little Bavaria because of German-style architecture in the town and restaurants, (250) 427–4881; (800) 667–0871. 2,300-foot vertical drop; longest night skiing run in North America; ski school; plenty of accommodations, entertainment, and restaurants.

Fernie Snow Valley, in the Canadian Rockies near Cranbrook, (250) 423–9221. 2,400-foot vertical drop; excellent accommodations, restaurants, and entertainment in the area; ski school.

Helicopter Skiing

Helicopters take you to mountaintops where there are unlimited runs of virgin powder. Top professional guides show you the way down, and the safety standards in equipment and on the runs are among the best in the world. Helicopter skiing in the Canadian Rockies is one of the thrilling wonders of this world. The following organizations offer helicopter skiing in the mountain ranges of British Columbia:

Canadian Mountain Holidays, the Bugaboos, Cariboos, Bobbie Burns, and Monashees; (403) 762–4531.

Mike Wiegele Helicopter Skiing, the Cariboos and Monashees; (403) 762–5548.

Kootenay Helicopter Skiing, the Selkirks and Monashees; (250) 265–3121 or (800) 663–0100.

Heli-Ski Panorama, the Purcells; (250) 342–3889 or (800) 661–6060.

Selkirk Wilderness Skiing, the Selkirks and Monashees; (250) 366–4424 or (800) 799–3499.

Snow-Cat Skiing

A twelve-passenger Snow-Cat vehicle will take a group to the top of a virgin powder run—no lifts, no crowds, the mountain mostly to oneself. This type of skiing offers all the advantages of helicopter skiing without the helicopter.

Selkirk Wilderness Skiing, five-day, all-inclusive packages; (250) 366–4424.

Great Northern Snow Cat Skiing, three- to six-day, all-inclusive packages; (250) 832–9500.

Nordic and Cross-Country Skiing

British Columbia has some of the most spectacular ski-touring areas in North America. Within or near the national and provincial parks are bed-and-breakfasts, ranches, motels, and resorts. A number of resorts have their own cross-country skiing trails.

National Parks: Yoho, Kootenay, and Glacier.

Provincial Parks: Assiniboine, Garibaldi, Manning, Alice Lake, Brandywine Falls, Champion Lakes, Kokanee Creek, Maclure Lake, Nancy Greene, Strathcona, Top of the World, Wells Gray, Whiteswan, Beaton, Bugaboo Glacier, Cypress, Kitsumkalum Mountain, Kokanee Glacier, Mount Seymour, Stageleap, Ten Mile Lake, Wasa, West Lake, and Mount Robson.

Call Tourism British Columbia at (800) 663–6000 for more information on recreation in these parks.

CHAPTER 5

Vancouver: Camelot by the Pacific

What Makes Vancouver Special

Several years ago Bob Hope played Vancouver and paid the city a most generous compliment: "People say that they've left their hearts in San Francisco. But they haven't seen Vancouver!" For those who have seen Vancouver, however, these words are well understood. Describing both cities as similar in many respects is fairly accurate—both enjoy laid-back lifestyles and excellence in creative and commercial efforts.

Vancouver has a mild climate most of the year, although it gets bountiful doses of rain from time to time, just as nearby Seattle does. The hazards of snow and ice rarely plague drivers here, but when the slush does hit, there is mayhem on the roads because people have forgotten or never learned how to drive in the mush. Vancouver offers skiing and sailing, both within an hour of each other. Its backyard sprawls over millions of acres of thick forests, tall mountains, wild rivers, and pure lakes. Some, such as native medicine men and scientists, say the legendary but shy Big Foot lives nearby in the deep woods.

Vancouver lacks much of the violent crime of California cities, and visitors from the States appreciate the generally law-abiding ways of Vancouverites. Stiff-upper-lip British traditions are very strong—more so in Victoria—but they've been slotted into the wider spectrum of cultures of the Poles, Greeks, Ukrainians, Chinese, Italians, Pakistanis, Indians, and Portuguese, to name but a few of the city's mosaic of peoples. Every kind of alternative lifestyle is here, too. Both the proper and the strange coexist without too many noses put out of joint. Perhaps this is the way people were meant to live, not as clones of one another but in diversity and harmony.

To Canadians living in the East, Vancouver is often thought of as their country's lotusland, the place to pull yourself together again after a divorce or any kind of bad luck. Once you feel psychically on top again, you can return to Ottawa, Montreal, Toronto, or Halifax. But few, it seems, end up going back east permanently. Life is that good in Vancouver.

Among the noteworthy persons who have lived in the Vancouver area are the artist/writer Emily Carr; Malcolm Lowry, author of *Under the Volcano;* and Ayn Rand, the famous writer and promoter of rugged individualism. The best of contemporary Canadian architecture has its roots here through such talented designers as Arthur Erickson. The city's University of British Columbia surely must be considered among the Ivy League of Canadian higher education. So-called beautiful people abound in Vancouver. The religions of health, fitness, and narcissism are pursued with the fervor of Ponce de León seeking the Fountain of Youth. But this is, after all, the west coast. The mind-set and ways are similar to those in California. Exceptional affluence is expressed everywhere in order to be seen—in fashions, cars, homes, and all sorts of other fancies. Poverty is hardly a virtue here, and the theological concept of predestination based on wealth beats mightily in the breasts of many well-heeled Vancouverites.

Vancouver is a city of opera, symphony, rock and roll, live theater, motion picture and television production, gourmet restaurants, diverse museums, and folk arts and crafts. Among the TV shows shot on location here have been *Wise Guy, 21 Jump Street, The X-Files, Millennium, The Commish,* and *MacGyver.* Vancouverites love sports—hockey, soccer, lawn bowling, golf, sailing, cricket. They are prime candidates for a major league baseball team. They are fanatical about sports oddities also, and in a nearby suburb, during the summer, there is an annual belly-flopping contest in which men weighing in the 350-pound-and-up range jump into a pool to determine who can make the biggest splash.

If Vancouverites have any hang-up about where they live, it's their sense of isolation from the eastern power centers of Canada. In the past they felt this apartness politically, economically, socially, and culturally. Now their loneliness is mainly political. No one would bet that a politician from Vancouver would ever become prime minister of Canada, although John Turner, leader of the Liberal party and representing the riding of Vancouver Quadra, was prime minister for a short time after the resignation of Pierre Trudeau—but even then Turner was more of an Ontario figure. Much to the nation's surprise, Kim Campbell, a true British Columbian and a woman, succeeded Brian Mulroney as leader of the Conservative Party and as Prime Minister in 1993, although she was subsequently defeated a few months later by the Liberals led by Jean Chretien. At any rate, Vancouver has wisely turned its face firmly to Asia—China, Japan, and the other thriving countries of the Pacific. The city's prosperous destiny lies more in this direction than toward the old boys' networks back east. Here in the Pacific Rim area, a brave new world is opening like the petals of the lotus flower at dawn, and Vancouver is very much a part of it all. What makes Vancouver special? Not any one tangible thing. It is something far more valuable: a continuing freshness combined with on-going potential.

A Brief Look at Vancouver's History

The first inhabitants of the area that is now the city of Vancouver were the Coast Salish people, noted for their high culture. Their descendants continue to live near the city, keeping alive an honored heritage through their arts and crafts. Captain James Cook was the first European to sail along here, and a few years later, Captain George Vancouver mapped this part of the northwest coast and claimed what he saw for George III, King of England—hence the name Strait of Georgia, the strait on which the city bearing the explorer's name lies.

It was not until the early 1860s, however, that any significant number of white people moved in to settle permanently. They were attracted by the prospect of making money in the lumber industry. In those early days, Vancouver was a raw, rough, grimy, but booming logging town, inhabited by tough timber and sawmill workers, shrewd entrepreneurs, and those who made big money on the periphery, such as Gassy Jack Deighton, a colorful saloon keeper who has been immortalized in local folklore. Another economic boost came with the completion of the transcontinental railroad, which linked this burgeoning port with the great cities of Eastern Canada, such as Toronto and Montreal. Sir William Cornelius Van Horne, chairman of the Canadian Pacific Railroad, helped to accelerate the city's growth as a major port by using it to ship grain from Alberta, Saskatchewan, and Manitoba to foreign buyers. Also from this port, in the nineteenth century, people crazed with "gold fever" sailed for fortune or misery up to major lodes in the Yukon and the Klondike. The opening of the Panama Canal in the early part of this century increased Vancouver's importance as a seaport. Although the early population was mostly of British and American origin, a sizable Chinese community began to develop from among those who had helped to build the transcontinental. During succeeding years, the city rapidly expanded as an influential business and population center, attracting new money and ever-increasing numbers of new people.

Unlike Montreal, Toronto, Halifax, and other east coast Canadian cities, Vancouver has had a relatively bland history. It has never experienced destruction from war or the anguish of rebellion and foreign occupation, as have places in Eastern Canada. Conflicts with coastal Indian tribes and later with Chinese tong societies do, however, give the Vancouver story some drama. The dismal years of the Great Depression of the 1930s, the sequestering in concentration camps of the city's native Japanese population in the World War II years, and the mistreatment of Pakistani immigrants during the 1960s and early 1970s are black marks on the proud heritage of an otherwise tolerant, highly civilized society.

Actually, the most exciting part of Vancouver's history is happening right now. The extraordinary success of Expo '86 was solid evidence of the city's present and future achievement. Because of its dynamism, location, climate, population, and financial strength, Vancouver is very much Canada's city of the future. Today it ranks second in economic importance, after Toronto. In little more than a hundred years, the progress of Vancouver from a rude logging camp to the bright jewel on the Pacific has been phenomenal. The use of such superlatives in Vancouver's case is not excessive.

The following are key dates and events in Vancouver's history:

1778 Captain James Cook, British explorer, sails into the area, but he keeps on going.

95

1792 Another Briton, Captain George Vancouver, takes possession of the area for the empire. Vancouver had been a junior officer when Cook first sailed into this part of the world.

1793 Another intrepid explorer, Alexander Mackenzie, treks to the Pacific Coast, becoming the first white person on record to journey across Canada.

1867 What is now downtown Vancouver—the West End—is sold for the minimal sum of 114 pounds, 11 shillings, and 8 pence. Today it is one of the most expensive real estate areas in North America. Also in 1867, Gassy Jack Deighton opens his saloon to satisfy thirsty lumber workers and gold seekers. Today a glitzy section of boutiques and cafés occupies this section, but it continues to be known as Gastown in Jack's honor.

1886 The town of Granville becomes a city and officially takes the name of Vancouver. During this year, Vancouver is destroyed by fire in just twenty minutes. The city acquires its first fire engine more than a month later.

1887 The first passenger train arrives from Montreal.

1897 The first Vancouver ship departs for the great gold rush in the Klondike.

1907 Vancouver's stock exchange is incorporated. Today it's the third most important exchange in Canada.

1909 The city gets its first skyscraper. Today's city center is a forest of gleaming skyscrapers.

1915 The Vancouver Millionaires hockey team wins the coveted Stanley Cup.

1944 Vancouver and Odessa, USSR, become sister cities.

1957 Queen Elizabeth, queen of Canada, and Prince Philip make their first of several visits to Vancouver.

1976 The University of British Columbia's outstanding Museum of Anthropology opens.

1986 Expo opens and logs twenty-two million visits, making it one of the most successful world's fairs in history. The Dr. Sun Yat-sen Gardens open in Chinatown. Vancouver celebrates its one-hundredth birthday as a city.

1987 The British Columbia World Trade and Convention Centre, one of the largest and best equipped on the North American continent, opens.

Vancouver is a city of adjectives—dynamic, big, frenetic, vibrant, beautiful,▶ progressive, tolerant, sophisticated, cultured, naughty. It has everything and gets better all the time.

1988 to the present Vancouver becomes "Hollywood North" with a full schedule of major motion picture and television production.

1990 to the present The first Vancouver Indy Race takes place on streets around B.C. Place Stadium. It's held on Labour Day weekend.

1991 Rock star Bryan Adams buys and restores the oldest brick building in Vancouver, the Oppenheimer Brothers grocery warehouse at Columbia and Powell Streets.

1993 Vancouver is the venue for a two-day summit meeting between presidents Bill Clinton of the United States and Boris Yeltsin of Russia.

1994 The Grizzlies, Vancouver's NBA entry, opens its first season at GM Place, the downtown home of hockey's Canucks and the Grizzlies.

1995 to the present The old warehouse district, Yaletown, north of False Creek, is converted into the latest chic and funky "in" place with condos, bistros, and shops carved from old brick buildings.

1996 The new Vancouver International Airport terminal opens, making travel into and out of the region easier. The Open Skies Treaty opens up Canada–U.S. intercity travel.

Vancouver Today: Some Basic Facts

Vancouver is located in the southwest corner of British Columbia, about 30 miles from the U.S. border.

Vancouver itself is only 44 square miles, but its metropolitan area, consisting of several municipalities, is 1,076 square miles.

Vancouver is Canada's third-largest city in terms of population. The city itself has close to 450,000 inhabitants; the metro area has nearly 1.6 million people.

Vancouver is one of North America's busiest seaports, especially for shipping raw materials produced in Canada (coal, metals, petroleum, potash, grain, timber, and others) to the industrial countries of Asia. It has companies involved in the lumber industries and in fisheries, which are mainstays of the region's economy. It is one of Canada's primary service and financial centers, in sectors such as banking and brokerage companies. Both federal and provincial governments have sizable operations in the metro area. Tourism is another large industry, with attractions and amenities among the finest anywhere.

University and medical facilities are known throughout the world for their excellence. They attract outstanding talent from throughout Canada, the United States, and other countries.

How to Get to Vancouver

A prominent North American city and Canada's door to the Pacific Rim region, Vancouver is served by major transportation companies—domestic and international airlines, transcontinental passenger rail service, buses, and cruise-ship lines from Los Angeles and Seattle (the ship itinerary usually includes the Yukon and Alaska as well). U.S. interstate and Canadian interprovincial highways, such as the Trans-Canada Highway 1, give direct, quick access to the city.

By Plane

The following air transportation companies provide service to Vancouver: Air Canada (from major Canadian, U.S., and international departure points); Air B.C. and Time Air (from British Columbia towns and cities, Seattle, and Calgary); Canadian Airlines; also United, Japan, Qantas, British Airways, Lufthansa, Canada 3000, Cathay Pacific, KLM, American, United, Delta, Continental, and Singapore, among others. Contact your local travel agent for schedules and fares.

Vancouver International Airport is located on Sea Island near Richmond, a short ride on Granville Street from Vancouver city center (about 12 miles; twenty-five minutes). It is one of Canada's busiest and most modern air travel facilities. Shuttle buses and cabs make frequent runs between the airport and city center, and a number of hotels in city center provide airport transportation services or are regular stops for the shuttles. All the major car-rental companies have booths in the main terminal, which itself has an array of dining places, lounges, money-changing offices, duty-free and gift shops, and bookstores. Adjacent to the airport are many fine hotels and restaurants. When you arrive at the airport, you must clear Canadian Customs. If you're returning to the States, you can also clear U.S. Customs at the airport.

By Car

The main road to Vancouver from Eastern Canada is the Trans-Canada Highway 1. The distance on the Trans-Canada, for example, from Calgary, Alberta, to Vancouver is 1050 km (652 mi). Highway 3 is another route from the Alberta border that takes you through some beautiful country in southern British Columbia, along the border with Montana, Idaho, and Washington. From the Trans-Canada you can pick up Highway 95 a few miles north of Banff; the highway goes by Kootenay National Park and connects with Highway 3 at either Cranbrook or Fort Steele.

If you are traveling north from U.S. west coast cities, Interstate 5 is your best route. The distance from Seattle to Vancouver is 144 miles, or a three-hour drive at 55 mph and a stop at Canadian Customs. Interstate highways from the East make a direct connection with Interstate 5 (check your map for routing). Interstate 5 connects at the U.S.–Canadian border with British Columbia Highway 99. Canada Customs is in the B.C. town of White Rock, and U.S. Customs is in Blaine, Washington.

A more interesting way of traveling to Vancouver from the South is first to tour the magnificent Olympic National Park area of Washington (the Olympic Peninsula), then take the car ferry from Port Angeles on the Strait of Juan de Fuca to the charming capital of Victoria, British Columbia, on Vancouver Island. From Sidney, take another car ferry through the Gulf Islands to the city of Vancouver (the ferry docks at Tsawwassen just south of the city center, a forty-five- to sixty-minute drive). You might also want to tour Vancouver Island, which is on the open Pacific (see page 165 for more details), and return to Vancouver via car ferries from Nanaimo.

By Train

Both VIA Rail (the Canadian passenger rail system) and Amtrak (passenger trains serving U.S. destinations) provide service to Vancouver. In the case of VIA Rail, you can count on regularly scheduled daily service from most points east of Vancouver. You can come into Vancouver either through the Rocky Mountain portals of Calgary and Banff National Park or through Edmonton and Jasper National Park. On the return trip east, you have the option of visiting the national park you missed on your way west. VIA Rail will also help you book hotels, rental cars, and package tours in Canada.

Amtrak will take you via Chicago to Seattle and through to

Vancouver. Amtrak trains provide service to Seattle from U.S. west coast cities too. Amtrak will help you make reservations for hotels, rental cars, and tours as well.

Vancouver's rail station is located at 1150 Station Street, in the False Creek section of the city, at Main and Terminal.

By Bus

Bus transportation from U.S. and Canadian destinations arrives at and departs from the Greyhound Bus Depot at 1150 Station Street.

By Boat

A number of cruise-ship lines, such as the "Love Boats" of Princess, include Vancouver as a major port stop on their Northwest Coast sailings through the Inside Passage and up to Alaska. Contact your local travel agent for details and prices.

As a leading port and sailing center, Vancouver has marina facilities for visiting yachtsmen, but docking space is especially tight during busy seasons.

How to Get Around in Vancouver

Vancouver city center, where most tourist and business activity is focused, is but a tiny part of this large metropolis. It is actually a huge peninsula. Along its north coast is a fjord known as the Burrard Inlet, which splits off into Indian Arm. To its south, the mighty Fraser River forms a delta and flows into the Strait of Georgia. Between Vancouver's Point Grey and the separate municipality of West Vancouver is English Bay, the city's broad front yard of water. Vancouver is surrounded by several municipalities that together compose Metro Vancouver—West Vancouver, North Vancouver, Burnaby, Coquitlam, New Westminster, and Richmond.

Except for side trips to certain attractions, you will probably spend most of your time in the central core of Vancouver, and so it shouldn't be too difficult to get around. Pender, Dunsmuir, Georgia, and Robson streets, running northwest/southeast, are parallel with one another. Burrard, Hornby, Howe, Granville, Richards, Homer, Hamilton, and Cambie bisect the others at right angles. These are the main streets of Vancouver city center, where you'll find some of the major hotels, shops, office buildings, art museums, and restaurants. The best way to orient yourself is to use the Hotel

METRO VANCOUVER

DOWNTOWN VANCOUVER

Vancouver, with its green copper, mansard roof, as your center point (Robson Square here will also do). Other landmarks in the area are the Birk's Clock and the Vancouver Art Gallery, both on Georgia Street. The hotel faces Georgia Street, which runs northwest toward Stanley Park. A few blocks beyond the back of the hotel is English Bay, and beyond that Vancouver Island. A few blocks past the front of the hotel is the waterfront on Burrard Inlet, the location of the new convention center and the cruise-ship docks. The nearby snowcapped mountains (Coast Mountains) that you see are north of the city. Most of the streets are nicely laid out in an easy-to-comprehend grid pattern.

Most city center attractions, including Stanley Park, can be seen the best and least expensive way on foot. Free maps are available at your hotel or at the **Tourism Vancouver Information Centre,** Suite 210, 200 Burrard Street, (604) 683–2000. The information center will also provide free literature and answer any questions you have about the city. It is an excellent place to start your tour of Vancouver.

Vancouver has superb public transportation to most sections of the city. **B.C. Transit** operates the city's bus system, with frequent service from 4:00 A.M. to midnight. Call (604) 521–0400 for fare and schedule information. A Seabus, actually two 400-passenger catamarans, connects city center with North Vancouver. The sail across the Burrard Inlet takes fewer than fifteen minutes. You can take aboard a bike on weekends and holidays for an additional, minor cost. The Seabus departs from the old CPR (Canadian Pacific Railroad) station near Granville Square in Vancouver city center and from Lonsdale Quay in North Vancouver. For more information, call (604) 521–0400. The Seabus, part of B.C. Transit, is a great tourist attraction, but avoid weekday rush hours.

The public transit ALRT (Advanced Light Rapid Transit) system is run by computers, although a security officer rides along. In city center ALRT is called Skytrain, part of B.C. Transit, because it moves on elevated rails. The ALRT system takes commuters and visitors all the way from New Westminster to the waterfront at the new trade and convention center. The return trip takes about an hour. Call (604) 521–0400 for schedules and fares.

Taxi cabs are everywhere, but nowhere when you need one the most. Have your hotel get a cab for you, or call Yellow Cab, (604) 731–1111, or Black Top, (604) 731–1111, or Maclure's, (604) 731–9211. Yellow Cab, by the way, will give you a tour of the city at the meter rate.

Useful Information

Emergencies: Police, fire, ambulance, dial 911.

Doctor: (604) 733–7758 (College of Physicians and Surgeons will provide referrals to foreign language–speaking doctors); after 5:00 P.M., 911.

Dentist: (College of Dental Surgeons of B.C.) (604) 736–3621.

Poison: (604) 682–5050 or 682–2344.

Rape: (604) 872–8212.

Crisis: (604) 872–3311

Veterinarian: (604) 734–7744.

Canadian Coast Guard (search and rescue): (800) 567–5111.

Vancouver Hospital and Health Sciences Centre: 855 West Twelfth Avenue, (604) 875–4111.

Road service (twenty-four-hour service): must be a member of an auto club, (604) 293–2222 in Vancouver.

Time zone: Pacific (three-hour difference from New York, Toronto, and Montreal).

Telephone area code: 604.

Climate: Sunny but not very hot summers; usually dry, invigorating weather. Rainy in autumn and winter, but very little snow at or near sea level. For the latest report on road conditions, call (800) 663–4997.

Special clothing: Bring a light raincoat, a hat, and an umbrella, plus a warm jacket and sweater for evenings.

Local holiday: B.C. Day, celebrated first Monday in August.

Mass media: The *Province* (morning newspaper) and the *Vancouver Sun* (morning newspaper); all other major national and international newspapers and magazines are available at newsstands. Both Canadian and American television, including cable programming, and radio are available at the flick of the dial.

Most hotels list the addresses of places of worship and their schedule of services.

Special Events

The two biggest special events are the **Sea Festival** in July and the **Pacific National Exhibition** in August and early September. Below is a listing of some of the other top events:

January/February
Chinese New Year Celebrations in Chinatown.

March
Spring Celebration on Granville Island.

April
B.C. Great Outdoors Show.
International Wine Festival.

May
Vancouver International Marathon.
Children's Festival.

June
North Vancouver Folkfest.

July
Vancouver Sea Festival, fireworks, salmon barbecues, parades, and
    the great Nanaimo-to-Vancouver bathtub race.
Vancouver International Chamber Music Festival.
Vancouver Folk Music Festival.

August
International Airshow at Abbotsford.

August/September
Pacific National Exhibition (PNE), one of the great agricultural
    and industrial fairs of the Pacific Northwest (the fifth-largest
    such fair in North America), held since 1910. There are
    countless exhibits and demonstrations, top-star entertain-
    ment, a demolition derby, a beauty contest, a midway, and
    lumberjack competitions. The PNE is held in Exhibition Park
    and operates from mid-August to Labour Day.
Greater Vancouver Open (PGA).
Vancouver Indy Car Race.

October
Vancouver International Film Festival.

November
Christmas Fair.

December
Christmas Craft Fairs in various parts of the city. Christmas carol
    music from boats: young carolers on board the *Carol Ship*,

which sails throughout the harbor to different locations on each of the three evenings of this beautiful event. They go as far as Point Grey, Deep Cove, and Port Moody.

Special Tours Outside Vancouver City Center

Royal Hudson Steam Train; board at B.C. Rail Station, 1311 West First Street in North Vancouver; call (604) 688–7246 for schedule and fares (advance reservations are advised).

The Royal Hudson, a vintage steam train, takes you along the beautiful coast north of Vancouver. This is a two-hour, 40-mile trip to the lumber community of Squamish. You pass by Horseshoe Bay with its many islands (Gambier and Bowen islands), near tall Douglas firs and the Coast Mountains. The views are spectacular; don't forget to bring your camera. If you let your imagination take wing, you could very well be in the fjord country of Norway. Squamish, the final destination, has restaurants and gift shops. You can return on the Royal Hudson or take a bus to a dock where you board the MV *Britannia,* a comfortable boat with such amenities as a snack bar offering sandwiches, soft drinks, and beer. The MV *Britannia* sails along the coast back to Vancouver, but the perspectives of the landscapes and seascapes from its decks are entirely different from the views out the windows of the Royal Hudson. Keep a sharp eye out for bald eagles. The round-trip consumes the better part of a day, but it's a memorable experience for all ages.

Marine drives. There are two marine drives: one that goes along the same basic route as the Royal Hudson, and another that goes around Point Grey on the opposite side of English Bay. When you take the **Northern Marine Drive,** you can visit Lighthouse Park; explore many of the small communities along the coast; stop awhile and cast a line for fish; take a ferry over to Nanaimo on Vancouver Island; hike trails in thick, primeval woods; and see awesome waterfalls on the way to Squamish via Highway 99. While on this northern route you can also drive—along with taking a couple of extra ferry rides—as far as Powell River on the mainland. The road stops a few miles above Powell River. After that are nothing but wilderness and a few coastal Indian reserves until Prince Rupert, B.C., and Alaska. If you wish to see more of this exceptionally beautiful north-

ern coast, take a cruise-ship voyage or a B.C. ferry from the northern tip of Vancouver Island through the Inside Passage to Prince Rupert, the Yukon, and Alaska. Such a voyage can be one of the great adventures of North America. The town of Squamish, north of Horseshoe Bay, is about as far as most people go in their brief forays from Vancouver. But if you continue inland on Highway 99, you will come to one of British Columbia's prize summer and ski resort areas, Whistler.

The second Marine Drive is less adventuresome but not without its rewards. This route is officially called **North West Marine Drive** and melds into **South West Marine Drive**. It goes around Point Grey, offering wonderful views of English Bay, the skyline of Vancouver city center, the Strait of Georgia, Vancouver Island, and the Gulf Islands. Along the way you will pass a number of beaches for swimming, sunbathing (including nude sunbathing), windsurfing, and picnicking. You will also circle the campus of the University of British Columbia, with its many museums, including the fabulous Museum of Anthropology; the exquisite Nitobe Memorial Garden (Japanese); and the extensive University Endowment Lands, where you can hike in the midst of botanical splendor. You can reach North West Marine Drive via Burrard and Cornwall. The private homes along the way are extraordinary, and so are their gardens and landscaping. They evoke envy in even the most innocent. There are several golf courses along the South West Marine Drive section; McCleery is open to the public.

Victoria. No visit to Vancouver would be complete without a side trip to Victoria, the tranquil, blossom-festooned capital of British Columbia. Regularly scheduled ferries connect the two cities at Tsawwassen, from Vancouver city center via Highways 99 and 17. (See chapter 6 for a complete description of Victoria.)

Gulf Islands, reached via ferries from Tsawwassen terminal; call B.C. Ferries at (604) 277–0277 for schedules and fares (reservations required).

In this part of the Strait of Georgia, the Canadian–U.S. international border zigzags to the extent that it's often difficult for a sailor to figure out just which country he or she is in on any given tack. Also here are numerous small islands, some belonging to

◄Vancouver's position between sea and mountains allows you to ski on fresh snow at a nearby peak one hour and windsurf or sail in the harbor the next hour.

British Columbia and others to the state of Washington. The Gulf Islands are Canadian, and the San Juan Islands are American, because they are nearest the Strait of Juan de Fuca, which separates the tip of Vancouver Island from the north shore of the Olympic Peninsula. If it all sounds confusing, it is, until you look at a map.

In addition to local fishing families, many professionals and people with artistic bents live on the Gulf Islands, which are small, rural islands tucked away from the frenetic pace of the city but also close enough to it so that one can easily go into Vancouver for a gourmet meal, a concert, or a stage show. You can visit these lovely islands by car, but a bike or good walking shoes are the best way for exploring them. Generally, the people who live on the islands are friendly, and the institution of the general store on some of them continues to be the center of gossip and simple fun. The many beaches, cliffs, and forest parks are good areas to see bald eagles and sea otters. Visit the studios of artisans and buy their elegant wares. The primary islands and their ferry ports are **Galiano Island** (Montague Harbour and Sturdies Bay), **Mayne Island** (Village Bay), **Saturna Island** (Saturna), **North Pender Island** (Otter Bay), and **Saltspring Island** (Long Harbour, Vesuvius Bay, and Fulford Harbour).

There are good accommodations on the Gulf Islands. For example, the **Cliff Bodega Bed & Breakfast,** on Galiano Island, (250) 539–2260, offers log chalets with fireplaces and stained glass windows, kitchen facilities, and two trout ponds, all on twenty-five acres of meadows and trees, overlooking mountains and sea. Moderate. Also consider Surf Lodge on Gabriola Island, (250) 247–9231, moderate; Cusheon Lake Resort on Saltspring Island, (250) 537–9629, moderate; and Mallard's Mill Inn (250) 537–1011. Some have dining and lounge facilities and recreational offerings, such as horseback riding, scuba diving, tennis, swimming pools, golf, and trout fishing. For more information on accommodations on the Gulf Islands, call Tourism British Columbia at (800) 663–6000.

Whistler Resort Area, located 75 miles north of Vancouver via Highway 99, is about a two-hour drive. (Use caution driving, as the road can be hazardous at times.)

The Whistler Resort Area has the best skiing closest to Metro Vancouver. Whistler has become one of the most fashionable four-seasons resort areas in North America, attracting scores of the rich and famous as well as ordinary folk. It features the highest vertical drop of any mountain in North America—5,208 ft (1,609 m), at

Blackcomb Mountain. It has chair lifts, T-bars, and a gondola to take you to the top. There are more than sixty runs, with the longest being 7 miles, and 50 percent of them are in the intermediate skill range. There are also trails for cross-country skiing and snowshoeing. Equipment rentals are available at Whistler Village Sports and other outlets. The Whistler area gets about 450 inches of snow a year, making for a long, satisfying season. Helicopter skiing is also offered here during the winter and helicopter hiking in the summer. These nimble whirlybirds take you high up on the Coast Mountains, and you come back down on your own over virgin snow or on foot through magnificent forests, picking a bouquet of wildflowers on the way. For more information and rates, call Whistler Heli-Skiing/Hiking, Ltd., (604) 932–4105.

In the warm-weather months, the Whistler area is a great getaway for fishing, horseback riding, tennis, golf—an eighteen-hole Arnold Palmer–designed course (604–932–4544), a Robert Trent Jones II course at the Château Whistler (604–938–2095), a Jack Nicklaus Course, Nicklaus North (604–938–9898)—and boating. The Whistler Mountain gondola gives a splendid high-rise ride, with the view from the top being outstanding. Dine at the restaurant on the summit or bring your own picnic.

Both mountains operate mountaintop sightseeing and dining facilities. Blackcomb utilizes a covered, high-speed quad chair, and Whistler operates a ten-passenger gondola. In its setup and ambience, Whistler is similar in concept to Vail and Aspen in Colorado, attracting the well-heeled, the young and beautiful, and just plain folks.

Whistler can be reached from Vancouver by train. For more information, call B.C. Rail at (604) 984–5246. Maverick Coach Lines provides bus transportation from downtown Vancouver; call (604) 662–8051.

Recommended places to stay in the Whistler area are numerous, for there is a wide selection of hotels, bed-and-breakfasts, and condos from which to choose. All are within easy reach of Whistler's recreational facilities. All hotels have restaurants or are next to restaurants, and the condos have full living facilities. Condos are spread out throughout the village and valley. Your best bet is to contact Whistler Central Reservations (800–944–7853 or, in Vancouver, 604–664–5625) for information and options. Here's a sampling of hotels and bed-and-breakfasts.

Hotels. Blackcomb Lodge, (604) 932–4155; Château Whistler,

(604) 938–2010; Crystal Lodge, (604) 932–2221; Delta Whistler Resort, (604) 932–1982; Glacier Lodge, (604) 938–3455; Greystone, (604) 932–2881; Holiday Inn Sunspree, (604) 938–0878; Le Chamois, (604) 932–8700; Listel Whistler Hotel, (604) 932–1133; Tantalus Lodge, (604) 932–4146; Westbrook Whistler, (604) 932–2321; Whistler Fairways, (604) 932–2522.

Bed-and-Breakfasts. Alta Vista Chalet, (604) 932–4900; Carney's Cottage, (604) 938–8007; Chalet Luise, (604) 932–4187; Durlacher Hof, (604) 932–1924; Edelweiss, (604) 932–3641; Lorimer Ridge, (604) 938–9722.

Recommended nonhotel restaurants include Il Caminetto di Umberto (604) 932–4442 for exquisite northern Italian cooking (moderate); The Keg (604) 932–5151 for steaks (moderate); Ristorante Araxi (604) 932–4540 for northern Mediterranean cuisine (moderate); Val d'Isere (604) 932–4666 for continental (moderate to expensive); Les Deux Gros (604) 932–4611 for French (moderate to expensive); The Border Cantina (604) 932–3373 for Tex Mex (moderate). For swinging nightlife try Crystal's Lounge (604–932–2221) in the Crystal Lodge, with live entertainment on weekends; the Savage Beagle Club (604–932–4540) for high-energy dancing until 2:00 A.M.; Garfinkle's (604–932–2323) for classic rock; The Longhorn Saloon (604–932–5999) with live entertainment every night. Best place for shopping is in the Château Whistler, where you'll find many shops in the concourse.

During the warm, dry-weather months, if you want to keep touring this beautiful, mountain- and lake-strewn part of the province, continue heading north on Highway 99 until you reach the town of Lillooet. From here, go south on Highway 12 to the community of Lytton, where you pick up the Trans-Canada Highway 1. Once you are on the Trans-Canada, you can easily come back to Vancouver or move east toward the great national parks of the Rockies (Banff and Jasper) and the cities of Calgary and Edmonton. Because of dangerous road conditions, this ordinarily pleasant tour beyond Whistler is not recommended in the winter or during any prolonged rainy period. The distance from Whistler to Lytton is about 169 km (105 miles).

Touring Services

Most of your best touring in Vancouver will be done on your own.

There will, however, be times when you want to let someone else make the effort while you just go along to learn and enjoy. The following companies offer sightseeing tours of Vancouver and nearby attractions:

Gray Line Tours, (604) 879–3363, from Hotel Vancouver or free pickup at your hotel. Trips to Capilano and Grouse Mountain areas, Stanley Park and Vancouver Aquarium, Victoria and Butchart Gardens; also a Royal Hudson/MV *Britannia* trip.

BC Rail Cariboo Dayliner, (604) 984–5246. Daily rail trips to Whistler and Lillooet.

SS *Beaver* Cruises, (604) 682–7284, located at Coal Harbour. Replica of B.C.'s first steamship (1835), built in 1966; provides day and evening cruises daily during the summer; also available for charters.

Pacific Coach Lines, (604) 662–7575, makes pickups at leading hotels. Tours of Metro Vancouver and Victoria.

Royal Hudson and MV *Britannia*, (604) 688–7246. Ride the steam train through gorgeous scenery to Howe Sound and Squamish, and cruise back to Vancouver on a ship. One of the best tours in Vancouver.

Harbour Air, (604) 688–1277. See Vancouver and the magnificent surrounding scenery from on high in a helicopter.

Neighborhoods

Four special neighborhoods are among Vancouver's most popular attractions: Chinatown, Granville Island, Gastown, and Robson Square/Robsonstrasse. These are walking places where discoveries are made and pleasures taken at a leisurely pace. To miss visiting them is to dismiss a significant part of the Vancouver experience.

Chinatown

Vancouver has the second-largest Chinatown in North America, although the Chinatowns of Los Angeles and Toronto will soon rival Vancouver's in population size (San Francisco's is still the first in size). Vancouver's Chinatown is located just east of city center, or a few minutes' walk from the Hotel Vancouver/Vancouver Art Gallery area. Pender, Keefer, Main, Gore, and Carrall are the principal streets in this section. The architecture of many of the buildings is reminiscent of that of the Orient. Both the Chinese Cultural

Centre and Dr. Sun Yat-sen Classical Chinese Garden, much of which was donated by the People's Republic of China, are worthwhile places to visit. Chinatown has many restaurants serving the varied cuisine of this most ancient culture—Cantonese, Mandarin, Szechuan, and Vietnamese. There are also plenty of dim sum places. The best part of Chinatown is exploring it on foot, poking in and out of Chinese grocery stores, curio shops, and herbal medicine stores. If you take a car, expect difficulty in finding a place to park, particularly on Sundays. Exploring Vancouver's Chinatown is a wonderful experience, and most of the people who live and work here will welcome your presence.

With political rule of Hong Kong having reverted to the People's Republic of China in July 1997 and the uncertainties this transition has caused, there has been a steady influx of wealthy Hong Kong Chinese into Vancouver, a large number of them multimillionaires. These new immigrants are becoming considerable centers of power in the city. They are purchasing established businesses and major pieces of real estate. They are also creating new businesses. Unlike the poorer and middle-class Chinese, these wealthy newcomers are building massive homes in the best residential sections of Vancouver. The impact has been both positive and negative. The entrepreneurial spirit and financial clout of the new Chinese-Canadians are helping to make Vancouver into one of the foremost business and trading cities on the dynamic Pacific Rim. The negative impacts include rapidly rising real estate values, which are making home ownership difficult for many native Vancouverites, and ensuing resentments at being priced out of one's own city.

Granville Island

Granville Island is in fact a peninsula in the False Creek area of Vancouver. Only a few minutes from city center, it can be reached under the Granville Street Bridge. It's best to take a car, a taxi, or a tour to this unusual part of Vancouver city center, or to take False Creek Ferry and bus service on #50 from city center. Bus #51 also goes to the island. Until the early 1970s, Granville Island was a grubby industrial area, but it has since been spruced up. The industrial companies have gone elsewhere, and a new, people-oriented community has come into being. The Granville Island Public Market is one of its major attractions; here you can buy almost every kind of food you like, from fresh basil to freshly caught or smoked salmon. You can rent a boat here, visit the galleries of the Emily Carr College of Art and Design, play tennis, fish in Alder Bay, see plays at three different theaters, and watch potters, printmakers, glassblowers, and goldsmiths create beautiful things you can purchase. Granville Island has a hotel and several seafood restaurants and cocktail lounges, and many excellent views of the harbor and city. It's a pleasant place within the city but removed from it by a more low-key attitude. The little Aquabus Ferries operating from the foot of Hornby Street and the False Creek Ferries from the Aquatic Centre make frequent runs to and from Granville Island seven days a week year-round.

Gastown

Gassy Jack Deighton, the local saloon proprietor mentioned earlier, bequeathed Gastown its unusual name. Once a rough-and-tumble area frequented by lumberjacks and seafarers, Gastown today is one of the most interesting areas in city center. Water, Cordova, Columbia, Richards, and Cambie are the main streets that run through Gastown. A statue of Gassy Jack himself in Maple Tree Square depicts him standing on a barrel of liquor near the spot where his saloon was located. At Water and Cambie streets is a steam clock, said to be the world's first. It blows its whistle on the quarter hour, delighting anyone passing near enough. Here you can browse in boutiques and unusual shops, take a bite at small restaurants and comfortable cafés, and wander in what was once skid row.

Robson Square and Robsonstrasse

Robson Square is the heart of Vancouver city center. Facing Georgia Street is the Vancouver Art Gallery. Behind it and sandwiched between Hornby and Howe streets is the two-block-long Arthur Erickson–designed complex that houses law courts, government offices, restaurants, a food fair, shops, an ice-skating rink, and a theater.

Robsonstrasse, or Robson Street (it crosses the middle of Robson Square), received its Teutonic name from German-speaking people who frequented the many shops that catered to their special tastes for food, fashions, and publications. The new name stuck, and it makes a nice tourist gimmick in a province that is mostly Anglo-Saxon. Along Robsonstrasse you can buy all kinds of sausages and dark breads and the latest magazines published west of the Rhine River. This is also a street of fashionable and expensive boutiques.

Strolling down the Robsonstrasse, chomping on wurst-on-rye, and eyeing Paris gowns priced in the thousands is chic and fun to do when bored with all else in attraction- and entertainment-rich Vancouver.

Yaletown

Yaletown, a rehabilitated former warehouse area adjacent to the old Expo '86 fairgrounds along False Creek, is the city's latest "in" place. As you read this, condos are being converted from warehouses and restaurants built from merchandise depots.

Located north of Pacific Boulevard and with the main activity on Mainland Street, Homer, and Cambie, you'll find small shops and new high-rise condos that are part of the new development of the old Expo grounds along and south of Pacific Boulevard.

Parks, Gardens, and Beaches

Because of its long growing season (as compared with those of other parts of Canada), its relatively mild climate, its high amount of rainfall, and the botanical knack of its citizens, Vancouver has some of the most lavish parks and gardens in North America. This penchant to grow plants and flowers and to manipulate their arrangement stems partly from the British and Japanese gardening influences that are so strongly expressed here. Gardening mania is everywhere, in both public and private places. Lawns surrounding homes appear so uniformly perfect that one would surely think there must be an inspector going around measuring the length of grass and comparing its lush tone of color against some official chart. At any rate, whatever way the landscaping is accomplished, one of the great joys of visiting Vancouver is smelling its lovely flowers (even roses in December) and walking among its giant trees.

Stanley Park: You haven't completed your visit to Vancouver if you haven't been through Stanley Park (named in honor of Governor-General Lord Stanley). This magnificent park, all one thousand acres of it, lies right next to Vancouver city center and a few minutes' walk from most of the top hotels. Established for the public's enjoyment in 1888, Stanley Park is one of the largest and most beautiful city parks in North America. You can walk or jog over its forested trails without worrying about cutting through the squads of

Picturesque scenes such as this one abound in Stanley Park. ▶

muggers that frequent many other urban parks. Stanley Park lies to the north of city center, between Burrard Inlet on the east and English Bay to the west. It's a peninsula that points to West and North Vancouver on the other shore. The city's famous Lion's Gate Bridge connects these communities with city center at Stanley Park. The attractions within the park are many and varied. Regardless of your age, there's something pleasant for you here. The children's zoo and the sensational aquarium are well worth visiting. In addition, there are trails through tall Douglas firs and western red cedars. A seawall walk that goes around the periphery of the park has a seaside part for walkers and a forestside part for bikers. It gives access to beaches for swimming and sunbathing and other areas for splendid views. This 5.5-mile-long seawall was built under the supervision of Master Stonemason James Cunningham, who worked on it for forty years, from the 1920s to the late 1960s—even after his formal retirement—as an expression of his desire to bring this unique project closer to completion. Also within Stanley Park is a lawn-bowling club that welcomes visitors, a display of B.C. coastal Indian totem poles (carved by Haida Kwakiutl artisans), and a small zoo of mammals. The charming Teahouse Restaurant, a Victorian garden house, is appreciated by Vancouverites and visitors alike. Take your favorite person here; sunset is a perfectly romantic time. You can take a car tour of the park and stop for a picnic. More vigorous souls can rent bikes, including tandems, or roller skates for enjoying the park; Stanley Park Bike Rentals, at 676 Chilco Street opposite Lost Lagoon, provides the wheels.

Perhaps the best part of Stanley Park can be had by going on a solitary walk among the giant trees and long ferns of the Northwest. You feel as if you are in the Garden of Eden and light-years from a bustling civilization. Every once in a while, you stop and remember that civilization is just beyond the treetops, and then, reluctant to leave, you find your pace slowing.

Queen Elizabeth Park, off Cambie Street, a few miles south of city center; best to take a taxi. From the highest hill at Queen Elizabeth Park you have the second-best view of the skyline of Vancouver (the first being from the top of Grouse Mountain, see page 120). Queen Elizabeth Park, named after the present monarch, contains superior botanical displays, with sunken gardens and creatively designed floral and shrubbery displays everywhere you walk. The floral exhibits within the park are so beautiful that it is hard to imagine that this site was once a dismal rock quarry. For the convenience of visitors, the park has a restaurant, picnic areas, tennis courts, and the Bloedel Conservatory.

Bloedel Conservatory, in Queen Elizabeth Park. Open daily, except for Christmas. Admission is charged. The Bloedel Conservatory sits on the highest hill within the jurisdictional limits of Vancouver. It is from here that you get the dramatic view of the city skyline with its background of snowcapped mountains. On the plaza surrounding the conservatory is a huge sculpture by Henry Moore. In the morning, on a nice day it is not unusual to see a number of elderly Chinese men and women performing solitary t'ai chi ch'uan exercises that are close to ballet movement in their grace and elegance. The Bloedel building itself is a Buckminster Fuller–style geodesic dome, inside of which are tropical and desert environments. Each one has its indigenous plants and flowers. A wide variety of tropical birds fly around the space at will. Bloedel is the park's pièce de résistance.

Nitobe Memorial Gardens, on the University of British Columbia campus, near the Museum of Anthropology. Open daily during the summer and weekdays the rest of the year. Admission is charged. Nitobe, a perfect example of Japanese skill and artistry in botany and landscape architecture, is my favorite garden in Western Canada. Exceptional balance and harmony are achieved through the arrangement of plantings (Japanese flowering shrubs and trees) within a limited area. There are also classical Japanese accents, such as a teahouse (for display only), a curved bridge, a gazebo overlooking a tranquil pond alive with prize carp, and a stone pagoda memorial in honor of Inazo Nitobe, the garden's benefactor. Inazo Nitobe was one of Japan's representatives to the League of Nations and a major force for linking the best interests of the nations of Asia with those of North America. His remains are interred in Victoria, British Columbia.

VanDusen Botanical Gardens, located at Thirty-seventh Avenue and Oak Street. Open daily. Admission charged. The VanDusen Gardens are famous for walks thickly flanked by pink, purple, red, and white rhododendrons. There is a wide assortment of trees, shrubs, flowers, and other plants, all well labeled. Band concerts are held within the park during the summer. There is a restaurant, and **MacMillan Bloedel Place** houses exhibits telling the fascinating story of the northwest Pacific coast lumber and paper industries.

Lighthouse Park, via Marine Drive in West Vancouver. Free. Lighthouse Park, a few minutes' drive from city center, offers wonderful woodland and sea-cliff walks. Site of picturesque Point Atkinson Lighthouse, this is a virgin forest of 200-foot fir trees that are some 2,500 years old. While hiking over the park's 13 kilometers of trails, keep a sharp eye out for bald eagles swooping to their nests in the trees. There are great views of the ships in English Bay, distant Vancouver Island, Vancouver city center, and Point Grey, where the campus of the University of British Columbia is located. You can climb or sunbathe on the rocks and enjoy a picnic in this exquisite wilderness setting.

Grouse Mountain Recreational Area, in North Vancouver, via Highways 1A and 99, over Lion's Gate Bridge and then to Capilano Road; (604) 984-0661. Admission charged for the aerial tramway ride to the top.

From the top of Grouse Mountain, 4,000 ft (1,200 m) high, you have the best view in this region of the lower mainland and greater Vancouver. You can see all of Metro Vancouver, a good swath of Vancouver Island, surrounding waterways—the Strait of Georgia, Burrard Inlet, English Bay—and even south to Mount Baker in the state of Washington. A thrilling aerial tramway ride takes you up and down the mountain, and folks of all ages enjoy the experience. It is not unusual to spot a black bear or a deer on the slopes below. At the summit are a restaurant with superb views, a café, and a gift shop. You can hike around Blue Grouse Lake or attend concerts and theatrical productions that are held from time to time. Brief but spectacular helicopter rides high above the Grouse Mountain area give you views of the surrounding lakes and forest wilderness and make you realize that sophisticated Vancouver is right on the edge of a vast, virtually uninhabited landscape extending to the North Pole.

During the winter, Grouse Mountain is the closest skiing area to city center. An adage in Vancouver says, "In the morning we go skiing on Grouse Mountain. In the afternoon we come down to go sailing in English Bay." There are easy runs for beginners, and instruction is available.

North Vancouver Parks, on the way to Grouse Mountain, via Lion's Gate Bridge. The main attraction here is **Capilano Suspension Bridge,** reputed to be the longest of its kind in the world. The great fun of walking across the narrow bridge is that it swings from side to side 450 feet above a raging river. It's an unforgettable experience, to say the least. A restaurant and gift shop are located here; (604) 985-7474. Admission charged. Also in·the area is the **Capi-**

lano **Regional Park and Salmon Hatchery,** offering tours showing British Columbia's top money-making fish in different stages of growth; (604) 666–1790. Free. The park has hiking trails and places for picnics. On the road to Grouse Mountain is **Cleveland Dam,** forming Vancouver's reservoir. There are picnic places and hiking trails in adjacent Capilano Park. This is a fine viewing point of the twin mountain peaks known as The Lions. North Vancouver has another swaying suspension bridge and an interesting ecology center with woodland walks at **Lynn Canyon Park,** best accessed from Second Narrows Bridge and via Lynn Valley Road. Free.

Beaches: The following public beaches for swimming, sunbathing, sailboarding, and picnicking are located in Vancouver.

Point Grey—Kitsilano Beach, Jericho Beach, Locarno Beach, Spanish Banks Beach, and Wreck Beach (nude).

Stanley Park—English Bay Beach, Second Beach (saltwater pool in this area), Third Beach. Most have facilities for picnics (tables, fireplaces) and can be reached by public transportation. Some have food concessions.

Attractions

Museum of Anthropology, on the campus of the University of British Columbia, (604) 822–5087. Closed on Mondays, Christmas Day, and Boxing Day. Admission is charged. The Museum of Anthropology is one of Vancouver's top three attractions (the other two being Stanley Park and the view from Grouse Mountain). If you have but a brief time to spend in the city, this museum should be at the head of your list. If you are staying in the city center, your best bet is to take a cab to the museum.

There are two impressive aspects to the museum: the architecture and the collection. Arthur Erickson's design is based on the Amerindian longhouses once so typical along the northwest coast. High windows, framed by a sequence of stark concrete post and lintel portals, look out on a set of fascinating, authentic totem poles. Beyond them are Point Grey Cliffs, English Bay, the towers of the city, and the Coast Mountains. The building is a photographer's delight because it offers so many striking angles. I consider the Museum of Anthropology to be one of Erickson's finest buildings.

The museum's collection, the best of its kind in the world, concentrates on artifacts from the northwest coast tribes. Many anthropological scientists consider the northwest tribes to have devel-

121

oped the most sophisticated and most beautiful visual arts and crafts in North America (the only exception being the advanced cultures of Mexico, Peru, and Ecuador). Artifacts from the cultures of the Pacific region, Asia, and Latin America are exhibited as well. Featured items are dramatically displayed and accessible to viewers; you can actually open the drawers of display cases and see the rare and precious. The museum offers both conducted and self-guided (audio) tours and a full schedule of special presentations.

Vancouver Aquarium, in Stanley Park, (604) 682–1118. Open every day. Admission is charged. In beautiful Stanley Park is Canada's largest aquarium. The stars here are the killer whales (*Orcinus orca*), which put on daily shows for visitors. A common sight along the British Columbian coast, these highly intelligent mammals are killers only in the sense that in the wild, one of their food sources is live seals. If you have ever visited Sea World or Sea Land, you know how smart and gentle they are. The thousands of other live sea species displayed at Vancouver Aquarium include beluga whales, sharks, and tropical fish. An Amazon River display is inhabited by tropical birds, boas, and piranhas. The whale pools have underwater windows through which you can see them look at you. The aquarium complex itself is one of the best on the continent.

Children's Zoo, in Stanley Park. Open every day. Free. Here is a perfect place for young children to see and pet gentle farm animals. Also in the area are pony rides and a miniature steam-train ride; there is a charge for the rides.

Vancouver Museum, in Vanier Park complex near Burrard Street Bridge, (604) 736–4431. Open every day. Admission is charged. The most distinctive architectural feature of the Vanier complex of museums is a circular, funnel-shaped roof symbolizing the ceremonial hats worn by northwest coast Indians. Within this striking complex is the Vancouver Museum, which has a number of interesting exhibits portraying the city's colorful history—among them Indian artifacts, a car from the first transcontinental passenger train to come into the city, furnishings from the Edwardian age, and a re-creation of an early trading post.

Gordon Southam Observatory, in Vanier Park complex near Burrard Street Bridge, (604) 738–2855. Call ahead for schedule; open during summer evenings in clear weather. Free. This is hands-on astronomy, enabling you to learn about the heavens from a scientist and see them for yourself through a telescope.

Maritime Museum, in the Vanier Park complex near Burrard

Street Bridge, (604) 736–8300. Open every day. Admission is charged. Vancouver's past, present, and future are inexorably linked to the sea. The city is Canada's door to the Pacific, with all its immense trading possibilities. The Maritime Museum chronicles this rich heritage. Among its exhibits is the *St. Roch*, a two-mast schooner, the first ship to sail through the fabled Northwest Passage.

City of Vancouver Archives, in the Vanier Park complex near Burrard Street Bridge, (604) 736–8561. Closed Saturday and Sunday. Free. The archives contain books, maps, papers, newspapers, and photographs of historical value. Both scholars and casual visitors are warmly welcomed.

H. R. MacMillan Planetarium, in the Vanier Park complex near Burrard Street Bridge, (604) 736–3656. Closed Mondays. Admission is charged. A trip through the galaxy is presented in the afternoon and in the evening. For those already well versed on constellations, planets, and interstellar happenings, there are more theatrical shows. A cafeteria in this part of the complex offers views of the harbor.

Vancouver Art Gallery, 750 Hornby Street in Robson Square; (604) 682–4700. Admission is charged. Housed in what was the city's old courthouse, of stolid neoclassical design graced by a brilliantly modern interior, Vancouver Art Gallery has four floors of well-lighted exhibition space. There is a special children's gallery on the ground floor. This art museum is best known for its extensive collection of paintings by Emily Carr, British Columbia's most famous artist. An impressionist of sorts, often considered as important as the Group of Seven (immortal Canadian artists), Carr painted scenes of the northwest coast and forests, totem poles, and remote native villages. There is a mystical quality to her works that sticks in one's imagination. The Vancouver Art Gallery is in the heart of city center and should be visited for the Carr collection alone.

University of British Columbia Museums, Point Grey section of Vancouver, a short drive southwest of city center. UBC, as it is called by local folks, is Western Canada's top institution of higher learning. Located on the end of Point Grey, UBC is worth visiting just to stroll its pleasant, attractive campus; there's very much of an "established, elite" feel to it. There are also low-cost dormitory accommodations here; see the "Accommodations" section on pages 125 to 131. Adjacent to the main campus is **Pacific Spirit Regional Park,** an area of 2,500 forested acres where you can hike or jog in lovely natural surroundings. The park is inhabited by small mammals, including deer, and it is not unusual to spot bald eagles, which are ubiquitous along British Columbia's coast. Marine Drive, which goes around Point Grey, offers some lovely views, and Wreck (nude bathing here) and Spanish Banks beaches are in this area. Among other reasons for visiting the UBC campus are its excellent museums:

Museum of Anthropology; see page 121.

M. Y. Williams Geology Museum; extensive mineral and fossil collection; (604) 822–5586. Closed weekends. Free.

Nitobe Memorial Garden; see page 119.

Fine Arts Gallery; (604) 822–2759; located in Main Library. Free.

TRIUMF; (604) 222–1047; one of the world's largest cyclotrons for subatomic research.

Fantasy Garden World, in Richmond, just off Highway 99, between turnoff roads for Vancouver International Airport and the ferry for Victoria; (604) 277–7777. Open daily. Admission is charged. If you are traveling to Vancouver from the state of Washington on B.C. Highway 99 or going south on this same road, visit Fantasy Garden World. This floral theme park features millions of flowers and beautiful landscaping, a farm with many small animals for the kids to pet, a miniature-train ride, a stocked trout lake, a biblical garden with a giant Noah's Ark, a European village where you can sample the foods from several nations, greenhouses, a pretty little chapel where many Vancouverites tie the knot, and a pavilion that serves English tea in the afternoon.

Simon Fraser University (SFU) Campus, located on Burnaby Mountain in Burnaby, an approximately forty-minute drive east of city center. Simon Fraser University, designed by architects Arthur Erickson and Geoffrey Massey, has one of the most stunning university campuses in the world, in terms of both its contemporary architecture and its setting on Burnaby Mountain with the backdrop of distant snowcapped mountains and great views of the city and sea inlets. Visit SFU's **Art Gallery** and its **Museum of Archaeology and Ethnology,** a fine display of artifacts from northwest coast Indian tribes. Open every day, noon to 3:00 P.M. on weekends. Free. Tours of the university; call (604) 291–3397.

Science World, 1455 Quebec Street; (604) 443–7740. Located within a former Expo pavilion. Open every day. Admission is charged. Offers exciting, hands-on science exhibits that are enjoyed by children and adults.

Burnaby Village Museum, 4900 Deer Lake Avenue in Burnaby; (604) 293–6500. Open daily; closed mid-October to mid-November. Admission is charged. Heritage Village takes visitors back to a simpler time. Here you can visit with a small-town blacksmith, see a sawmill in operation, taste the treats at an ice-cream parlor, and poke into an early log cabin, general store, and schoolhouse. **Canadian Craft Museum,** 639 Hornby Street, (604) 687–8266. Canada's first national cultural facility dedicated to craft is a showplace for both Canadian and international craft artists. Located in a beautiful new building, its 10,000 square feet (900 square meters) are on three levels. Small admission fee.

Accommodations

Vancouver, as the third most important city in Canada and as Western Canada's number one destination, has a large number of hotels, motels, and guest houses. Most are priced in the moderate-to-expensive range, although some decent inexpensive accommodations are available, generally outside city center. During the busy tourist season—from late May to mid-September—rooms at the more desirable hotels are difficult if not impossible to book on short notice. In addition, during other peak periods delegates to large conventions make booking a room frustrating for the casual traveler. It's smart to make reservations anytime; during busy times, they are essential.

Consult with your local travel agent and auto club for their accommodation reservation services, which are usually available at no extra cost. Many places require a cash deposit prior to arrival and/or evidence of credit; both can be accomplished through a major credit card.

Some places of accommodation in this listing are described as "good-value accommodations with many amenities," which means that they are recommended and offer such features as swimming pools, pleasant settings, and/or other conveniences to make your stay comfortable. This designation has been used to increase the number of recommended places to stay during peak seasons.

If you would like to stay at a Vancouver-area bed-and-breakfast, contact this agency for more information and rates: Best Canadian Bed & Breakfast Network, 1090 West King Edward Avenue, Vancouver, B.C. V6H 1Z4; (604) 738–7207. Old English Bed and Breakfast Registry, P.O. Box 86818, North Vancouver, British Columbia V7L 4L3, (604) 986–5069, is another resource to try.

City Center Accommodations
The following hotels are located in the city center, with convenient access to major attractions (parks, museums, etc.), business and government offices, shopping areas, entertainment and sporting venues, and restaurants.

Vancouver's Finest
The hotels in this first category are considered by travelers to be the best in Vancouver in terms of customer satisfaction, guest services, facilities, and management. They are also among the most expensive, averaging well over $100 a night.

Four Seasons Hotel, 791 West Georgia Street, (604) 689–9333; (800) 268–6282. Certainly one of the premier hotels in the city, with excellent amenities and service. Its main restaurants are Chartwell's (named after Winston Churchill's estate in Kent, England) and Harvester; lunch is served in the Garden Lounge and, in the summer, beside the outdoor pool. There's an indoor/outdoor pool. The Four Seasons is connected to Pacific Centre Mall, which has more than 150 shops. Expensive.

Metropolitan Hotel, 645 Howe Street, (604) 687–1122; (800) 268–1133. This hotel is near the Pacific Centre. The rooms and suites are luxurious, and the service is first-rate. It features a health club, squash and racquetball courts, a billiard room, a swimming pool, and a sauna. Excellent restaurants. Expensive.

Westin Bayshore, 1601 West Georgia Street, (604) 682–3377; (800) 228–3000. This excellent hotel in the Westin chain is located near beautiful Stanley Park. There are both an indoor and an outdoor pool, as well as a marina with services for your yacht. The Westin offers a family plan and free parking. Its restaurants include Trader Vic's and the Garden Restaurant. Expensive.

Hotel Vancouver, 900 West Georgia Street, (604) 684–3131; (800) 828–7447. The first Hotel Vancouver was opened in 1887. The present and third Hotel Vancouver, completed in 1939, is the city's landmark place of accommodation, much in the same manner as the Château Frontenac in Quebec City is. It would be difficult to imagine Vancouver city center without this venerable hotel. The service here is high class, and the rooms are spacious and pleasant. Dining and dancing in the Panorama Roof restaurant is a city tradition. There are also the Timber Club and the Roof. Expensive.

Sutton Place Hotel, 845 Burrard Street, (604) 682–5511; (800) 543–4300. The former Meridien hotel provides luxury in the

European manner, with regard to both rooms and service. Its restaurants include Gerard and Café Fleuri. Expensive.

Pan Pacific Vancouver Hotel, 999 Canada Place, (604) 662–8111; (800) 663–1515. A deluxe hotel, the Pan Pacific is part of the dramatic Canada Place complex, located on the waterfront. Its main function is to provide top accommodations to convention delegates, but other travelers are also welcomed. It features a pool, health club, racquetball courts, and twenty-four-hour room service. For dining there are a Japanese restaurant, Five Sails for continental cuisine, and Café Pacifica. Expensive.

Hyatt Regency Vancouver, 655 Burrard Street (in Royal Centre), (604) 683–1234; (800) 228–9000. This Hyatt—more than thirty sparkling floors—offers luxury and all the amenities you need, including a charming lounge and a gourmet restaurant. The Hyatt's situation couldn't be better. It's in the heart of downtown Vancouver and connected to the Royal Centre, an attractive indoor shopping mall. Expensive.

Waterfront Centre Hotel, 900 Canada Place Way, (604) 691–1991; (800) 268–9420. Located directly across from the Pan Pacific Vancouver Hotel. Operated by Canadian Pacific Hotels, it has all of the amenities expected of a first-class hotel. Direct access to the Vancouver Trade and Convention Centre. Expensive.

Sheraton Wall Centre Garden Hotel, 1088 Burrard, (604) 331–1000; (800) 331–1001. Vancouver's newest hotel and the latest definition of luxury living. Expensive.

Other Fine Accommodations

Hotel Georgia, 801 West Georgia Street, (604) 682–5566; (800) 663–1111. A fine, centrally located hotel with friendly, personal service. An English pub called George V, restaurants, and lounges. A favorite with frequent visitors to the city. Expensive.

Day's Inn Vancouver, 921 West Pender Street, (604) 681–4335; (800) 325–2525. Located in the financial center. An older hotel with newly refurbished rooms. Restaurants and lounges. A good value in downtown Vancouver. Moderate.

Best Western Chateau Granville, 1100 Granville Street, (604) 669–7070; (800) 663–0575. Offers discounts to seniors. Rooms have balconies or patios, with views of the city, waterfront, or mountains. There are a dining room and a place for cocktails and live entertainment. Moderate to expensive.

The Georgian Court, 773 Beatty Street, (604) 682–5555;

(800) 663–1144. An intimate, high-class hotel in the European manner. Its William Tell restaurant is one of the best in the city. Near B.C. Place Stadium. Expensive.

Coast Plaza at Stanley Park, 1733 Comox Street, (604) 688–7711; (800) 268–8998. A nice location near Stanley Park and English Bay. Rooms have balconies and refrigerators; some have kitchens. There are an indoor pool, a rooftop restaurant, and a bar. Moderate to expensive.

Parkhill Hotel, 1160 Davie Street, (604) 685–1311; (800) 663–1525. Rooms have balconies with excellent views of English Bay. Pool and free parking; dining room and lounge. Close to beaches and city center. Expensive.

Landis Hotel and Suites, 1234 Hornby, (604) 688–1234; (800) 426–0670. In midtown, this facility has spacious studio suites with kitchenettes. Moderate.

Century Plaza Hotel, 1015 Burrard Street, (604) 687–0575; (800) 663–1818. An apartment-type accommodation with large rooms; some have balconies and kitchen facilities. Indoor pool and sauna; dining room, coffee shop, and nightclub. Live entertainment in the Rum Runners Lounge. Moderate to expensive.

Holiday Inn Downtown, 1110 Howe Street, (604) 684–2151; (800) HOLIDAY. Downtown location, close to Pacific Centre. Restaurant, indoor pool; lounge offers live entertainment. Expensive.

Pacific Palisades Hotel, 1277 Robson Street, (604) 688–0461; (800) 663–1815. Offers full kitchen facilities; Puffin's dining room; health club and indoor pool; free parking; executive suites. Expensive.

Landmark Hotel, 1400 Robson Street, (604) 687–0511; (800) 325–3535. Rooms with balconies. A revolving restaurant on top, called Cloud Nine, gives superb views of the city, ocean, and mountains. Jazz bar with live entertainment. Family plan. Expensive.

Listel O'Doul's Best Western Hotel, 1300 Robson Street, (604) 684–8461; (800) 663–5491. Has smoking and nonsmoking floors, twenty-four-hour room service, indoor pool, Jacuzzi, exercise room; also restaurant, lounge, and sidewalk café. Moderate to expensive.

Wedgwood Hotel, 845 Hornby Street, (604) 689–7777; (800) 663–0666. City center location. Balconies, fireplaces, and the Wedgwood Room—one of the best restaurants in the city. Expensive.

Sylvia Hotel, 1154 Gilford Street, (604) 681–9321. This is the hotel "in-the-know" visitors go to for a terrific view of the water and a comfortable, small hotel flavor. Older establishment that has character. Decent restaurant. Moderate.

Sunset Inn Apartment Hotel, 1111 Burnaby Street, (604) 684–8763. A former apartment block, this converted facility offers condo suites within walking distance to Stanley Park and English Bay. Moderate to expensive.

Vancouver Vicinity

The following places of accommodation are within a thirty- to forty-five-minute drive of downtown Vancouver and should be considered when hotels in the city center are filled. Accommodations in suburban Richmond, located south of city center, are close to the Vancouver International Airport and may be preferable to businesspeople.

Delta Pacific Resort & Conference Centre, 10251 St. Edwards Drive in Richmond, south of Vancouver city center and near the airport; (604) 278–9611. Next to the airport and a twenty-minute drive from downtown. A resort on twelve acres, offering three swimming pools, tennis and squash courts, exercise and game rooms. It even has a special fun place for children. This resort offers Japanese ambience in its restaurants and lounges. The best accommodation in the airport area. Expensive.

Best Western Coquitlam Inn, 319 North Road in Coquitlam, east of Vancouver city center; (604) 931–9011; (800) 528–1234. Located about 10 miles from city center. Pool, sauna, tropical courtyard, Beef 'n Barrel restaurant, and a lounge with live entertainment. Moderate to expensive.

Best Western Kings Inn, 5411 Kingsway Street in Burnaby, east of Vancouver city center; (604) 438–1383; (800) 528–1234. Comfortable accommodations with many amenities. Restaurant. Moderate to expensive.

Best Western Richmond Inn, in downtown Richmond, 7551 Westminster Highway, south of Vancouver city center and near the airport; (604) 273–7878. Nice rooms, heated pool, saunas, health club; restaurants and lounge with entertainment. Moderate.

Clarion Hotel Villa, 4331 Dominion Street in Burnaby, east of Vancouver city center; (604) 430–2828; (800) 325–3535. Indoor/outdoor pools, dining facilities, and live entertainment. Family rates. Moderate to expensive.

Best Western Abercorn Inn, 9260 Bridgeport Road in Richmond, south of Vancouver city center and near the airport; (604)

270–7576. In architecture and ambience, a wee bit of rural Scotland in B.C. Restaurant and whirlpool. Moderate to expensive.

Radisson President Hotel and Suites, 8181 Cambie, Richmond, (604) 276–8181; (800) 333–3333. This new hotel has 184 deluxe rooms, including 39 luxury suites. Close to Vancouver International Airport; focus is business travel. Moderate to expensive.

Best Western Tsawwassen Inn, in Tsawwassen, about 3 miles from the Victoria ferry terminal and about a forty-minute drive south of Vancouver via Highways 99 and 17; (604) 943–8221; (800) 528–1234. Good-value accommodations with many amenities. Dining room. Moderate to expensive.

Park Royal Hotel, in West Vancouver, north via the Lion's Gate Bridge, on the Capilano River; (604) 926–5511. A Tudor-style country inn set in beautiful surroundings. Minutes from Vancouver city center. Dining room. Moderate to expensive.

Lonsdale Quay Hotel, 123 Carrie Cates Court, North Vancouver, (604) 986–6111. Located above the Lonsdale Quay market, it is one of the most unusual settings in the Vancouver area. On the waterfront and next to the Seabus terminal, it offers wonderful Vancouver skyline views. Moderate.

Inexpensive but Good Places to Stay

University of British Columbia, Student Union Boulevard, southwest of Vancouver city center, (604) 882–1010. Low-cost accommodations for singles, doubles, and families on this attractive campus—a major area attraction in itself—are available from early May until late August. Meals are available at the student union. Downtown is about twenty minutes away. The University of British Columbia offers one of the best accommodation values in this popular travel destination; highly recommended. Inexpensive.

Simon Fraser University, in Burnaby, (604) 291–4503. Fully furnished single and twin rooms; shared bathrooms; lounges on each floor. Guests can use recreational facilities. Inexpensive.

YWCA Hotel, 733 Beatty Street, (604) 895–5830. This is a new, coed accommodation (welcomes couples and families) located in downtown Vancouver.

Camping near Vancouver

Contact your camping association and auto club for a complete listing of privately operated campgrounds. Here's one well-established camping spot.

Parks Canada Recreational Vehicle Inn, Highway 17, via Fifty-second Street exit, northeast of the ferry terminal to Victoria; (604) 943–5811. In operation from April to October. Facilities include washrooms, toilets, a heated pool, and a recreation lounge; near a water-slide park, grocery and gift shops, and golf.

Dining

There are hundreds of excellent restaurants in Vancouver, representing the cuisines of about twenty ethnic groups. The deluxe hotels in Vancouver pride themselves on having at least one superb restaurant each, and you probably won't be disappointed in dining at least one evening at yours. Throughout the city there are also the familiar fast-food franchises when you need something fast and cheap. Regardless of your budget, kids seem to prefer fast-food burgers, french fries, and pizza to chateaubriand and flaming pepper steak. Vancouver's best foods are those that come from nearby areas—such as fresh seafood, especially salmon; fresh vegetables; and fruit. Wines are being produced in British Columbia, and you should sample some of them. Vancouver, with the second-largest Chinese population in North America, has an abundance of superb Chinese restaurants; it's a bit of an adventure going into Chinatown and discovering the one that may become your favorite. Other ethnic groups have their eateries as well. There are, for example, more than eighty-five Japanese restaurants scattered throughout the greater Vancouver region, with the majority within easy access of downtown. Those serving continental cuisine—meaning French—are among the best of all restaurants. There are also fine Italian, Greek, and Portuguese places. As long as you have money to spend, you won't go hungry for great food to eat in Vancouver. The following recommended places are a small sampling of what's available:

La Gravroche, 1616 Alberni Street, (604) 685–3924. La Gravroche is considered one of Canada's finest restaurants. French cuisine is superbly prepared by its chefs and served with style in an elegant environment. An excellent wine list. Make this a special dining treat. Expensive.

The Teahouse Restaurant, in the Ferguson Point area of Stanley Park, (604) 669–3281. The Teahouse in Stanley Park is Vancouver's sentimental favorite place for a light snack or a full-course meal. It is a traditional British greenhouse with a most uplifting decor and splendid views from its windows. The atmosphere is relaxed and civilized in the English manner. Toasting an achievement or a loved one seems to take on special meaning at the Teahouse. Moderate to expensive.

Cloud 9 Revolving Restaurant, at the Landmark Hotel, (604) 687–0511. An exceptional restaurant offering continental cuisine and fresh B.C. salmon, as well as panoramic views from your table of the city, mountains, and sea. Famous for its Sunday brunch. Moderate to expensive.

Naniwa-Ya Japanese Seafood Restaurant, 745 Thurlow Street, (604) 681–7307. Traditional Japanese seafood dishes, including sushi and sashimi. Moderate to expensive.

Chartwell's, at the Four Seasons Hotel, 791 West Georgia Street, (604) 689–9333. One of Vancouver's elegant restaurants. Menu selections, wines, ambience, decor, and service are excellent. Continental and nouvelle cuisine prepared with artistry and with strict emphasis on fresh ingredients available in season. Expensive.

Bishop's Restaurant, 2183 West Fourth Avenue, (604) 738–2025. Continental and West Coast cuisine. A mainstay on trendy Fourth Avenue, this intimate restaurant continues to be one of the city's finest year after year. Moderate to expensive.

Five Sails in the Pan Pacific Hotel, 300–999 Canada Place, (604) 662–8111. West Coast cuisine. Moderate to expensive.

Bacchus Restaurant in the Wedgewood Hotel, 845 Hornby Street, (604) 689–7777. Northern Italian. Inexpensive to moderate.

Star Anise, 1485 West Twelfth Avenue, in Vancouver, south of the Granville Street Bridge, (604) 737–1485. Progressive Pacific Rim cooking served up by one of the city's finest restaurants. Expensive.

Monk McQueen's, 601 Stamps Landing on the south shore of False Creek, (604) 877–1351. Casual dining amid the waterfront sea character of sailboat moorings. Great view of the city and mountains. Moderate.

Imperial Chinese Seafood Restaurant, 355 Burrard, downtown, (604) 688–8191. Cantonese cuisine with a view of the mountains and Coal Harbor. Moderate.

Grouse Nest, atop Grouse Mountain and accessed via the Grouse Mountain Skyride, 6400 Nancy Greene Way in North Vancouver, (604) 984–0661. Not the finest fare in town, but the greatest view of the city, the Strait of Georgia, and Vancouver Island. Moderate.

Pink Pearl Chinese Seafood Restaurant, in Chinatown, 1132 East Hastings Street, (604) 253–4316. A favorite restaurant with both Chinese and Caucasian patrons. A vast menu of Cantonese specialties will whet your appetite. Peking Duck and Rainbow Lettuce Wrap are just two of innumerable delicious dishes. Moderate to expensive.

Salmon House on the Hill, 2229 Folkestone Way, West Vancouver, (604) 926–3212. One of the best places in the Vancouver area for Pacific salmon grilled over alderwood, Amerindian style. Get it served with wild rice and fiddleheads. This is also the place for romantic views of the harbor and distant Vancouver Island. Moderate to expensive.

William Tell, 765 Beatty Street, (604) 688–3504. Seafood and steak dishes are well prepared. Both service and dining comfort get high marks. Expensive.

The Cannery, 2205 Commissioner Street, (604) 254–9606. Get a table with a view of the harbor and order your choice of seafood. The decor is that of an early, northwest coast fish cannery. Moderate.

Bridges, 1696 Duranleau Street, (604) 687–4400. Meals served alfresco on a spacious deck in the quaint ambience of Granville Island and the marina world of boats, flapping sails, and screeching gulls. Bridges has a formal, enclosed dining room and a wine bar as well. Moderate to expensive.

A Kettle of Fish, 900 Pacific Street, (604) 687–6661. A fine seafood place with a menu that changes according to the availability of fresh finfish and shellfish. Congenial environment in a greenhouse packed with plants, making for an uplifting meal on an overcast day. Moderate.

Wedgwood Room, 845 Hornby Street, in the Wedgwood Hotel, (604) 689–7777. North American, West Coast, and French cuisines. Moderate to expensive.

Mulvaney's Restaurant, Granville Island, (604) 685–6571. Since 1975 this popular restaurant has been serving fresh seafood and Cajun classics in a casual, New Orleans atmosphere. Moderate.

Sprinklers Restaurant, 5251 Oak in the VanDusen Botanical Gardens, (604) 261–0011. West Coast continental cuisine, overlooking the peaceful surroundings of the gardens. Moderate.

Caffe de Medici, 1025 Robson, (604) 669–9322. Northern Italian cuisine featuring veal, pasta, and fresh seafood. In the heart of the city. Moderate to expensive.

Kilimanjaro, 332 Water Street, (604) 681–9913. Colorful art deco surroundings and a cuisine that consists of unique African foods. Moderate.

Liliget, 1724 Davie Street, (604) 681–7044. Authentic northwest coast native cuisine such as bannock bread, baked sweet potato with hazelnuts, alder-grilled salmon. Native music, masks on the walls. Moderate.

Il Giardino di Umberto, 1382 Hornby Street, (604) 669–2422. This is a light-splashed restaurant styled after a Tuscany home. Reindeer filet and pheasant are the house specialties. Moderate to expensive.

Entertainment

Vancouver, as is typical of large, important cities, has all forms of entertainment, from the highbrow to the seamy. If you are staying at a major hotel or motel, in addition to dining and lounge facilities, there is a good chance it offers some form of live entertainment—a dance band, pop singers, comedians, dancers, stage revues. There are movie houses throughout the city. Nightclubs and theaters are listed below. You can buy tickets to concerts, plays, sport games, and special events through **Ticketmaster,** (604) 280–3311 or 280–4400; charge tickets by phone, using major credit cards.

Nightclubs

The following are chic drinking and dancing places, where you can bring a date or come yourself and see the possibilities:

Beatty Street Bar & Grill, 733 Beatty Street, (604) 682–6265.

The Purple Onion, 15 Water Street, Gastown, (604) 687–6794.

Yuk Yuk's Komedy Kabaret, 750 Pacific Boulevard, (604) 683–5233.

Richard's on Richards, 1036 Richards Street, (604) 687–6794.

BaBalu, 654 Nelson, (604) 605–4343.

George V Pub and Lounge, Hotel Georgia, 801 West Georgia, (604) 682–5566.

Graceland, 1250 Richards, (604) 688–2648.

The Commodore Ballroom, 870 Granville Street, (604) 681–7838.

Music and Theater

The music and theater scene in Vancouver is active, with enough offerings to satisfy the interests of most visitors. Local talent and performers from other parts of Canada put on splendid shows, and some go on to be stars. Both Michael J. Fox and Arthur Hill, leading actors in films and television, originally came from the area. Vancouver is a main stop on the tours of top international performers; there's a good chance you can see some of your favorites when you visit. In addition to the theaters listed below, both **B.C. Place Stadium** and **Pacific Coliseum** at Exhibition Park are major venues for important concerts and performances.

Orpheum Theatre, on Seymour Street, Ticketmaster (604) 280–3311. Built in 1927 and recently renovated, this highly ornate theater is now the home concert hall for the **Vancouver Symphony Orchestra,** the **Vancouver Chamber Choir,** the **Vancouver Bach Choir,** and other music groups.

Queen Elizabeth Theatre, on Georgia Street, (604) 665–3050. The Queen Elizabeth Theatre seats 2,800 and is home for four major performances a year by the **Vancouver Opera.** The 650-seat Playhouse has its own resident company, which puts on experimental and popular productions from autumn to spring. The **Festival Concert Society** and the **Vancouver Recital Society** have concerts at the Playhouse, which also is the venue for the **Playhouse Theatre Company.**

Bard on the Beach, 1101 West Broadway, (604) 739–0559.

Vancouver TheatreSports League, Pacific Space Centre, (604) 688–7013.

Firehall Arts Theatre, 280 East Cordova Street, (604) 689–0926. Various dramatic productions and concerts.

Theatre under the Stars, outdoors in Stanley Park from July through August, (604) 687–0174. Popular Broadway musicals.

Waterfront Theatre, on Granville Island, (604) 669–3410. Performs works by British Columbia writers.

Arts Club Theatre, Granville Island, (604) 687–5315. A small theater with three stages, operating throughout the year. Also has two stages at Granville Island, where full-scale dramas and musicals are performed, including cabaret-style productions with table service.

Ford Centre for the Performing Arts, 777 Homer, (604) 844–2801. Newly constructed theater and the home of megaproductions like *Show Boat* and similar shows.

Shopping

Vancouver is Western Canada's largest shopping center—it has everything you need. Considering the favorable exchange rate, there are a number of bargains for visitors from the United States. Fashions for women and men are of as high style and quality as those you would find in New York and Toronto. Yet you can also purchase some special products here that would be hard to get elsewhere, such as alderwood-smoked Pacific salmon and northwest coast Amerindian arts and crafts. Department stores of large national chains—Eaton's, the Bay—are here.

Some of Vancouver's most interesting shopping sections include Robson Street (Robsonstrasse), Robson Fashion Centre for Canadian and international designs, Gastown, Chinatown, Granville Island, and the South Granville Street area.

The major multistore malls in city center are listed below:
Pacific Centre, Georgia at Granville—130 shops and three department stores; **Eaton's** and eight floors of departments in this mall. Also in the area are the **Bay** and **Holt Renfrew**.

The Landing, Water Street, near Convention Centre—two levels of exclusive shops and boutiques.

Royal Centre, on Burrard and Georgia.

Harbour Centre, on Hastings Street, between Seymour and Richards.

In West Vancouver, **Park Royal Centre** sprawls for acres on both sides of Marine Drive. As can be expected, it has a large number of shops, several department stores, and supermarkets.

The following is a list of shops that may be of special interest to visitors:
Bushlen Mowat Gallery, 1445 West Georgia; Canadian contemporary art.

Inuit Gallery, 345 Water Street in Gastown; Inuit and west coast Indian art and crafts.

Kaya Kaya, 2037 West Fourth Avenue; exquisite Japanese porcelains.

Duthie Books, B.C.'s largest bookstore, newly opened in the old Birk's Building at the corner of West Georgia and Granville, houses 250,000 books, and 2,000 magazines; (604) 689–1802. Also 919 Robson Street; beautiful coffee-table books and travel guides.

Murchie's, 970 Robson Street; a large selection of fine china, crystal, and flatware.

Model Shipyard, 278 East First in North Vancouver; a wide selection of hard-to-get model-boat building kits and hobby supplies.

Professional Sports

The **Canucks,** National Hockey League, is Vancouver's top professional sports team. The team plays at the newly constructed General Motors Place in downtown Vancouver, opposite B.C. Place Stadium; (604) 899–4625 or 681–2280.

Vancouver Grizzlies, National Basketball Association, is a new NBA franchise beginning play in the 1995/96 season with games at General Motors Place, an arena it shares with the Vancouver Canucks; (604) 899–4667 or 681–2280.

The **B.C. Lions,** Canadian Football League, play their home games at B.C. Place Stadium, 777 Pacific Boulevard, (604) 661–3664.

Thoroughbred racing takes place at Exhibition Park, at Hastings and Renfrew streets, (604) 254–1631.

Harness racing is at the Cloverdale Raceway, 6050 176th Street in Cloverdale. Call (604) 579–9141; the season runs from October to April.

The **Vancouver Canadians,** a baseball club, play at a field adjacent to Queen Elizabeth Park, Thirty-third Avenue at Quebec Street, (604) 872–5232.

The **Vancouver '86ers,** a soccer club, are based at the Swangard Stadium, at Boundary and Kingsway, (604) 299–0086.

Recreation

Sports play a big role in this health-conscious city. Most sports activities are organized ad hoc or just enjoyed individually. **Sport British Columbia** is a central source for information regarding most sports activities taking place in the province. The people in this agency will be happy to answer your questions and suggest how you can participate in a sport of interest to you; (604) 687–3333.

Public Golf Courses

Contact your own club about playing the private courses in the Vancouver area.

The University Golf Club, 5185 University Boulevard, pro shop, (604) 224–1818.

McCleery Golf Course, 7170 MacDonald Street, pro shop, (604) 257–8191.

Langara Golf Course, 290 West Forty-ninth Avenue, pro shop, (604) 257–8400 (to reopen July 1998).

Fraserview Golf Course, 7800 Vivian Street, pro shop, (604) 257–8400.

Burnaby Mountain Golf Course, 7600 Halifax Street, pro shop, (604) 421–7355.

Seymour Golf and Country Club, 3723 Mount Seymour Parkway, North Vancouver, pro shop, (604) 929–2611.

Mayfair Lakes Golf Centre, 5400 North Seventh Road, Richmond, pro shop, (604) 276–0505.

Peace Portal Golf Course, 16900 Fourth Avenue, Surrey, pro shop, (604) 538–4818.

Tennis
Stanley Park, (604) 257–8400.
Queen Elizabeth Park, (see page 118).

Public Indoor Pools
Most of the major hotels and motels listed in this guide have swimming pools.
University of British Columbia Aquatic Centre, (604) 228–4521.
Vancouver Aquatic Centre, 1050 Beach Avenue, (604) 665–3424.
YMCA Downtown, (604) 681–0221.

Outdoor Saltwater Pools
Kitsilano Beach, (604) 257–8400.
Second Beach at Stanley Park.

Skiing
Whistler Resort Area, (see page 110).
Grouse Mountain, (see page 120).
Mount Seymour Provincial Park, 10 miles from city center in North Vancouver; three runs, chair lifts, and rope lifts.
Cypress Bowl Ski Area in West Vancouver, downhill and cross-country, (604) 922–0825.

Excellent downhill skiing is also available at Mount Baker in the state of Washington.

Ice-skating
Lower level of Robson Square in city center.

Sailing
Sea Wing Sailing School, (604) 669–0840, 1818 Maritime Mews, Granville Island; rentals of vessels can be bareboat or with captain.
Jericho Sailing Centre Association, 1300 Discovery, (604) 224–4177.
Cooper Boating Centre, 1620 Duranleau, (604) 687–4110.

Scuba Diving
For such a northerly area in the Pacific, the sea life here is fabulous—close to 200 varieties of animals, including whales and octopuses, and more than 325 kinds of fish—making for many fascinating dives. For suggestions on where to dive and equipment to rent, contact the Diving Locker, (604) 736–2681.

Sailboarding
Windsurfing is a big sport on the waters off Vancouver. Many of the beaches (see page 121) have people giving instruction. For more information on the popular spots and equipment rentals, contact Windsure Windsurfing, Ltd., (604) 224–0615.

Running/Jogging
The best place for running in the city is Stanley Park. Also try the Endowment Lands at the University of British Columbia.

Salmon Fishing Charters
The following companies, among others, offer salmon-fishing trips from Vancouver:
Westin Bayshore Yacht Charters, (604) 691–6936
Paradise Yacht Charters, (604) 273–7865
Sewell's Landing Marina, (604) 921–3474
These companies supply everything you'll need—food for the fish and you, gear, and even the fishing license.

Small Boating
You can rent kayaks at Granville Charter Centre, (604)

683–1447, and Deep Cove Canoe and Kayak Rentals, in North Vancouver, (604) 929–2268.

Bicycling

For information on routes and laws regarding biking, call (604) 687–3333. The scenic routes in the city for biking are in Stanley Park (see page 116) and the Pacific Spirit Regional Park.

Rentals are available at Bayshore Bicycle Rentals, (604) 689–5071, and Stanley Park Rentals, (604) 681–5581.

CHAPTER 6

Victoria: England by the Pacific

Victoria • Vancouver Island • The Inside Passage • Prince Rupert to Prince George

What Makes Victoria Special

No city in Canada is more British in mood and trappings than Victoria, British Columbia. Just as Quebec City expresses the essence of *ancien régime* France in North America, Victoria does the same for Canada's other founding nation/culture, Great Britain. And just as Halifax, Nova Scotia, was a major seaport for the Royal Navy on the North Atlantic, so was Victoria on the Pacific. Through several decades, British naval officers found the climate and lifestyle of Victoria to their liking, and many retired here, thus permeating a good portion of the city's institutions with their homeland's styles, manners, and attitudes: Afternoon tea with crumpets, scones, and delicate sandwiches served on English bone china with bright sterling settings is as common as the red double-decker London buses plying Government Street. Downtown stores sell Scottish woolens, Waterford crystal, Doulton china, tweed jackets, Stilton cheeses,

141

and exquisitely wrapped bonbons. You can order a made-to-measure suit from a London tailor. Union Jack flags in all sizes and souvenirs with pictures of members of the royal family are available just about everywhere. The genuine and the pseudo Brits of Victoria tend to be a bit more prim and proper, stodgy and stiff-upper-lipped than are the citizens of the home country—yet each contributes to the special atmosphere that many tourists, especially Anglophiles, seem to enjoy and expect. While the British influence is undeniably strong, residents from many other ethnic backgrounds contribute to the high quality of life here—Dutch, Germans, and Chinese, to name but a few. While the British reserve is often a temporary facade, the people are more often than not warm, smiling, and helpful.

Although metropolitan Victoria is large in both area and population, the downtown section, where most visitors tend to stay, gives the impression of being smaller and more intimate than it really is. You can visit most of the attractions, shops, restaurants, and entertainment spots on foot. Victoria is an immaculately clean city. Most of the older buildings have been declared heritage places and have been refurbished into boutiques, dining spots, and professional offices. Visually, the city is most attractive—particularly around the Inner Harbour area, which is used primarily for pleasure boats—with its parks and shore walks and flower baskets hanging from lampposts. Victoria has a slower pace, compared with that of Vancouver.

Victoria has the mildest weather in British Columbia. Although there is a great deal of rain in the winter, as is the case all along the coast, many colorful flowers bloom in February, and during this otherwise harsh season, duffers in tweed knickers are out shooting a round of eighteen holes at the local golf clubs. Spring, summer, and early autumn are truly magnificent, with mostly bright skies and dry air. The grass is lush, and flowers abound. Almost everywhere are views of the sea and distant mountains—those on Vancouver Island and in the state of Washington. Washington's snowcapped volcano, Mount Baker, is a familiar sight, and so are the peaks of the Cascades and those in Olympic National Park.

Victoria is a city of walkers, joggers, bikers, sailors, golfers, and tennis players. All ages participate in exercise and recreation that they like. The Christmas season is a special time in Victoria; both the hotels and the city attempt to create a Dickensian holiday feel, and people come here just to enjoy a Victorian Noel. It takes a little extra effort to get to Victoria, but few visitors come away disappointed. Most, in fact, plan to return in the near future.

A Brief Look at Victoria's History

The human history of the Victoria area is many millennia old. Northwest coast aboriginal peoples developed an advanced civilization based on fishing and hunting and created art that many connoisseurs consider the finest produced by the indigenous peoples of North America. Their culture went into decline with the coming of the Europeans. In 1843, James Douglas, who was the chief factor for the Hudson's Bay Company at Fort Vancouver (on the Columbia River in what is now the state of Washington), chose the tip of this peninsula jutting into the Strait of Juan de Fuca as the site of Fort Victoria. The political reason a trading fort was established here is that the United States and Great Britain were in the process of establishing the forty-ninth parallel as the international boundary between much of British North America (Canada) and the United States. The tip of Vancouver Island at Fort Victoria extended a considerable distance below the forty-ninth. By maintaining sovereignty over all of Vancouver Island and its valuable resources in this manner, further U.S. territorial claims were blunted. If you look at a map, you'll see that the U.S.–Canada border follows the forty-ninth parallel for thousands of miles until it hits the west coast, where it loops around the southern end of Vancouver Island.

As fur trading faded away in Victoria, the settlement became a major port for the processing and shipment of the island's rich lumber and mineral resources. Gold was also discovered in the Fraser River region in 1858, and Victoria became a boomtown for people en route to seeking wealth there. During the mid-1800s, the port was a contrast of bawdy houses and saloons, beautiful mansions and churches, the rough and crude, the gentle and cultivated. It became a city in 1862. At nearby Esquimalt Harbour, in 1865, the British Admiralty established a naval base. Victoria became first the capital of Vancouver Island and later, in 1871, a part of the province of British Columbia. It remained the major city of British Columbia until the transcontinental railroad linked the vast territory between the Atlantic and Pacific coasts to Vancouver. From then on the economic importance of Victoria diminished while

Vancouver's rose. The provincial capital was originally in New Westminster, former name of the city of Vancouver, but protests forced the seat of government to be moved in 1868 to Victoria, where it has remained since.

Victoria Today: Some Basic Facts

Although some light manufacturing (furniture, machinery, food, rubber and plastic products, etc.) takes place in the city, Victoria's main occupation and preoccupation is government, both provincial and federal. Thousands of people are employed in the government bureaucracy. The second most important economic activity is tourism, followed by education, retail sales, and various kinds of personal and professional services. Fishing, ship repair, agriculture, and the shipment, through its seaport, of the island's natural resources (lumber, fish, minerals, and farm products) are other principal ways the people of Victoria make their living.

The population of greater Victoria is about 331,000. The people live in Victoria proper and in the surrounding communities of Esquimalt, Oak Bay, and those on the Saanich Peninsula.

Victoria is a popular retirement community, attracting hundreds of new inhabitants because of its mild climate, high quality of life, and excellent services for the elderly. There is, however, a good mix of all ages here.

The central city has no excessively tall buildings, except for a few multistory hotels. Almost every structure is on a human scale. There are plenty of nice parks and walking areas, gardens and floral displays, magnificent views of mountains and sea, and top-quality goods in stores. The cultural life—music, stage, and the visual arts—is quite rich and diverse. When discussing Victoria, one finds few defects to complain about.

How to Get to Victoria

Although situated on an island, Victoria is easy to reach by private or rented car, by bus, and by air. On Vancouver Island the Trans-Canada Highway itself extends from Nanaimo and ends at "mile 0" in Victoria. The B.C. ferries are modern, large-capacity vessels that link the island with the mainland at several points and also provide trips through the famous Inside Passage (see page 177).

By Car

From Vancouver: The quickest way to get here is by Highway 99 South to Highway 17, which leads to the ferry terminal at Tsawwassen. (This is also the best way for those coming up from Washington, Oregon, and California. Highway 99 North, connecting with U.S. Interstate 5, is your best route in B.C.) Another way—one that allows you to tour more of Vancouver Island—is to take the Lion's Gate Bridge to North Vancouver, then the Trans-Canada Highway to the ferry terminal at Horseshoe Bay.

From Seattle, Washington: The ferry terminal is located off Elliott Avenue at Elliott Bay.

From Anacortes, Washington: Take U.S. Interstate 5 North to Highway 20 West to the ferry terminal in Anacortes.

From Olympia, Washington, via the Olympic peninsula to Port Angeles: Take Highway 101, which circles the peninsula. If you have extra time, tour the west side of the peninsula, which borders on the open Pacific and Olympic National Park, one of the most splendid natural areas in the United States.

By Ferry

The most pleasant way to get to Victoria/Vancouver Island is on one of the B.C. ferries. It's amazing how many cars and campers these modern vessels can carry (the average for vehicles is 320). Tractor-trailer trucks go into the bottom hold, while cars are carried on the second level. The enclosed passenger decks have comfortable nonsmoking and smoking sections, a coffee bar, a cafeteria, a buffet lounge, and a newsstand. The open decks have benches for relaxation and plenty of space for strolling about. En route the scenery is gorgeous, with lovely islands and plenty of birds to see, including bald eagles.

From Vancouver to Victoria, using the terminals of Tsawwassen on the mainland and Swartz Bay on the island: During the summer (late June to early September) there are sailings every hour from 7:00 A.M. to 10:00 P.M.; the same schedule applies for return trips. The sailing time is approximately ninety minutes.

From Vancouver to Nanaimo, using the terminals at Horseshoe Bay on the mainland and Departure Bay on the island: same schedule and sailing time as above. From Nanaimo, you can go farther "up island" to Port Hardy, across the island to Port Alberni and the Pacific Rim National Park, or "down island" to Victoria, which is 112 km (67.2 mi) south via the Trans-Canada.

You should be at the ferry terminal at least an hour prior to sailing. Travel is on a first come, first served basis; no reservations are available (except for the Inside Passage trip). You can purchase a book of tickets for assured loading between Victoria, Vancouver, and Nanaimo. Check on length of waiting time during the peak months of July and August. For more information, call B.C. Ferries' twenty-four-hour recorded messages—Vancouver, (604) 277–0277, Victoria, (250) 656–0757; and Nanaimo (250) 753–6626.

Ferry service is also available on Washington State Ferries— (206) 464–6400 in Washington; (604) 656–1531 in B.C.—via Anacortes, Washington; there are three sailings daily in the summer and one during the winter. Sailing time is three hours and twenty minutes. Blackball Transport—(206) 457–4491 in Port Angeles, (250) 386–2202 in Victoria—has four sailings daily between Port Angeles, Washington, on the Olympic peninsula, and downtown Victoria. Sailing time is one hour and thirty-five minutes.

The *Victoria Clipper* ferry provides two-and-a-half-hour service between Victoria and Seattle. Passengers only; no vehicles. Call (250) 382–8100 in Victoria and (206) 448–5000 in Seattle.

By Plane

The following airlines provide regularly scheduled service between the mainland at Vancouver International Airport and Victoria: Air Canada (with connections to major North American and international cities), Air B.C. (this airline provides service throughout the province, even to remote coastal areas), Burrard Air, Canadian Airlines, San Juan Airlines (has several trips daily to and from Seattle), and Skyline Airlines. The Victoria International Airport itself is located in Sidney, off Highway 17, 30 km (18 mi) north of Victoria and a few miles south of the Vancouver ferry terminal at Swartz Bay. Rental cars are available at the airport.

By Bus

Frequent, comfortable bus/ferry service is available between Vancouver and Victoria on Pacific Coach Lines. In Victoria, call (250) 385–4411; the terminal is at 710 Douglas Street, near the Empress Hotel. In Vancouver, call (604) 662–7575; the terminal is at 1150 Station.

By Rail

VIA Rail—(800) 561–8630 from Western Canada—provides

Vancouver Island rail service between Victoria and Courtenay, with stops at Nanaimo. From the Victoria area, you can get ferries to the United States and to Vancouver via Swartz Bay. From Nanaimo, you can take the ferry to the mainland—Horseshoe Bay to the city of Vancouver.

How to Get Around in Victoria

The best way to get around in downtown Victoria is on foot. Most of the major attractions are here—the Royal British Columbia Museum, the boutiques and specialty stores, the wax museum, Inner Harbour, afternoon tea served at the Empress Hotel and other establishments, and so forth. You can orient yourself on the front steps of the Empress Hotel. Directly across from you is Inner Harbour with its promenade and yacht moorings. The street in front is Government Street. If you go north on Government, you will pass by most of the fine shops selling woolens, china, books, and so on. Government Street will take you to Fisgard Street, which, in this section of the city, is Chinatown. From the Empress going north, Government bisects Humboldt, Courtney, Broughton, Fort, View, Yates, Johnson, and Pandora; it runs parallel with Gordon, Broad, Douglas, and Blanshard. Within this general area are shops, department stores, boutiques, cafés, restaurants, malls, and theaters. Going south on Government, you cross Belleville Street, on which are located the Parliament buildings (at a right angle to the Empress on Inner Harbour), Royal London Wax Museum, Undersea Gardens, hotels, the Archives, the Royal British Columbia Museum, Thunderbird Park, the bus station, Crystal Garden, and Victoria's new Conference Centre. Douglas Street, which runs parallel to Government, heading south, goes by Beacon Hill Park and ends at Dallas Road, part of the Marine Drive. Other areas and their attractions can be easily reached by car, taxi, kabuki cab, horse and buggy, or bus and double-deckers—for example, the campus of the University of Victoria is off Highway 17, via McKenzie Avenue. Butchart Gardens is off Highway 17 North; follow signs. As a matter of fact, signs leading to attractions are very good in the Victoria area, and you should not get lost.

Public Bus Service
B.C. Transit provides bus service on downtown routes from

6:00 A.M. to midnight every day of the week. The company sells day passes for unlimited rides. Call (250) 382–6161 for information and rates.

Taxis, Rental Cars, and Bikes

Ask the concierge or desk clerk at your hotel or motel for assistance in securing a cab, or call Bluebird (250) 384–1155 or 382–4235. Budget Rental Car can be reached at (250) 388–5525. Island Sun Rentals, (250) 383–4424, at 434 Kingston Street, rents cars, scooters, jeeps, tandems, mopeds, and motorcycles.

Visitor Information Center

At the junction of Wharf and Government—812 Wharf Street, on the Inner Harbour and across from the Empress Hotel—the Travel Infocentre is a good source for maps, brochures, directions, and information on accommodations in Victoria. Call (250) 382–2127 for tourism information at any time of the year. For hotel reservations, call this toll-free information number: (800) 663–3883.

Parking

A number of public parking garages are scattered throughout downtown. The *P* sign will lead you to one in the area you want to visit. There is metered street parking, but pay attention to the time limits and keep the meter honest. Victoria has a reputation for having its tow trucks waiting in the wings to scoop up the vehicles of visitors and residents alike; this situation is one of the few blemishes on an otherwise superb city.

Useful Information

Police: (250) 384–4111
Medical: 911
Royal Jubilee Hospital: (250) 595–9200
Victoria General Hospital: (250) 727–4212
Emergency road services: (250) 383–1155 (twenty-four hours)

Special Events

January
Polar Bear Swim
Victoria Symphony

February
Various musical, theatrical, and
    visual arts events
Bloomin' Flower Count

March
Various musical, theatrical, and
    visual arts events

April
Hobby Show
Dixieland Jazz Party

May
Victoria Day holiday
Annual Exhibition and Fair
Crystal Garden Spring Craft
    Fair
Swiftsure (yacht race)

June
Oak Bay Tea Party
Folkfest International Village

July
Canada Day holiday

August
All Day Logger Sports
Market Square Jazz Festival
Sunfest
Classic Boat Festival
International Festival

September
Classic Boat Festival
The Saanichton Fair

October
Royal Victoria Marathon
Goldstream Salmon Run

November
Christmas Craft Fair, Crystal
    Gardens
Christmas at Craigdarroch

December
Christmas at Craigflower Manor
Christmas Craft Fair, Empress
    Hotel
Nutcracker, Royal Theatre

Touring Services

The following touring services provide sightseeing in Victoria:
   Grayline Tours, (250) 388–5248. Free pickup at major hotels.
Sightseeing of local area attractions; trips to Butchart Gardens.
   Tally-Ho Sightseeing, (250) 479–1113. Located beside Parliament buildings and opposite Royal London Wax Museum. Provides one-hour, horse-drawn tours of Victoria.
   Walk-A-Bout Victoria, (250) 382–2127, Visitors and Information Centre, 812 Wharf Street. A guided walking tour through some

METRO VICTORIA

of the city's most interesting and colorful sections; operates during the summer only.

Attractions

Butchart Gardens, located 14 miles north of Victoria, via Highway 17. Call (250) 652–5256 (recorded information) or 652–4422 (questions). Open throughout the year. Because of heavy traffic during the peak months of July and August, admittance into the gardens may be limited. Admission is charged.

If there is a North American paradise for horticulturists and simple lovers of flowers and landscaping, it is Butchart Gardens. Here you will be dazzled by splendid displays of innumerable kinds of flowers, plants, shrubs, and trees, all arranged along a walking tour that takes you through the very heart of Eden itself. Butchart

150

features Italian, English Rose, Japanese, and Sunken Gardens. There are ponds, waterfalls, a dancing fountain, two restaurants, and a coffee bar. Books, seeds, plants, and gardening tools can be purchased at the Seed and Gift Shop. Entertainment—fireworks, stage shows, and music—is provided every day except Sunday from mid-May through September. Write or phone for a copy of the *Butchart Gardens Entertainment Guide*. When you're on site, the staff will loan you umbrellas, cameras, wheelchairs, and pushcarts for babies. Moorages are also available for visitors in the area on their own yachts. Buses provide frequent transportation to Butchart Gardens from Victoria and from the city of Vancouver. When you walk through the sumptuous gardens, it is hard to imagine that this place was once a drab limestone quarry. The late Jennie Butchart was the main force in transforming gouged-out land into one of the premier horticultural attractions in the world (the work began in 1904). To visit British Columbia and miss experiencing Butchart Gardens is to turn one's back on the beauty that the hands of God and human beings have wrought together.

Marine Drive follows the coastline along Dallas Road and offers spectacular views of the distant Olympic Mountains across the Strait of Juan de Fuca. It passes through parts of the swank Rockland residential area and continues past the lovely Victoria Golf Course, which is in full operation during the winter, and through the prestigious Oak Bay community. The drive continues through the high-priced area of Uplands to the Saanich Peninsula and on to Cordova Bay. There are many stopping places along the way where you can enjoy the views and stroll or jog the promenades.

Thunderbird Park, located at the corner of Belleville and Douglas, next to the Royal British Columbia Museum, is a small grass area decorated with tall totem poles and a Kwakiutl dance house. Here's a perfect spot to take pictures of your friends in front of the fantastic carvings of the region's Amerindians.

Beacon Hill Park, between Douglas and Cook streets and bordering Marine Drive (a five-minute walk from the Empress Hotel), is a 154-acre enclave of flower beds, ponds, oaks, and cedars. There are communities of royal swans and many different birds, including the giant black raven. At the Marine Drive end of the park is one of the world's tallest totem poles. Also within Beacon Hill Park is a children's farm replete with chickens, pheasants, peacocks, goats, and lambs. Children have a place where they can pet the young animals.

Parliament Buildings, Belleville Street, facing Victoria Harbour and at a right angle to the Empress Hotel. Call (250) 387–3046 for tour information. Tours given in not only English but French, Japanese, Italian, and German; tours conducted during the summer months, but buildings are open throughout the year. Free. These buildings were designed by Francis Mawson Rattenbury, an Englishman who was also the architect of the Empress Hotel and the Crystal Gardens. The Parliament (provincial legislative) buildings are impressive enough to grace the capital of a good-size country; they could certainly accommodate Canada's federal Parliament, should it ever decide to move out of Ottawa. Completed in 1898, this complex for enacting legislation and governing the province is a massive building of domes, towers, and arches. The interior is rich with marble. If the legislature is in session while you're passing through, you may observe the proceedings of the lawmakers. During the evening, the outline of the complex is illuminated with thousands of bulbs, giving it a Christmasy feel even in midsummer. A large expanse of lawn flows from the center building down toward Victoria's Inner Harbour. Set back a few feet from Belleville Street and in a straight line to the main portal of the complex is a majestic statue of Queen Victoria (one of the best sculptures of her in Canada), from whose patronage this city takes its name.

Royal British Columbia Museum, 675 Belleville Street, near the Parliament buildings, (250) 387–3014. Open daily, except Christmas Day and New Year's Day. Admission is charged. This extensive museum is one of Victoria's best attractions. The B.C. museum concentrates on the peoples, industries, and ecology of the province. The displays of Amerindian art are superb. There are mounted animals (the woolly mammoth is awesome), fish, and birds common to B.C. One display re-creates a frontier town, allowing the visitor to walk through as one who has zoomed backward several decades in time. A tearoom and a gift shop are on the main floor.

Helmcken House, 10 Elliot Street, (250) 387–3440. Open daily. Donations are accepted. This historic 1852 residence belonged to Dr. J. S. Helmcken, a man who brought medical science to a needful community in its pioneering days. You can see the original furnishings and medical instruments of that bygone era.

The Empress Hotel on the yacht harbor in Victoria is one of the world's ▶ **most famous hotels. Here the tradition of English-style afternoon tea is sacred, ample, and punctual.**

Point Ellice House Museum, 2616 Pleasant Street, (250) 385–4697. Open daily. Donation accepted. A magistrate named Peter O'Reilly built this fine house in 1861. The house itself, its original furnishings, and displays will give you a fair idea of how well the Establishment lived at a rugged and woolly time in the city's early history.

Pacific Undersea Gardens, 490 Belleville Street, (250) 382–5717. Open daily. Admission is charged. This museum of marine life is well worth a visit. In an undersea gallery, you see living specimens of thousands of marine animals. The northwest coast is an exceptionally rich environment for a wide diversity of marine life, including the world's largest octopuses. A scuba diver puts on a show working with a huge Pacific octopus.

Victoria Heritage Village, 321 Belleville Street. Open daily. Admission is charged to some attractions. Heritage Village is a complex of shops and tourist attractions.

Royal London Wax Museum, 470 Belleville Street, (250) 388–4461. Open every day, with extended hours during the summer. Admission is charged. Figures of British royalty, Canadian greats, and famous and infamous figures from throughout history—more than 180 of them, made in London—are here authentically costumed and set in displays portraying their times. The kids love the horror and fantasy displays, and Anglophiles adore the renditions of the queen and members of her family.

Crystal Garden, 713 Douglas Street, (250) 381–1213. Open daily. Admission is charged. The setting is that of a tropical garden containing 150 species of plants and 50 species of exotic birds, monkeys, and reptiles. The attraction has several souvenir boutiques and restaurants as well.

Miniature World, 649 Humboldt Street (at the Empress Hotel), (604) 385–9731. Open daily. Admission is charged. Things miniature have always been popular with people. At this attraction you'll see what is purported to be the "world's largest doll house," a neighborhood in "ye olde London," and "one of the world's largest rail scenes and the world's smallest operational sawmill."

Mile "0," where Douglas Street meets Dallas Road. Although Mile "0" doesn't sound like much of anything, it is the western starting point of the Trans-Canada Highway, *the world's longest national highway—7,820 km/4,860 mi.* For those of us who have traveled long stretches of the Trans-Canada in all kinds of weather, this is a major attraction indeed.

The Emily Carr Gallery of the Provincial Archives of British

Columbia, 1107 Wharf Street, (250) 384–3130. Closed Sundays. Free. The gallery shows paintings by Emily Carr, B.C.'s most famous artist, and documents relating to her life and work. Exhibitions of the works of other artists are also held. Films about Emily Carr are shown, and special tours give visitors a fuller appreciation of the contributions of one of Canada's cultural immortals. Reproductions of Carr's paintings are for sale here.

Bastion Square, entrance off Government Street, between Yates and Fort streets at the foot of View Street. Here was the original site of Fort Victoria, established by James Douglas of the Hudson's Bay Company in 1843. Several buildings of historic importance are in Bastion Square: the Board of Trade Building (1893); the Court Building (1889), Victoria's first concrete building, which now houses a maritime museum; Law Chambers (turn of the century), which now has several shops; Burns House (1882) once a brothel; and Strousse Warehouse (1885), which supplied gold miners.

Maritime Museum of British Columbia, 28 Bastion Square, (250) 385–4222. Open daily. Admission is charged. The Maritime Museum has a wide assortment of marine artifacts; ship models; exhibits centering on Captain Cook, who sailed hereabouts in the eighteenth century; and displays portraying the history of Britain's Royal Navy and the Canadian Navy as they pertain to British Columbia. The museum houses the *Tilkum* and the *Trekka,* two famous B.C. sailing vessels that circumnavigated the globe.

Art Gallery of Greater Victoria, 1040 Moss Street, (250) 384–4101. Open daily. Admission is charged. The Art Gallery collection includes European prints and drawings, English decorative art, and Canadian art, both historical and contemporary. Its excellent collection of Japanese art is one of the finest on the continent. The Art Gallery has the only Shinto shrine outside Japan. A café and shop are within the Spencer Mansion complex.

Government House, 1401 Rockland Avenue, (250) 387–2080, is the official residence of the lieutenant governor of British Columbia and the place where Elizabeth II, queen of Canada, and other members of the monarchy stay when visiting this part of the province. The beautiful grounds are, however, open to the public, except, of course, when royalty is in residence or during special events. There are a sunken rose garden, formal lawns and other gardens, a lily pond, and many exquisite botanical features, both indigenous and specially planted.

Craigdarroch Castle, 1050 Joan Crescent, (250) 592–5323. Open daily. Admission is charged. Scots have a penchant for building grand castles for themselves. This was so with Robert Dunsmuir, who in 1851 left the heather-covered hills of Scotland to settle in Victoria. Dunsmuir, known as the coal king of British Columbia, made a great deal of money and spent $650,000 (a king's ransom in those days) building Craigdarroch Castle. Completed in 1889, Craigdarroch is not a castle in the classic medieval sense. But as an immense, impressive mansion, Craigdarroch can be topped by few other similar places in Canada. There are guides to answer questions to make a visit here memorable.

Craigflower Manor Farmhouse, 110 Island Highway, (250) 387–4697. Phone for hours. Free. The farmhouse and schoolhouse on this site were part of a Hudson's Bay Company farm established in 1853. The farmhouse contains furniture from this mid-nineteenth-century period (most of the pieces are originally from Scotland).

Craigflower School, 2765 Admirals Road, (250) 387–4697. Open daily during the summer by appointment only. Free. For those interested in Canada's pioneering heritage, Craigflower School is the oldest standing schoolhouse in Western Canada, built around 1855.

Dominion Astrophysical Observatory, 5071 West Saanich Road (best taken in when going to or from Butchart Gardens), (250) 388–0012. Open daily in the summer. Free. There are a giant telescope here and interesting exhibits dealing with astronomical phenomena. The public can view the heavens through the telescope on Saturday evenings. A fine panoramic view of the countryside can be had from this facility.

Chinatown, on Fisgard Street, is a compact section of small restaurants and stores selling Oriental goods. The food is quite good here. The Chinese community has a number of festivals throughout the year. The entrance to Chinatown is marked by an ornate gate where Fisgard bisects Government Street.

Centennial Square, off Douglas Street, is the location for City Hall and the McPherson Theatre, where many entertainments are performed. Shops and restaurants surround a landscaped courtyard.

Fable Cottage Estate, 5187 Cordova Bay Road, (250) 478–5526. Open from the end of March to the third week in October. Admission is charged. Fable Cottage is a lovely estate on the waterfront, featuring a handcrafted mansion (à la Disney), an outdoor animation display, beautiful gardens, great views of the sea, gift shops, and a tea pavilion.

Fort Rodd Hill National Historic Park and Fisgard Lighthouse, 603 Fort Rodd Hill Road, (250) 363–4662. Open daily, except certain holidays. Free. The Fort Rodd/Fisgard Lighthouse area (designated a national park) offers many acres of lovely, tranquil parkland overlooking Esquimalt Harbour. Explore the nineteenth-century artillery installations. Fisgard is British Columbia's oldest lighthouse, built in 1859.

Maltwood Art Museum and Gallery, at the University of Victoria, (250) 721–8298. Open daily, except Saturdays. Free. By visiting this art museum you will also have a chance to stroll the pleasant campus of the University of Victoria. The main gallery, located in the University Centre building, features art exhibits and the Katharine Maltwood collection of decorative arts, paintings, sculptures, graphics, archaeological artifacts, glass, textiles, ceramics, and furniture. Exhibitions by contemporary artists are held at the McPherson Library Gallery.

The Carillon, at the corner of Belleville and Government streets in Heritage Court. Recitals given every Sunday at 3:00 P.M. and on all holidays at noon. Concerts are given during the Advent/Christmas season as well. With sixty-two bells, this is the largest carillon in Canada and the seventh largest in the world. You can climb eighty-five steps to the carillonneur's playing cabin and see him or her in performance. The Carillon is a gift to the province from Canadians of Dutch ancestry.

All Fun Waterslide Park, north on the Trans-Canada Highway 1, 13 km (8 mi) from Victoria, (250) 474–4546. Open late May to mid-June on weekends and every day from mid-June to Labour Day. Call for hours and fees. The park has fifteen water slides, a whitewater river ride, a car museum, minigolf, and other attractions.

Accommodations

Victoria is one of Canada's most popular tourist cities, and reservations during the summer season and over the Christmas holidays are essential. Call ahead, or have your travel agent do so.

The Empress, 721 Government Street, (250) 384–8111; toll-free, (800) 268–9411 or (800) 828–7447 in the United States. The

157

Empress is a landmark hotel known to sophisticated travelers throughout the world. It reflects the essence of bygone elegance in its neo-Gothic architecture, ambience, service, and civility. Central to all attractions and within steps of the Parliament buildings, the hotel overlooks Victoria Harbour and the moorings of luxurious yachts. The Empress features fine restaurants, shops, and many amenities. It has become a popular place to stay during the Christmas season, when Victoria takes on a Dickensian feel, and a number of tour companies offer special Christmas holiday trips to Victoria with stays at the Empress; contact your travel agent for details. The most popular tradition at the Empress is afternoon tea, in the English manner. The best of the house is served on bone china with sterling: English honey crumpets, fruit salad, homemade scones with jersey cream and strawberry jam, assorted tea sandwiches, Empress cakes, and Empress blend tea. There are four sittings during the summer months and three during the winter. Because of its popularity, having afternoon tea at the Empress requires a reservation and proper dress. The Empress has undergone a $45-million renovation. Improvements include the addition of a swimming pool and a health and fitness facility, the total renovation of all guest rooms, a more beautiful and serviceable lobby, and the restoration of the stunning stained-glass ceiling in Palm Court. Expensive.

Clarion Hotel Grand Pacific, 450 Quebec Street, (250) 386–0450; (800) 663–7550. A new, deluxe hotel offering many services and amenities—swimming pool, sauna, whirlpool, health and fitness facilities, restaurant, lounge. Good downtown location. Expensive.

Executive House, 777 Douglas Street, (250) 388–5111. Excellent accommodations, including luxury penthouse suites. Indoor pool, sauna, free parking, and Raven's, a fine restaurant. This hotel is central to everything—attractions and government and commercial offices. Moderate to expensive.

Ramada Huntington Manor Inn, 330 Quebec Street, (250) 381–3456. A top-of-the-line hotel with most amenities. Excellent location. Moderate to expensive.

The Gatsby Mansion, 309 Bellville Street, (250) 388–9191; (800) 563–0656. This is the new name of The Captain's Palace. The mansion turned 100 in 1997 and it has lost none of the charm of the former owners. This is one of Victoria's great B&Bs, a return to the 1920s with 20 rooms in a house of crystal chandeliers, stained-glass windows, a martini bar, and hand-frescoed ceilings. A restaurant that specializes in upscale Northwest cuisine overlooks Victoria Harbor. Expensive.

Laurel Point Inn, 680 Montreal Street, (250) 386–8721. One of Victoria's best hotels—a superb location; all rooms with balconies and a water view, swimming pools, tennis, dining room, and lounges. Free parking. Expensive.

The Beaconsfield Inn, 998 Humboldt Street, (250) 384–4044. Elegant rooms in an English-style mansion located near Inner Harbour. Some rooms have canopy beds. There are fireplaces and down comforters, a guest library, and a sunroom. Moderate to expensive.

Best Western Carlton Plaza, 642 Johnson, (250) 388–5513; (800) 663–7241. All amenities, European–style hotel in central downtown. Moderate to expensive.

Queen Victoria Inn, 655 Douglas Street, (250) 386–1312. A nice location facing Thunderbird Park and other downtown attractions. Offers comfortable rooms, whirlpool and sauna, restaurant, suites with Jacuzzi and marble fireplace. Expensive.

Best Western Inner Harbour, 412 Quebec Street, (250) 384–5122. An excellent hotel in a superb location, facing Inner Harbor and Quadra Park. Amenities include swimming pool, sauna, Jacuzzi, kitchenettes, penthouse suites with fireplaces. Expensive.

Oak Bay Beach Hotel, 1175 Beach Drive, via Marine Drive, (250) 598–4556. A lovely Tudor-style hotel right on the water's edge, with views of snowcapped mountains in the distance. In addition to the usual hotel amenities, Oak Bay has an English-style pub and a fine dining room overlooking the water and mountains. This is a very friendly place whose staff members are eager to please. Oak Bay also has a yacht for cruising and fishing trips and evening dinner sails. Moderate to expensive.

Harbour Towers, 345 Quebec Street, (250) 385–2405; (800) 663–5896. A full-service hotel near the Inner Harbour, shopping areas, and downtown attractions. Moderate to expensive.

Chateau Victoria, 740 Burdett Avenue, (250) 382–4221; (800) 663–5891. One of Victoria's top hotels, offering an indoor pool, a sauna, satellite TV, free parking, a central location, and the city's only rooftop restaurant, called the Parrot House. Expensive.

James Bay Inn, 270 Government Street, (250) 384–7151. Comfortable accommodations, convenient location, reasonable rates, restaurant. Inexpensive to moderate.

Embassy Motor Inn, 520 Menzies Street, (250) 382–8161. Located next to the Parliament buildings and within a few steps of the promenades circling the Inner Harbour; has kitchenettes, a sauna, a pool, parking, and a restaurant. Moderate.

Old England Inn, 429 Lampson Street, (250) 388–4353. A well-known accommodation that transports you to Elizabethan times. You can sleep in a canopy bed that was previously used by royalty and feast on roast beef and Yorkshire pudding—along with several pints of good stout ale, of course. Part of this complex is Anne Hathaway's Cottage, an authentically furnished sixteenth-century dwelling that seems as though it had been plucked from a street in Stratford-on-Avon itself. The cottage is filled with furnishings from that period, and the guides are costumed as comely Tudor wenches. Moderate to expensive.

Royal Scot Motor Inn, 425 Quebec Street, (250) 388–5463; (800) 663–7515. The Royal Scot gives you good value by providing a suite for the price of a room. Free local calls, indoor pool, saunas, Jacuzzi, masseur, tearoom, exercise facilities. Moderate to expensive.

Cherry Bank Hotel, 825 Burdett Avenue, (250) 385–5380. Dating from the 1890s, this old building in a quiet residential area has some family suites and kitchens, rooms with canopied beds, plus a lounge and restaurant. No phones or TVs. Three blocks from the downtown area. Moderate.

Crystal Court Motel, 701 Belleville Street, (250) 384–0551. Downtown location, some housekeeping units. Moderate.

University of Victoria Housing Services, P.O. Box 1700, Victoria, B.C. V8W 2Y2; (250) 721–8396. From May 1 to August 30, comfortable rooms are available at the University of Victoria, located a few minutes' drive north of downtown, as well as on the bus route. Price includes breakfast and free parking. An excellent value for the thrifty. Inexpensive.

Other Good Places to Stay

Bed and Breakfast Victoria, Vancouver Island and the Gulf Islands, Box 5511, Station B, Victoria, B.C. V8R 6S4, (250) 595–BEDS.

Dogwood Manor Apartment Lodge, 1124 Fairfield Road, (250) 361–4441. A 1910 interesting "character" home that offers suites and kitchens and welcomes families. Moderate.

The Henderson House, 522 Quadra Street, (250) 384–3428. Considered one of the most photographed houses in the city; features nicely furnished rooms with antiques. Located near all downtown attractions. Furnished full breakfasts in oak-paneled dining room. Moderate.

Dining

Victoria offers a wide choice of restaurants. Seafood and traditional British dishes are featured. Ethnic fare, such as Chinese, Japanese, Greek, and Italian, is also widely available. French cuisine is excellent. The Bombay Room at the Empress serves Indian dishes with chutney and other condiments; its seafood with chutney on Fridays is a must.

Camille's Restaurant, 45 Bastion Square, (250) 381–3433. Delicious French cooking, including mouth-watering breads and cakes. Moderate.

Cherry Bank Hotel Spare Rib House, 825 Burdett Street, (250) 385–5380. Here's where you can satisfy your hunger for pork baby back ribs, also steaks and seafood. Inexpensive to moderate.

Chez Daniel, 2522 Estavan Avenue, (250) 592–7424. One of Victoria's old standbys, it is located in Oak Bay. High calorie cuisine. Expensive.

Don Mee Restaurant, 538 Fisgard Street, (250) 383–1032. A full menu of Chinese delicacies representing the different culinary regions of China. Inexpensive to moderate.

Gazebo Tea House and Gallery, 5460 West Saanich Road, between Victoria and Butchart Gardens, (250) 479–7787. Lunch, afternoon tea, and early dinner served in the English manner in a lovely country garden. Inexpensive to moderate.

Harbour House, 607 Oswego Street, (250) 386–1244. A top seafood place in a convenient location on the Inner Harbour and near the Empress Hotel. Moderate.

Izumi Japanese Restaurant, 739 Pandora, (250) 995–8432. If sushi is your choice of cuisine, you won't do better than this cozy and authentically Japanese eatery.

Koto, 510 Fort Street, (250) 382–1514. Private tatami rooms provide an authentic character. There's a wide variety of sushi. Inexpensive to moderate.

La Cucina, 920 Gordon Street, (250) 381–4556. Fine northern Italian food. Moderate.

Larousse Restaurant, 100–1619 Store Street, (250) 386–3454. Special French colonial and provincial cooking. Moderate to expensive.

Le Petit Saigon Vietnamese Restaurant, 1010 Langley Street, (250) 386–1412. This restaurant is generally regarded as Victoria's best place for Vietnamese food, with a menu that combines a hint of French with exotic elegance.

Ming's Restaurant, 1321 Quadra Street, (250) 385–4405. A gourmet's Chinese restaurant. Inexpensive to moderate.

Pagliacci's, 1011 Broad Street, (250) 386–1662. Italian. Pasta servings are made on site. Chicken in marsala sauce with fettuccine is one of several house specialties. Moderate.

Periklis, 531 Yates Street, (250) 386–3313. Delicious Greek food—lamb dishes, seafood, and steaks. Guests are treated to Greek dancers and belly dancers. Moderate.

Pablo's Dining Lounge, 225 Quebec, (250) 388–4255. You can't beat this for casual fine dining. French continental cuisine that includes seafood, paella, lamb, and poultry. And, like everywhere else in Victoria, you don't have to dress to the gills.

Princess Mary, 344 Harbour Road, (250) 386–3456. A fine restaurant in an old ship. Seafood and beef dishes; special children's menu. Moderate.

Rathskeller Restaurant, 1205 Quadra Street, (250) 386–9348. German and Bavarian cuisine. Inexpensive to moderate.

Rattenbury's, 703 Douglas Street, (250) 381–1333. Summer salmon barbecue, prime rib, steaks; alfresco dining in good weather. Moderate.

The Gatsby Mansion, 309 Belleville Street, (250) 388–9191. Breakfast, luncheon, afternoon tea, and dinner elegantly served in a historic Victoria mansion. Good location on the Inner Harbour. Bed-and-breakfast accommodation also available here. Moderate.

The Keg, 500 Fort Street, (250) 386–7789. Serves what it considers the ultimate sharing snack—strips of steak or chicken sauteed with green peppers and onions and served hot with relish, cheeses, and a soft tortilla. Also has seven-layer dip, two-way salmon, and Cajun popcorn shrimp. An unpretentious, fun place where the British stiff upper lip is out of place. Inexpensive.

Yokohama Japanese Restaurant, 980 Blanshard Street, (250) 384–5433. If you lust for sushi, this is the place to get your fill. Moderate.

Entertainment

Most of the major hotels have live entertainment (singers, comedians, dance bands, etc.) in their lounges and some in their dining rooms. For current entertainment events ask your concierge or call the organizations listed below. The following groups and theaters feature plays, dance, and musical events, throughout the year or in their formal seasons:

Victoria Symphony Society, 631 Superior, (250) 385–6515

Pacific Opera Association, 1316 Government, (250) 385–0222

The Royal Theatre, 805 Broughton Street, (250) 386–6121

Phoenix Theatre, at the University of Victoria, (250) 721–8000

McPherson Playhouse, 3 Centennial Square, (250) 386–6121

New Bastion Theatre Company, 625 Superior, (250) 382–0402

Kaleidoscope Theatre Productions, 520 Herald, (250) 475–4444

Sports and Recreation

For the visitor, most sports and recreation will involve touring Victoria on foot. It is also a wonderful city for jogging. Almost everywhere, you'll see people of all ages briskly walking, jogging, or cycling. The following additional options are offered:

Public Golf Courses
Gorge Vale Golf Club, 1005 Craigflower, (250) 386–3401. Long and tough.

Cedar Hill Municipal Golf Course, 1400 Derby off Cedar Hill Road, (250) 595–3103. Eighteen holes, par 67.

Henderson Park Golf Course, 2291 Cedar Hill Road (Oak Bay recreational area), (250) 595–7946. Nine holes, par 3.

Olympic View Golf Club, 643 Latoria Road, (250) 474–3671. Great view, 6,450 yards (5,805 meters) long.

Cordova Bay Golf Course, 5333 Cordova Bay Road, (250) 658–4075. Completed in 1991, 6,558 yards (5,902 meters) long.

Royal Colwood Golf and Country Club, 629 Goldstream Avenue, (250) 478–8331. Ranked number 1 in B.C. by many.

Public Swimming Pools
Crystal Pool, 2275 Quadra, (250) 380–7946

Recreation Oak Bay, 1975 Bee, (250) 595–7946

Public Tennis Courts
Beacon Hill Park Courts, off Cook Street
Recreation Oak Bay, 1975 Bee, (250) 595–7946

Public Skating Rinks
Memorial Arena, 1925 Blanshard, (250) 384–0444
Recreation Oak Bay, 1975 Bee, (250) 595–7946

Racquet Sports
Quadra Court House, 3950 Quadra, (250) 727–2277
YMCA/YWCA, 880 Courtney Street, (250) 386–7511

Fishing Charters
Oak Bay Charters, 2141 Newton, (250) 598–1061
Brentwood Inn Boat Charters, 7212 Penden Lane, Brentwood Bay,
    near Butchart Gardens, (250) 652–3151

Sailing Charters
Victoria Sailing Academy, 481 Head, (250) 384–7245

Harness Racing
Sandown Harness Raceway, thirty minutes north of downtown via
    Highway 17; 1810 Glamorgan, Sidney; call (250) 656–1631 for
    information

Shopping

Your best buys are imported goods from Great Britain, locally made
candies, Amerindian-made sweaters, jewelry (B.C. jade and silver)
and carvings, books on Canada, and arts and crafts by the
province's other artists (weavings, pottery, fashions, paintings, etc.).
   Crystal Garden Shopping Mall, located across from the Royal
British Columbia Museum, offers a fine selection of specialty shops.
   Market Square, 201–560 Johnson Street, in the heart of "Old
Town"; more than thirty stores and restaurants are set in refurbished heritage buildings, surrounding an old-style covered market.
This is an enjoyable place for all ages, whether you buy or just poke
around. Special entertainment and recitals are held here through-
out the year.

Harbour Square Shopping Mall, 910 Government at Broughton Street, an indoor mall with many shops and eateries.

Hudson's Bay Company, 1701 Douglas at Fisgard, Canada's well-known department store, featuring furs; more than 300 patterns of top brands of English china; the Canadiana Shop offering works by local artists and artisans (10 percent off on purchases made in the shop); woolens from England and Scotland; and famous Hudson's Bay point blankets.

Mayfair Shopping Center, 221 Mayfair, 1 mile from downtown at Douglas and Finlayson, more than one hundred fashion boutiques. Mayfair is one of the most elegant shopping malls on Vancouver Island. Bus service is available from downtown.

Rogers' Chocolates, 913 Government Street, the place for connoisseurs of fine chocolate goodies. Rogers' has been in business for more than one hundred years, and its Victoria Creams make taste buds sing heavenly tunes. Dieters beware.

Bolen Books, Hillside Centre, 1644 Hillside Avenue, offers a wide selection of general interest books and guidebooks.

Montague Bridgman, Ltd., 650 Broad Street, the city's oldest store selling fine china and crystal. The shop stocks more than 300 dinnerware patterns.

Munro's Books, 1108 Government Street, one of the finest bookshops in Western Canada; browsing through the extensive collection is an unhurried pleasure. Housed in one of Victoria's heritage buildings, with high ceilings and colorful wall hangings by Carole Sabiston.

Victoria Limited Editions, 919 Fort Street, has Victoria's largest selection of stemware. Offers low prices on Waterford crystal.

Trounce Alley, off Government Street. A quaint little passage with stores and dining places.

Vancouver Island

Touring "Up Island"

Most visitors to the coast of British Columbia concentrate on the cities of Victoria and Vancouver. Both certainly have enough attractions to keep you busy for an extended period—fishing, golf, touring, whale watching, crafts shopping, hiking, camping, mountain climbing. Nonetheless, while you are in this area it would be a shame to miss out on experiencing the natural magnificence of

Vancouver Island. Here are long stretches of unspoiled beaches, impressive mountains, and forests containing some of the tallest trees in the world. If you've never seen whales or bald eagles, you can do so here; this is their natural habitat. All you need is a sharp eye, binoculars, and a camera. You can fish for salmon and trout and not be disappointed. There are beaches for swimming and slopes for skiing. And while it rains a lot in winter, Vancouver Island is Canada's mildest zone during this otherwise-harsh season: Unless you go to a high elevation, there's generally no snow, nor is it unusual to see flowers growing outdoors during the cold-weather months—in contrast to most of Canada and the United States, which have to wait until April to enjoy the first blossoms.

Vancouver Island is 405 km/252 mi long and 64 to 128 km/ 40 to 80 mi wide, making it the largest Pacific island off the coast of North America (for comparison's sake, whereas the province of Prince Edward Island is 2,184 square miles, Vancouver Island, which is part of a province, is 12,408 square miles). The island extends from just below the fiftieth parallel to about the forty-eighth. About one-fifth of the island—the southwestern tip containing the city of Victoria—extends close to one degree below the forty-ninth parallel, along which almost the entire U.S.–Canadian boundary line runs. In fact, the city of Victoria is far closer to Washington's Olympic National Park than either Bellingham or Seattle, major cities in that state.

The center spine of the island is a range of high mountains; on the east coast, facing the Strait of Georgia, are most of the communities and broad expanses of agricultural land; and the west coast, facing the open Pacific, is very rugged, wind- and rain-swept through much of the year, and relatively uninhabited. As you tour Vancouver Island, search out west coast Indian sites and villages that reveal an ancient way of life. There's a mystical aspect to the native people, a depth of understanding about life and nature, that seems more profound than our own.

Highway 14 goes around the southern tip of Vancouver Island, from Victoria to Sooke, Jordan River, and Port Renfrew. At **Sooke** visit the **Sooke Region Museum,** (250) 642–6351, which has a collection of weavings and carvings by the Salish and Nootka people and exhibits on early pioneer life; open through the year. Free. Be sure to see **Leechtown Gold Rush Site**—call Sooke Region Museum, above, for details—where gold was discovered in 1864. **Botanical Beach,** between Sooke and **Port Renfrew** at Botany Bay, has natural aquariums, tidal pools, and a great deal of intertidal marine life to see. Be careful of rough seas and winds when exploring in this area. At Port Renfrew you can get over to the west coast hiking trail with some effort, but you would be better off to start the trail at Bamfield, which can be reached from Port Alberni, about a third of the way "up island."

Camping at Provincial Parks

Provincial parks that offer camping facilities are listed below. Call Tourism British Columbia (800–663–6000) for more information. Camping is on a first come, first served basis. There is a small fee for use of camping facilities. Most campgrounds have showers, firewood, and toilets, but the actual range of facilities may vary from park to park.

Bamberton, on the Saanich Peninsula, north of Victoria
Elk Falls, on the Quinsam River, near Campbell River
Englishman River Falls, in the Parksville/Qualicum area
Goldstream, just north of Victoria on the Trans-Canada
Gordon Bay, on Cowichan Lake, north of Victoria
Little Qualicum Falls, off Highway 4 between Parksville and Port Alberni
McDonald, close to Swartz Bay, near the Vancouver ferry terminal
Rathtrevor Beach, south of Parksville
Sproat Lake, near Port Alberni
Buttle Lake Campground and Ralph River Campground, both in Strathcona Park

The following tour starts in Victoria and moves in a northwest direction "up island":

As you drive from the outskirts of Victoria on the Trans-Canada Highway 1, you go over Malahat Drive, which offers remarkable views of deep forests and distant islands. **Goldstream Provincial Park** is here and a good place to stop and grab a bite to eat and walk among the tall trees.

In **Duncan** you can purchase thick, exceedingly warm Cowichan sweaters knitted by native women who live in or around this community. Be sure to visit the following:

British Columbia Demonstration Forest Museum, off Trans-Canada Highway 1, (250) 746–1251. Open from May to September. Admission is charged. Indoor/outdoor exhibits on the forest industry in B.C., woodland walking trails, and steam-train rides.

Cowichan Valley Museum, Duncan Railway Station, (250)

746–6612. Donations are accepted. Small, local historical museum. Pioneer house. Indian art and historic photographs.

The Glass Castle, off the Trans-Canada, (250) 746–6518. Open throughout the year. Admission is charged. An eccentric house made from 180,000 glass bottles.

Whippletree Junction, off the Trans-Canada, (250) 748–1100. Open daily. Admission is charged. Re-creation of turn-of-the-century pioneer village; includes an early Chinatown.

Twenty-four giant murals decorate the buildings of **Chemainus**. These beautifully rendered murals depict this tiny town's heritage from the time of the native people to pioneering days and great moments in its history. A charming, unique place that's well worth the side trip on Highway 18.

In **Ladysmith** stop at the **Black Nugget,** 12 Gatacre Street, (250) 245–4846 (call for hours and admission fee), a local historical museum in an 1881-vintage hotel.

Ladysmith Arboretum, on the Trans-Canada, (250) 245–2218, is open throughout the year. Free. Tree specimens from all over the world; early logging and railroad equipment displays.

Accommodations in Yellowpoint, 13 km (8 mi) north of Ladysmith, are available at the **Inn of the Sea,** Yellowpoint Road, (250) 245–2211. A full-facility waterfront resort offering fireside dining, a pool, tennis, and Jacuzzi. Moderate to expensive.

Nanaimo is the second-largest community on Vancouver Island. There are plenty of accommodations, restaurants, and shopping malls. The terminal for ferries to the mainland and the city of Vancouver is here; sailing time is one hour and thirty-five minutes. One of British Columbia's oldest remaining Hudson's Bay Company bastions still guards the harbor. Killer whale-watching trip services operate out of Nanaimo. Attractions here include the following:

Historic buildings in the downtown area, south of the ferry terminal, include **Nanaimo Courthouse** (1886); the **Palace Hotel** (1889); **Central Drugs,** a 1900-style drugstore that was built in 1985 (in the 1911-vintage Dakin Building); old-fashioned light posts, cobblestone streets, and brick sidewalks.

The Bastion, corner of Bastion and Front streets, (250) 754–1631 in summer; (250) 754–8474 in winter. Housed in the original Hudson's Bay Fort, the Bastion's collection includes memorabilia from the 1850s to the 1880s. Each day, during the summer, Bastion guardsmen, dressed in colorful naval uniforms of the

1850s, are led to the Bastion by a piper. Under the orders of an officer, the cannon is elaborately cleaned and then fired as a salute to visiting ships—of which there are always many in the harbor.

Nanaimo District Museum, 100 Cameron Street, (250) 753–1821. Open throughout the year. Donations are accepted. Historical and art exhibitions, Chinese art, coal-mine re-creation, local archives.

Annual Events
Empire Days, May
Heritage Days, June
Nanaimo Festival, June and July
Vancouver Island Exhibition, August
Jazz Festival and Vintage Car Challenge, September
Highland Games, September

For dining, try the following restaurants:

The Lighthouse, 50 Anchor Way, (250) 754–3212. An unusual lighthouse restaurant on the water; serves seafood. Moderate.

The Grotto, 1511 Stewart Avenue, (250) 753–3303. Specializes in seafood. Waterfront. Inexpensive.

Accommodations can be found at **Coast Bastion Inn,** 11 Bastion Street, (250) 753–6601. The best in town. Rooms have water views. Gourmet restaurant, health facility, nightclub, and lounge. Moderate to expensive.

The following inns also have dining rooms, lounges, and other amenities:

Days Inn Harbourview, on Trans-Canada South, (250) 754–8171. Moderate.

Tally-Ho Island Inns, 1 Terminal Avenue, (250) 753–2241. Moderate.

Nanaimo has several large shopping malls where you can find just about any kind of item. It's about equal to Victoria in having such retail complexes. Woodgrove Centre, on the North Island Highway, is one of the largest on the island. Harbour Park Mall is in downtown. Rutherford Mall is on the North Island Highway.

The main route heading north out of Nanaimo becomes Highway 19.

The **Parksville-Qualicum Beach** area is best known for its long sandy beaches, and during the summer season it is a primary vacation spot for both B.C. residents and visitors. It's also popular with anglers, hikers, and spelunkers. Visit **Craig Heritage Park** in

Parksville, (250) 248–6966. Open mid-May to the end of August. Free. Collection features Amerindian and pioneer artifacts. Qualicum Beach is perfect for swimming and sunbathing. Golf, lawn bowling, live theater, and nature hikes are also offered. **Qualicum Falls Provincial Park** has hiking trails and provides areas for overnight camping. The Sand Castle Competition is held in July.

Recommended restaurants:

Maclure House Inn, 1015 East Island Highway, (250) 248–3470. Beautiful oceanfront restaurant and country inn. Continental food. Moderate.

All of the following accommodations have dining rooms and other amenities:

Tigh-Na-Mara Resort Hotel, off the Trans-Canada, (250) 248–2072. Moderate to expensive.

The Best Western Bayside Inn Resort, 240 Dogwood Street, (250) 248–8333; (800) 663–4232. Best in town. Moderate to expensive.

Qualicum College Inn, Qualicum Beach, (250) 752–9262. Moderate.

Island Hall Beach Resort, 181 West Island Highway, (250) 248–3225. Moderate.

From Parksville you can travel to the western side of the island and the Pacific Rim National Park by taking Highway 4.

Cathedral Grove, on Highway 4 going west to Port Alberni, has splendid stands of tall, 800-year-old Douglas firs and west coast cedar. Cathedral Grove is within **MacMillan Provincial Park,** which also includes Cameron Lake. A small bathing beach is off the road.

Cameron Lake Resort, via Highway 4, (250) 752–6707, has housekeeping cottages, a store, and boat rentals. Moderate.

Port Alberni, the largest community in the center of the island, has several motels and restaurants. Port Alberni is famous for salmon fishing and has an annual derby offering a cash-rich first prize for a record catch. From here you can take a passenger ferry to Bamfield, where the West Coast Trail begins, or to Ucluelet, a section of the Pacific Rim National Park located at the southern end of Long Beach.

Port Alberni attractions are as follows:

Alberni Valley Museum, 4255 Wallace Street, (250) 723–2181. Open Tuesdays to Sundays. Free. Forestry and Amerindian displays.

Martin Mars Water Bombers, via Highway 3, Lakeshore Road,

(250) 723–6225; call ahead for visiting information. The world's largest fleet of flying water bombers used to fight forest fires. A "must visit" for aviation buffs.

All of the following accommodations have dining rooms, lounges, and other amenities:

TimberLodge Motor Inn and RV Campground, on Highway 2, (250) 723–9415. Moderate.

Coast Hospitality Motor Inn, 3835 Redford Street, (250) 723–8111. Moderate.

The Barclay, 4277 Stamp Avenue, (250) 724–7171. Moderate.

Ucluelet is a favorite departure point for divers; they can explore shipwrecks around the Broken Group Islands and encounter giant octopuses, king crabs, and other inhabitants below the surface.

A listing of street addresses for the following accommodations is unnecessary since once you get into town you can't miss them; unless otherwise noted, all have dining rooms:

Canadian Princess Resort, (250) 726–7771. A historic steamship permanently moored in the harbor; cabin accommodations, dining room, and lounge. Moderate.

West Coast Motel, (250) 726–7732. Moderate.

Thorton Motel, (250) 726–7725. Moderate.

Pacific Rim Motel, (250) 726–7728. Housekeeping units. Restaurants nearby. Moderate.

The West Coast Trail, part of the Pacific Rim National Park, runs from **Bamfield** to **Port Renfrew** (72 km/44 mi). This challenging trek requires a great deal of preparation and physical stamina and takes several days to complete. There are dangers from wind, rain, and rough seas, as well as on the rugged trail itself. Its rewards are many—opportunities to see surprises in nature, such as the marine, bird, and mammal life of the area; the quickly changing moods of the weather; and the joy of being solitary in a magnificent and dramatic natural environment. In the early part of the century, this trail provided a route for shipwreck victims to find their way to the safety of human civilization; when the winds are right, you can almost hear the voices of those lost at sea off this beautiful but hazardous and mystical coast. To reach Bamfield, take the ferry from Port Alberni.

Bamfield accommodations include the following:

Bamfield Trails Motel, (250) 728–3231. Restaurant nearby. Moderate.

Pinkerton Lodge, Barkley Sound, (250) 683–4187; (800)

501–9611. A small, full-range marine resort that accommodates twenty-eight guests. Moderate.

McKay Bay Lodge, (250) 728–3323. Harbor view. Moderate.

Pacific Rim National Park, contact Superintendent, Pacific Rim National Park, Box 280, Ucluelet, B.C. V0R 3A0; (604) 726–7721.

Pacific Rim National Park faces the open Pacific and comprises three sections: the West Coast Trail, the Broken Group Islands, and Long Beach. When you stand facing the Pacific here, the entire, immense nation of Canada is to your back. For most visitors to the park, the Long Beach area is the most accessible. You can get to Long Beach by car and easily tour its 34-km (20-mi) length. By strolling its hard-packed sand surface, you can catch sight of sea lions, seals, schools of porpoises, and pods of orca whales. Within the woodland areas are blacktail deer, bald eagles, and many different species of birds. Inasmuch as a great deal of rain falls along this coast, take along "dirty weather" gear—slickers, warm sweaters, and water-shedding hats. The road that goes the length of Long Beach doesn't always hug the shoreline; you'll have to look for access roads to get to the beach. Sea Lion Rocks can be seen not far from the main road. To visit the Broken Group Islands, inhabited by many bald eagles, make arrangements in Ucluelet to hire a boat. At Bamfield, or Port Alberni Pacific gray whales pass close to shore starting in late February, as they journey from the Bering Sea to the warm waters of Baja California. Regardless of what season you visit, be sure to bring binoculars and/or cameras with telephoto lenses. Various whale-watching trip services operate out of Tofino and Ucluelet.

The main beach areas from Ucluelet to Tofino are Wya Point, Florencia Bay, Quistis Point, Wickaninnish Bay, Sandhill Creek, Long Beach, Cove Box Island, and Schooner Cove. There are dramatic cliffs at Florencia Bay and Green Point. The Rain Forest Trail will take you into thick stands of cedar and hemlock.

Wickaninnish Centre, (250) 726–7333, in the Ucluelet area, is open daily during the summer. Free. Exhibits on the ecology of the park: the sea, land, birds, marine life, mammals, winds, tides, rain. You'll see the Seabird Mural, the Offshore Zone Mural, and *Explorer 10* submersible, as well as exhibits on the local Nuu-Chah-Nulth (Nootka) people. By way of excellent outdoor interpretive programs, guides take you on walks through the different ecological zones and explain what you see. There's an interpretive theater at Green Point.

172

The two campgrounds in the park are at Green Point, for those with vehicles, and Schooner Walk-In, which has limited facilities (water, wood, toilets, etc.) for those with tents. More basic (frills-free) camping is on the Broken Group Islands, at Benson, Dodd Hand, Clark, Gibraltor, Gilbert, Willis, and Turret islands. Accommodations and restaurants are available in Tofino and Ucluelet. Access is only by boat. Travelers must make their own arrangements.

Boats can be chartered in Tofino and Ucluelet. You must get a license to fish; licenses are available in Tofino at most marinas and federal fisheries offices and in Ucluelet. Taking shellfish from the beach or waters for eating is usually not advised, because of red tide—potentially lethal dinoflagellates consumed by shellfish. Check with local authorities if red-tide warnings are up. The water around here is too cold for swimming, except for polar-bear types, although there's a supervised swimming area at North Long Beach. This is the right place, however, for other water sports—surfing (great waves here), kayaking, and scuba diving (lots of unusual marine life to see). Although the powerful rollers coming off the ocean make canoeing dangerous, there are plenty of inlets, coves, bays, lakes, and streams for you to explore.

If you want to get away from civilization but still have a roof over your head, **Tofino** is the place. In addition to enjoying the beaches and woodlands of Pacific Rim National Park, you can go deep-sea fishing and bathe in natural hot springs. You might also want to curl up beside a log fire and finally read *War and Peace* while a turbulent surf and fierce winds rage outside. Golf, whale-watching trips, and restaurants are here. Since this is a very popular spot for visitors, it is recommended that you reserve accommodations. Call the Tofino Travel Infocentre (250–725–3414) for a list of bed-and-breakfast places.

For accommodations, choose among the following:

Pacific Sands Beach Resort, (250) 725–3322. Moderate.

Crystal Cove Beach Resort, (250) 725–4213. Moderate.

Duffin Cove Motel, (250) 725–3448. Moderate to expensive.

Middle Beach Lodge, Pacific Rim Highway, (250) 725–2900. A spectacular setting on the open Pacific. Moderate to expensive.

From Tofino, you can return on Highway 4 to Highway 19, which runs north and south along the eastern side of the island.

The Wickaninnish Inn, Osprey Lane at Chesterman Beach, (250) 725–3100. This spectacularly located inn, set on a rocky promontory at the westernmost point of Chesterman Beach, is one of British Columbia's "must-stay" facilities. Besides having panoramic ocean views, it has a world-class restaurant, conference rooms, and facilities for storm watching, whale viewing, and beachcombing. Rooms have fireplaces, in-room bars, and balconies. Off-season rates. Expensive.

Wilp Gybuu (Wolf house), 311 Leighton Way, (250) 725–2330, is a B&B in a contemporary home with a view of Duffin Passage and Clayoquot Sound. Adult-oriented, near the beach with full breakfast, library, and coffee room. Restaurants are nearby.

Courtenay and **Comox** are sister communities located along Highway 19. In Courtenay, see the exhibits at the **District Museum**—360 Cliffe Avenue; (250) 334–3611—which include a Coast Salish longhouse, logging equipment, and Chinese and Japanese artifacts. Open daily in the summer; closed Sundays. Donations are accepted. Wonderful fishing and birdwatching are in the area, as are cruises to nearby islands. Swimming and hiking can be enjoyed at Comox Lake. In Comox, visit the Air Force Museum, at the Canadian Forces Base, (250) 339–8162. Open Tuesday through Sunday, April to October. Donations are accepted. A good collection of vintage aircraft. At Little River you can take the ferry to Powell River, which is on the mainland's Sunshine Coast, just above the city of Vancouver; sailing time is one hour and fifteen minutes.

All of the following hotels have dining rooms and other amenities:

Coast Westerly Hotel, 1590 Cliffe Avenue, Comoy, (250) 338–7741. Moderate.

The Washington Inn, 1001 Ryan Road, Courtenay, (250) 338–5441. Moderate.

The Alders Beach Resort, in Comox, (250) 337–5322. Housekeeping cottages with fireplaces; on the beach; salmon fishing. Moderate to expensive.

If there is a mecca for salmon fishing in B.C., it is **Campbell River**. In August and September, Campbell River is "tooth by jowl" with anglers going after the giant "king" and "tyee" salmon. There's great fishing throughout the year here—especially for trout in the local lakes—with accommodations ranging from rustic fishing camps to comfortable resorts. Visit the **Campbell River Museum and Archives,** depicting native cultures, (250) 287–3103. Open year-round. Donation accepted. Take the ferry to Quadra Island to see excellent aboriginal arts and crafts at the **Kwakiutl Museum** at Quathiaski Cove, (250) 285–3733. Open July through August. Donation accepted.

Campbell River also gives access, via Highway 28, to **Elk Falls Provincial Park** and **Strathcona Park,** the largest parks on Vancouver Island. Strathcona offers superb camping, mountain climbing, and canoeing. Highway 28 continues to **Gold River** on the Muchalat Inlet—Canada's "caving capital," with North America's deepest vertical cave. A cruise boat will take you for a sail down the inlet to the site of an ancient Indian village where Captain Cook visited in 1778. It is said that his first contact with the native peoples of the coast was made here.

You can take a ferry from Campbell River across a narrow part of the Strait of Georgia to **Whale Town,** which is on an island adjacent to the B.C. mainland and its Sunshine Coast (see page 58). From Whale Town via ferries and Highway 101 to 99, you can get back to the city of Vancouver. This trip is convoluted and time-consuming but also truly worthwhile, in that you'll experience wonderful scenery and see the interesting ways people live so far from civilization yet so close to it.

Accommodations in the area include the following:

Coast Discovery Inn, 975 Tyee Plaza, (250) 287–7155. Rooms with water views; dining room, lounge, and marina. Moderate to expensive.

Marina Inn Resort, 1430 South Island Highway, (250) 923–7255. Moderate.

Bachmairs Hotel Apartment Hotel, 492 South Island Highway, (604) 923–2848. Moderate.

April Point Lodge and Fishing Resort, on Quadra Island, (250) 285–2222. One of the best fishing resorts in the region. Expensive.

The Best Western Austrian Chalet Village, 462 South Island Highway, (604) 923–4231. Moderate.

Peppercorn Trail Motel and RV Park, Mill Road, Gold River, (250) 283–2443. Sleeping units with combination baths, satellite and cable TV, fishing charters. Inexpensive.

Ridgeview Motel, 395 Donner Court, Gold River, (250) 283–2277. A panoramic setting over the townsite with 48 units including executive and honeymoon suites. Moderate.

A ferry from Port McNeil will take you to **Alert Bay** on Cormorant Island, where you will find the tallest totem pole in the world. Visit the Alert Bay **Library and Museum** on Front Street, (250) 974–5721. Open Monday to Saturday, July and August. Donations are accepted. Exhibits of Kwakiutl Indian culture, as well as **St. George's Anglican Chapel.** Also Visit **U'Mista Cultural Centre** on Front Street (250) 974–5213. Open May to September. Admission is charged. This cedar building looks like a Kwakiutl longhouse and has a potlatch collection.

Accommodations are available at **Haida-Way Motor Inn,** in Port McNeil (250–956–3373; moderate), and at the **Orca Inn,** in Alert Bay (250–974–5322). Moderate.

Port Hardy—the departure point for the famous Inside Passage journey on the B.C. ferries—was named after Vice Admiral Sir Thomas Masterman Hardy of the British Royal Navy. During the battle of Trafalgar, as captain of the HMS *Victory,* Hardy, according to depictions, held the dying Lord Nelson in his arms. Once a Hudson's Bay Company post, Post Hardy is the last major town of any size or importance on the northern tip of Vancouver Island. Kwakiutl arts and crafts are available for sale in this area. You can take a ferry from here through the Inside Passage (see below) to Prince Rupert on the B.C. mainland and then to southern Alaska. While in Port Hardy, visit the following:

Port Hardy Museum and Archives, 7110 Market Street, (250) 949–8143. Open daily during the summer. History of white settlers in the area.

Fort Rupert, Beaver Harbour. Open in the summer. Hudson's Bay Company fort and trading post built in 1849.

Whaling Station, Coal Harbour. A place where whales were processed for various markets. There's a twelve-foot-high whale-jawbone arch here.

All of the following hotels have restaurants:

Thunderbird Inn, 7050 Rupert Street, (250) 949–7767. A large, full-facility motor lodge with dining room, recently renovated. Pub, beer and wine store, entertainment. Moderate.

Pioneer Inn, 4965 Byng Road, (250) 949–7271. In a quiet, parklike setting; complimentary in-room coffee. Free local calls, kitchen units. Moderate.

Seven Hills Golf and Country Club, 2 km (1 mi) west on Highway 19. Located on a nine-hole golf course; for self-contained RVs only. Electric and water hookups, central washrooms; $15 per vehicle including electricity and water.

The Inside Passage

A voyage through the magnificent Inside Passage is one of the great trips of the world. It's an adventure that takes you through thickly forested mountains that rise up from the sea and whose walls are almost perpendicular to the surface of the water. The scenery is truly spectacular. As you sail through the passage, you'll see bald eagles, orca and humpback whales, sea lions, loons, porpoises, and many other kinds of wildlife. The traditional way to travel is on a luxury cruise ship, beginning the voyage in Los Angeles, San Francisco, Seattle, or the city of Vancouver, then sailing between the magnificent islands along the British Columbia coast to destinations in Alaska. The voyage takes several days and can be quite expensive. There is, however, another way to experience the Inside Passage that's quicker and less expensive. It also allows you to go ashore to explore remote communities en route and to take your vehicle along: B.C. Ferries operates the MV *Queen of the North,* which sails from Port Hardy to Prince Rupert, the province's largest city on the upper coast of its mainland. Prince Rupert is just a few miles south of the B.C.–Alaska border. From the mainland of B.C., you can sail down the Inside Passage on the MV *Queen of the North* from Prince Rupert to Port Hardy. Port Hardy itself is about an eight-hour drive from the city of Victoria. You can also get on Vancouver Island and thence to Port Hardy from the mainland by taking a B.C. ferry from Horseshoe Bay (Metro Vancouver) or Powell River on the Sunshine Coast (north of Metro Vancouver).

Northbound sailings on the MV *Queen of the North* begin in the first week of June. The last sailing is in late September. Southbound sailings are also on this schedule. For reservations, write B.C. Ferries, 1112 Fort Street, Victoria, B.C. V8V 4V2. For information, call (604) 669–1211 (Vancouver) or (250) 386–3431 (Victoria).

The summer cruise between Port Hardy and Prince Rupert takes fifteen hours one-way, most of it during daylight; the length of the voyage is 274 nautical miles. The MV *Queen of the North* carries 750 passengers and 157 vehicles. Long-term parking is available at both the Port Hardy and the Prince Rupert terminals. The vessel itself offers overnight cabins, a buffet dining room with a dance floor, a cafeteria, a children's playroom, a video arcade, a bar, a parents' room, an observation lounge, promenade decks, a newsstand, a gift shop, and other amenities.

Sailing north en route to Prince Rupert, you will pass Scarlett Point, site of many shipwrecks in the past; Pine Island, with its lighthouse that marks the entrance to the Inside Passage; Queen Charlotte Sound, where countervailing currents create danger for inexperienced mariners; Egg Island Lighthouse, which marks approaches to Fitz Hugh Sound and to Smith and Rivers inlets; Addenbroke Island, site of an unsolved murder (Namu whirlwinds blow in the area with great strength, and mountains tower in excess of 1,000 m/3,279 ft); and Pointers Island, where the Goldville family operated the lighthouse here for forty-two years. At Dean Channel, the great Canadian explorer Alexander Mackenzie ventured into this area. Ocean Falls is a lumber-producing community; Bella Bella, a prosperous fishing and logging town. Dryad Point marks Lama Passage for ships; Ivory Island is the site of an 1898 lighthouse; and Milbanke Sound is an active salmon-fishing area. In the waters of McInnes Island, many marine tragedies took place. Boat Bluff is where the lighthouse keeper wanted a transfer because of the many wolves on the island; Swanson Bay is where paper and shingle mills once operated. In Butedale, fishing, lumbering, and mining once thrived. Grenville Channel is considered the most spectacular channel in the Inside Passage, surrounded by mountains that rise 1,500 to 3,000 feet, densely wooded with pine and cedar. And Ridley Island is a modern bulk-shipping terminal, with goods going to all points around the world.

Prince Rupert to Prince George

The end (or beginning) of the Inside Passage voyage for our purpose is **Prince Rupert,** named after the cousin of King Charles II of England and Grand Factor of the Hudson's Bay Company. Before the coming of the whites, this area was a gathering place for Tshimshian and Haida peoples. Prince Rupert, with a population of some 18,000, is called the City of Rainbows and the Halibut Capital of the World; its main economic activity is serving as a terminal for natural resources (coal, lumber, and wheat) and finished goods being shipped to all parts of the world. The city also has fish canneries and pulp-and-paper processing factories. During World War II, many American military personnel departed from here for service in Alaska and in the Pacific.

Located at the mouth of the Skeena River and set in the midst of fjords, islands, and mountains, Prince Rupert is often also called the gateway to the north. Fishing, hunting, sailing, diving, and exploring the interior mainland are some of the activities of this area. The city has a mild climate, with very little snow, mostly rain; gardens thrive here. A few miles north of Prince Rupert are Wales and Pearse islands, which form part of the border between British Columbia and mainland Alaska.

While in Prince Rupert, visit the **Museum of Northern British Columbia,** First Avenue and McBride Street. Open mid-May to the end of August. Local history of the settlement and exhibits on northwest coast Amerindian cultures.

The Prince Rupert accommodations listed below have dining rooms and other amenities:

Crest Motor Hotel, 222 First Avenue West, (250) 624–6771. Moderate.

Best Western Highliner Inn, 815 First Avenue West, (250) 624–9060. Moderate.

Coast Prince Rupert Hotel, Second Avenue at Sixth Street, (250) 624–6711. Moderate to expensive.

Inn on the Harbour, 720 First Avenue, (250) 624–9107. Moderate.

From Prince Rupert you can take a B.C. ferry to visit Skidegate and Masset on the **Queen Charlotte Islands**. At Second Beach, Skidegate, Queen Charlotte City, visit the **Queen Charlotte Islands Museum**, (250) 559–4643. Open throughout the year. Exhibits are of Haida totem poles, maritime history, and pioneer settlement. The Queen Charlottes are wonderful for camping, exploring, and fishing. If you're up in the province to fish, stay at **Langara Fishing Lodge,** (250) 873–4228 (call collect), on Langara Island off Graham in the Charlottes. The lodge offers a package that includes fine accommodations, meals, equipment, air transportation from the city of Vancouver, the advice of fishing experts, and catch care. Expensive, but a good value for the dedicated fisherman.

You can also go from Prince Rupert to Alaska on the Alaska State ferry system. Between May 1 and September 30, Alaska ferries sail four times a week from Prince Rupert to Skagway (Highway 98 connects Skagway with Whitehorse in the Yukon and the Alaska Highway). Service between Ketchikan, Alaska, and Stewart, B.C., gives you access to the magnificent alpine scenery on Highway 37— the Stewart-Cassiar Highway (37 heading north links up with the Alaska Highway; communities are far apart on this highway, so have supplies and extra gas).

For more information on ferry service between B.C. and Alaska, contact the Alaska Marine Highway System, Box R, Juneau, AK 99811; (907) 465–3941 Juneau; (250) 627–1744, Prince Rupert; or (800) 642–0066, other locations.

If you and your vehicle arrive at Prince Rupert by ferry, you have several touring options on the mainland: You can take the Yellowhead Highway 16 (see also page 86) to Prince George (721 km/ 433 mi) and, on the same route, continue east to the great national parks of the Canadian Rockies and the cities of Edmonton and Calgary in Alberta. From Prince George you can also head north to Dawson Creek and Fort St. John, which are on the Alaska Highway, and then northwest to the Yukon, the Northwest Territories, and Alaska. Going south from Prince George via Highway 97 to the Trans-Canada takes you to Vancouver.

When you are traveling between Prince Rupert and Prince George, although it seems as if you are at the northern part of the province, you are only in the middle of the province—north of you stretches a vast wilderness with few communities. The hardy people who live in this region farm, harvest timber, fish, trap fur-bearing animals, work in mining, provide services to the local people and to tourists, and work in government agencies. Pioneering is very much alive in these parts. This is also native peoples country, and you'll have the opportunity to experience something of a culture that predates the arrival of Europeans on this continent. This is a region of high mountains, thick forests, wild rivers, and sparkling lakes— home to eagles, moose, coyotes, grizzly and black bears (they are dangerous, so don't feed them and don't get out of the car when they're near). The many recreational opportunities along the way include camping, fishing, trail riding, and wild-river rafting. Bring your camera and capture the beauty. Use common sense when traveling on remote stretches, plan your stops, and don't be the cause of a forest fire. Otherwise, it's all there for you to enjoy.

Terrace is a sizable community about 140 km (84 mi) from Prince Rupert. Here you can find accommodations, gas, restaurants, tennis, swimming pools, theaters, and museums. **Terrace Heritage Park,** on Kalum Street, open from mid-May to end of August, has several old log buildings—a dance hall, a barn, a gold miner's cabin, and others—that represent pioneering life. Snow-capped Sleeping Beauty Mountain is a beautiful local landmark. On Copper River Road is a large bed of marine shell fossils. Highway 37 south from town takes you to **Lakelse Provincial Park** and the community of **Kitimat,** site of one of the largest aluminum-processing plants in the world (which you can tour). There's terrific salmon fishing in the Kitimat area. Visit the **Kitimat Centennial Museum,** at 293 City Centre (250–632–7022), open year-round, which depicts the history of Kitimat's growth from a missionary village to an industrial town. Call for hours and fees.

All of the accommodations listed below have restaurants and other amenities:

Coast Inn of the West, 4620 Lakeside Avenue, Terrace, (250) 638–8141. Moderate.

Sandman Inn, 4828 Highway 16 West, Terrace, (250) 635–9151. Moderate.

At **Kitwanga** you can connect with Highway 37—the Stewart-Cassiar Highway—going north to the Alaska Highway. Kitwanga itself is famous for its number of hundred-year-old totem poles.

'Ksan Village, on the bank of the Skeena River, has one of the province's premier exhibitions of northwest coast Amerindian arts and crafts. No admission charge to the village itself and to open buildings. Open from late April to mid-October (250) 842–5544. It features six decorated tribal houses: the treasure, or carving shed, where native artisans create beautiful objects from their ancient heritage; the studio, where silkscreen prints are produced by 'Ksan artists; the 'Ksan shop, where you can purchase authentic arts and crafts; the firewood house, where you can try your hand at craft making; the wolf, or feast, house, where the potlatch feast is described; and the frog house, portraying the ways of a stone-age culture. 'Ksan is a few miles north of Hazelton and well worth the diversion from the main route. There is a campground here.

Smithers is a regional transportation center. Ranching, mining, lumbering, and services are the main economic activities here. Visit the **Smithers Art Gallery,** 1425 Main Street, with exhibitions by local artists and traveling shows. Call (250) 847–3898 for hours and fees.

The following accommodations have dining rooms and other amenities:

Hudson Bay Lodge, on Highway 16, East, (250) 847–4581. Moderate.

Aspen Motor Inn, on Highway 16, (250) 847–4551. Moderate.

Fort Fraser is one of B.C.'s oldest communities. Simon Fraser established a post here for the North West Company, which later merged with Hudson's Bay Company. In addition, in this area the last spike of the Grand Trunk Pacific Railway, Canada's second transcontinental railroad, was driven in, in 1914.

Fort St. James makes an interesting side trip via Highway 27 North off 16. Once capital of New Caledonia (the Scottish dream for a free homeland), it is the second-oldest community in B.C. and was founded by Simon Fraser and John Stuart in 1806. At Fort St. James National Historic Park the old fort has been reconstructed, and summer tours of the grounds, buildings, wharf, and other facilities are offered. In this area, at Necoslie Reserve, is the grave of the famous Chief Kwah. There are also memorials to Father Morice, a missionary who served the native people of the area. Our Lady of Good Hope, Father Morice's church, still stands and is open to visitors. Near the church is a propeller memorial to Russ Baker, a bush pilot who founded Canadian Pacific Airlines (CP Air merged with Pacific Western in 1987 to create Canadian Airlines). A hike up Mount Pope (1,465 m/4,803 ft) gives great views of the surrounding wild landscape. The annual twenty-five-kilometer "Pope Peak Run" has a 650-meter (2,131-foot) uphill section.

Vanderhoof is a good place to stop for the night en route to Prince George. In July there's the two-day **Vanderhoof International Airshow,** which is the top one of its kind in Canada. Visit the **Nechako Bird Sanctuary**, with its many different species and thousands of Canada geese. The local museum displays a photograph of Herbert Vanderhoof, an oddball Chicago businessman who gave the town its name.

Grand Trunk Inn, 2351 Church Street (250–567–3188), a dining room and lounge. Moderate.

Prince George, British Columbia's third-largest city, is at the junction of the Yellowhead 16 (east/west) and the Alaska 97 (north/south) highways. This city traces its history back more than 200 years, to when the explorer Alexander Mackenzie came here and noted the location for his employer, the North West Company. Simon Fraser came later, and Fort George was developed on the site. At that time, Fort St. James was the capital of this region, and Fort George had a secondary position. Today Prince George is one of the most important communities in B.C. It is a key place for finding accommodations, getting car repairs and extra supplies, and relaxing a bit before heading north on the Alaska Highway, east to the Rockies, or south to the city of Vancouver. The city is enjoying a renaissance of growth. The new University of Northern British Columbia's main campus sits atop Cranbrook Hill, overlooking the city. Opened in 1994, the school's studies emphasize programs of the first Nations, environmental, northern, and women's studies.

The university's presence has spurred other construction, like the new 1,800-seat Prince George Civic Centre Complex at Seventh and Dominion (which includes one of the finest concert halls in the province), a new domed courthouse, shopping and recreational facilities. Cappuccino parlors have sprung up around the city.

Prince George Art Gallery, 2820 Fifteenth Avenue, (250) 563–6447, is open daily. Free. Exhibitions by artists from the region and traveling shows.

All of the following accommodations have dining rooms and other amenities:

Ramada Hotel Prince George, 444 George Street, (250) 563–0055; (800) 272–6232. Moderate to expensive.

Connaught Motor Inn, 1550 Victoria Street, (250) 562–4441. Moderate.

Coast Inn of the North, 770 Brunswick Street, (250) 563–0121. Moderate to expensive.

Simon Fraser Inn, 600 Quebec Street, (250) 562–3181. Moderate.

Sandman Inn, 1650 Central Street, (250) 563–8131. Moderate.

Esther's Inn, 1151 Commercial Drive, (250) 562–4131. Moderate.

CHAPTER 7

Touring Alberta and the Canadian Rockies

Calgary · Banff · Lake Louise
Jasper · Icefields · Edmonton

Alberta in Brief

One might assume that Alberta was named after Prince Albert, the beloved consort of Queen Victoria. Queen Victoria played such an important role in Canadian history that her name has been liberally applied to cities, mountains, glaciers, and all sorts of things—she was that well loved, except perhaps in Quebec. It would, then, make sense to name a province after Prince Albert, but, in fact, the Marquis of Lorne named the province in honor of Princess Louise Caroline Alberta, the fourth daughter of the Great Queen. First, as governor-general of Canada he had the authority to do so. Second, the princess was his wife.

Until the coming of white explorers, trappers, mountain men, fur traders, settlers, ranchers, the Northwest Mounted Police, and the builders of the transcontinental railroad, the people residing on this magnificent land of prairies and mountains were Amerindians. These native people have lived here in what they call the "land of four directions" for thousands of years—some say 5,000 years, others close to 8,000; both may be gross underestimates. these people are known by the names of Cree, Blackfoot, B Assiniboine, Piegan, Sarcee, and Chipewyan.

The first whites—that is, those from Europe or of European ethnic origin—were fur traders and missionaries who came into this region of Canada in the early eighteenth century. By and large, relations between the whites and the Amerindians were amicable. The whites wanted to trade and make money, but they were not interested in developing the land. Appropriating ancestral lands here was not a major issue in the nineteenth century, as it was below the border in the United States. Trouble did, however, come up north from the States in the form of rough-and-tough whiskey traders who built their own forts in the southern part of the province, exploited the native people, and created so much tension that in 1873 the Canadian federal government established the Northwest Mounted Police (today's Royal Canadian Mounted Police), under the command of such legendary strongmen as Colonel Macleod, and sent them to this part of the prairies in 1874 to bring law and order by driving out the whiskey traders, protecting the native peoples, and opening up the area for development and settlement.

Settlement boomed after the tracks of the transcontinental railroad went through in the latter half of the nineteenth century. Villages, towns, and cities sprang up along the railroad as entrepreneurs seeking new ventures and immigrants from many foreign countries, hungry for freedom and opportunity in this promised land, flooded into the area. They turned Alberta into cattle ranches, wheat farms, and mining and forestry operations. Manufacturing, services, education, and culture blossomed, and by 1905 Alberta had grown enough to become a full-fledged province in the Canadian Confederation.

Vast reserves of oil and natural gas were discovered here in the early part of this century, and Alberta found it had more in common with Texas than Ontario or Quebec—the oil and cowhand images were essentially the same in both places. The Great Depression of the 1930s hurt, but the post–World War II oil boom made Alberta exceedingly affluent, the envy of the rest of the country, and thousands of Canadians flocked here to get their piece of the pie. By the 1970s, such cities as Calgary and Edmonton were transformed into urban showplaces, and everyone seemed to be doing all right. But good times don't last forever, and Alberta's economy was dampened by the slide in oil prices during the 1980s.

Nevertheless, this is a "can do" province, and optimism for the future is part of the essence of life here.

Geographically, Alberta is located between 60 degrees latitude north and 49 degrees at the Canadian–U.S. border. This is a large province of 661,000 square kilometers (255,200 square miles), with diverse topography, including many rivers, lakes, streams, and glaciers, and even sections of badlands (arid stretches of land with little or no vegetation), suitable more for trekking than development. In the southern region, some of the most important paleontological finds in the world have been made. On Alberta's western border is British Columbia; on the east, the province of Saskatchewan. To the north are the Northwest Territories, and to the south is the state of Montana. Although the southern and central regions of the province are prairie farms and cattle ranches, the north is mostly forested wilderness and muskeg. Along the western border run the great Rocky Mountains, with their world-famous national parks and resorts—Banff, Lake Louise, and Jasper.

Alberta winters are long and cold, with low humidity and dry, crisp air; its summers are typically warm and pleasant. A great deal of snow falls in mountain areas—a boon for skiers and winter sports enthusiasts. During the winter, chinook winds—warm, dry winds that descend from the eastern slopes of the Rockies and across the prairies—lessen the severity of the cold and make living here, at times, quite enjoyable. Because Alberta doesn't experience the amount of heavy rainfall that the Pacific coast does, travelers are assured, on the one hand, of many sunny days to enjoy their vacations. On the other hand, when in the high mountains, don't be surprised to see brief periods of heavy snow falling in late June—though at that time of year, the snow quickly melts in the bright sun.

The population of Alberta is about 2.5 million, and the people represent many different ethnic and racial backgrounds— British (the majority), as well as German, Ukrainian, French, and Amerindian. Indeed, there are more than 1,200 ethno-cultural groups throughout Alberta that are eligible to receive support from the province's cultural and linguistic programs.

Before the building of the transcontinental railroad, the only persons who traveled to this region were those in quest of fortune or the salvation of souls; once the railroad was built, however, close to two-thirds of the Canadian continent was opened up for exploration and/or enjoyment by more ordinary folk. With the development of such resort areas as Banff, Lake Louise, and Jasper, tourism here began in grand style. More and more people came to vacation in Western Canada, particularly the Rockies of Alberta, and they in turn told their friends of the natural glories and the highly civilized, plush resorts set in the middle of a wilderness. More and more people came to Alberta, and the tourism infrastructure grew and became more sophisticated to satisfy their demands. Today tourism is Alberta's third-largest economic activity. The diversity of tourism/vacation offerings is vast. You can be joyfully indolent in the midst of some of the most glorious scenery in the world or work your tail off climbing some of the highest mountains in the world. But the bottom line here is neither the scenery nor the attractions. It is the quality of the people of Alberta themselves, who welcome you with open arms and genuinely warm smiles, western style.

Travel Alberta—
Tourism Information

Travel Alberta, the provincial government's tourism agency, maintains a year-round, toll-free telephone number that can be used throughout the continental United States and throughout Canada. To request information, brochures, or maps, call (800) 661–8888.

You will find Travel Alberta visitor information centers at these locations:

Walsh, on the Trans-Canada at the Alberta-Saskatchewan border

Milk River, on Highway 4 near the Alberta-Montana border

West Glacier, Montana, junction of U.S. Highway 2 and Going-to-the-Sun Road

Sentinel, on the Crowsnest Highway 3 at the Alberta-British Columbia border

Oyen, Highway 9

Jasper, Highway 16

Field, in Field, British Columbia

Canmore, near the Trans-Canada Highway in Canmore

Mountain resort towns offer fine accommodations, dining, entertainment, ➤ and shopping. They are also at the doorstep of the best in outdoor sports—skiing, hiking, skating, golf, white-water rafting, horseback riding, and a lot more.

Lloydminster, on the Yellowhead (Highway 16) at the Alberta-Saskatchewan border

Edmonton, third floor, City Centre Building, 10155 102nd Street, open Monday through Friday except holidays, 8:15 A.M. to 4:30 P.M.

Alberta's Extraspecial Attractions

Southern Alberta

Cardston, via Macleod Trail Highway 2. The **C. O. Card Home and Museum,** 337 Main Street. Open mid-June to the end of August. Admission by donation. A log cabin home that belonged to Charles Ora Card, the leader of eleven Mormon families, with whom he emigrated from Utah in 1887. A **Mormon Temple,** 348 Third Street West, (403) 653–3552, offers tours of its visitor center. The **Remington Alberta Carriage Centre,** 623 Main Street, (403) 653–5139, is a 65,000-square-foot (5,850-square-meter) facility housing one of North America's largest collections of horse-drawn vehicles. Open year-round.

Crowsnest Pass, via the Crowsnest Highway 3 near British Columbia. Within this municipality are the following points of interest: 100-million-year-old volcanic rocks; Sulphur Springs, cold waters used for their curative powers by the native peoples; the Frank Slide Interpretive Centre (ninety million tons of rock from Turtle Mountain crashed on the town of Frank in 1903 and killed seventy persons); Hillcrest, site of one of Canada's worst coal-mining disasters in 1914; and Leitch Collieries, tours of an old coal-mining complex, guided tours in summer, self-guided September through April. Admission by donation.

Cypress Hills Provincial Park, via the Trans-Canada to Highway 41 and then south (located at the Alberta-Saskatchewan border in the southeast corner of the province). This park, situated on a plateau that was untouched by ancient glaciers, not only supports fourteen species of orchids but also contains two hundred species of nesting birds and is the habitat of deer, elk, moose, and beaver. An archaeological dig found a seven-thousand-year-old native encampment. Fishing, boating, camping, and hiking are all possible here. Rent boats at Cypress Hills.

Dinosaur Provincial Park, via the Trans-Canada and Highway 36 North (watch for signs for other access roads). A World Heritage site (designated as such by UNESCO), this important park (15,000 acres) protects one of the most extensive dinosaur fields in the world. Bus tours take visitors through the park for a small charge; camping facilities are available.

Fort Macleod, at the Crowsnest Highway 3 and Macleod Trail Highway 2. The Fort Macleod Museum is a re-creation of the original Northwest Mounted Police fort built in 1874. A mounted police ride is held here daily during the months of July and August. The fort's official season is from mid-May to mid-October. Call (403) 553–2522 or 553–2500. A guided walking tour of Fort Macleod takes you through the streets and thirty buildings, describing the way the police, pioneers, and native people lived in this area; these free tours run from May to the end of August. Also within this area, via Highways 2 and 516, is **"Head Smashed In" Buffalo Jump,** a World Heritage site (designated as such by UNESCO). Here, for more than fifty-six hundred years the natives drove buffalo over the cliff and to their deaths to obtain food and materials for clothing and shelter. Open year-round. Call (403) 553–2731 for more information.

Lethbridge, via the Crowsnest Highway 3 and Macleod Trail Highway 2 or via Highway 4 from the Alberta-Montana border. Lethbridge is a thriving city just south of Calgary and north of the international border. In the 1800s it was a well-known coal-mining town, and American whiskey-trading forts were strung out over the landscape in this region. Visit Fort Whoop-up, located in Indian Battle Park; call (403) 329–0444. A great battle took place here in 1870 between the Cree and the Blackfoot peoples. Near the park is the **Helen Schuler Coulee Centre,** which has several nature trails. Free. At Seventh Avenue South, in Lethbridge, is the **Nikka Yuko Japanese Gardens,** (403) 328–3511. Open mid-May to the end of September. Admission is charged. The **Sir Alexander Galt Museum,** First Street and Fifth Avenue South, housed in a hospital built in 1891, has displays of local history; (403) 320–3898. Free. The city's crown jewel is the campus of the **University of Lethbridge,** a stunning complex designed by Arthur Erickson. Call (403) 329–2111 for free campus tours.

All of the following accommodations have dining rooms and other amenities:

Lethbridge Lodge Hotel, 320 Scenic Drive, (403) 328–1123 or (800) 661–1232. Moderate to expensive.

Sandman Hotel Lethbridge, 421 Mayor Magrath Drive, (403) 328–1111 or (800) 663–6900. Moderate.

Lethbridge Lodge Motel, 2210 Seventh Avenue South, (403) 329–0100.

Best Western Heidelburg Inn, 1303 Magrath Drive, (403) 329–0555 or (800) 528–1234. Moderate.

Medicine Hat, at the junction of the Trans-Canada and the Crowsnest Highway 3. If you are traveling west in the southern part of the province, Medicine Hat is the first large community you will come into after you pass the Saskatchewan border. From here you can go to Calgary on the Trans-Canada or straight to British Columbia through Lethbridge via the Crowsnest Highway.

In 1907, Rudyard Kipling said that Medicine Hat was a city "with all hell for a basement," in reference to its extensive natural gas field (discovered here in 1883). Today, Medicine Hat—a name that evokes images of the Old West—is a center for manufacturing and the distribution of agricultural products.

Medicine Hat Museum and Art Gallery, 1302 Bomford Crescent SW; museum, (403) 527–6266; art gallery, (403) 526–0486. The museum has interesting displays on the native peoples and pioneers of its region. Open throughout the year. Free. The gallery presents exhibits of art, natural and ethnological history, and science. Open year-round.

Downtown Historical Walking Tour, Tourist Centre, (403) 527–6422. A self-guided tour of the turn-of-the-century architecture still in use. Excellent examples of homes, churches, businesses.

Most of the following accommodations have dining rooms and other amenities:

Best Western Inn, 722 Redcliff Drive, (403) 527–3700 or (800) 528–1234. Moderate.

Circle T Lodge, 950 Thirteenth Street SW, (403) 527–2275 or (800) 442–8729. Moderate.

Imperial Inn, 3282 Thirteenth Avenue SE, (403) 527–8811 or (800) 661–5322. Moderate.

Medicine Hat Lodge, 1051 Ross Glen Drive SE, (403) 529–2222 or (800) 661–8095. Moderate.

Travelodge Motor Inn, 1100 Redcliff Drive SW, (403) 527–2275 or (800) 255–3050. Moderate.

Turner Valley, 54 km (34 mi) southwest of Calgary via Millarville and Highway 22. Turner Valley was one of Canada's richest oil-producing areas. Visit the Dingman #1 and Royalite #4 wells, Christ Church (Anglican, circa 1910), the Fisher Ranch, the John Ware cairn (John Ware was a famous black cowboy who had his own ranch in the area), and the Black Diamond Mine.

There are also a number of working ranches in Turner Valley, and though they are private operations, you may, as you tour the countryside, see cattle grazing and ranch hands riding or doing chores.

Writing on Stone Provincial Park, via Highway 2 to Milk River and then east on Highway 501. This park has many ancient petroglyphs (carvings and paintings in sandstone cliffs by the native people who lived here). Naturalists conduct guided tours. There's a camping area among large cottonwood trees.

Central Alberta

Camrose, via Highway 21, south of Edmonton. Visit the **Centennial Museum,** Fifty-third Street and Forty-sixth Avenue, (403) 672–5456. Open mid-May to September. Donations accepted. The museum has a pioneer church, an early schoolhouse, a log house, a mill, and a fire hall, all from settlement days.

Cochrane Ranch, on Highway 1A at junction of Highway 22 west of the town of Cochrane, (403) 932–2902. Open mid-May to September. Donations accepted. Alberta's first large-scale cattle ranch was established here in 1881. The present site has 150 acres of parkland, lush with wildflowers and nature trails. On a hilltop is a large statue of a cowboy on his horse, the figure sitting frozen in time as a perpetual symbol of Alberta's heritage.

Devon, west of Edmonton on the Yellowhead Highway 16. Here in Devon are the excellent University of Alberta **Devonian Botanic Gardens**, (403) 987–3054. Open early May until the end of September. There are an herb garden, a Japanese garden, a butterfly house, a native people's garden, an alpine garden, and indoor floral and plant displays. A nature trail leads past a wide variety of plants, including those that grow in the desert.

In the **Drumheller** area, via the Trans-Canada to Highway 9 North, is the exceptional **Royal Tyrrell Museum,** (403) 823–7707. Open year-round. Half price mid-October to mid-May. This museum is well worth the side trip. The Tyrrell Museum, housed in a stunning modern building, tells the story of millions of years of the earth's history, through dinosaur, fossil, and geological exhibits, some of which interact with the viewer. Named in honor of the explorer and geologist Joseph Burr Tyrrell, who found the first dinosaur bones in this area in 1884, this is a wonderfully educating attraction for all ages.

Hoodoos, via Highway 10 southeast of Drumheller and toward East Coulee. The Hoodoos are huge geological mushroom-shaped rocks, formed by wind and water erosion. To walk among them is like walking on a planet in a science-fiction movie.

Gleichen, via the Trans-Canada east from Calgary to Highway 21. **Siksika Museum of Human History,** (403) 734–3070, is located on the third floor of Old Sun College, 1 km (0.6 mi) west of town. The historical displays and artifacts of the Siksika (Blackfoot) tribe interpret four major life transitions of Siksika. Open year-round by appointment only.

Markerville, via Highway 54. The **Stephansson House Provincial Historic Site,** (403) 932–2902, is located 7 km (4.4 mi) north of Markerville, off highways 592 or 781. In this pleasant house lived Stephan G. Stephansson (1853–1927), Iceland's national poet. Guided tours take you through this furnished literary home in which traditional Icelandic handicrafts are displayed. Open from mid-May to September. Admission charged.

Polar Park, via Highway 14, east of Edmonton, (403) 922–3013. Open year-round. Admission charged. This is a special reserve for cold-climate mammals—fifty species, more than 500 animals from Canada, Northern China, Russia, and other countries.

West Central Alberta

Rocky Mountain House National Historic Park, via Highway 11A, (403) 845–2412. Open May to October. Donations accepted. The interpretive center tells the story of fur trading and the forts serving the traders in this region between 1799 and 1886. There are nature trails and a buffalo paddock.

Siffleur, White Goat, and Ghost River wilderness areas, located along the eastern side of Banff and Jasper national parks, are preserved to protect their natural beauty and character. Visitors on foot are welcome; development, impairment, hunting, fishing, trapping, motor vehicles, horses, and pack animals are prohibited.

Grande Cache, via Highway 40, is the gateway to the Willmore Wilderness and site of the second leg of the Smoky River's Great Canadian Riverboat Race.

Willmore Wilderness Park, located north of Jasper National Park, permits some activities, such as horseback riding, mountain biking, hunting, and fishing. For more information, call Alberta Tourism at (800) 661–8888.

Wetaskiwin, Highways 13 and 2A, **Reynolds Alberta Museum,**

(403) 361–1351, opened in the fall of 1992. This world-class facility interprets the history of ground and air transportation, agriculture, and selected industries in Alberta. It is also home to Canada's Aviation Hall of Fame, located in a hangar amidst vintage aircraft. A 1929 Duesenberg Phaeton Royale is also on display.

Stettler, Alberta Prairie Steam Tours, (403) 742–2811. Round-trip day excursions on train powered by a 1920 steam locomotive. The nostalgic 304-km (190-mi) journey is a unique way to experience the culture and history of prairie towns. Tours vary four to eight hours in length, May to October.

Northern Alberta

Elk Island National Park, via Highway 16, just east of Edmonton. Call (403) 922–6380. A relatively small national park, Elk Island is a tranquil place of meadows, lakes, and forests of aspen and spruce. It is also a preserve for elk and buffalo, which roam free in the park. There are hiking trails throughout the park and an interpretive program.

Fort McMurray, via Highway 55 from Athabasca to Highway 63, (403) 743–7167, is in the Athabasca Oil Sands region, a vast area of oil-bearing sand that will become a critical source of energy when other sources of petroleum dry up. The interpretive center explains the technology used to separate oil from sand. Open year-round. Donations accepted.

Saint Albert, via Highway 2, north of Edmonton, established in 1861, was one of the first independent communities in Western Canada. It was named after Father Albert Lacombe, a legendary missionary and friend of the native, Métis, and pioneering peoples of this region. His chapel, restored to look as it did in the 1860s, stands at St. Vital Avenue and welcomes visitors. Visit the museum here, the religious shrine, and Father Lacombe's crypt. The complex is open from mid-May to September, (403) 459–7663. Donations accepted.

Ukrainian Cultural Heritage Village, 50 km (30 mi) east of Edmonton on Highway 16. Open mid-May to September, (403) 662–3640. Admission half price after Labour Day. This unique heritage village re-creates an early Ukrainian settlement in Alberta. Canada's famous Giant Ukrainian Easter Egg—7 m long, 5.5 m wide, and weighing 2,270 kg is located at Vegreville, nearby. The egg's decorations tell the story of settlement, religious faith, culture, good harvests, and protection received from the Royal Canadian Mounted Police. During the first weekend in July, the annual **Pysanka Festival** features Ukrainian food, song, dance, and crafts.

Wood Buffalo National Park, located in the extreme north of Alberta and overlapping into the Northwest Territories, is accessible by air or by road from Fort Smith, N.W.T. (no road access from Alberta). Wood Buffalo, one of the largest national parks in the world, is very much a wilderness area of great rivers, large lakes, extensive bogs, and thick forests that is home to moose, wolves, lynx, black bears, and eagles. It's a secure nesting ground for the endangered whooping crane as well. The park, which covers an area larger than Switzerland, has areas for camping, boating, and swimming. If you want to get away from it all, literally and figuratively, this is the right place. For more information, contact Superintendent, Wood Buffalo National Park, Box 750, Fort Smith, NWT X0E 0P0; (403) 872–2349.

Calgary: A World-class City and Southern Doorway to the Canadian Rockies

What Makes Calgary Special

Calgary is a modern, sophisticated city, with skyscrapers rising up from the flatlands of the prairies, which end abruptly at the high walls of the Canadian Rockies. The image of the Old West persists in Calgary—it annually holds the largest rodeo in the world, the Calgary Stampede, and authentic cattle ranches with real cowhands are but a short drive from city limits—yet Calgary can be best equated with such great cities of Texas as Dallas and Fort Worth, for Calgary is one of Canada's major petroleum centers. The oil companies are here, and this is where the deals are cut. The prosperity brought by the petroleum industry is reflected in the affluence of most of the people who live here, the modern city itself, and the recreational and cultural amenities it offers to residents and visitors alike. In addition to its many attractions, this most modern city is the southern gateway to the great national parks of the Canadian Rockies: Banff and Jasper, with their awesome beauty, famous resorts, and many recreational opportunities. If you have never been to Calgary, you're in for a few surprises regarding a former Northwest Mounted Police post that in less than a hundred years has become a booming, gleaming, twenty-first-century city, very much in a class by itself.

A Brief Look at Calgary's History

The native peoples of the Calgary–southern Alberta prairie region can trace their history back 12,000 years. Their civilizations were based on hunting, particularly the buffalo, herds of which were in great abundance. Although explorers and fur traders for the North West Company and Hudson's Bay Company came through this area en route to what is now British Columbia, there were few white habitations as such. In the mid-1800s, American buffalo hunters and whiskey traders, however, rode into this area, slaughtering these noble animals and exploiting the native people. The whiskey sellers in fact set up a string of their own forts to protect themselves and to discourage competition. Their presence became so objectionable that the Canadian federal government formed the Northwest Mounted Police to drive out these dangerous entrepreneurs, protect the native tribes, and establish law and order throughout Western Canada. This outstanding military police force not only did its job exceedingly well but prevented the lawlessness and brutality plaguing several American states from happening in Canada. In addition, after the battle of the Little Bighorn, such chiefs as Sitting Bull fled with their tribes to the prairies of Western Canada, because they knew they would be protected by the Mounties. Not only did these people find safety, but also they received provisions and land for encampment from the government of Canada.

Calgary itself was founded in 1875 as a Mountie post called Fort Calgary, located where the Bow and Elbow rivers come together, and in 1883 became an important center in the development of the transcontinental railroad. Calgary was incorporated as a city in 1893 and continued to grow, serving as a conduit for processing cattle from local ranches into meat and for handling other agricultural products from area farms. For much of its history, until the boom times of petroleum, Calgary was primarily known as Canada's cow town, much the same as Fort Worth, Texas. The first oil find was made nearby in Turner Valley in 1914, and the province's first refinery started operating in Calgary in 1923. The early promoters of Calgary as Canada's oil center were R. A. Brown, W. S. Herron, and A. W. Dingman. In 1947 a major reserve of oil was found at Leduc, and from that post–World War II time to just

recently, Calgary has been an oil-boom town, and its skyline, affluence, and attractions reflect the money that has been made here.
During its boom years, thousands of Canadians from slower-growth
areas of the country flooded into Calgary to seek their fortunes,
and most of them prospered. When, however, the price of oil sank
to distressing lows, the glow faded, and thousands left Calgary for
more promising opportunities in other areas, such as coastal British
Columbia and southern Ontario. Yet the impressive characteristic
about the more than 790,500 people of Calgary is their "can do"
spirit. After several years of economic downturn, Calgary's economy
is booming again. The city now has the second-highest number of
corporate head offices in Canada, having overtaken Montreal, and
is now behind only Toronto.

How to Get to Calgary

By Plane

The following airlines serve Calgary International Airport: Air
Canada, American Airlines, Canadian Airlines, Delta, Lufthansa,
KLM, and United. The airport is approximately 11 km (7 mi) or
about thirty minutes, from Calgary city center via Barlow Trail,
McKnight Boulevard, and Centre Street. The terminal itself is modern, with full facilities, including restaurants, a duty-free shop, gift
shops, new Kidsport area, lounges, magazine and book shops, and
the booths of car-rental agencies. There are taxis, limousines, and
buses. The airport bus picks up on the half hour to and from various downtown hotels.

By Car

From the east: Trans-Canada Highway 1.

From the west: Trans-Canada Highway 1, or the Crowsnest
Highway 3 to Macleod Trail Highway 2 North.

From the south: U.S. Interstate Highway 15 to the border at
Sweetgrass, Montana, and Coutts, Alberta, which merges with Highway
4 North to Lethbridge and then via Macleod Trail Highway 2 North.

**Just over a hundred years ago, Calgary was a small Mountie post on the ▶
prairies that was not far from the Rockies. There were few human beings
in this southern area of Alberta, except for Indian bands, roaming moun-
tainfolk and whiskey traders, and the Mounties. Today Calgary is Dallas
and Houston rolled into one sharply focused city, Western Canadian style.**

From the north (the city of Edmonton): Calgary Trail Highway 2.

By Bus

Greyhound provides service to and from Calgary. It operates from a terminal at 850 Sixteenth Street NW. Call (403) 265–9111 for schedules and fares. The Red Arrow Express provides luxury bus service four times a day between Calgary and Edmonton. Its terminal is at 205 Ninth Avenue SE, main floor, with pickups at the Quality Inn Airport Hotel, 4804 Edmonton Trail NE; call (403) 531–0350.

By Rail

VIA Rail bypasses Calgary, linking Alberta to Vancouver through Edmonton. Rocky Mountaineer Railtours, (604) 984–3131 or (800) 665–7245, a private railway operated by the Great Canadian Railtour Company, links Vancouver to Calgary via Banff in luxury style. The two-day trip of 840 km (600 mi) is during daylight hours, stopping overnight in Kamloops, British Columbia, so you don't miss a thing along the way. Operates late May to early October.

How to Get Around in Calgary

The city, logically laid out in a grid pattern, is divided into four sections (quadrants), according to points on the compass—NE, NW, SE, and SW. City streets run north and south; avenues go east and west. Numbering of streets and avenues starts from city center, which is at Centre Street and Ninth Avenue, at the base of the Calgary Tower (190.9 m/626 ft), the city's primary landmark. Between Fourth and Ninth avenues in city center is where much of the city's daily hustle and bustle takes place.

The **Calgary Transit System** provides C-Train (light rail transit) and bus service throughout the city and to outlying shopping malls; call (403) 262–1000 for routes, schedules, and special unlimited-ride passes. The C-Train is free between Tenth Street West and Third Street East; like most of the system's buses, it is accessible for wheelchairs.

City center parking is available at metered street spaces and parking garages. The best bet is to park in a garage, to avoid fines

METRO CALGARY

and towing. Free parking is available during summer at many locations and at meters.

Taxis are readily available. The best locations are in front of downtown hotels.

Visitor Information

For current information on accommodations, dining, attractions, sports, tours, and entertainment, call the Calgary Convention and Visitors Bureau, (403) 263–8510, or visit the Visitor Service Centre, Tower Centre, main floor, 101 Ninth Avenue SW. Call (800) 661–1678 toll free in North America, write the bureau at 237 Eighth Avenue SE, Calgary, Alberta T2G 0K8, or visit their Web site at http://www.visitor.calgary.ab.ca.

Useful Information

Local holiday: Heritage Day, first Monday in August.
Time zone: Mountain.
Area code: 403.
Emergencies of all kinds: Dial 911.
Entertainment and sports tickets: CCUB at (800) 661–1678 or Ticketmaster at (403) 270–6700.
Religious Services: Calgary has most mainline Protestant churches, Roman Catholic churches, and Jewish temples, all of which welcome visitors to their weekly services. Ask the concierge or guest relations person at your hotel for locations and times of services.
Road emergency service: (403) 246–0606 (twenty-four hours).
Road-condition reporting service: (403) 246–5853 (twenty-four hours). Alberta Motor Association.

Extraspecial Events

The Annual Calgary Exhibition and Stampede, ten days from the beginning of July to mid-month. Call (403) 261–0101 or (800) 661–1260 for information. The Calgary Stampede takes place at Exhibition Grounds/Stampede Park, just south of city center via Macleod Trail Highway 2. Whether you are a rodeo buff or have never been to one, the Calgary Stampede is the biggest and best in the world. But the rodeo is just part of this old-time western extravaganza:

A half-million-dollar, three-hour rodeo show held every afternoon features bull riding, steer wrestling, and saddle-bronc, bareback, and wild-horse riding. The Calgary Stampede made championship chuck-wagon racing, held during evening shows, the biggest thrill at rodeos; compared to Calgary-style chuck-wagon racing, the old Romans and their chariots seem tame.

At night, singers, dancers, comedians, and acrobats entertain audiences at the Grandstand Spectacular. A Las Vegas–style revue, top-star performers, and a spectacular display of fireworks are among the highlights.

You can visit the agricultural displays and purebred livestock shows; take midway rides, eat everything from fast food to broiled Alberta steaks or ethnic dishes, compete in the annual big-prize-money Blackjack Tournament, tour an Indian prairie village and see people demonstrating skills used in pioneering days, and watch the blows and hammers taking place at the World Championship Blacksmith Competition.

Touring Service

Brewster/Gray Line Transportation and Tours, Calgary, (403) 221–8242 or (800) 661–1152; Banff, (403) 762–6700; Jasper, (403) 852–3332. Brewster provides tours of the city of Calgary, Banff and Jasper national parks, Lake Louise, and the Athabasca Glacier, as well as glacier touring on a Snocoach, gondola rides up steep mountains, and boat trips on Maligne Lake and Lake Minnewanka. Reasonable rates.

Attractions

Glenbow Museum, 130 Ninth Avenue, in city center, (403) 268–4100. Open daily. Admission is charged. The Glenbow, housed in modern facilities, is one of the best Western Canadian history museums in North America. Here you can see exceptional exhibitions on the tribes of the Canadian prairies and those of the American plains (actually, for the native people themselves, theirs was a "land of four directions," without the white person's borders and topographical designations). There are exhibits telling the stories of the fur trappers, the explorers, the missionaries, the Northwest Mounted Police, Louis Riel and the Métis people, and the building of the transcontinental railroad. If you have time to visit only one attraction in Calgary, see the Glenbow Museum.

    Calgary Tower, 101 Ninth Avenue SW, in city center, (403) 266–7171. Open daily. Admission charged. The Calgary Tower is the city's landmark. At 190.9 m (626 ft) high, it offers a spectacular view of the city and surrounding countryside, including the snow-capped Canadian Rockies themselves, from its top observation deck. The tower has a revolving restaurant from which you can see the views while you dine on western or continental cuisines. Call the Panorama Room for reservations, (403) 266–7171.

    Calgary Science Centre, 701 Eleventh Street SW, (403) 221–3700. Open daily. Admission charged. This is an excellent facility for exploring the wonders of the cosmos: You're a space traveler in the Star Chamber visiting destinations throughout the heavens. A Rock and Roll Laser Show entertains. There are displays featuring of space-shuttle tiles and the Millarville Meteorite, as well as traveling exhibits. The centre is newly renovated and has the finest multimedia theater in Canada.

Fort Calgary, 750 Ninth Avenue SE, (403) 290–1875. Open throughout the year. Here is where the original Fort Calgary (1875) stood and where the city began. Exhibits depict the early history of the city and the role the Northwest Mounted Police played in facilitating and securing civilization in this part of the country. Displays show clothing and tools used by Calgary's early pioneers. From the fort—currently being rebuilt—you can walk down to the spot where the Bow and Elbow rivers converge, a nice area for a picnic or a rest in the sun. The interpretive center is open May through October. Park site open year-round.

Heritage Park, west of Fourteenth Street and Heritage Drive SW, (403) 259–1900. Open daily. Admission charged. One of Canada's most popular heritage parks, this full-scale prairie town is restored to what it was in the early 1900s. There are more than a hundred buildings, most of which have demonstrations and/or guides. There are antique railroad cars and a train trip through sixty-six acres of the park, or visitors can ride aboard a vintage paddle-wheeler as it plies Glenmore Lake.

Calgary Zoo, Botanical Gardens, and Prehistoric Park, on St. George's Island, 1300 Zoo Road NE, near city center, (403) 232–9372. Open throughout the year. Admission charged. This park contains life-size exhibits of dinosaurs and other prehistoric animals from the Mesozoic era, an aviary of exotic birds, and beautiful floral displays. The zoo has one of the largest populations of lowland gorilla in North America, as well as some 1,400 other animals, both from foreign lands and from the Western Canadian wilderness. Two sections of the five–part Canadian Wilds exhibit are now complete: the Aspen Woodland and the Rocky Mountains.

Devonian Gardens, on the fourth level of Toronto Dominion Square, (403) 268–3830. Open daily. Free. Calgary has created two and a half acres of exquisite gardens, waterfalls, and reflecting pools—all enclosed within a modern city-center office complex. Escape winter winds or broiling summer sun in climate-controlled Devonian Gardens, a special world of beauty, tranquility, and comfort. On a mini-scale, these enclosed gardens, which are connected by enclosed passageways that lead to all parts of city center, demonstrate that it is possible to create a pleasant year-round environment in climates far more rugged than Calgary's. Perhaps the future of northern Canada has its roots here.

Spruce Meadows Equestrian Centre, via Macleod Trail Highway 2 to Highway 22X West, (403) 254–3200. Open daily. Free. Spruce Meadows is Western Canada's premier equestrian facility, not to be missed if you love any aspect of this multifaceted sport. You can see riders practicing their jumps on magnificent Hanoverians, which are bred at this ranch, or attend a competition.

Every year a series of major equestrian competitions takes place at Spruce Meadows. For example, the Spruce Meadows National, one of North America's top jumping competitions, was held here; the Texaco Invitational attracted leading Canadian and U.S. riders; and the Spruce Meadows Masters drew the finest riders from around the world.

Calaway Park, 9.6 km (6 mi) west of Calgary on the Trans-Canada, (403) 240–3824. Open from mid-May to mid-October. Admission is charged. Calaway is Western Canada's largest theme park. Twenty exciting rides, attractions, live entertainment, food and gift shops, games, and a nice park environment provide fun and relaxation.

Aero Space Museum of Calgary, Hangar 10, 64 McTavish Place North, (403) 250–3752. Open daily except Saturday. Donations are accepted. Here you can see aircraft being restored and displays of engines and aviation memorabilia.

Museum of the Regiments (Lord Strathcona's House), 4520 Crowchild Trail SW. Open daily. Free. Artifacts from cavalry and armored history of the regiment, including full-sized dioramas, models, and miniatures.

Nickle Arts Museum, on the University of Calgary campus; main entrance is from Thirty-second Avenue NW, (403) 220–7234. Open throughout the year; closed Monday. Free on Tuesdays. This museum has a fine collection of ancient coins and exhibitions of contemporary and historical art.

Naval Museum of Alberta, 1820 Twenty-fourth Street SW, (403) 242–0002. Royal Canadian Navy memorabilia including the only collection of three fighter craft (Seafire, Sea Fury, and Banshee jet) used by the navy. Open year-round. Admission by donation.

Tsuu T'ina Culture Museum, 3700 Anderson Road SW, (403) 238–2677. Open Monday through Friday. Free. Displays on the life and culture of the Tsuu T'ina nation include artifacts, a model tepee, and clothing.

Canada Olympic Park/Olympic Hall of Fame, Highway 1 west of the city, (403) 247–5454. Open daily. Admission is charged for tours. Exhibits relating to the fifteenth international Olympic Games held in February 1988 in the Calgary area. The attraction features exciting ski-jump and bobsled-run simulations.

Accommodations

The following hotels and motels are recommended choices when staying overnight in Calgary:

Palliser Hotel, 133 Ninth Avenue SW, (403) 262–1234; (800) 441–1414. Superior accommodations, considered by many travelers to be Calgary's finest. Restored to a new grandeur. Central to businesses and attractions in city center; a Calgary landmark in itself. Some rooms with minibars, a nonsmokers' floor, exercise facilities. Rimrock Dining Room with large fireplace; Oak Room Lounge with entertainment; a deli and boulevard café. Expensive.

Westin Hotel, 320 Fourth Avenue SW, (403) 266–1611; (800) 228–3000. Superior accommodations. Top-notch in most respects; many travelers return to the Westin repeatedly. Suites, swimming pool, and numerous services and amenities. Expensive.

Château Airport, within the Calgary International Airport complex, 2001 Airport Road NE, (403) 291–2600; (800) 441–1414. Excellent accommodations with top-quality amenities Expensive.

Delta Bow Valley Inn, 209 Fourth Avenue SE, (403) 266–1980; (800) 268–1133 (Canada); (800) 877–1133 (U.S.). City center location. Conservatory Dining Room, two lounges, indoor pool, whirlpool, saunas, and exercise room. Expensive.

Marriott, 110 Ninth Avenue SE, (403) 266–7331; (800) 228–2800. Excellent accommodations; twenty-four-hour room service, sundeck, nonsmoking floors, swimming pool. Centrally located; limousine service; dining at the Trader's Room and at the Wheatsheaf Café. Expensive.

International Hotel, 220 Fourth Avenue SW, (403) 265–9600. An executive-suite hotel (two rooms); swimming pool and other amenities. Moderate to expensive.

Sandman Hotel, 888 Seventh Avenue SW, (403) 237–8626; (800) 736–3626. Excellent accommodations; nightclub, swimming pool, many other amenities. Moderate.

Other Fine Places to Stay

All the places listed below offer fine accommodations and many amenities (such as swimming pools, dining rooms, and lounges), and some have nightclubs.

Best Western Hospitality Inn, 135 Southland Drive SE, (403) 278–5050; (800) 528–1234. Moderate.

Best Western Village Park Inn, 1804 Crowchild Trail NW, (403) 289–0241; (800) 528–1234. Moderate.

Blackfoot Inn, 5940 Blackfoot Trail SE, (403) 252–2253; (800) 661–1151. Moderate.

Sheraton Cavalier, 2620 Thirty-second Avenue NE, (403) 291–0107; (800) 325–3535. Moderate.

University of Calgary, 2500 University Drive NW, (403) 220–3202. Open during the summer months when the resident population is on vacation. Pleasant accommodations in a campus setting. An excellent value for families, couples, or the single traveler. Inexpensive.

Other inexpensive places to stay in summer include **Mount Royal College,** (403) 249–7224, and **Southern Alberta Institute of Technology (SAIT),** (403) 284–8013. To find inexpensive accomodations year-round, call the Bed and Breakfast Association, (403) 531–0065.

Calgary International Hostel, 520 Seventh Avenue SE, (403) 269–8239.

Dining

Calgary has a wide assortment of restaurants serving all kinds of foods in every price category. Below are some of the city's worthy eateries:

Hy's, 316 Fourth Avenue SW, (403) 263–2222. Well known in Western Canada for excellent beef dishes served in an elegant setting. A fine selection of wines. Moderate to expensive.

Traders, at the Radisson Plaza, Ninth Avenue and Centre Street, (403) 266–7331. One of the better restaurants in the city; noted for its excellent cuisine, service, and atmosphere. Expensive.

La Chaumière, 121 Seventeenth Avenue SE, (403) 228–5690. French cuisine at its best served in an elegant environment. Moderate to expensive.

Teatro, 200 Eighth Avenue SE, (403) 290–1012. Italian market cuisine served in a renovated old bank building. Moderate to expensive.

Grand Isle Seafood, 200–128 Second Avenue SE, (403) 269–7783. Excellent Chinese restaurant with buffet and dim sum plus regular menu. View of the Bow River. Moderate.

River Café, Prince's Island Park, (403) 261–7670. Delightful island location, open all year except January and February. Fusion cuisine. Moderate.

Owl's Nest, at the Westin Hotel, 320 Fourth Avenue SW, (403) 266–1611. Beautiful interior. High-class, Old World service. Continental cuisine and dishes made with Western Canadian prime ingredients—salmon and Alberta beef. Moderate to expensive.

Panorama Room, Calgary Tower, Ninth Avenue and Centre Street SW, (403) 266–7171. Revolving restaurant on top of the tower, offering great views and Alberta beef dishes. Moderate to expensive.

Japanese Village, 302 Fourth Avenue SW, (403) 262–2738. Traditional Japanese favorites. The food is sliced, diced, and grilled at your table. Moderate.

Cannery Row Restaurant, 317 Tenth Avenue SW, (403) 269–8889. Fresh seafood and Creole restaurant. Live New Orleans jazz. Moderate.

Cross House Garden Cafe, 1240 Eighth Avenue SE, (403) 531–2767. Set in a historic home in the Inglewood district with a grand lawn and garden. Alberta beef, salmon, Arctic char specialties.

McQueen's Upstairs, 317 Tenth Avenue SW, (403) 269–4722. Chicago speakeasy-style atmosphere. Same building as Cannery Row Restaurant. Seafood and Alberta beef. Moderate.

Dean House Historic Site & Tea Room, 806 Ninth Avenue SE, (403) 269–7747. Elegant 1906 Edwardian home, a must visit. Lunch or afternoon tea in glass-enclosed veranda. View of Elbow River. Inexpensive to moderate.

Entertainment

The focus of the city's cultural life is the **Calgary Centre for Performing Arts,** in city center. It is home for the Calgary Philharmonic Orchestra, Theatre Calgary, Alberta Theatre Project, and One Yellow Rabbit Theatre Company. This complex consists of the Jack Singer Concert Hall, the Max Bell Theatre, and the Martha

Cohen Theatre. For information on events and tickets, call (403) 266–8888, or Ticketmaster, (403) 270–6700.

The following clubs offer entertainment, food, and drink:

King Edward Hotel, 438 Ninth Avenue SW, (403) 262–1680. Home of the blues in Calgary; line music and dancing.

Ranchman's, 9615 Macleod Trail South, (403) 253–1100; country-and-western music and dancing.

McQueen's, 317 Tenth Avenue SW, (403) 269–4722; blues, jazz, seafood, and drinks.

Stage West, 727 Forty-second Avenue SE, (403) 243–6642; dinner theater.

Garry Theatre, 1229 Ninth Avenue SE, (403) 233–9100; drama productions.

Jesters Comedy Club, 239 Tenth Avenue SE, (403) 269–6669; amateur and professional comics.

Cowboy's Dance Hall, 826 Fifth Street SW, (403) 265–0699. Dancing, live entertainment.

Dusty's Saloon, 1088 Olympic Way SE, (403) 263–5343. Dancing, country-and-western music.

Kaos Jazz & Blues Bistro, 718 Seventeenth Avenue SW, (403) 228–9997. Live jazz.

Shopping

Calgary city center, between Ninth and Fourth avenues, is the main shopping district. The C-Train or bus will also take you to other large shopping malls where you will find the large department stores—Eaton's, the Bay—and a wide assortment of shops, from those selling local arts and crafts to high-fashion boutiques.

Calgary has several other interesting shopping districts:

Kensington, the area between Tenth and Fourteenth streets along Kensington Road and Tenth Street.; small shops, casual dining, coffee bars.

Mount Royal Village, along Seventeenth Avenue SW between Fourteenth Street and Fourth Street SW; shops and restaurants.

Atlantic Avenue, along Ninth Avenue SE between Twelfth Street and Fort Calgary; antiques and coffee bars.

Eau Claire Market, along the Bow River next to Prince Island Park; a new market full of shops and restaurants.

The following are some interesting shops worth your time and credit cards:

Lammle's Western Wear, nine locations, (403) 255–0272; cowboy hats, boots, and other gear.

Cottage Craft Gifts, 6503 Elbow Drive SW; a wide variety of high-quality gifts to bring home.

Chase Cattle Company, TD Square, third floor, (403) 269–6450; Old West and native clothing, jewelry, sculpture.

Professional Sports

Calgary Flames of the NHL—former Stanley Cup Champions; call Ticketmaster, (403) 270–6700, for ticket information and the home schedule. The Flames play at the Canadian Airlines Saddledome in Stampede Park.

Calgary Stampeders of the Canadian Football League; call Ticketmaster, (403) 270–6700, for ticket and schedule information. The Stampeders play at McMahon Stadium, adjacent to the University of Calgary.

Calgary Cannons Professional Baseball Club; call (403) 284–1111 for ticket and schedule information. The Cannons are members of the Pacific Coast League and play at Foothills Stadium.

Thoroughbred and harness racing takes place at Stampede Park. Call (403) 261–0214 for schedules.

Recreation

The people of Calgary have created four-season indoor environments that simulate summertime at the beach. The many leisure centers throughout the city provide warm indoor beaches, swimming, water slides, and even bodysurfing, which is possible because of machine-made waves that rival those on a real ocean beach. In addition, these centers contain indoor rinks, weight-lifting areas, racquet courts, restaurants, and many other facilities. Most of the major hotels have swimming pools and health and fitness facilities. Golf, jogging, biking, tennis, and horseback riding are also in the area. For details on recreation during your stay, your hotel

The resorts of the Canadian Rockies offer an excellence of hospitality that ▶ has made them famous around the world. Visitors also get the added benefit of some of the best scenery anywhere in the world.

concierge or guest relations person is your best source for information and for making arrangements for your enjoyment.

Calgary has a unique pathway system joining all areas of the city. It is used by cyclists, joggers, walkers, and in-line skaters. Pathway maps detailing the 300 km (186 mi) of trails are available at many locations. The visitors centers operated by the Calgary Convention and Visitors Bureau are at the airport and at the base of the Calgary Tower.

The Fabulous Canadian Rockies

Waterton Lakes National Park

Waterton Lakes National Park can be reached via Highways 2 and 6 South from Calgary, Highway 5 West from Lethbridge, or U.S. Highway 17 from Great Falls, Montana, to Alberta Highway 5. For more information, contact Superintendent, Waterton Lakes National Park, Waterton Lakes, Alberta T0K 2M0; (403) 859-2445.

Located at the extreme southwestern corner of the province on the Alberta-Montana border, Waterton Lakes National Park and Glacier National Park (to the south into Montana) were joined to form Waterton-Glacier International Peace Park, the first of its kind in the world. Waterton itself has been described as the place "where the mountains meet the prairies." The transition between these two topographical zones is abrupt here, as there are no foothills as such (the same can be said for much of the western length of the Rockies in Alberta). Ancient glaciers, however, did carve out lakes and valleys, leaving moraines, eskers, and kames (different kinds of rock and dirt formations). Upper Waterton Lake, the park's deepest (148 m/485 ft), juts from Alberta into Montana, crossing the international border. Some unique aquatic species live here—deep-water sculpins, pygmy whitefish, and opossum shrimps. The park also has zones of shortgrass prairie, aspen groves, and alpine meadows lush with wildflowers. There are many species of birds and waterfowl, elk, mule deer, bighorn sheep, black bears, and grizzly bears. The Waterton-Glacier area supports many grizzlies. If you are hiking or camping, please heed the park's warnings and precautions—people have been severely mauled and killed by these animals.

For your hiking enjoyment, the park has 183 km (113 mi) of trails that lead to lakes, canyons, waterfalls, forested valleys, and alpine meadows. Scenic auto drives, such as the Promenade Akamina Parkway, wind throughout the park. Cruise boats on Upper Waterton Lake provide tours. You can also tour the park on bus or horseback. The park offers an interpretive program and camping facilities at Crandell Mountain and Belly River. There are boat rentals and fishing (get a permit at Cameron Lake). An eighteen-hole public golf course, surrounded by magnificent scenery, is near the park.

Accommodations

Prince of Wales Hotel, (403) 226–5551; reservations are a must. Whenever pictures of Waterton Lakes National Park are published, the baronial structure of the Prince of Wales Hotel is in the foreground, sitting on a bluff overlooking a sparkling lake and surrounded by snowcapped mountains. The building and the setting are superior, although the hotel lacks some of the amenities typical of other equally expensive places. Moderate to expensive.

Aspen Village Inn, (403) 859–2255. Excellent accommodations with many amenities. Moderate.

Bayshore Inn, (403) 859–2211. Excellent accommodations with many amenities. Moderate to expensive.

Kilmorey Lodge, (403) 859–2334. Year-round accommodations. Moderate.

Banff–Lake Louise Area

Banff National Park

Banff National Park can be reached from the west (Vancouver) and from the east (Banff is 130 km [78 mi] west of Calgary) via the Trans-Canada Highway 1; also via Highway 93 from southern B.C. and through the Kootenay region; and from Edmonton via the Yellowhead Highway 16 West and then on Highway 93 South; also from Edmonton via Highway 2 South to 11 West to 93. For more information, contact Superintendent, Banff National Park, Box 900, Banff, Alberta T0L 0C0 (403–762–1500) or Banff/Lake Louise Tourism Bureau, Box 1298, Banff, Alberta T0L 0C0 (403–762–8421).

Banff is Canada's most popular national park, not just for its natural beauty but also for its many recreational and cultural offerings throughout the four seasons. The Banff and Lake Louise region was originally developed as a prime resort and recreational area by the Canadian Pacific Railroad, which built the transcontinental railroad in the 1800s. The great resorts of Banff Springs

Hotel and Chateau Lake Louise, among the world's most famous, have attracted the rich, the celebrated, and the ordinary for generations. The park itself is in the heart of the Canadian Rockies, with awesome, snowcapped mountains in every direction. The mountain scenery is accented by the ultramarine waters of lakes, the greenish-tan rush of streams and rivers, and the dark blue-green shades of deep evergreen forests—habitats for grizzlies, elk, bighorn sheep, and coyotes. Because the mountains often pierce through fast-moving clouds and the temperature varies so greatly at different levels of elevation, the weather is very changeable. One minute it is a marvelous sunny day, perfect in every way; the next, fierce winds blow and rain or hail beats down. The effects, however, are stunning: rainbows, mountains emerging from and disappearing into clouds, dark blotches highlighted and revealed in detail as stands of aspen and evergreen. This is a place where you need a loaded camera close at hand at all times. Perhaps one of the most inspiring experiences of the park is to go off by yourself—even if it's off the road a bit—and listen to the wind and view the mountains and clouds. Whether you're just plain folk or a big shot, you'll be humbled and elevated in spirit at the same time.

One of the most photographed scenes in the park is Mount Rundle with the Vermilion Lakes in the foreground, at the town of Banff; the best view is from the Trans-Canada. The town of Banff is the major tourism center in the park, offering accommodations, dining, shopping, and entertainment.

Northwest of the town, via the Trans-Canada (west), is **Lake Louise,** named in honor of Princess Louise Caroline Alberta, fourth daughter of Queen Victoria and wife of the Marquis of Lorne, governor-general of Canada. (The province of Alberta was named in her honor also.) Watch for the side road off the Trans-Canada that takes you through the village into higher country and then to the lake itself. What has made Lake Louise famous for generations is the ethereal atmosphere here: the clear waters, the high surrounding mountains, the Victoria Glacier and Mount Victoria at the western end of the lake, and the hotel Chateau Lake Louise. The best way to describe Lake Louise is that it is at the bottom of a deep bowl with steep, beautifully decorated, fluted sides. A trip to the Canadian Rockies would not be complete without a visit to Lake Louise; for some it is a pilgrimage of sorts.

Banff National Park's 1,600 km (980 mi) of trails encourage you to get into the beautiful countryside on foot or horseback or by rock climbing or cross-country skiing. A number of interpretive programs are given by professional naturalists and guides. The park has thirteen campgrounds (2,799 campsites for those with vehicles).

The Bow Valley Parkway (a secondary highway that parallels the Trans-Canada Highway) gives access to all attractions and to Lake Louise and the town of Banff. Just north of Lake Louise, as the Trans-Canada turns west toward Vancouver, Icefield Parkway (Highway 93) continues north to Columbia Icefields, Jasper National Park, and the resort town of Jasper.

Sports and Recreation

Downhill Skiing

These four ski areas are known throughout the world as being among the best in North America:

Nakiska, in the Kananaskis area, was the site of alpine events during the 1988 Winter Olympic Games. This new ski area is world class in every way. At nearby Kananaskis Village are deluxe hotels, fine restaurants and shops, and some of the best après-ski fun anywhere. The highest elevation is 2,250 m/7,381 ft; vertical rise is 918 m/3,012 ft. The longest run is 3,196 m/10,486 ft. Skiing terrain is 16 percent novice, 70 percent intermediate, and 14 percent expert. There are one double chair lift, one triple chair lift, and two detachable high-speed quad lifts; lift capacity is 8,000 persons per hour. Nakiska offers a ski school, day-care, downhill and cross-country equipment rentals, and many other recreational opportunities. For more information, contact Nakiska, P.O. Box 1988, Kananaskis Village, Alberta, T0L 2HO, (403) 591-7777.

Kananaskis village accommodations:

Hotel Kananaskis, (403) 591-7711; (800) 268-9411. Top place in this recreational area. Expensive.

Kananaskis Inn, (403) 591-7500. Suites with fireplaces. Steam room and hot tub. Expensive.

The Lodge at Kananaskis, (403) 591-7711; (800) 268-9411. Excellent accommodations. Expensive.

Banff Mount Norquay, the area's oldest resort, has been totally redesigned and expanded to world-class standards. Long famous for its beginner and expert terrain, it has now expanded its intermediate skiing area on Mystic Ridge by a full 70 acres. Ten minutes from downtown Banff, overlooking the Bow River, its season is from early December to mid-April. Lift capacity is 6,300 persons an hour; snowmaking covers 90 percent of the terrain. The runs are split between 11 percent novice, 45 percent intermediate, 28 percent advanced, and 16 percent expert. Lessons and ski equipment are readily available. For more information, contact Banff Mount Norquay, Box 219, Suite 7000, Banff, Alberta T0L 0C0; (403) 762–4421, or Calgary snow phone, (403) 221–8259, available twenty-four hours.

Sunshine Village, located 22 km (13.2 mi) from the town of Banff and at the tree line in a high alpine bowl, is noted for an abundance of powder and the longest ski season in the region— from early November to late May. Highest elevation, 2,806 m/9,200 ft; vertical rise, 1,070 m/3,514 ft; longest run, 8 km/5 mi; skiing terrain, 15 percent intermediate, 25 percent expert, and 60 percent novice; lift capacity, 1,600 persons per hour; annual snowfall, 1,000 cm/400 in. A ski school, cross-country skiing, mountain tours, equipment rentals, and restaurants and accommodations are all here. For more information, contact Sunshine Village, Box 1510, Banff, Alberta T0L 0C0; (403) 762–6500 or a twenty-four-hour snow phone (403) 762–6543.

Lake Louise (see page 214), via the Trans-Canada Highway, is famous for its beauty, and many travelers have said that it is the most beautiful part of the Canadian Rockies. The ski area has facilities on two mountains—Mount Whitehorn and Mount Lapalian. There are open slopes, bowls, mogul fields, gladed timberline, and a great deal of delightful powder. The season runs from November to mid-May. Highest elevation, 2,636 m/8,650 ft; vertical rise, 1,000 m/3,257 ft; longest run, 8 km/5 mi; skiing terrain, 45 percent intermediate, 30 percent expert, and 25 percent novice; lift capacity, 15,499 persons per hour; annual snowfall, 360 cm/140 in. There are a ski school for various levels of expertise and specialties, equipment rentals, mountain tours, cross-country skiing, ice skating, and sleigh rides. For more information, contact Skiing Louise, Box 5, Lake Louise, Alberta T0L 1E0; (403) 522–3555.

Helicopter Hiking/Skiing

Helicopter hiking/skiing has become a popular sport in the Canadian Rockies. Here a helicopter takes you to the top of a mountain and drops you off with a top-notch guide and supplies; you then hike or ski down through a pristine wilderness that seems to belong to you alone. The following companies provide helicopter skiing in the Canadian Rockies, both in the mountains of Alberta and those nearby in British Columbia (also consult your travel agent; several package-tour operators do provide helicopter skiing/hiking vacations in the Canadian Rockies):

Canadian Mountain Holidays, (403) 762–7100

R.K. Heli-Skiing, (403) 762–3771

Assiniboine Heli Tours, (403) 678–5459

Alpine Helicopters, (403) 678–4802

Mountaineering

Banff Alpine Guides, Box 1025, Banff, Alberta T0L 0C0; (403) 678–6091. Operates a school and conducts guided hikes in the Canadian Rockies.

The Lac des Arcs Climbing School, 1116 Nineteenth Avenue NW, Calgary, Alberta T2M 0Z9; (403) 289–6795. Courses in rock climbing, mountaineering, bush survival, river kayaking, and mountain rescue.

Yamnuska, Inc., 1316 Railway Avenue, Canmore, Alberta, T1W 1P6; (403) 762–4164. Canada's leading mountain school and guide service offers the usual training plus wilderness treks and hikes to some of the most spectacular points in the national parks. Ideal for those who want the adventure but not the climb.

Wild-River Rafting

Hunter Valley Recreational Enterprises, Box 1620, Canmore, Alberta T0L 0M0; (403) 678–2000. White-water rafting trips, rafting and trekking packages, canoe and kayak clinics.

Rocky Mountain Raft Company, Box 1771, Banff, Alberta; (403) 762–3632. One- and three-hour tours on the scenic Bow River. June 1 to mid-September.

Bicycle Tours

Bactrax Bike Rentals, (403) 762–8177.

Park N' Pedal, (403) 762–3191.

Peak Experience, (403) 762–0581.

Performance Ski & Sports, (403) 762–8222.

Boat Cruises

Minnewanka Tours, located at Lake Minnewanka, just east of downtown Banff; (403) 762–3473, fax (403) 762–2800. Cruises around this beautiful lake at the foot of Mount Norquay and to various scenic points. The organization also provides fishing trips.

Fishing

Banff Fishing Unlimited, (403) 762–4936, fax (403) 678–8895. Provides licensed guides, tackle, foul-weather gear, lunch. Staff clean and pack your catch.

Monod Sports, (403) 762–4571.

Mountain Fly Fishers, (403) 678–2915.

Golf Courses

Kananaskis Country Golf Course, a Robert Trent Jones course of thirty-six holes (the facility has two eighteen-hole courses), clubhouse, restaurant, equipment rentals, and pro shop. For tee times, call (800) 661–1581.

Canmore Golf Course, eighteen holes, clubhouse, lounge, restaurant, pro shop, equipment and cart rentals. In operation from May to mid-October. One-day advance booking is recommended; call (403) 678–4784/4785.

Banff Springs Hotel Golf Course, twenty-seven holes; 147 sand traps! This course is smack in the middle of some of the most inspiring scenery in the world. It's not unusual to see elk race across the fairways. The facility has a driving range, practice green, equipment and cart rentals, restaurant, lounges, pro shop, and clubhouse. Book your game well in advance by calling (403) 762–6801.

Trail Rides

Holiday on Horseback, Box 2280, Banff, Alberta T0L 0C0; (403) 762–4551, (800) 661–8352, fax (403) 762–8103. From weekend-long to six-day trips into the remote area of the Canadian Rockies.

Timberline Tours, Box 14, Lake Louise, Alberta T0L 1E0; (403) 522–3743. Outdoor packages.

Hostelling

Southern Alberta Hostelling Association, headquarters in Calgary, (403) 283–5551, has facilities at Calgary, Ribbon Creek, Spray River, Banff International, Castle Mountain, Mosquito Creek, Ramparts Creek, and Hilda Creek.

Gondola Sightseeing

Sulphur Mountain Gondola Lift; (403) 762–2523, fax (403) 762–8101. Admission charged. Takes you to the summit (2,285 m/

7,500 ft high) where on a clear day you can truly see forever. The ride up is exciting and fun, and there's a restaurant in the observation complex.

Lake Louise Sightseeing Lift and Gondola, (403) 522–3555. In operation from June to September. Admission is charged (pay for going up and hike down free).

Hot Springs Bathing

Upper Hot Springs Pool, Mountain Avenue, near the Banff Springs Hotel, (403) 762–1515. Open throughout the year. Bathing-suit and towel rentals. Upper Hot Springs Pool has attracted bathers from all over the world to its therapeutic waters of natural hot springs. In this pool, the ordinary have bathed along with the rich and famous, seeking relaxation and/or cures to their aches and pains. The Banff experience would not be complete without a good hot soaking here.

Special Events

Banff Festival of the Arts, from June to August. This is one of Western Canada's premier arts festivals. It brings together the finest professional talent and the best of young Canadian talent at the Banff Centre School of Fine Arts. During the summer, the public can partake of more than a hundred events in classical music, jazz, ballet, opera, musical theater, drama, and literary readings. These superior performances are held at Margaret Greenham Theatre, Eric Harvie Theatre, Roubakine Auditorium, Max Bell Auditorium, and Donald Cameron Hall. There are workshops in musical theater, dance, and opera. Art exhibitions are held at the Walter Phillips Gallery. The Banff Festival of the Arts makes summer here splendid, and it all happens right in town. Tickets are scarce close to performance dates and must be obtained *in advance.* This festival is as much a part of the Banff experience as the Rockies themselves. For schedule and ticket information, call (403) 762–6300; (800) 413–8368.

Museums

Natural History Museum, 112 Banff Avenue, (403) 762–4747. Open daily, free. Displays and a diorama showing the geological history and present structure of the Canadian Rockies.

Banff Park Museum, 93 Banff Avenue, (403) 762–1558. Open daily. Built in 1903 and housed in the park's old administrative building, this museum has displays on the diverse natural history of the area. It also has prints of Robert Bateman, a Canadian artist who has become world famous for his wildlife studies.

Luxton Museum, One Birch Avenue, (403) 762–2388. Open daily. Closed Monday and Tuesday in winter. Admission is charged. An excellent collection of Plains Indian artifacts.

Cave and Basin National Historic Site, (403) 762–1557. Open daily. Admission charged. The center has historical and geological exhibits, including the replica bathhouse (1887), and the Discovery Trail, a natural history walk. Interpretive center and restaurant that is open only in summer.

Whyte Museum of the Canadian Rockies, 111 Bear Street, (403) 762–2291. Open daily. Call for hours and fees. Has exhibition galleries that show the works of Canadian artists and those from other countries. The **Archives of the Canadian Rockies** is also here.

Walter J. Phillips Gallery, Banff Centre Complex, St. Julien Road, (403) 762–6281. Open daily. Free. Named in honor of W. J. Phillips, a prominent Canadian landscape artist, this gallery shows works by leading artists as well as students and faculty of the Centre of Fine Arts.

The Town of Banff

Banff, Alberta, has only one reason for being—tourism. When the transcontinental railroad was being built, Banff (named after a county in Scotland), because of its surrounding beauty and natural hot mineral springs, was selected as a spa for the wealthy to relax and regain their zest for pursuing their various social, political, and commercial interests. The huge, sprawling Banff Springs Hotel was built just to serve such clients. When the late Duke of Windsor was a young Prince of Wales, he vacationed at Banff Springs Hotel, and his presence served as a magnet that drew more of the "carriage set" to the Canadian Rockies. As time went on, many others came here to vacation, and a thriving, lovely community grew on the valley flats. For much of the town's history, the only way to get here from distant points was by the Canadian Pacific Railroad. Banff and Lake Louise have remained the highlights of this world-renowned rail trip across Canada, which continues to bring visitors (via Calgary or Vancouver). In the post–World War II period, the Trans-Canada Highway was built, and today Banff and Lake Louise are easily accessible to all.

The main street of Banff, running north and south, is Banff

Avenue, where you will find many shops, restaurants, and services. Going northeast on Banff Avenue will take you to Tunnel Mountain Campground. The Trans-Canada, the train station, and Mount Norquay are all directly north of downtown; west of downtown are the Vermilion Lakes. Banff Avenue will also take you across the Bow River, past the national park administrative building and its lovely floral displays to Spray Avenue, which leads to the Banff Springs Hotel. Even if you are not staying in the hotel, you should go in and see the beautifully decorated public rooms and the fantastic view from the terrace overlooking the golf course (elk come out on the fairways at dusk to feed), Bow Valley, and the surrounding mountains. Once you see this view, you'll instantly know why Banff became such a popular vacation paradise and has continued as such for so long. The dining and lounge facilities of the hotel are open for use by nonresidential guests.

Tourist Information
Banff/Lake Louise Tourism Bureau Information Centre, 224 Banff Avenue, Banff, Alberta T0L-0C0; (403) 762–8421, fax (403) 762–8163.

Touring Services
Brewster Independent Travel, (403) 762–6700 or (800) 661–1152
Mountain Park Tours, (403) 762–5652
The Trail Rider, 132 Banff Avenue, (403) 762–4551; provides horse-drawn carriage rides to Banff Springs Hotel and other attractions and horseback trail rides of two to six days

Accommodations
Banff has many places to stay; the ones listed here are the best in town. If you require lower-priced accommodations, contact the Banff/Lake Louise Tourism Bureau, (403) 762–8421. Since Banff is one of Canada's most popular resort towns during the high seasons of summer and winter, reservations for accommodations are essential. For camping information, call the Parks Information Centre, (403) 762–1550.
Banff Springs Hotel, Spray Avenue, (403) 762–2211; in Canada, (800) 441–1414. One of Canada's best-known hotels, this huge baronial castle surrounded by the splendor of the Rockies has undergone extensive renovations that have greatly helped in spruc-

221

ing up the rooms (those with views of Bow Valley are superior). The hotel has three dining rooms serving excellent cuisine, and the main dining room is one of the most elegant in Western Canada. There are lounges, a world-class spa, a great twenty-seven-hole golf course, several tennis courts, hot springs, shops, live entertainment, and many other services and amenities. Expensive.

Rimrock Resort Hotel, at Sulphur Mountain, (403) 762–3356; (800) 661–1587 Canada and United States. A new four-diamond hotel with grand views of Bow Valley and surrounding mountains. Classico restaurant, Primrose dining room, and the Larkspur lounge. Indoor pool, sauna, hot tub, and exercise room. Expensive.

Banff Park Lodge, Lynx Street, (403) 762–4433; (800) 661–9266. Excellent accommodations, Terrace and Chinook dining rooms, Glacier lounge with nightly entertainment, indoor pool. Close to ski areas, cross-country trails, boating, fishing, and other sports. Expensive.

Banff Rocky Mountain Resort, off the Trans-Canada near Tunnel Mountain Road, (403) 762–5531; (800) 661–9563. Chalet units with fireplaces and various kitchen conveniences. Restaurant, lounge, squash and tennis courts, indoor pool. Expensive.

Inns of Banff, 600 Banff Avenue, (403) 762–4581; (800) 661–1272. Deluxe rooms, Reflections dining room, Belvedere lounge with entertainment, indoor pool, squash court. Expensive.

Lake Louise Accommodations

Chateau Lake Louise, on the shore of Lake Louise, (403) 522–3511; (800) 441–1414. Lake Louise is not all that large a body of water. What makes it mystical and beautiful are the high, steep, snowcapped mountains surrounding it; the high Victoria Glacier at the opposite end of the lake from the hotel; the dark-green forests all around; and the sky often made moody by fast-moving clouds. All these facets reflect off the lake and give it a pantheism that other lakes lack. It's a memorable experience to be here just for a few moments, and so much better if you can stay for a few days. The Chateau itself is not as impressive as its sister hotel in Banff—taken out of this setting, it would appear as a sprawling ark of a place. But, fortunately, renovations have brought it up to contemporary standards; the grounds, interior public places, and rooms are first-class. Its Victoria dining room offers excellent cuisine and service. There are an indoor pool, steam room, exercise room, and tanning room, as well as canoeing on the lake, ice-skating, fishing, hiking, horseback riding, and other activities, one of the best of which is simply walking lakeside, drink in hand, and meditating on the glories of nature before you. Expensive.

Lake Louise Inn, in Lake Louise Village, (403) 522–3791; (800) 661–9237, Canada and United States. Excellent accommodations and facilities in a superb natural area; restaurant, swimming pool, health club, lounge, and dance floor. The best all-around choice in Lake Louise, except that it does not front the lake itself as Chateau Lake Louise does. Moderate to expensive.

Deer Lodge, near the lake, (403) 522–3991; (800) 661–1595. A pleasant inn that has a fine restaurant. Moderate.

Dining

For a small resort town, Banff has a broad choice of fine restaurants. The high quality of restaurant offerings makes sense when you consider the large number of sophisticated travelers who come here every year and are not afraid to take local chefs to task for any slip below standards. For the average traveler, this extra attention to detail is a bonus, for in Banff you know you can dine very well. The following is but a sampling of fine Banff eateries.

Banff Springs Hotel, Spray Avenue, (403) 762–2211. The Rob Roy Room for continental cuisine and dancing. Expensive.

Guido's Ristorante, 116 Banff Avenue, (403) 762–4002. Tender veal dishes, linguine, smoked filet of trout. Inexpensive to moderate.

Balkan Restaurant, 120 Banff Avenue, (403) 762–3454. Greek fare—shrimp and herbs baked with feta, broiled marinated lamb chops, moussaka, and baklava for dessert. Moderate.

Le Beaujolais, corner of Buffalo Street and Banff Avenue, (403) 762–2712. Excellent French restaurant, perhaps the best in the Canadian Rockies. Chateaubriand, lobster soup, filet mignon, and other haute cuisine dishes. Very nice decor and a good wine list. Expensive.

The Grizzly House, 207 Banff Avenue, (403) 762–4055. An eclectic restaurant, indeed. Specialties include fondues of buffalo, venison, lobster, prawns, rattlesnake, and wild game. Telephones at every table lead to strange meetings with fellow diners.

Joe BTFSPLK's Diner, 221 Banff Avenue, (403) 762–5529. This is 1950s Canada, complete with jukebox, red vinyl booths, and great, affordable food. Save room for made-from-scratch apple pie.

Entertainment

The larger hotels and motels in both Banff and Lake Louise have lounges with live entertainment, and a number of independent lounges in town offer bands, singers, dancers, and comedians. Banff Springs Hotel has both sedate ballroom dancing and a frenetic disco. The Rose and Crown, at 202 Banff Avenue, is a British-style pub that offers live entertainment and darts.

Wild Bill's Legendary Saloon, 210 Banff Avenue, second floor, (403) 762–0333. Liveliest spot in town. Call for group bookings.

Shopping

What would a resort town be without lots of shops to keep tourists busy and happy? Banff has its share.

Art of Man Gallery, Chateau Lake Louise; Inuit sculptures.

Mountain Magic Sportswear, 224 Bear Street; outdoor sports equipment.

Monod Sports, 111 Banff Avenue (also at Chateau Lake Louise); climbing and camping gear, clothing for the out-of-doors, swimsuits.

Beautiful Jasper

Jasper National Park

Jasper National Park can be reached from the south (Banff) via Highway 93 and from Edmonton or Vancouver via the Yellowhead Highway 16. For more information, contact Superintendent, Jasper National Park, Box 10, Jasper, Alberta T0E 1E0 (403–852–6176), or the Jasper Tourism and Commerce, Box 98, Jasper, Alberta T0E 1E0 (403–852–3858).

Jasper National Park is one of North America's largest natural areas preserved for present and future generations. Within the boundaries of this magnificent park are high mountains, many lakes—including Maligne Lake—forests, alpine meadows, Columbia Icefield, Athabasca Glacier, and Sunwapta Falls. This is the terrain of grizzly bears, elk, bighorn sheep, and elusive mountain goats. Native peoples, trappers, botanists, geologists, prospectors, and mountain people have been through here. Explorers such as David Thompson, Captain John Palliser, Sir Sanford Fleming, and Philadelphian Mary Schaffer trekked through this inspiring country; their records of and enthusiasm for Jasper (named after the fur trader Jasper Hawes) have attracted countless numbers of people since.

At the southern end of Jasper National Park is the Icefield Parkway (Promenade Champs de Glace), actually Highway 93. This 230-kilometer (138-mile) scenic highroad will take you to the awe-inspiring Columbia Icefield (125 km [75 mi] north of Lake Louise, 105 km [63 mi] south of Jasper), with its Athabasca and Dome glaciers. Access to this 325-square-kilometer (130-square-mile) expanse of ice and snow is possible, at least at its tip, from the edge of the road. If you have never seen a glacier close up, here it is in all its imposing glory. In the distant west on a clear day, you will be able to see Mount Athabasca (3,491 m/11,637 ft high) and its glacier. The best way to experience this ice field is to take a ride over its bumpy surface in a Snocoach, in operation from the end of May to the end of September. An interpretive center here has a model of the entire Columbia Icefield, highlighting its unique features.

The park has 1,000 km/600 mi of trails for hiking; campgrounds (Whistler's, Wapiti, Pocahontas, Snaring River, Wabasso, Mount Kerkeslin, Honeymoon Lake, Jonas Creek, Columbia Icefield, and Wilcox Creek); and places for fishing, boating, trail riding, scuba diving, downhill and cross-country skiing, and body soaking at Miette Hot Springs. The resort town of Jasper offers fine accommodations, dining, entertainment, and shopping.

Sports and Recreation
Downhill Skiing
Marmot Basin, located 365 km/225 mi west of Edmonton on the Yellowhead Highway 16 and 19 km/12 mi southwest of the town of Jasper on Highway 93A, has a season that lasts from early December to early May. Highest elevation, 2,423 m/7,950 ft; vertical rise, 701 m/2,300 ft; longest run, 5.5 km/3.5 mi; skiing terrain, 30 percent expert, 35 percent intermediate, and 35 percent novice; lift capacity, 8,684 persons per hour. Marmot Basin offers ski instruction, equipment rentals, and dining facilities. For more information, contact Marmot Basin, Box 1300, Jasper, Alberta T0E 1E0; (403) 852-3816.

Other Winter Sports
In addition to downhill skiing, Jasper National Park offers Nordic skiing, canyon crawling, helicopter skiing, ice climbing, ice fishing, ice-skating, sleigh rides, and snowshoeing.

Mountaineering

Jasper Climbing School, Box 452, Jasper, Alberta T0E 1E0; (403) 852–3964. Instruction in mountaineering, alpine ski touring, avalanche safety, and ice climbing.

Golf

Jasper Park Lodge, call (403) 852–6090 for tee-off reservations. A superior eighteen-hole golf course in the middle of fantastic scenery. Watch out for such hazards as deer or coyotes darting across the fairways.

Trail Riding

Skyline Trail Rides, Jasper Park Lodge; (403) 852–4215.

Amethyst Lake Pack Trips, Box 23, Brille, Alberta T0E 0C0; (403) 865–4417.

Jasper Wilderness and Tonquin Valley Pack and Ski Trips, Box 550, Jasper, Alberta T0E 1E0; (403) 852–3909. Trail riding and outdoor packages.

Hot Springs Bathing

Miette Hot Springs, 61 km (37.8 mi) east of Jasper on Highway 16, then right at Pocahontas Junction. Open during the summer. This large outdoor pool has some of the hottest water coming up from the bowels of the Canadian Rockies.

Gondola Sightseeing

Jasper Tramway, (403) 852–3093. The tramway is in operation from mid-April to Canadian Thanksgiving. It takes you to the top of Whistler's Mountain. During both the ride up and the ride down, the views from the summit are spectacular.

Wild-River Rafting

Rocky Mountain River Guides, 600 Patricia Street, (403) 852–3777.

Maligne River Adventure, 626 Connaught Drive, (403) 852–3370.

Whitewater Rafting, 702 Connaught Drive, (403) 852–7238. Trips down the mighty Athabasca River.

Jasper Raft Tours, 314 Connaught Drive, (403) 852–3613. River rafting packages.

Bike Rentals

◀ **Beautiful Maligne Canyon at Jasper National Park.**

Beyond Bikes, 4 Cedar Street, (403) 852–5922.
Freewheel Cycle, 611 Patricia Street, (403) 852–3898.
On-Line Sport & Tackle, 600 Patricia Street, (403) 852–3630.
Beauvert Boat & Cycle, at Jasper Park Lodge, (403) 852–5708.
Bicycle rentals and touring information.

Maligne Lake Boat Tours

Maligne Lake, intensely explored by Mary Schaffer, an affluent Quaker from Philadelphia, is, in terms of its beauty and mystical qualities, close to the natural splendor of Lake Louise. Maligne
Tours takes you out in its boats for two hours, and you can experience a bit of what Mary Schaffer did. These boat tours operate from
June through September. Call (403) 852–3370 for information.

Boat Rentals

Canoes, sailboarding equipment, and fishing boats are all
available for rent.
Beauvert Boat & Cycle, at Jasper Park Lodge, (403) 852–5708.
Pyramid Lake Boat Rentals, at Pyramid Lake, (403) 852–3536.

Fishing

Curries's Guiding, 622 Connaught Drive in Jasper, (403)
852–5650.
Fish Maligne Lake, at Maligne Lake or 626 Connaught Drive
in Jasper, (403) 852–3370.
On-Line Sport & Tackle, 600 Patricia Street, (403) 852–3630.

The Town of Jasper

Jasper is the second most important resort town in the Canadian Rockies. It's the human oasis within Jasper National Park. Because Jasper is neither as large nor as bustling as Banff, its pace and
intimacy make Jasper an excellent choice for travelers staying for a
time in the Canadian Rockies. The Jasper Park Lodge, a superior
resort, is as well known as its sister hotels in the south, Banff Springs
and Chateau Lake Louise. VIA Rail provides service to Jasper from
points east and west in Canada. Greyhound has daily trips to and
from the city of Edmonton. Jasper is easy to reach by car via the Yellowhead Highway 16 (East or West) or Highway 93 from the south.
Connaught Drive, which parallels the tracks of the railroad and the
Yellowhead Highway, is Jasper's main street; Patricia Street also has
a number of services for tourists. Most places to stay (except for

Jasper Park Lodge), restaurants, and shops are within a few steps of one another. There are many lakes, such as Patricia and Pyramid, and the Athabasca River is the major waterway. For more information, including accommodations options, contact Jasper Tourism and Commerce at Box 98, 632 Connaught Drive, Jasper, Alberta T0E 1E0, (403) 852–3858.

Accommodations

Reservations are essential during peak summer and winter months. The following places are the best that Jasper has to offer. There are also budget places and campgrounds.

Jasper Park Lodge, via Lodge Road, (403) 852–3301; (800) 441–1414. The popular image of Jasper Park Lodge that comes to mind is that of waiters riding bikes around the resort while carrying trays of cocktails. The facilities here are superior, possibly among the best in the Canadian Rockies. The list of offerings includes an eighteen-hole golf course, swimming pool, tennis, horseback riding, fishing and touring trips, health club, sailboats, bikes, and excellent restaurants. Book well in advance. Expensive.

Alpine Village, junction of Highways 93 and 93A, (403) 852–3285. Moderate.

Chateau Jasper, corner of Juniper and Geikie streets, (403) 852–5644; (800) 661–9323. Fine accommodations and dining room. Moderate to expensive.

Jasper Inn, at Bonhomme and Geikie streets, (403) 852–4461; (800) 661–1933. Moderate to expensive.

Lobstick Lodge, at Juniper and Geikie streets, (403) 852–4431; (800) 661–9317. Moderate.

Marmot Lodge, on Connaught Drive, (403) 852–4471. Moderate.

Sawridge Hotel Jasper, on Connaught Drive, (403) 852–5111; (800) 661–6427. Moderate to expensive.

Dining

Jasper Park Lodge; for reservations, call (403) 852–3301. Beauvert Dining Room, overlooking Lac Beauvert, serves continental cuisine; expensive. Edith Cavell offers four-star dining; expensive. Meadows Café has light and casual fare; moderate. Tonquin Dining Room has gourmet food; expensive. Moose's Nook for dining and dancing; moderate to expensive.

Beauvallon Dining Room at the Chateau Jasper, (403)

852–5644. Superb French cuisine, great steaks, freshly made desserts. Moderate to expensive.

Amethyst Dining Room at the Andrew Motor Lodge, 200 Connaught Drive, (403) 852–3394. Fresh pasta dishes, Alberta steaks, veal piccata milanaise, apple strudel. Moderate to expensive.

Tonquin Prime Rib Village, Juniper Street, (403) 852–4966. Excellent place for prime rib of beef, fresh salmon, Arctic char, and west coast oysters. Moderate.

Becker's Gourmet Restaurant, Jasper/Banff Highway, (403) 852–3535. Beautiful views of the Athabasca River from the dining room. Menu features fine continental cuisine. Moderate to expensive.

Entertainment

The lounges at many of the better places of accommodation feature live entertainment and/or dancing. Check with the desk person at the place you are staying to find out what's happening at night when you're there.

Shopping

Malowney's British Woolens, 606 Patricia Street. Imported woolens and cashmeres.

Sherriff's of Jasper, 610 Connaught Drive. English china, Italian silver, Ammolite jewelry.

Edmonton: Canada's Festival City

What Makes Edmonton Special

To lovers of malls and theme parks, the West Edmonton Mall and Galaxyland makes Edmonton special. To business wheeler-dealers working the rich oil and natural gas fields near the city, Edmonton is prime playing field. To those who want the magnificence of the great national parks of the Canadian Rockies with their resorts and many recreational opportunities, Edmonton's proximity to Jasper and Banff makes it special. And to those who want to kick up their heels at a rip-roaring festival, the rooting-tooting Klondike Days do.

Before the white explorers and fur traders, Amerindian cultures had inhabited this region of Alberta for more than 5,000 years. Their descendants still live here, both in the city and in rural reserves. In 1795, the North West Company built Fort Augustus near what is now the town of Fort Saskatchewan. That same year, William Tomison set up a competing fur-trading post for Hudson's Bay Company, an enterprise he called Fort Edmonton, in honor of the birthplace in England of Sir James Winter Lake, deputy governor of Hudson's Bay Company. By 1821, Fort Edmonton had become the dominant post. In 1830 it was moved to where the Legislature Building now stands; the fort was demolished in 1915.

In 1897, Edmonton became the gateway for the gold rush to the Yukon. There was no clear route as such, and some who had gold fever perished en route; others turned back and went home with empty pockets; and still others stayed in Edmonton and helped to expand the city's population. Edmonton, with 9,000 residents, was incorporated as a city in 1904, and when Alberta itself became a province in 1905, Edmonton was designated its capital. A. C. Rutherford was Alberta's first premier.

When, in 1942, construction began on the Alaska Highway, thereby making the country north of Edmonton accessible by car, the city clearly became the gateway to the North. Perhaps the most important date in its history was February 13, 1947, when the Leduc #1 well spouted black gold. This discovery made Edmonton the "oil capital of Canada," though Calgary might also apply this sobriquet to itself. Thousands of oil and gas wells were found within a 160 km (96 mi) radius of the city.

Today Edmonton is, in land area, one of Canada's largest metropolitan centers. Its present metropolitan population exceeds 862,600. Close to half the people here are of British background, and other large ethnic groups are German, Ukrainian, French, Scandinavian, Polish, Chinese, and Hungarian.

The thriving economy of the city is based on manufacturing, tourism, food processing, petroleum refining, agriculture, government and professional services, transportation/distribution, retailing, medicine, and education. Edmonton is a city of grace, vitality, culture, and vision.

How to Get to Edmonton

By Plane

Edmonton International Airport is located 29 km/18 mi south of the city center. This facility has restaurants, lounges, newsstands, and a duty-free shop; nearby are accommodations. Sky Shuttle provides shuttle-bus service to and from city center. There are also taxis and limousines. Several major rental-car firms have booths at the airport and offices in city center. The following airlines are among those that serve Edmonton: Air Canada, Canadian Airlines, Northwest, Canada 3000, Delta, NWT Air, Horizon, West Jet, Air B.C., and Canadian Regional Airlines.

By Car

Edmonton is 294 km/184 mi north of Calgary, via Calgary Trail Highway 2 and 362 km/226 mi east of Jasper, via the Yellowhead Highway 16. If you are coming from the East, take the Trans-Canada Yellowhead west from Saskatoon, Saskatchewan.

By Bus

The Edmonton bus station is located at 103rd Avenue and 103rd Street. Service to Jasper and Calgary is provided by Greyhound, (403) 413–8747.

By Rail

VIA Rail provides service to Jasper and Vancouver in the west and to Saskatoon, Winnipeg, and major eastern cities. The VIA Rail station is located at 104th Avenue and One-hundreth Street. VIA Rail's toll-free number in Alberta is (800) 561–8630.

How to Get Around in Edmonton

Edmonton is spread out in an easy-to-comprehend grid pattern. The city center is where 101st Street bisects Jasper Avenue. The Alberta Telephone Tower, at One-hundreth Street and One-hundreth Avenue, is a landmark you can use in finding your way around. Another landmark is Edmonton Centre—with its three black towers—at 101st Street and 102nd Avenue. The city's LRT (Light Rail Transit) and bus systems will take you to most places you want to see, including the West Edmonton Mall.

Useful Information

Local holiday: Heritage Day, first Monday in August
Time Zone: Mountain
Area Code: 403
Emergencies of all kinds: Dial 911

METRO EDMONTON

Tourist information: Edmonton Tourism, 9797 Jasper Avenue, (403) 496–8400; (800) 463–4667

Touring Services: Bus tours of the city, Royal Tours, (403) 435–6069

Special Events

Jazz City International Festival, late June through early July.

Klondike Days, mid- to late July. Celebrating the heritage of Edmonton and its role as the gateway to the gold fields of the Yukon. There are parades, pancake breakfasts, gambling casinos, gold panning, a Taste of Edmonton, the World Championship Sourdough Raft Race, and the Sunday Promenade.

Heritage Festival, early August. Ethnic food, dance, culture, and fun.

Folk Music Festival, early to mid-August. The city comes alive with music—folk, country, bluegrass, string band—and dancing.

Fringe Theatre Event, mid- to late August. Old, new, and experimental plays in the city's Old Strathcona district; more than

650 performances; the largest alternative-theater festival in Canada.

Attractions

The West Edmonton Mall, 170th Street and Eighty-Seventh Avenue, (800) 661–8890 and (403) 444–5200. Open every day. Admission is charged for nonshopping attractions. Shuttle-bus service is provided to and from the mall from some Edmonton hotels. The mall has become one of Western Canada's prime attractions. A visit here is like nothing else you've experienced and should not be missed.

There is no doubt about this fantastic place—it is the world's largest and most pleasurable shopping mall, with more than 800 stores, as well as numerous other attractions. Actually, it is a major theme park that has been merged with a mall. Within this sprawling complex are the world's largest indoor amusement park, with more than twenty rides, including a triple-loop roller coaster and a thirteen-story free-fall ride; World Waterpark, a five-acre indoor lake with twenty-two water slides, surfing on 6-foot waves and a wild-river ride; Deep Sea Adventure, an indoor lake 400 feet long and 30 feet deep that offers rides and four submarines, a marine theater with trained dolphins, and a replica of the 80-foot *Santa Maria* galleon; Pebble Beach Miniature Golf, an eighteen-hole minigolf course Europa Golf; Ice Palace Skating, an NHL-size skating rink with equipment rentals; and animal displays that include aviaries, saltwater aquariums, shark tanks, alligators, and penguins. There are thirteen Italian marble fountains throughout the mall. The Europa Boulevard features boutiques with Parisian storefronts. Bourbon Street has nightclubs, jazz, and restaurants. Motorized carts are available for those who want to ride to shops and attractions. The mall cost more than $1 billion to build and employs more than 15,000 persons.

The mall incorporates the Fantasyland Hotel, which has 127 themed, 355 rooms in total, depicting different cultures and periods in history, such as the Polynesian Room (with a waterfall), the Roman Room (with marble sculptures and an authentic Roman bath), the Truck Room, the Coach Room, the Hollywood Room, igloo- and African-themed rooms, and the Arabian Room. Excellent restaurants and lounges are in the hotel; kosher food is served on request. This is also a convention hotel, one that would delight delegates. Call (403) 444–3000 or (800) 661–6454. With accommodations like these, the price is expensive.

Alberta Legislature Building, 107th Street and Ninety-seventh Avenue, (403) 427-7362. Open daily. Free. This provincial capitol is noted for being constructed out of terra-cotta blocks. The terra-cotta and steel-reinforced dome has never shown a crack. Beautiful gardens, as well as a reflecting pool and water displays, surround the building. Carillon bells sing every day at noon. The cornerstone was laid in 1909 by Earl Grey, governor-general of Canada, and the building was officially opened in 1912 by another governor-general, the Duke of Connaught.

Alberta Railway Museum, 24215 Thirty-fourth Street, (403) 472-6229. Open daily May to September. Admission is charged. Displays of early railroading equipment used in the development of Western Canada—steam and diesel engines, rolling stock, vintage 1877 to 1950.

Edmonton Art Gallery, 2 Sir Winston Churchill Square, (403) 422-6223. Open throughout the year. Admission is charged. Exhibitions of classical and contemporary art.

Edmonton Police Museum, 9620 103A Avenue, (403) 421-2274. Open Monday to Saturday. Free. Displays portraying the history of law enforcement in Alberta.

Fort Edmonton Park, via Whitemud and Fox Drive, (403) 496-8787. Open mid-May to September. Admission is charged. On the banks of the North Saskatchewan River and south of city center, Fort Edmonton is a re-creation of a noteworthy early Hudson's Bay trading post (circa 1846). Within this park are several of Edmonton's historic homes and replicas of early street scenes; the Reverend George McDougall Shrine, honoring a pioneering missionary; and rides on an old-time streetcar. Visit Kelly's Saloon for soda and ice cream, the Jasper House for good meals, and the Masonic Hall, where you can relax and sip sarsaparilla. This large historic park is divided into two main sections: (a) the Fort Complex and (b) the settlement, consisting of streets that capture their eras—1885 Street, 1905 Street, and 1920 Street. Fort Edmonton Park is an interesting, enjoyable attraction for all ages.

John Janzen Nature Centre, located next to Fort Edmonton Park, (403) 496-2939. Open throughout the year. Free. Exhibits of Edmonton flora and fauna, including bees, ants, snakes, and salamanders. Nature walks.

Edmonton Space and Science Centre, 111th Avenue and 142nd Street, (403) 493-9000 or 452-9100. Open throughout the year. Admission is charged. This is Canada's largest planetarium, featuring the Star Theatre; the IMAX theater, which uses special effects; and science exhibits.

John Walter Museum, 10627 Ninety-third Avenue; open Sundays; (403) 496–7275. Four historic homes (circa 1875–1915) owned by John Walter, one of the city's first settlers. Displays portray the early development of the province.

Muttart Conservatory, Ninety-sixth Avenue and 96A Street, (403) 496–8755. Open daily. Admission charged. Four pyramid-shaped glass buildings containing plantings of the arid, tropical, and temperate climatic zones; the fourth structure has changing exhibits.

Provincial Museum of Alberta, 12845 102nd Avenue, (403) 453–9100. Open daily. Admission. Provincial Museum tells the story of Alberta's natural and human history—paleontology, zoology, Amerindian cultures, fur traders, and settlers.

Rutherford House, 11153 Saskatchewan Drive on the University of Alberta campus, (403) 427–3995. Open year-round. Admission. Home of Alexander Cameron Rutherford, the first premier of Alberta. Restored and furnished to its early 1900s appearance. Costumed interpretive guides. This is an impressive mansion for a "man of means and considerable influence"—which Rutherford clearly was.

Great Divide Waterfall, located on the High Level Bridge, 109th Street, (403) 496–8400. Niagara Falls in miniature during the summer holiday weekends.

***Edmonton Queen* Riverboat Company,** (403) 424–2628. A 145-foot (44-m) Mississippi-style riverboat cruising along the North Saskatchewan River. Five cruises a day May to October.

Ukrainian Canadian Archives and Museum of Alberta, 9543 110th Avenue, (403) 424–7580. Open year-round. Donations are accepted. The largest Ukrainian museum in Alberta.

Ukrainian Museum of Canada (Alberta Branch), 10611 110th Avenue, (403) 483–5932. Open May to August. Free. Displays of beautiful, embroidered tablecloths; wood carvings; hand-painted Easter eggs; ceramics; sculptures; and paintings.

Valley Zoo, 134th Street and Buena Vista Road, (403) 496–6911. Open year-round. Admission is charged. Many different animals displayed in their natural habitats. Amusement rides for children.

Edmonton's Klondike days celebrate the city's heritage. ➤

Accommodations

Edmonton has accommodations ranging from deluxe to budget. There are places to stay along all major routes leading to the city. The deluxe hotels at city center are among Canada's finest. For additional suggestions, contact your travel agent or auto club, or call Edmonton Tourism, (403) 496–8400; (800) 463–4667.

Sheraton Grande Edmonton Hotel, 10235 101st Street, (403) 428–7111; (800) 263–9030. One of Edmonton's top hotels. Located in city center and adjoining Edmonton Centre shopping mall, this Hilton offers fine service and many luxurious amenities, elegant dining, an indoor pool, and saunas. Expensive.

Westin Hotel, 10135 One-hundreth Street, (403) 426–3636; (800) 228–3000. City center location. Fine service and amenities, gourmet dining, indoor pool, and exercise facilities. Expensive.

Crown Plaza/Château Lacombe, 101st Street at Bellamy Hill, (403) 428–6611; (800) 227–6963. A modern, circular tower structure in city center. Dining at La Ronde, a revolving restaurant. Expensive.

Fantasyland Hotel, at West Edmonton Mall, (403) 444–3000; (800) 661–6454. Moderate to expensive.

Mayfield Inn, 16615 109th Avenue, (403) 484–0821; (800) 661–9804. Excellent accommodations and service. Indoor pool, health club, trade center, four racquetball courts. Dining room, lounge, and live entertainment. Moderate.

Other Fine Places to Stay

All the places listed below offer fine accommodations and many amenities, such as swimming pools, dining rooms, and lounges; some have nightclubs.

Renaissance Edmonton, 10155 105th Street, (403) 423–4811; (800) 423–4811. Expensive.

Econolodge, 10209 One-hundreth Avenue, (403) 428–6442. Inexpensive to moderate.

Mayfair Hotel, 10815 Jasper Avenue, (403) 423–1650. Moderate.

Royal Inn West Edmonton, 10010 178th Street, (403) 484–6000; (800) 661–4879. Five blocks from the West Edmonton Mall. Full service. Moderate.

Dining

In Edmonton cuisine, the emphasis is on Alberta beef, which in my opinion is the best in North America. Fancy continental and hearty ethnic cuisines are also the pride of Edmonton's chefs.

Japanese Village, 10126 One-hundreth Street, (403) 422–6083. Traditional Japanese dishes prepared at your table; also has a sushi bar. Moderate to expensive.

La Ronde Revolving Restaurant, at the Crowne Plaza/Château Lacombe, (403) 428–6611. This restaurant gives you views of the city "from the top," while you dine on prime roast beef, steak, or a fancy continental dish. Moderate to expensive.

The King and I, 8208 107th Street, (403) 433–2222. Voted the city's best Thai restaurant. Inexpensive to moderate.

Syrtaki Greek Island Restaurant, 16313 111th Avenue, (403) 484–2473. Bright, Greek island setting. Inexpensive to moderate.

Mirabelle Restaurant, 9929 109th Street, (403) 429–3055. Continental cuisine. Moderate to expensive.

La Boheme, 6427 112th Avenue, (403) 474–5693. French cuisine located in a historic setting. Moderate to expensive.

Bones, 10220 103rd Street, (403) 421–4747. Ribs, burgers, prime rib. Casual and robust eating. Inexpensive to moderate.

Ginger, Etc., 11003 124th Street, (403) 452–2282. Authentic northern- and southern-style Chinese. Casual. Inexpensive to moderate.

That's Aroma, 11010 101st Street, (403) 425–6708. A new restaurant whose menu is devoted to garlic dishes.

Entertainment

The Citadel Theatre, 9828 101A Avenue; for ticket and schedule information, call (403) 426–1820. This is a beautiful, modern complex of several theaters. Plays are performed in the Shoctor, Rice, and Maclab theaters. The Tucker Amphitheatre in the Lee Pavilion is set amidst indoor gardens that have 4,000 tropical plants, a reflecting pool, and a 30-ft (9-m) waterfall.

Jubilee Auditorium, Eighty-seventh Avenue and 114th Street, is the home of the Edmonton Opera; for performance dates and ticket information, call (403) 427–2760.

The **Francis Winspear Centre For Music** is a new $35 million, 1,800-seat concert hall located adjacent to the Citadel Theatre and

Churchhill Square, the cultural hub of downtown Edmonton. Home of the Edmonton Symphony Orchestra. (403) 429–1992.

Shopping

If you want to spend hours of enjoyable shopping, go to the West Edmonton Mall, which not only is the largest in the world but also combines amusements and theme parks—enough diversions to keep you busy for several days. It's one of the city's great attractions (see the description on page 232). In city center, the Edmonton Centre Mall has a large number of shops, from glitzy to budget-busting boutiques.

The following are interesting shops for gifts:

Bearclaw Gallery, 10403 124th Street. Canadian Indian and Inuit arts and crafts.

Alberta Crafts Council Gallery, 10106 124th Street, (403) 488–6611. A collection of local and provincial crafts.

Northern Images Gallery, West Edmonton Mall, Inuit and Native art and clothing.

Professional Sports

Edmonton Oilers, five-time Stanley Cup champions (1984, 1985, 1987, 1988, and 1990), play at Edmonton Coliseum, 118th Avenue and 74th Street. For game dates and tickets, call (403) 451–8000.

Edmonton Eskimos, of the Canadian Football League, play at Commonwealth Stadium, 11100 Stadium Road. For game dates and tickets, call (403) 448–3757.

Edmonton Drillers Soccer Club, 10233 Ninety-six Avenue, (403) 471–5425. Indoor professional soccer from November to March at the Edmonton Coliseum.

Thoroughbred and harness racing, at Northlands Park, 115th Avenue and Seventy-ninth Street. Call (403) 471–7379 for racing dates.

Canadian Finals Rodeo, at Edmonton Coliseum, 118th Avenue and Seventy-fourth Street. Call (403) 471–7210 for dates.

Edmonton Trappers, of the Triple-A baseball Pacific Coast League, play at the new Telus Field, 10233 Ninety-sixth Avenue, (403) 429–2934.

Recreation

Edmonton offers visitors a wide assortment of recreational activities and venues—golf, tennis, swimming pools, family recreation centers, health clubs, ice-skating, and so on. Your hotel concierge or guest relations person will be happy to offer suggestions and make arrangements.

Traveling from Edmonton to Alaska or Yellowknife

If you are traveling from Edmonton to the Yukon, the Northwest Territories, and/or Alaska, take Highway 43, which begins just west of the city, via the Yellowhead Highway 16. Continue on Highway 43 until you reach the town of Valleyview (a more scenic but longer route is Highway 2 from Edmonton via Lesser Slave Lake to Valleyview or Grande Prairie). At Valleyview, turn west on Highway 34, which will take you to Grande Prairie. From here, take Highway 2 to Dawson Creek, British Columbia; it is at Dawson Creek that the Alaska Highway officially begins. From Dawson Creek, follow Alaska Highway 97 North to Highway 4 and/or 2, via Whitehorse, in the Yukon and thence to the state of Alaska.

To reach Yellowknife, the capital of the Northwest Territories, from Edmonton, take Highway 43 North to Valleyview, then Highway 35 North, which connects with Northwest Territories Highway 1. Highway 1 West will take you to Highway 3 North (around the southwest shore of Great Slave Lake) and then on to Yellowknife via Highway 4 East.

CHAPTER 8

Touring Saskatchewan

Regina · Saskatoon

Saskatchewan in Brief

Although wheat is grown in all three prairie provinces (Alberta, Saskatchewan, and Manitoba), Saskatchewan can claim the title of Breadbasket of Canada. If you are in the province just before harvesting, you can stand in the middle of a field and it will seem as if for countless miles in every direction there is only a seamless, thick carpet of burnished gold. Here is part of the great wealth of Canada. Here is food for the nation itself and for people all over the world. Just as the Atlantic and Pacific are awesome and inspiring in their particular ways, so, too, is the vast ocean of Saskatchewan's wheat-laden prairie land.

When traveling east or west across Canada, many tend to rush through Saskatchewan. But Saskatchewan is full of surprises and delights, and it reveals these only to those who make the effort to discover them. There are two brilliant cities, national parks and historic sites, rodeos and Indian powwows, lakes and rivers for swimming and fishing, and more varied cultural offerings than you would have time to sample.

The human history of the province is one of noble men and women from many different backgrounds who shaped and made productive a land that was not easy to tame. The first inhabitants of

Saskatchewan were the native peoples—Chipewyan, Cree, and Assiniboine. In the north their culture developed around hunting such animals as the moose and the caribou; in the south they hunted buffalo.

One of the first whites to come into this region was Henry Kelsey. Kelsey, an employee of the Hudson's Bay Company, explored the Saskatchewan River in 1690. In the decades that followed, other explorers left their footprints on Saskatchewan soil, and their visions motivated others—Pierre Gaultier de Varennes de La Vérendrye, Peter Pond, David Thompson, Peter Fidler, Sir John Franklin, Dr. John Richardson, John Palliser, and Henry Hind.

Several key events in the nineteenth century radically changed the development of Saskatchewan: Canadian Confederation in 1867; the relinquishing by the Hudson's Bay Company of lands in Saskatchewan to the federal government of Canada in 1869; the founding of the Northwest Mounted Police in 1873 to establish and maintain law and order in the Canadian West; through treaties, the confinement of the native peoples into reserves; the final defeat in 1885 of the Métis; the building of the transcontinental railroad connecting Saskatchewan to the rest of Canada; and the Dominion Lands Act, which opened up the land to homesteading and immigration. And the immigrants came in droves: Doukhobors, Ukrainians, Germans, Hutterites, Mennonites, Scandinavians, French, Americans, Chinese, and many others. They came to this fertile part of Canada fleeing religious and/or political persecution or simply because they saw better opportunities here than those available from where they came. With a great deal of hard work and sacrifice, they put plows to the tough prairie soil and made it bloom with an overflowing cornucopia of nutritious food.

On September 1, 1905, Saskatchewan entered the Canadian Confederation (the alliance of provinces that created a self-governing Dominion of Canada) and has been a province of significance ever since. Among the many outstanding men and women Saskatchewan has contributed to the national life of Canada was John George Diefenbaker. Although born in Ontario in 1895 and having lived some of his early years in the Northwest Territories, Diefenbaker (called Dief by his friends and foes) was more closely associated with Saskatchewan than with any other province. After distinguishing himself in local and provincial politics, he was elected in 1940 to the federal Parliament in Ottawa. As leader of the Progressive Conservative party from 1956 to 1967, Dief was constantly a thorn in the side of the ruling Liberals, but he had a high-minded vision for Canada, based on the values of democracy and self-reliance he had learned on the prairies and rough country of Saskatchewan. In 1957 he became prime minister of Canada, giving the nation its first Tory government since R. B. Bennett's (1930–35).

Diefenbaker was responsible for the first wheat sales to the People's Republic of China, the momentum that eventually led to the Canadian Charter of Rights, and the granting of the native people's right to vote in federal elections. His stand against apartheid led to South Africa's leaving the Commonwealth of Nations in 1961. In 1963, the Liberals regained control of the federal government, but not by much. John Diefenbaker, the man from Prince Albert who was frequently ridiculed by those with different ideas—including President John F. Kennedy—passed away in August 1979. As his funeral train slowly went from Ottawa to Saskatoon, Canadians and others around the world mourned a giant who had done much for others and remained true to his vision.

Another noteworthy Canadian from Saskatchewan, Jeanne-Methilde Sauvé (née Benoit), born at Prud'homme, was the first woman in the nation's history to be appointed (in May 1984) governor-general. As governor-general, Madame Sauvé, previously a journalist and politician, represented the queen (Elizabeth II) in Canada and as such held the highest government position in the country, although without the considerable executive powers of the prime minister, who is elected by House of Commons members of the majority party.

Saskatchewan is also a province of many natural wonders. Its Cree name is Kisiskatchewan, "the river that flows swiftly," namely the Saskatchewan River. The province—651,900 square kilometers/251,700 square miles—is wide open and almost the size of Texas. To the north, Saskatchewan borders the Northwest Territories; to the south, the states of Montana and North Dakota; to the west, Alberta; and to the east, Manitoba. Prairies dominate much of the landscape in the south; parklands, in the center—a transitional zone of farms and rolling terrain with forests; and thousands of square miles of Precambrian wilderness, with more lakes and streams than an angler could enjoy in several lifetimes, in the northern portion. Winters, even in the southern portion, can be very cold. Summers, however, are typically warm, dry, and pleasant. The hottest temperature ever recorded in Canada was 45°C/113°F, occurring in the southern part of the province. During June, July,

and August the weather is perfect for all kinds of outdoor recreation. Moreover, during the summer just about every town and city has festivals, rodeos, ethnic events, heritage days, or cultural happenings.

The North and South Saskatchewan, the Assiniboine, and the Churchill are the province's major river systems, and they all flow in a northeasterly direction and empty into Hudson's Bay. The largest lakes in northern Saskatchewan are Athabasca, Lac la Ronge, Cree, Wollaston, Reindeer, Churchill, and Peter Pond. There are more than 100,000 throughout the province, and the many beaches, such as Waskesiu in Prince Albert National Park, are good places to cool off or get a terrific tan. Cypress Hills in southeast Saskatchewan (1,392 m/4,564 ft) is the highest point of land between Labrador and the Rockies.

The province has approximately one million inhabitants. Regina is the capital and second-largest city; Saskatoon is slightly larger. Canada's only training academy for the Royal Canadian Mounted Police is located in Regina.

The economy is based on agriculture, mining, manufacturing, construction, oil and petroleum, and tourism. The province produces 60 percent of all wheat grown in Canada, and more than half of the world's known recoverable potash reserves (used in making fertilizer) are located here.

Saskatchewan Tourism

To get the best out of traveling in Saskatchewan, use the province's information and travel-planning assistance services, both of which are available free of charge. The folks at **Tourism Saskatchewan** will answer your questions, make suggestions, and send you free maps and brochures. If you are interested in destination attractions, accommodations, fishing, hunting, canoeing, white-water rafting, mountain biking or bike touring, houseboat charters, hiking, nature tours, outfitting organizations, or wilderness lodges, ask for the booklet *Saskatchewan Vacation Guide* or the *Saskatchewan Fishing and Hunting Guide,* which have everything you need to know (plus maps).

◄**The first people of Western Canada are those who have lived here for thousands of years. Their progeny keep the unique cultures alive, sustaining themselves and teaching us how to live in harmony with nature.**

247

Saskatchewan tourism literature describes the many provincial parks and the facilities they provide to the public. The main provincial parks in Saskatchewan are Cypress Hills, Danielson, Saskatchewan Landing, Douglas, Buffalo Pound, Echo Valley, Katepwa Point, Rowan's Ravine, Pike Lake, Good Spirit Lake, Duck Mountain, Greenwater, Meadow Lake, the Battlefords, Narrow Hills, Lac la Ronge, and Moose Mountain. Most of these parks have campgrounds that provide electricity and other conveniences (Katepwa Point has no camping, and Nipawin has no electric sites).

Other free guides from Tourism Saskatchewan that you may find useful are *Saskatchewan Accommodation, Resort, and Campground Guide* (including camping, hotels/motels, and farm vacations), *Events Guide, The Angler's Guide,* and *The Hunting and Trapping Guide.*

Tourism Saskatchewan can be reached throughout the year at (800) 667–7191; Regina area, (306) 787–2300.

Tourism Saskatchewan has five visitor reception centers located at strategic border crossings across the province that are open mid-May to September:

Fleming on Highway 1 East
Langenburg on Highway 16 East
Maple Creek on Highway 1 West
Lloydminster on Highway 16 West
North Portal on Highway 39 South on the U.S.–Canada border

Useful Information

Time zone: Central
Area code: 306

Saskatchewan Special Events

Saskatchewan has a great variety of festivals and special events. Some, such as rodeos, are familiar. Others, such as bee beard competitions, snowmobile grass drags, and world bannock championships (a Russian game played with horse-ankle bones), are just plain strange but are terrific fun. Here's a sampling of some of the best special events taking place in the province during the summer vacation season:

May

Kinsman International Band and Choral Festival, Moose Jaw, mid-May
Yorkton Short Film and Video Festival, Yorkton, late May to early June
Vesna Festival, Saskatoon, early May
Thoroughbred Racing, Saskatoon, mid-May to October

June

Mosaic, multicultural celebration, Regina, early June
Folk Festival, Regina, mid-June
Yellowhead Arabian Horse Show, Yorkton, mid-June
Model Air Plane Show, Moose Jaw, mid-June
Western Canada Farm Progress Show, Regina, mid- to late June
World Championship Chicken Chariot Races, Wynyard, late June
Frontier Days/Regional Fair and Rodeo, Swift Current, late June to early July
Bazaart (arts and craft sale), Regina, mid-June
SaskTel, Saskatchewan Jazz Festival, Saskatoon, mid-June
Humboldt Summerfest, Humboldt, late June

July

World Championship Gopher Derby, Eston, beginning of July
Heritage Wagon Trek (pioneer wagon trip and festival), Foam Lake, early July
Trial of Louis Riel (dramatic reenactment), Regina, July through August
Shakespeare on the Saskatchewan Festival, Saskatoon, late July to late August
Saskatoon Exhibition, Saskatoon, early to mid-July
Wood Mountain Stampede (oldest continuous rodeo in Canada), Wood Mountain, early July
RCMP Sunset Retreat Ceremonies, Regina, July to mid-August
Saskatchewan Handcraft Festival, Battleford, late July
Yorkton Threshermans Show and Seniors Festival, Yorkton, late July to early August
Prince Albert Exhibition, Prince Albert, late July
Saskatchewan Air Show (one of the largest air shows in North America, featuring the famed Snowbirds precision-flying team) Moose Jaw, mid-July
Big Valley Jamboree, (country-and-western music), Craven, mid-July
Northwest Territorial Days, North Battleford, mid July

August
Standing Buffalo Indian Pow-Wow, Fort Qu'Appelle, mid-August
Craven Valley Stampede (largest chuck-wagon races in the world), Craven, mid-August
Piapot Indian Pow-Wow, Cupar, mid-August
Folkfest (large ethnic festival), Saskatoon, late July
Chautauqua '93, Moosejaw, late August
Buffalo Days, Regina, early August
Saskatchewan Premier's Cup, Nipawin, mid-August
Royal Red Arabian Horse Show, Regina, late August
Western Canada Old Time Fiddling Championship, Swift Current, early October

September
Regina Dragon Boat Festival, Regina, early September
Lumsden Duck Derby, Lumsden, early September
Cowboy Poetry Gathering/Western Art Show, Maple Creek, late September

October
COA Finals Rodeo, Lloydminster, late October
Chokecherry Festival, Lancer, early October

November
Canadian Western Agribition, Regina, late November
Saskatoon Fall Fair, Saskatoon, mid-November
Agribition Rodeo, Regina, late November

National Parks

Grasslands National Park, located in the south central part of the province, two separate sections on the border of Montana; access to the western section is via Highway 4 through the town of Val Marie. For more information, contact Superintendent, Grasslands National Park, Val Marie, Saskatchewan S0N 2T0. Landowner permission required for access in some areas; for more information call (306) 298–2257.

Grasslands National Park was established in 1981 to protect a special ecosystem of rolling terrain covered with spear grass and other vegetation and inhabited by pronghorn antelope, prairie rattlesnakes, sage grouse, prairie dogs, and a variety of birds, including the threatened Ferruginous Hawk and Burrowing Owls. This is the only preserve of its kind in North America. Before extensive human settlement, this prairie ecosystem covered thousands of square miles of the continent. Within the proposed park boundaries are also the Killdeer Badlands, a sinking fault and the site where in 1874 Sir George Mercer Dawson made the first recorded discovery of dinosaur remains in this area. This was once a prime buffalo-hunting area for Plains Indians and the Métis. In 1876, Chief Sitting Bull and his Sioux people found temporary refuge here from the U.S. Army after the battle of Little Bighorn. The area surrounding the park boundaries is the former site of the Wood Mountain Northwest Mounted Police post, the Jean-Louis Legaré Trading Post; the Fort Walsh–Wood Mountain Trail runs through the area, including within park boundaries. Today, farming and ranching operations surround the park. As yet there are few visitor facilities in the park; its main function is to protect a vastly diminished ecosystem. There are, however, tourist services in the town of Val Marie; call (306) 298–2257.

Prince Albert National Park, located due north of Saskatoon, can be reached via Highway 2 North from the city of Prince Albert. Highways 263 and 264 lead to the entrance of the park, as well as to some of the key areas within it. For more information on facilities and services, contact Superintendent, Prince Albert National Park, Box 100, Waskesiu Lake, Saskatchewan S0J 2Y0; (306) 663–5322.

Located in the center of the province, Prince Albert National Park, named in honor of Queen Victoria's beloved consort, is a vast, oblong-shaped ecological bridge between the aspen parkland of central Saskatchewan and its vast northern forest. Prince Albert has many lakes, streams, and bog areas and supports abundant wildlife—badgers, coyotes, black bears, otters, elk, deer, moose, loons, bison, pelicans, foxes, wolves, lynx, caribou, ospreys, and eagles. The three largest lakes are Waskesiu, Crean, and Kingsmere, which along with the many other lakes are favorites with anglers; perch, walleye, whitefish, trout, and northern pike are among the species waiting to be caught. The town of Waskesiu Lake, on the shores of the lake bearing the same name, is a resort community catering to anglers, boaters, campers, swimmers, and those seeking the solitude and beauty of the park. One early naturalist, author, and orator who lived in this wilderness was Archibald Stansfield Belaney. Taking the name of Grey Owl and believing himself to be the son of a Scottish father and an Apache mother, this eccentric Englishman became immortal for his work in the cause of conservation and as author of *The Men of the Last Frontier, Pilgrims of the Wild, The Adventures of Sajo and her Beaver People,* and *Tales of an Empty Cabin.* Grey Owl's writings on the beavers he raised—Jellyroll and Rawhide—became almost as famous as he. To those of us urban and suburban dwellers, Grey Owl said, "You are tired with years of civilization and I come to offer you, what? . . . a single green leaf." Grey Owl's cabin, at Lake Ajawaan (a 19.5-km/12-mi hike from the end of Highway 264), is preserved. You can visit it and hear his voice in a gentle breeze, "I offer you . . . a single green leaf."

Prince Albert National Park offerings include interpretive programs; campgrounds at Beaver Glen, Narrows, Trapper's Lake, Namekus, Sandy Lake, and Kingsmere Lake; swimming from the park's main beach at Lake Waskesiu, as well as at all other lakes except Lavalle; an eighteen-hole golf course in town plus another eighteen-hole course outside the park limits via Highway 264; bike rentals; hiking trails; canoe rentals and canoe routes; horseback riding; and fishing with a park permit.

In **Waskesiu Lake** take advantage of the following:
Paddlewheeler Tours, (306) 663–5253
Nature Centre, open June through August, (306) 663–4522
Country Crafts, (306) 764–7575
Accommodations include the following:
Lakeview Hotel, (306) 663–5311. Open May 1 to October 1. Dining room. Moderate.
Haywood Inn, (306) 663–5911. Year-round, luxury rooms, self-contained suites, licensed dining room. Moderate to expensive.
Chateau Park Chalets, (306) 663–5556. Year-round self-contained chalets. Moderate to expensive.
Kapasiwin Bungalows, (306) 663–5225, May 1–October 15. Modern cabin accommodations. Moderate to expensive.
Skyline Motel, (306) 663–5461. Efficiency units. Moderate.
The city of **Prince Albert,** the gateway to the national park, has many attractions of interest:
Diefenbaker House, 246 Nineteenth Street West, (306) 764–2992 or 953–4863. Open mid-May to September. Free.
Grace Campbell Art Gallery, in the John M. Cuelenaere Library, 125 Twelfth Street East, (306) 763–8496. Open throughout the year. Free.
Also visit the **Nisbet Church, Prince Albert Forest Nursery, Prince Albert Historical Museum,** and historic **La Colle Dam.**

Accommodations are listed below:
Madison Inn, Sixth Avenue, (306) 922–9595. Moderate.
Imperial 400 Motel, Highways 2 and 3, (306) 764–6881.
Moderate.
Comfort Inn, Second Avenue and Marquis Road, (306)
763–4466; (800) 228–5150. Moderate.
Marlboro Inn, 67 Thirteenth Street, (306) 763–2643; (800)
661–7666. Moderate.
Prince Albert Inn, 3680 Second Avenue, (306) 922–5000;
(800) 922–5855. Moderate.

National Historic Parks

Fort Walsh National Historic Site, (306) 662–3590, open mid-May
to mid-October, near the Alberta-Saskatchewan border, can be
reached via the Trans-Canada, then south on Highway 271 from
Maple Creek (adjacent to Cypress Hills Provincial Park, an important attraction and recreational area in itself). For more information, contact Superintendent, Fort Walsh National Historic Park,
P.O. Box 278, Maple Creek, Saskatchewan S0N IN0.

In 1873 the Cypress Hills Massacre took place in this region,
known as Whoop-up Country, because of the frenetic trading and
whiskey drinking that went on here. A group of white wolf-hunters
got into a drunken brawl with Assiniboine Indians, and twenty of
the natives, as well as one of the wolf-hunters, were killed. With the
territory on the verge of anarchy, the Northwest Mounted Police established a base of operations here at Fort Walsh (named after the
first superintendent, James Walsh, a flamboyant but popular com-
mander). From Fort Walsh the Mounties chased out the American
whiskey traders operating in this region, secured the international
border, and protected the Indians. Superintendent Walsh offered
Chief Sitting Bull and his people refuge after the battle of Little
Bighorn.

Today, Fort Walsh has been re-created and looks as it did in
the late 1800s. A high wooden wall encircles and thus protects several buildings. Nearby are Solomon's and Farewell's trading posts.
If you let your imagination go, you can almost hear bugles, the
voices of troops, and the sounds of horses preparing to venture
forth and tame a wild land.

There are camping and recreational opportunities at the

45,000-acre **Cypress Hills Inter–Provincial Park,** (306) 662–4411.
Open throughout the year. Park entry fee is charged. Supplies and
various tourist services can be obtained in the town of Maple Creek.
Fort Battleford National Historic Site Area, (306) 937–2621,
is located near the town of Battleford, 153 km (92 mi) northeast of
Saskatoon. The best access is off Yellowhead Highway 16. For more
information, contact Superintendent, Fort Battleford National Historic Park, Box 70, Battleford, Saskatchewan S0M 0E0.

A great tragedy took place here in 1885—one of the battles of
the North West Rebellion, conducted by one of the proudest and
noblest leaders of the native peoples of the Plains, Cree Chief
Poundmaker, adopted son of a great Blackfoot leader, Chief Crowfoot. According to one version, this uprising occurred because by
the late 1880s the native Cree and Blackfoot peoples felt hemmed
in by the white settlements, whose inhabitants believed that the
land was for the taking, and by the building of the transcontinental
railroad. The Indians could no longer move freely across this limit-
less landscape; their primary food source—the buffalo—was disappearing; and their liberty was increasingly controlled by white
people's laws. According to another version, the battle took place
because of the traditional, long-standing antagonism between the
Cree and the Blackfoot.

At any rate, the Mounties built Fort Battleford to serve as a
buffer between the two tribes. From the fort the police could serve
the Indians by distributing annuity payments, enforcing the laws,
and settling them on reserves. In 1885, Chief Poundmaker and his
Cree warriors laid siege to the fort, where 112 men were sta-
tioned—the largest mounted police division then in Western
Canada. The Mountie Superintendent, Colonel William Otter, pursued Cree warriors from the fort and engaged them in battle at Cut
Knife Hill. Eight warriors were found guilty of murder by the
Mounties and were hanged within the stockade. Although pleading
innocent to treason and felony charges, Chief Poundmaker was
sentenced to three years in prison but was released after one year.
He died shortly thereafter, on July 4, 1886, and is buried on a hill
where the battle of Cut Knife was fought. Visit Chief Poundmaker
Historical Centre and Teepee Village where Poundmaker's grave is
on site. The museum features historical displays, artifacts, and
videos interpreting the history of Poundmaker's Cree Nation.

The residence of the commanding officer, General Frederick
Middleton, still stands within the stockade; it is furnished with deco-

rations and items from the late nineteenth century. Government House, a two-story building constructed in 1877, was the seat of the territorial capital. In the late 1870s Battleford was the capital of the North West Territories, as much of Western Canada was then known. In 1882, the capital was moved to Regina, which was right on the line of the transcontinental railroad and thus linked to primary urban centers throughout Canada.

Batoche National Historic Site, located 88 km (53 mi) northeast of Saskatoon on the east bank of the South Saskatchewan River, can be reached from Saskatoon via Highway 11 North to Highway 312. For more information, contact Site Coordinator, Batoche National Historic Site, Box 999, Rosthern, Saskatchewan S0K 3R0; (306) 423–6227.

Batoche was the site of the epic battle in 1885 between the Métis and the established authority of Canada. The Riel Rebellion was the closest Canada ever came to civil war, although there were other rebellions in the nineteenth century. The Métis considered themselves a distinct people, neither French nor Indian but a merging of cultures and genes from both. They were the sons and daughters of men who were French or Scottish voyageurs (trappers and/or haulers of furs) and women who were Cree, Saulteaux, or Ojibwa.

Batoche, located on the Carlton Trail, a trade route between Fort Garry, Manitoba, and Fort Edmonton, Alberta, was part of a larger district known as the Saint-Laurent Settlement. In the mid-1880s this territory was embroiled in conflict. There were battles between the Indians and the Northwest Mounted Police, and the Métis expressed grievances against encroachments by the Canadian federal government. Some took up arms against the Mounties, who moved in on the Métis at Batoche. General Frederick Middleton's force of 800 attacked 100 Métis and Indians. His first attack failed, but the Mounties bombarded the Métis with their artillery for about three days. On May 12, 1885, General Middleton and 130 of his men drew the Métis to an area where a Mountie Gatling gun was firing (a Gatling gun is on display at the park), and then a Mountie force rushed down on the Métis, who by this time were firing nails and stones from their rifles. Within a few minutes the battle was finished, and so was the Métis cause—at least from a military perspective.

Both Louis Riel, the charismatic political leader of the Métis cause, and General Gabriel Dumont, its military chief, escaped. Riel surrendered later and was eventually tried and convicted of treason in Regina. He was hanged in that city on November 16, 1885. The trial and the sentence have been controversial in Canada ever since, especially among those French-Canadians who believe that the severity of Riel's sentence was due as much to his ethnic background and religion as to the severity of his crime. Gabriel Dumont escaped to the United States, where he joined Buffalo Bill Cody's Wild West Show as a trick rifle shooter. General Middleton was found to have illegally confiscated furs from a Métis prisoner; he returned to England, where Queen Victoria made him Keeper of the Crown Jewels in the Tower of London. The Batoche Park has become a kind of shrine in Canada, expressing the struggle of a people both to retain their liberty and to preserve their culture. The park contains the church and rectory of Saint-Antoine-de-Padoue, the East Village, the battlefield itself, and General Middleton's encampment. An interpretive center features a presentation, diorammas, and displays.

Other locations associated with the North West Rebellion in Saskatchewan are Steele Narrows, Fort Pitt, Frog Lake, Frenchman Butte, Prince Albert, and Fort Carlton.

Motherwell Homestead National Historic Site is reached via the Trans-Canada east from Regina to Highway 10, at Balgonie and then 9 km (15.5 mi) south of Highway 10 on Highway 22. For more information, contact Area Superintendent, Motherwell Homestead National Historic Park, Box 247, Abernethy, Saskatchewan S0A 0A0; (306) 333–4801 or 333–2202.

William Richard Motherwell, one of many settlers from Ontario who contributed considerably to the development of Saskatchewan, created an oasis of refined civilization on his prairie lands. He named his estate Lanark Place, after Lanark County in Ontario. The Italianate-style mansion he built in 1897 was of cut fieldstone with a double-pitched gambrel roof; this became one of the most popular architectural styles for the nouveaux riches on the prairies. Motherwell had a distinguished career as cofounder and president of the Territorial Grain Grower's Association at Indian Head. He was the province's first minister of agriculture and, as a member of the House of Commons in Ottawa, served as federal minister of agriculture. The mansion, buildings, and grounds ("the homestead") have been being restored to reflect the peak period of Motherwell's career.

Saskatchewan's Ukrainian Connection

Ever since the lands of Saskatchewan were opened for settlement in the late nineteenth century, people from all over the world have come to the province to start new lives. One ethnic group that has contributed much to the development of Saskatchewan, particularly in agriculture, is the Ukrainians, who for the most part came to this part of Canada from the Bukovyna and Halychyna regions of the western Ukraine. In many ways, the terrain and climate of the prairies were not unlike the fertile steppes of the Ukraine. Just as the Ukraine was the "breadbasket" of the old Soviet Union, so, too, is Ukrainian Canada the breadbasket here.

Along with their commitment to the land, the Ukrainians have contributed aspects of their rich culture to Canada. You can experience this influence in their beautiful onion-dome churches, Byzantine or Latin rituals, and elaborate decorations or icons; in their festivals; and most particularly in their exuberant dancing groups, which have thrilled audiences throughout the world. You can visit Ukrainian places of interest (museums, churches, schools) located along or near the Yellowhead Highway 16 from Lloydminster at the Alberta border to North Battleford, Radisson, Saskatoon, Wynyard, Foam Lake, Sheho, Insinger, Theodore, Yorkton, and Rokeby near the Manitoba border (admission charges, if any, and hours are individually posted). Even in some small communities, don't be surprised to see two Ukrainian churches, one aligned with the Orthodox hierarchy and the other with the Roman Catholic Church. In Saskatoon, visit the **Musée Ukraina Museum,** 202 Avenue M South, (306) 244–4212. Open throughout the year. Donations are accepted. This museum has 2,000 artifacts describing the Ukrainian culture in Europe and in Canada.

Saskatchewan's Special Attractions

The treasure chest that is Saskatchewan requires exploring and discovery. You won't be disappointed with the new experiences and perceptions you'll find. The following is just a sampling of what a few Saskatchewan communities have to offer.

Wanuskewin Heritage Park, 3 km/2 mi north of Saskatoon, just off Highway 11, (306) 931–6767. Open year–round. (See page 272.)

Manitou Springs Mineral Spa, 6 km/4mi north of Watrous, located at Manitou Beach, south central Saskatchewan. One of the oldest and best-known resorts in Western Canada. Manitou Beach has long been a popular destination because of the supposed curing properties of briny Little Manitou Lake, known as the lake of "healing waters" by early Plains Indians. The spa is connected to a resort hotel. (306) 946–2233; (800) 667–7672. Open daily.

In Gravelbourg (reached via the Trans-Canada and Highway 58), a French-Canadian cultural center on the prairies, visit **Our Lady of Assumption Cathedral,** Main Street, (306) 648–3322. Open throughout the year. Beautiful interior with paintings by Charles Maillard. Built in 1918, it has been declared a Provincial Historic Site.

Stop in Maple Creek, on the Trans-Canada near the Saskatchewan-Alberta border, to see the **Old Timer's Museum,** 218 Jasper Street, (306) 662–2474. Open year-round. Admission is charged. This is the oldest museum in the province, with a fine collection of pictures and artifacts of the native people and early settlement.

Moose Jaw is located on the Trans-Canada. Legend says that during the 1800s a Red River cart (a wagon mounted on two large wheels that was better able to traverse the rough and soggy ground than other vehicles of the times) broke down in this area and was fixed by an Englishman using a moose's jawbone. Impressed Indians named the place Moose Jaw, and the name has stuck ever since. The most popular and believable theory notes the warm, prevailing winds and concludes that Moose Jaw is derived from "moosegaw," a Cree word meaning "warm breezes." Today, Moose Jaw, on the line of the transcontinental railroad and the Trans-Canada Highway, is one of the province's largest cities, with an economy based on agriculture and industry. Moose Jaw is home to **Saskatchewan Air Show** in mid-July, featuring the Snowbirds, a precision-flying team. Visit the **Temple Gardens Mineral Spa Hotel and Resort,** 24 Fairford Street E, (306) 694–5055; (800) 718–7727. Open year-round, this

In many parts of Saskatchewan, the second language, after English, is ▶ **Ukrainian. Here in Western Canada the cultural mosaic shines with ethnic diversity and concord.**

geothermal mineral spa features indoor and outdoor pools fed by naturally heated therapeutic mineral water, a spa salon with massage therapy, and a spa shop.

In St. Victor (reached via Highway 2), visit **St. Victor Petroglyphs Historic Park,** (306) 694–3659, which features rock carvings made by ancient native peoples. Open throughout the year. Free. **Wood Mountain Post Historic Park,** in Wood Mountain on Highway 18, (306) 694–3659. Open end of May to September. Reconstructed buildings have displays on the lives of the Sioux Indians and the Northwest Mounted Police in this area of the province. **Wood Mountain Stampede,** held in early July, is the oldest continual rodeo in Canada.

Worth a visit is **Eastend,** a small town nestled in the Frenchman River Valley on Highway 13. Tour the **Eastend Fossil Research Station,** which features a world-renowned Tyrannosaurus Rex skeleton excavated in 1994–95—one of only a dozen or so such skeletons in the world. Open year-round. Admission. (306) 295–4144.

In Esterhazy (reached via Highways 16, 80, and 22), stop at the **Kaposvar Historic Site Museum,** (306) 745–2692. Open mid-May to mid-October. Free. Here is the site of the first Hungarian colony in the province, settled more than a hundred years ago. The museum complex contains a pioneer homestead, a barn, a smokehouse, a school, and various artifacts.

Fort Qu'Appelle can be reached via Highway 10, east of Regina. Located in the beautiful Qu'Appelle Valley is **Fort Qu'Appelle Museum,** Bay Avenue and Third Street, (306) 332–6443. Open July to September. The museum is joined to an original 1864 Hudson's Bay Company post and displays Indian artifacts, Hudson's Bay Company articles, pioneer photos, and more.

The lovely Qu'Appelle Valley runs almost across the central/southern part of the province. The name Qu'Appelle has been adopted by the Cree and means "Who calls?" This is a wonderful touring area of productive farms, meandering rivers and streams, many lakes, and fine parks for the recreational pleasure of visitors. If you have extra time, a sojourn through Qu'Appelle would be most worthwhile. In a very real sense, it does call the traveler and answers the Cree legend.

Visit the **National Doukhobour Heritage Village** in Veregin on Highway 5. Early homes reveal lifestyles and habits of pioneer Doukhobours. Included are a bathhouse and prayer room, a museum, barns, a blacksmith shop, and agricultural equipment.

Open year-round. Admission. (306) 542–4441.

Duck Lake Regional Interpretive Centre is in Duck Lake (reached via Highway 11), (306) 467–2057. Open throughout the year. Admission is charged. The museum features thousands of items related to the North West Rebellion and to pioneer life in this region. Also visit nearby **Fort Carlton Provincial Historic Park,** reached via Highway 212; (306) 467–4512. Open mid-May to September. This reconstructed stockade has buildings of a fur-trading post with furnishings from the 1800s. There are interpretive programs and walking trails. Stop, too, at **St. Laurent Shrine,** (306) 467–2212. Open June to September. Free. This structure was inspired by the shrine at Lourdes; pilgrimages are held once in July and once in August.

Fort Pitt Provincial Historic Park, is south of Frenchman Butte (reached via Highway 3), (306) 787–9573. Open throughout the year. Free. Interpretive panels tell the story of the fur trade. Nearby is **Frenchman Butte Historic Site,** where you can see gun pits used in the 1885 skirmish.

In Loon Lake (reached via Highways 55 and 26), visit **Steel Narrows Provincial Historic Park,** (306) 837–2092 or 787–2854, Open throughout the year. Free. The skirmish between the Cree and the Mounties, which was the last military engagement of the North West Rebellion, took place at this site.

The Battlefords—The city of North Battleford and its neighbor, the town of Battleford, form the Battlefords, a popular vacation spot in the historic heart of Saskatchewan. The two communities are linked by the largest bridge in the province, spanning the fast-flowing North Saskatchewan River. While in the Battlefords, be sure to stop at the following:

Allen Sapp Gallery, 1091 One Hundredth Street (306) 445–1760, in the old Carnegie Library. Open year-round, it's a public gallery that will open you to the sensitive and powerful images of the Northern Plains Cree through the art of renowned Cree artist Allen Sapp.

Golden Eagle Casino, north side of Highway 16, (306) 446–3833. A new casino features video lottery terminals, eight blackjack tables, roulette wheels, poker tables, and coin-in, coin-out slot machines.

Western Development Museum, at Highways 16 and 40, (306) 445–8033. Open April to September. Admission is charged. Exhibits tell the story of settlement and agricultural development, including demonstrations of farming techniques (summer only). Also here you can walk through the re-creation of a small town in the early twentieth century. **Northwest Territorial Days,** held in late July at North Battleford Exhibition Grounds near the museum features exhibits, entertainment, chuck-wagon races, chariot races, a fiddlers' hoedown, fiddlers' contest, parade, and demolition derby.

Regina: Queen City of the Prairies

What Makes Regina Special

The Cree name for Regina was Oskana, meaning "pile of bones." On the bank of Wascana Creek, near the present-day Legislative Building, the early Indians created a huge pile of buffalo bones as a religious landmark and oblation to the diety for successful hunts. The buffalo, or bison, was essential to their way of life and supplied them with nourishing food and with materials for clothing, shelter, and weapons.

Fur traders came through the Wascana area and settled for a time, only to move on when the prospect of riches beckoned elsewhere. The development of a permanent settlement at "Pile O' Bones" (the name of the first settlement) was made possible by the Northwest Mounted Police, who provided protection to the Indians from American whiskey traders and security for immigrants developing the region's agriculture. In 1857 the name was misunderstood and recorded as Wascana, by which name the creek has since been known. With the Canadian Pacific Railway's decision to build its main line across the southern prairies, the actual town site of Regina was established. Anxious to find a suitable territorial capital to replace Battleford, which was too far north of the proposed railway line, Sir John A. Macdonald—Canada's prime minister at the time—left the decision of the town location in the hands of the CPR. The Mounties provided the security needed for expansion of the Canadian Confederation across the prairies. Today, although the RCMP headquarters is in Ottawa, the only training academy for this elite force is in Regina.

In 1882 the city became the capital of the province of the Northwest Territories, which at that time encompassed much of Western Canada (later the prairie provinces and the Yukon Territory evolved out of this vast land area and entered Confederation). The name "Leopold" had been proposed for the town, but when

Princess Louise, wife of the governor-general, suggested "Regina" in honor of her mother, Queen Victoria, her suggestion was accepted.

In 1905 Regina became the official capital of the province of Saskatchewan. Today, it is a modern city of 180,000 persons, a center for agriculture, manufacturing, government, finance, medicine, tourism, education, transportation, and food processing. Although the dominant ethnic groups are British Isles and German, Regina is a cosmopolitan city in which many different cultures merge and contribute their own unique flavors and perspectives. The bottom line here, regardless of one's heritage, is good old-fashioned prairie friendliness.

How to Get to Regina

By Plane

The following major airlines provide daily service to Regina: Northwest Airlines, Air Canada, and Canadian Airlines. The Regina Airport is located in the southwestern part of the city. Its terminal has full facilities, including rental cars. Travelers from the United States can reach Regina via connecting flights.

By Car

Regina is located on the Trans-Canada Highway 1 in the southern part of the province. U.S. Highway 16 from Sidney, Montana, and U.S. Highway 52 from Minot, North Dakota, provide direct access to Regina. U.S. Highway 16 connects with Saskatchewan Highway 6 North, and U.S. Highway 52 connects with Saskatchewan Highway 39 to 6. If you are traveling the Yellowhead Highway 16 from Alberta, take Highway 11 south in Saskatoon, which will bring you directly into Regina.

By Bus

Regina Bus Depot, 2041 Hamilton Street. Greyhound has daily service to Regina from many destinations in Western Canada. For information on fares and schedules, call (306) 787–3340.

Saskatchewan Transportation and Moose Mountain Lines connect Saskatchewan communities.

How to Get Around in Regina

Regina is laid out in a logical grid pattern. Its two main streets, which bisect each other in city center, are Albert Street and Victoria Avenue. The heart of the city is Wascana Centre, which comprises the Legislative Building, the Royal Saskatchewan Museum, and other attractions, is located at Albert and College. Many of the biggest hotels are on or near Victoria.

Regina Transit provides bus service throughout the city; call (306) 777–7433. There are a number of taxi services in the city.

For additional information on the city, visit Tourism Regina, Highway 1 East, (306) 789–5099, or Tourism Saskatchewan at 1900 Albert Street, (306) 787–2300.

Touring Services

Ferry Boat Tours, thirty-minute cruises on Wascana Lake; (306) 522–3661.

Attractions

Royal Canadian Mounted Police Centennial Museum, Depot Division, Dewdney Avenue West, (306) 780–5838. Open throughout the year. Free. The RCMP museum is one of Regina's finest attractions. Here thousands of men and—more recently—women have been trained to be members of Canada's elite police force, highly respected throughout the country and the world. The standards to get in are high, and the training is comparable to that of the U.S. and Royal Marines. Mounties serve on highway patrols, as law officers in remote communities and areas, as security for political leaders, and as the nation's intelligence service.

The RCMP museum, officially opened by Queen Elizabeth in 1973, contains uniforms, weapons, flags, documents, and many other artifacts relating to the history and heritage of the Mounties. It has the uniform belonging to Superintendent Walsh, who gave refuge to Chief Sitting Bull and his people after the battle of Little Bighorn; exhibits on the mad trapper of Rat River; and the crucifixes that Louis Riel carried to his hanging here in Regina. Within the complex is also the chapel—the spiritual heart for the RCMP—

originally built as a mess hall in 1883. It is decorated with stained-glass windows depicting noble moments in the Mountie heritage and with flags from past campaigns, such as the North West and Indian rebellions; its baptismal font honors a comrade who fell at the battle of Cut Knife Hill. Outside, in Parade Square, is a monument to the *St. Roch,* an RCMP boat that was the first to sail through the Northwest Passage. The *St. Roch* is now permanently on exhibit in Vancouver at the Maritime Museum. There are other memorials as well. An old cemetery is nearby.

Be sure to attend the stirring Sergeant Major's drill parade, 12:45 P.M. weekdays, and the Sunset Retreat ceremonies, Tuesday evenings in midsummer.

Wascana Centre, bounded by Twenty-third Avenue, Albert Street, and College Avenue, (306) 522–3661, is the most beautiful part of Regina. It covers 2,500 acres, through which flows Wascana Creek, forming man-made Wascana Lake. Within the park are located some of Regina's most important attractions: the Legislative Building; a band shell and marina; Wascana Place, which features films and exhibits and provides tourist information; Wascana Waterfowl Park; the Royal Saskatchewan Museum; the Saskatchewan Centre; and the University of Regina. During the summer, live entertainment and boat cruises are offered. Picnic areas are provided, and walks through the beautifully landscaped park lead you past colorful flower beds. You can take a brief ferry ride to Willow Island, where there are picnic areas. Of all of Canada's provincial capitols, Saskatchewan's in Wascana Centre is the most beautifully sited in terms of the surrounding landscaping, extensive lawns, flower beds, and promenades and of its axis on Wascana Lake. The modern campus of the University of Regina is also within Wascana Centre, and you are welcome to stroll the grounds.

Legislative Building, in Wascana Centre, (306) 787–5357. Open throughout the year; tours (free). This fine, domed structure, in cruciform shape, imitates the architecture of eighteenth-century England and France, but it is also solidly North American. The rotunda area, jewel of the building, is faced with marble and decorated with a mural painted by Edward Morris. An art gallery here (open daily; free) displays portraits, photographs, and other objects relating to Saskatchewan history.

Saskatchewan Science Centre, Winnipeg Street and Wascana Drive in Wascana Centre, (306) 791–7914 or 352–5811 (recorded twenty-four-hour message), is Saskatchewan's number-one year-round family tourist attraction with eighty hands-on exhibits, demonstrations, and world-class visiting exhibits. Experience the Kramer IMAX Theatre.

Saskatchewan Centre of the Arts, Lakeshore Drive in Wascana Centre, (306) 565–0404. This modern facility is home of the Regina Symphony Orchestra. Other groups also present performances here—ballet, opera, top star talent, and so on.

Diefenbaker Homestead, in Wascana Centre, (306) 522–3661. Open mid-May to the first of September. Free. Dief's boyhood, three-room pioneer home is furnished with Diefenbaker family artifacts. It was moved to this site from Borden, Saskatchewan.

Royal Saskatchewan Museum, in Wascana Centre on the corner of College Avenue and Albert Street, (306) 787–2815. Open throughout the year. Free. The First Nations Gallery traces 10,000 years of aboriginal culture. The Earth Sciences Gallery depicts two billion years of geological evolution. A must-see attraction.

Regina Plains Museum, 1801 Scarth Street, fourth floor of historic Old Post Office downtown, (306) 780–9435. Admission is charged. Here are displays on the history of the Indians, Métis, and pioneers who lived in the Regina area. There are pioneer artifacts and period rooms, including a sod hut, schoolroom, kitchen, and parlor.

Government House, Dewdney Avenue at Connaught Street, west of Lewvan Drive, (306) 787–5726. Open throughout the year. Free. This was the official residence of Saskatchewan's lieutenant governors from 1891 to 1945. You are allowed to tour the rooms, whose period furnishings are elegant.

Saskatchewan Archives, 3303 Hillsdale near Saskatchewan Center of the Arts, (306) 787–4068. Open Monday through Friday. Free. Open to those seeking historical and genealogical information.

Art Galleries

Regina, for its size and distance from art centers like Montreal, Toronto, and New York, has a large number of galleries that feature outstanding art and crafts works by artists from the province as well as other areas of Canada and the world. Many of these works are for sale—perfect souvenirs that tend to appreciate in value with time.

MacKenzie Art Gallery, 3475 Albert Street, southwest corner of Wascana Centre, (306) 522–4242. Open year–round. Excellent collection of historical and contemporary works by Canadian,

American, and international artists. Gallery shop, cafeteria, 175-seat theater that stages *The Trial of Louis Riel* during the month of August.

Rosemont Art Gallery, Neil Balkwill Civic Arts Centre, 2420 Elphinstone Street, (306) 522–5940.

Accommodations

Hotel Saskatchewan Radisson Plaza, 2125 Victoria Avenue, (306) 522–7691; (800) 667–5828. After a $20 million renovation, this classic hotel has been restored to its original Georgian character. All 215 rooms, 26 suites, and amenity rooms and parlors are as fresh as when the hotel was first constructed in 1927. Expensive.

Sands Hotel & Resort, 1818 Victoria Avenue, (306) 569–1666; (800) 665–1666. The Delta Regina, one of Regina's top hotels, has a beautiful lobby, nice rooms, fine restaurants, and many amenities, plus a swimming pool and whirlpool. Moderate to expensive.

Regina Inn, 1975 Victoria Avenue, (306) 525–6767; (800) 667–8162. A good-value hotel, offering fine accommodations, dining, and health club. Its restaurants and lounges include the Courtyard, Reflections, Splendidos, and the Lauderdale's. Moderate to expensive.

Ramada Plaza Hotel, 19191 Saskatchewan Drive, (306) 535–5255; (800) 667–0400. A deluxe hotel located near the Convention Centre and downtown attractions. Excellent accommodations, restaurants, lounges, nightclub, three-story water slide, swimming pool, and other amenities. Moderate to expensive.

Regina Travelodge Hotel, 4177 Albert Street, (306) 586–3443; (800) 578–7878. Award-winning hotel, indoor waterslide, Oscar's Restaurant, Blarney Stone Irish Pub. Moderate.

Other Good Places to Stay

Chelton Inn, 1907 Eleventh Avenue, (306) 569–4600; (800) 667–9922. Moderate.

Imperial 400 Motel, 4255 Albert Street, (306) 584–8800. Moderate.

Landmark Inn, 4150 Albert Street, (306) 586–5363; (800) 667–8191. Moderate.

Howard Johnson's, 1717 Victoria Avenue, (306) 569–4656; (800) 446–4656. Moderate.

West Harvest Inn, 4025 Albert Street, (306) 586–6725. Moderate.

Seven Oaks Best Western, 777 Albert Street, (306) 757–0121; (800) 667–8063. Moderate.

Turgeon International Hostel, 2310 McIntyre Street, (306) 791–8165. Inexpensive.

YMCA, 2400 Thirteenth Avenue, (306) 757–9622. Inexpensive.

YWCA, 1940 McIntyre Street, (306) 525–2141. Inexpensive.

Dining

Diplomat House, 2032 Broad Street, (306) 359–3366. Elegant restaurant with steak at its best. Expensive.

Memories, 1711 Victoria Avenue, next to the Howard Johnson's, (306) 522–1999. Continental cuisine. Expensive.

Victoria's Regina Inn, Victoria Avenue and Broad Street, (306) 525–6767. Good food from an extensive menu; good service, ambience, and entertainment. Expensive.

C. C. Lloyd's, 1907 Eleventh Avenue, (306) 569–4650. The atmosphere re-created here is that of New York City in the 1930s. The dishes are traditional gourmet: veal Oscar, roast rack of lamb, chicken en croute, shellfish bisque with champagne, and aristocratic desserts—strawberry savarin and Grand Marnier cream. Expensive.

Neo Japonica Japanese Restaurant, 2176 Hamilton Street, (306) 359–7669. Convenient downtown location; offers irresistible tempura, sushi, teriyaki, and sukiyaki. Moderate to expensive.

Alfredo's Fresh Pasta, Old City Hall, Scarth Street Mall, (306) 522–3366. Best of Italian cuisine. Contemporary dining in a relaxed heritage setting. Moderate.

Chimney Restaurant, 2710 Montague Street, (306) 584–7777. Dine around the fireplace in Regina's only log cabin setting. Greek, ribs, and seafood. Moderate.

Park Place, next to the marina in Wascana Place, (306) 522–9999. Regina's only restaurant on the lake. Casual dining, picnic baskets, outdoor patio. Inexpensive.

Melrose Place, 4030 Albert Street, (306) 347–9999. Family restaurant, ribs, pizza, souvlaki, pasta, seafood. Inexpensive to moderate.

Entertainment

Call the following performing arts organizations for their schedules and ticket information (for information on current "hot" night spots and meeting places, ask your hotel concierge or guest relations person for recommendations):

The Saskatchewan Centre of the Arts, Lakeshore Drive in Wascana Centre, (306) 565-4500, is home for the Regina Symphony Orchestra, which plays in the 2,000-seat Centennial Theatre. Within this complex is Jubilee Theatre, used for recitals and dramatic productions.

The Globe Theatre, in Old City Hall, on Scarth Street, (306) 525-9553, is Regina's main stage for plays professionally produced.

Regina Little Theatre, 1077 Angus, (306) 352-5535.

Regina Summer Stage, 1077 Angus, (306) 522-9078.

Applause Feast and Folly Dinner Theatre, in the Regina Inn (306) 525-6767.

Professional Sports

Professional football: The Saskatchewan Roughriders play at Taylor Field, (306) 525-2181.

Amateur hockey: The Regina Pats play at the Agridome in Exhibition Park, (306) 527-0688.

Standardbred and harness racing, at Queensbury Downs in Regina Exhibition Park, (306) 757-2674.

Baseball: The Regina Cyclones play in the Prairie League of professional baseball, (306) 949-2255.

Recreation

Regina has many recreational opportunities for visitors—tennis, golf, swimming, jogging, horseback riding, water parks, and lots more. Your hotel concierge or guest relations person will be happy to offer suggestions and make arrangements for you.

Shopping

Regina has major shopping centers. Downtown, visit the **Cornwall**

Centre, which has a hundred stores, including two large department stores, Sears and Eaton's; the **Golden Mile Centre,** at Albert and Twenty-fifth; and the **Scarth Street Mall.** The **Galleria at Scotia Centre** has more than seventy stores and services. It is located at Hamilton and Eleventh. The city's two other large shopping centers, located on either end of Albert Street, are the **Northgate Mall** and **Southland Mall.**

Book and Brier Patch, 4065 Albert Street. The largest independently owned bookstore in Saskatchewan. The largest selection of books in Regina.

The **Children's Corner Bookstore,** 2335 Eleventh Avenue. Fun and educational books, toys, videos, games, and records for children.

Derek Olson Goldsmith, 2333 Albert Street. Custom-designed and handcrafted jewelry.

Saskatoon: Hub City of Saskatchewan

What Makes Saskatoon Special

Saskatoon, also known as the City of Bridges, is a fast-growing, modern city, but also one that has retained traditional prairie friendliness. Saskatoon, considered a hub city because of its transportation facilities, moves the province's grain, minerals, and lumber to customers in all parts of the globe. Among the fascinating architectural features surrounding Saskatoon—for that matter, in many places throughout the prairies—are the grain elevators by the side of the railroad tracks. These geometrically pleasing structures are the trademarks of the prairies.

Saskatoon was founded in 1882 by John Lake and his congregation of 113 Ontario Methodists. Granted 200,000 acres, the Methodists wanted to create a utopia based on their denomination's values, which include temperance. They called their new community Minnetonka, after a local lake. The community's name was later changed to Saskatoon, after "Misakwatomin," the Cree name for the purple berries that grow along the river. Unfortunately, utopias can survive as such only in isolation. Starting in the late 1800s, the migration into Western Canada of great numbers of people seeking land transformed Saskatoon into a more ethnically diverse community. Ukrainians, for example, who were expert grain farmers in the Old Country, were among the new people who produced food for millions from the rough prairie land. Meat processing and various kinds of manufacturing became important industries. Large deposits of potash and uranium, as well as reserves of petroleum and natural gas, were discovered and have been developed. Today, Saskatoon is a city of gleaming office towers, beautiful parks, and clean streets, and it has a thriving cultural life.

How to Get to Saskatoon

By Plane

Air Canada, Northwest Airlines, and Canadian Airlines provide daily service to Saskatoon. The Saskatoon Airport is located northeast of city center, via Circle Drive. Its terminal has full facilities, including rental cars.

The Western Aero Centre, (306) 652–9121, is a new facility for private, corporate, and business planes.

By Car

Saskatoon is located south of the geographic center of the province, on the trans-Canadian Yellowhead Highway 16. From Regina, the city can best be reached by taking Highway 11 North; from Prince Albert, Highway 11 South.

By Rail

VIA Rail provides service to and from Saskatoon. Call (800) 561–8630 in Canada or (800) 561–3949 in the United States.

By Bus

Greyhound provides bus service to and from Saskatoon and many other Western Canada destinations; Saskatoon Bus Depot, 50 Twenty-third Street East, (306) 933–8000.

How to Get Around in Saskatoon

Saskatoon is located on the South Saskatchewan River. The main streets of city center are Spadina Crescent, Queen Street, First through Fifth avenues, and Twentieth to Twenty-fifth streets. Saskatoon Transit provides bus service throughout the city, and there are taxi services. For information on the city, call Tourism Saskatoon, (306) 242–1206.

Touring Services

Northcote River Cruise, along the South Saskatchewan River, (306) 382–1166. Tours depart from their main dock behind the Mendel Art Gallery.

Saskatoon Cycling Club Tours, (306) 244–7332. Start from Mendel Art Gallery.

Attractions

Mendel Art Gallery, 950 Spadina Crescent, (306) 975–7610. Open throughout the year. Free. The Mendel is one of Western Canada's most important public art galleries. It was given to Saskatoon by Frederick Mendel, a German immigrant who made his fortune from meat packing. The permanent collection has works by Emily Carr, David Milne, Feininger, Utrillo, Chagall, and Pissarro. There are also significant traveling exhibitions throughout the year. The Mendel has a conservatory of rare plants and flowers as well as a gift shop.

Little Stone School House, on the University of Saskatchewan campus, (306) 966–8382. Free. This is Saskatoon's first school and the city's oldest public building. It was called the Old Victoria School.

Musée Ukraina Museum, 202 Avenue M South, (306) 244–4212. Open throughout the year. Donations are accepted. A superior collection of Ukrainian artifacts and arts and crafts.

Wanuskewin Heritage Park, 3 km (2 mi) north of Saskatoon, just off Highway 11, (306) 931–6767. Open year-round. New Indian heritage park interpreting 6,000 years of history. There are nineteen archaeological sites in a serene valley, many twice as old as King Tut's tomb. Cultural demonstrations, restaurant, art exhibit, amphitheater, buffalo-pound model, overnight tepee programs. Entrance fee.

Gordon Snelgrove Art Gallery, in the Murray Memorial Building at the university, (306) 966–4208. Features work by students and faculty from the art department and local artists. Open weekdays, 9:00 A.M. to 4:30 P.M.

Kenderdine Gallery, in the Agriculture Building at the university, (306) 966–6816. Exhibits historical and contemporary art from the university's permanent collection. Open weekdays, 11:30 A.M. to 4:30 P.M.

Saskatoon Western Development Museum, 2610 Lorne Avenue South, on Exhibition grounds, (306) 931–1910. Open throughout the year. Within this museum is a re-creation of a street, circa 1910, containing an early bank, stores, Chinese laundry, church, school, hotel, railroad station, pool hall, and theater. Walking down this street you really feel as if you're in boomtown Saskatchewan. There's also a gallery of Saskatchewan arts and crafts and a gift shop.

St. Thomas More Art Gallery, on the University of Saskatchewan campus, (306) 966–8953. Open from mid-September to mid-April. Free. Exhibitions of paintings by provincial and regional artists. Be sure to see the stunning Kurelek mural in the St. Thomas More Chapel. The late William Kurelek was one of Canada's most distinguished contemporary artists. His paintings of ordinary life were highly realistic and also highly mystical in a religious sense.

The Diefenbaker Canada Centre, on the campus of the University of Saskatchewan, (306) 966–8384. Open throughout the year. Free. Diefenbaker museum and archives. Dief's grave is next to the building.

Ukrainian Museum of Canada, 910 Spadina Crescent East, (306) 244–3800. Open throughout the year. Admission is charged. Displays on Ukrainian culture and family life in Canada.

Accommodations

Delta Bessborough, 601 Spadina Crescent East, (306) 244–5521; (800) 268–1133. Saskatoon's landmark hotel has the château-style exterior so characteristic of similar places throughout Canada. It has two fine restaurants—the Samurai Japanese Steak House and Garden's Bistro. There are a swimming pool, steam bath, exercise facilities, and many other services. Moderate to expensive.

Sheraton Cavalier, 612 Spadina Crescent East, (306) 652–6770; (800) 325–3535. This Sheraton has a wonderful complex of swimming pools, water slides, hot tubs, and other recreational facilities. It offers excellent accommodations, and fine dining. Moderate to expensive.

Radisson Hotel, 405 Twentieth Street East, (306) 665–3322; (800) 333–3333. This bright, modern hotel offers excellent accommodations and services. It has a swimming pool with a great water slide, a restaurant, and a health club. Moderate to expensive.

Ramada Hotel, 90 Twenty-second Street, (306) 244–2311; (800) RAMADA. This hotel, located downtown, across from the Centennial Auditorium, has a special executive section called the Commonwealth Club. Its top restaurant is R. J. Willoughby's. There are a swimming pool and other facilities. Moderate to expensive.

Other Good Places to Stay

Best Western Inn, 1715 Idylwyld Drive North, (306) 244–5552; (800) 528–1234. Moderate.

Country Inn & Suites, 617 Cynthia Street, (306) 934–3900. Moderate.

Imperial 400 Motel, 610 Idylwyld Drive North, (306) 244–2901. Moderate.

ParkTown Hotel, 924 Spadina Crescent East, (306) 244–5564; (800) 667–3999. Moderate.

Saskatoon Inn, corner of Circle Drive and Airport Drive, (306) 242–1440; (800) 667–8789. Moderate to expensive.

Travelodge Hotel, 106 Circle Drive West, (306) 242–8881; (800) 578–7878. Moderate.

The Sands and Golf Dome, 806 Idylwyld Drive North, (306) 665–6500; (800) 667–6500. Moderate.

YWCA, 510 Twenty-fifth Street East, (306) 244–0944. Inexpensive.

Dining

The Granary, 2806 Eighth Street East, (306) 373–6655. Prime rib is the house specialty, and the setting is prairie memorabilia.

Jamieson Street Restaurant, #3 305 Idylwyld Drive North, (306) 664–9555. Fine dining in a Victorian atmosphere. Located in the historic CPR station. Moderate to expensive.

Samurai Japanese Steak House, at the Delta Bessborough, (306) 244–5521. Here you can feast on hibachi steak or scallops—a shogun special that includes steak, chicken, and lobster—or a vege-

Saskatchewan has a variety of recreational facilities, including the most golf ▶ courses per capita of any place in North America. Saskatoon's Willows, pictured here, is one of many courses where the score is secondary to the scenery.

tarian platter of onions, green peppers, Japanese mushrooms, and other vegetables. Moderate.

Saskatoon Station Place, Idylwyld Drive and Twenty-third Street, (306) 244–7777. Located in an old railroad station, this is Saskatoon's most colorful restaurant. It features an extensive menu of goodies: ribs, shrimp, stuffed mushrooms, Greek salad, French onion soup, pork chops, lobster tails, halibut steak, stuffed sole, omelets, burgers, pasta, souvlaki, prime roast rib of beef, steaks, lamb, and more. Moderate.

Cheers Brew Pub, 32, 2105 Eighth Street East, (306) 955–7500. An in-house brewery featuring Southern Cajun specialties, Italian food, and smoked prime rib.

Boomtown Cafe, Western Development Museum, 2610 Lorne Avenue South, (306) 931–1910. Home-cooked specialties that include Saskatoon berry baking—all in a 1910 setting.

St. Tropez Bistro, 243 Third Avenue, (306) 652–1250. A touch of Europe here, featuring homemade soups, bakery, pasta, and salads; specials every day. Very popular place in town. Inexpensive.

Martini's, 410 Twenty-second Street East, top of the TD building, (306) 244–7770. Offers great food and panoramic views of the city and surrounding countryside. Moderate.

Blue Diamonds, 1428 Twenty-second Street West, (306) 652–6464. A tasty place for ribs, pizza, scampi, steaks, barbeque chicken. Inexpensive.

Taverna, 219 Twenty-first Street East, (306) 652–6366. Located in the heart of downtown and serving huge portions of Italian goodies—pasta, meats, and seafood. Inexpensive to moderate.

Entertainment

For suggestions on the currently popular night spots, dramatic offerings, and music events, ask your hotel concierge or guest relations person for recommendations.

Saskatoon Centennial Auditorium, 35 Twenty-second Street East, (306) 975–7777. A major venue for the city's performing arts groups and for visiting talent. Box office is 938–7800.

Other Saskatoon cultural groups include the **Saskatoon Symphony,** (306) 665–6414; **Saskatoon Youth Orchestra; Saskatoon Opera Society,** (306) 374–1630; **Saskatoon Jazz Society,** (306) 653–1421; **Persephone Theatre,** (306) 384–7727; **Twenty-fifth**

Street Theatre, (306) 664–2239; Greystone Theatre, (306) 966–5188; Gateway Players, (306) 653–1200; and the Shakespeare Festival, (306) 653–2300.

Sports and Recreation

Consult with your hotel concierge or guest relations person about recreational opportunities in the city—golf, tennis, jogging, family and water parks, and so forth.

Junior hockey at Saskatchewan Place, (306) 975–3155.

Shopping

Midtown Plaza, located in city center at First Avenue and between Twentieth and Twenty-second streets, has many shops and services, including an Eaton's department store. The Bay is nearby on Twenty-second and First. Scotia Centre, with twenty-five shops, is located downtown at Second Avenue South and Twenty-second Street.

The Trading Post, 226 Second Avenue South (306) 653–1769. Unique Canadian crafts, including Inuit carvings and Indian jewelry.

Homespun Craft Emporium, 250A Second Avenue South, (306) 652–3585. Quilts, quilting supplies.

Antique Cellar, 38 Twenty-third Street, (306) 244–0488. More than 3,600 square feet of quality antique glass, china, and collectibles from throughout Canada.

CHAPTER 9

Touring Manitoba

Winnipeg · Churchill on Hudson Bay

What Makes Manitoba Special

When you take a look at the map of Canada—that line of huge provinces from the Atlantic to the Pacific—you'll see that Manitoba is smack in the middle. Manitoba is like a keystone that cements the different blocks of an arch into a strong, symmetrical whole. Although Manitoba sits north of Minnesota and North Dakota, states usually associated with the American Midwest, in Canada the province is very much within the western region of the country. Manitoba was and still is considered the gateway to Western Canada when traveling from the east. Here is where Western Canada began for settlers, entrepreneurs, and developers from Ontario, Quebec, and Atlantic Canada and for the thousands of immigrants from many foreign countries seeking a new life in the New World.

Manitoba is a very large province—250,946 square miles (403,772 square kilometers) and the only one in Western Canada (excluding the Northwest Territories) that has extensive shoreline on Hudson Bay. In the province you can travel from southern wheat fields to northern wilderness areas where polar bears roam in large numbers. Manitoba has the largest lake—Lake Winnipeg—within its interior of any province in Canada. (The Great Lakes are not within the interior of any province but share shoreline and territorial waters with various American states.) Specifically, Manitoba

has both the Hudson Bay and the province of Ontario at its eastern border; the states of Minnesota and North Dakota on its southern edge (the forty-ninth parallel, the straight-line international border between Canada and the United States); Saskatchewan on its western border; and the Northwest Territories to the north.

In the southern portion of the province, where the majority of the one million Manitobans live, the climate is similar to that of the other prairie provinces—cold, invigorating winters and warm, pleasant summers. The climate in the south is so congenial, in fact, that agriculture flourishes: Wheat and other grains, vegetables, and fruits grow here. In the south, where Winnipeg, the province's capital, is situated, spring tends to come in sooner than in other places. Topographically, Manitoba is a relatively flat landmass, patterned over by many lakes and rivers. The land in the south has been extensively developed for agriculture; in the midsection it is thick with forests; and in the north the land is subarctic with boreal forests and tundra. The climate in the north during the summer, particularly near Hudson Bay, tends to be cooler than northern sections of Alberta and Saskatchewan, but it is a very attractive area to those interested in experiencing the particular ecology created by this climatic zone.

Human habitation in Manitoba has existed for thousands of years. The first Europeans to arrive and put down stakes were the fur trappers and traders of the Hudson's Bay Company, which established a post and fort at York Factory in 1682. Furs brought into York Factory from countless inland points of origin were placed on ships that sailed up Hudson Bay, through Hudson Strait, into the Atlantic, and on to markets in England (during the summer months Churchill had a direct link with Liverpool, England, 2,936 miles [4,698 kilometers] away). For close to 200 years, Manitoba, known as Rupert's Land (an appellation given to most of Western Canada in honor of Prince Rupert, one of the founders of the Hudson's Bay Company), was virtually a "factory" that produced furs for English merchants and European fashions. In 1812, however, the first Selkirk settlers, under the leadership of Thomas Douglas, Fifth Earl of Selkirk, arrived and, along with fur trading, began a serious effort at expanding agriculture, transforming the rich potential of the grass prairies. With burgeoning agriculture, stable communities were built and grew as more people, seeing potential for themselves in Manitoba, arrived and settled. Lord Selkirk formed a habitation of new hope called the Red River Settlement, composed mainly of dispossessed Scottish sharecropping farmers. Rupert's Land was sold by the Hudson's Bay Company to Canada in 1870, and in 1871 the first legislature of Manitoba met, consisting of twelve English-Canadian and twelve French-Canadian members. A year earlier, in 1870, Manitoba actually became the fifth province in the Canadian Confederation as a result of the Manitoba Act, which received assent from Queen Victoria.

Although the majority of Manitobans are of British extraction (Scots, English, Irish, Welsh), there are also sizable groups of French, German, Polish, Icelandic, and Ukrainian. The Mennonites, a German-speaking religious sect, are another large group. Many of the early French fur trappers and a smaller number of Scottish trappers married native Indian women. Their progeny became the Métis, who formed a colony at Red River, from which Louis Riel and his people launched a rebellion in 1869 and 1870 when the land was transferred from Hudson's Bay Company to the Canadian government. Métis settlements were in the Red River Valley, in and around Winnipeg, and the Métis influence continues to be strong in a number of communities in southern and central Manitoba.

Today Manitoba's economy is based on agriculture, mining (nickel and precious metals), hydroelectric energy, forestry, food processing, manufacturing, transportation, and tourism. Winnipeg, because of its central location, is a major transportation hub for all of Canada. The city is also well known throughout the world for its cultural life, particularly its Royal Winnipeg Ballet. For the vacation traveler, Manitoba has it all: a sophisticated city, significant history, beautiful scenery, many attractions and recreational opportunities, adventure north to the polar bears and Hudson Bay, and friendly people who say "Welcome!" in many different languages.

Manitoba Tourism

Travel Manitoba, the provincial government's tourism agency, provides this toll-free number for your use: (800) 665–0040, ext. SD8 (operative throughout the continental United States and Canada). Or you can write to Travel Manitoba, Department SD8, Seventh Floor, 155 Carlton Street, Winnipeg, Manitoba, R3C 3H8.

Travel Manitoba will provide free maps, brochures, and personal counseling on how you and your party can get the most out of your travels and vacation time in the province. Travel Manitoba has information centers at the following locations, open mid-May through early September:

Manitoba–U.S. border, at Highways 75 and 10

Manitoba-Ontario boundary, at the Trans-Canada Highway 1

Manitoba-Saskatchewan boundary, at the Trans-Canada Highway 1

Manitoba-Saskatchewan boundary at Highway 16

Downtown Winnipeg at the Travel Idea Centre at the Forks and the Manitoba–U.S. border at Highway 10 are open year-round.

Many local communities also maintain their own tourism information bureaus.

Touring Services

The following is a partial listing of companies that provide tours to the major attractions in Manitoba. For a complete listing, contact Travel Manitoba and ask for the *Manitoba Explorer's Guide.*

Churchill Wilderness Encounter, (204) 675–2248; one- to nine-day trips to the Churchill area to see wild birds, beluga whales, and local communities on Hudson Bay.

Great Canadian Travel Company, (204) 949–0199; sightseeing tour packages customized for groups and individuals.

Manitoba Country Vacations Association, (204) 436–2599; vacations on family farms.

North Star Tours, (204) 675–2629; trips to Churchill attractions and to Eskimo Point in the Northwest Territories.

Riding Mountain Nature Tours, (204) 636–2968; hiking, trail riding, mountain biking, birdwatching, and wildlife safaris in Riding Mountain National Park.

Fehr-Way Tours, (204) 989–7011. Escorted motor-coach tours of Manitoba.

Frontiers North, (204) 949–2050. Group tour packages of Manitoba.

Overland Canada Adventure Expeditions, (204) 866–3075. Adventure, nature, and cultural packages throughout the province.

Sea North Tours, (204) 675–2195; boat trips to Fort Prince of Wales on Hudson Bay and beluga whale watching.

Trailhead Outfitters, (204) 848–7649; trail-riding trips in Riding Mountain National Park.

Tundra Buggy Tours, (204) 675–2121; summer nature tours

of the Churchill area and fall expeditions to see polar bears.

Paddlewheel River Rouge, (204) 942–4500; British double-decker bus tours of the city of Winnipeg, including dining/dancing cruises.

Useful Information

Emergencies: Throughout the province, dial 911
Time zone: Central
Area code: 204

Manitoba Special Events

International Music Camp and Athletic Camp, Peace Gardens, all summer

Festival du Voyageur, St. Boniface, mid-February
Winnipeg International Airshow, Winnipeg, early June
Winnipeg International Children's Festival, Winnipeg, June
Manitoba Summer Fair, Brandon, mid-June
Red River Exhibition, Winnipeg, late June
La Fête de la Saint-Jean Baptiste, La Broquerie, late June
Trout Festival, Flin Flon, late June to July 1
National Strawberry Festival, Portage la Prairie, early July
Winnipeg Folk Festival, Winnipeg, early July
Highland Gathering, Selkirk, early July
Threshermen's Reunion and Stampede, Austin, late July
Sunflower Festival, Altona, late July
Northwest Round-up, Swan River, late July
Manitoba Stampede and Rodeo, Morris, mid- to late July
Opasqwayak Indian Days, The Pas, late August
Oktoberfest, Winnipeg, early to mid-September
Manitoba Fall Fair, Brandon, early November

Some of Manitoba's most entertaining and unusual festivals are held during the month of August:

Islending a dagurinn, the Icelandic Festival of Manitoba, takes place in Gimli in early August.

Canada's **National Ukrainian Festival** is held in Dauphin during the first week in August. The festival features stirring, beautiful, and wild Ukrainian dancing and singing; Old Country food; and traditional arts and crafts. One of the most impressive moments in the festival is Obzhynky, the Ukrainian harvest ritual in which an honored guest is presented with bread and salt, an ancient custom symbolizing warmth and hospitality. Another highlight is the enactment of a traditional four-phase Ukrainian wedding—the matchmaking, the engagement, the marriage, and the wedding feast—which in past times went on for several days.

Steinbach Pioneer Days, in Steinbach, held early in August, is a unique festival celebrating the Mennonite heritage in Manitoba with traditional foods, arts and crafts, demonstrations of pioneer life, and entertainment.

The **Canadian Turtle Derby,** in Boissevain, is held in mid-July and features the international turtle racing championships.

Frog Follies, Canadian national frog-jumping championships, are held in St. Pierre-Jolys in early August.

Folklorama, in Winnipeg, held for two weeks in early August, is Manitoba's great ethnic festival, in which Manitobans representing ethnic, racial, and cultural groups from all over the world celebrate their uniqueness and their contribution to the Canadian cultural mosaic. You visit pavilions located throughout the city, each one representing a different culture and featuring traditional foods, arts and crafts, and entertainment. In effect, you travel from country to country without ever leaving Winnipeg.

Winnipeg:
Where Western Canada Begins

What Makes Winnipeg Special

Winnipeg, located where the Assiniboine and Red rivers converge, is nearly equidistant from the Atlantic and Pacific oceans and 100 km/60 mi north of the U.S.–Canadian border where the states of Minnesota and North Dakota meet. Ever since the mid-1800s, Winnipeg has been known as the Gateway City to Western Canada, much in the same manner as St. Louis, Missouri, and the American West.

La Vérendrye, the French explorer and entrepreneur, set up a trading post called Fort Rouge here at the "Forks" in 1738. Thomas Douglas, Fifth Earl of Selkirk, a Scot with big ideas for his beleagured Highlanders, created the Red River Settlement in 1812. Saint-Boniface, one of the Métis settlements in this area, is now a part of Greater Winnipeg and is considered the largest center of French culture in Canada outside of Quebec. In 1816 the Seven Oaks Massacre took the lives of twenty pioneers in the Red River Settlement. Under Lord Selkirk's leadership, the colony again took hold, expanded, and became prosperous. The Red River (along with trails using the famous Red River carts, distinctive by their two huge wheels) became the main highway of commerce between Winnipeg and St. Paul, Minnesota. This interchange of business, ideas, and people became so intensive that some in the region were saying that Manitoba would become part of the United States. But Louis Riel's visions for his country and the creation of Manitoba as a province quashed any prospect of merging with the United States. Today, Winnipeg and St. Paul, Minnesota, share a sisterly relationship based on a common pioneering heritage.

In 1873, Winnipeg was incorporated as a city. Its growth boomed when in 1881 the transcontinental railroad came in, making Winnipeg the distribution center for almost all of Western Canada. (It still plays that role for the heartland of the country. If you take a VIA Rail trip across Canada—one of the great rail adventures of the world—Winnipeg will be the midpoint in your journey.) The city became the grain-market center for the prairies with the establishment of the Winnipeg Grain Exchange in 1887. What oil is to Calgary and cod is to St. John's, grain is to Winnipeg; it's the main commodity of economic prosperity for thousands of people. In 1919 the city went through the Winnipeg General Strike; social upheaval caused basic services to cease operating, stores and factories to close their doors, unemployment to soar, and extreme bitterness between fellow citizens to burst into violence. Just as the wounds from the strike were being soothed, Winnipeg became one of the many North American casualties of the Great Depression of the 1930s. The supply and human resource demands of World War II helped to boost Winnipeg's economy, and it has been on an upswing ever since because of the optimism, hard work, and intelligence of its citizens.

In the sphere of international culture, most people outside Canada may never have heard of Manitoba, but they surely know of the Royal Winnipeg Ballet, one of the foremost classical dance companies in the world. Sometimes it is difficult to reconcile in one's mind the ethos of the prairies with great cultural institutions, but in Winnipeg the blend works exceedingly well. In addition to dance, there's excellence in visual arts and in dramatic art.

Although the first people of Winnipeg were native Indians, French, Scots, Irish, and English, succeeding waves of immigrants seeking their fortune were Germans, Ukrainians, Poles, Dutch, Italians, Scandinavians, Hungarians, Jews, and Asians. As a result, Winnipeg, although English on the surface, is a merging of many nationalities into one people working together for the common good, yet distinct within their own noble heritages.

Today Winnipeg is a modern city that has been able to blend its historical heritage nicely with gleaming skyscrapers. Its population now numbers more than 616,000 people, who are employed in various industries and services: manufacturing, tourism, food processing, transportation, aerospace, electronics, government, medicine, and education. The standard of living is quite high here, with abundant cultural, educational, shopping, and recreational opportunities for residents and visitors.

When you arrive in Winnipeg, you are where Western Canada begins or ends. This is a significant geographical point, one also rich in human history, particularly as concerns the development of Canada as an independent nation-state. To stay awhile in Winnipeg is not only to absorb this significance but also to enjoy the treasures of a cultural oasis in a vast prairie land.

How to Get to Winnipeg

By Plane

Winnipeg International Airport is located a few miles west of Winnipeg city center; the terminal has full facilities: restaurant, lounge, gift and duty-free shops, and so on. Rental-car booths are also here. The following major airlines serve Winnipeg: Air Canada, Canadian Airlines, Air Manitoba, American Airlines, and Northwest, plus several regional carriers.

By Car

Traveling from Calgary and Regina, continue on the Trans-Canada Highway 1; from Edmonton and Saskatoon, stay on the Yellowhead Highway 16. Traveling from Ontario and Eastern Canada, take the Trans-Canada to Winnipeg. Coming north from Minnesota and North Dakota, use Interstate Highway 29 to the border and then Manitoba Highway 75, which will take you straight into Winnipeg.

By Rail

VIA Rail provides train service to and from Winnipeg. The terminal is located on Main Street near the Upper Fort Garry Gate. Call (800) 561–8630 for the toll-free VIA Rail number serving your area code. In Winnipeg, call (204) 944–8780 for schedule information and for fares and reservations. If you are traveling to Western Canada from the east, you have a choice in Winnipeg: to go due west to Regina, Calgary, Banff, Lake Louise, and Vancouver or northwest to Saskatoon, Edmonton, Jasper, and Vancouver.

By Bus

Greyhound provides bus service throughout much of Western Canada. The terminal is located at 487 Portage Avenue; (204) 775–8857 or (800) 661–8747.

How to Get Around in Winnipeg

Winnipeg is a very easy city to get around in. City center is laid out in a grid pattern. To the south of city center is the Assiniboine River and to the east are the Red River and the French-speaking community of Saint-Boniface. Portage Avenue and Main Street are among the primary streets. The provincial Legislative Building is located at Osborne and Broadway. If you require additional information regarding your stay in the city, call Tourism Winnipeg at (204) 943–1970 or (800) 665–0204, or visit its facilities at 320–325 Forks Market Road or at the airport.

Winnipeg Transit operates bus service throughout most of the city; call (204) 986–5700 for information.

The following companies provide taxi service: Duffy's, (204) 775–0101; Yellow, (204) 942–7555; Preston Limousine, (204) 633–6715; Grosvenor, (204) 947–6611; and Unicity, (204) 947–6611.

Attractions

Centennial Centre, opposite City Hall, north of Portage and Main, (204) 956–1360, encompasses the Planetarium, the Museum of Man and Nature, Manitoba Theatre Centre, terraced gardens, and fountains.

Museum of Man and Nature, 190 Rupert Avenue at Main Street, (204) 956–2830. Open throughout the year. Admission is charged. This exceptional museum, part of the Manitoba Centennial Centre complex, includes the Planetarium—call (204) 943–3142 for information. The museum contains fascinating exhibits depicting Métis on horseback hunting buffalo, the life of the prairie farmer, the geological history of the province, the role of Hudson's Bay Company in the exploration and development of Manitoba, the ecology of the grasslands, and human settlement of the prairies. Its planetarium presents exciting shows describing the wonders of our cosmos.

The Exchange District, a several-block area in city center. This visually and architecturally rich district has a fine collection of turn-of-the-century commercial buildings that have been preserved and restored: Massey-Harris Building (1885), Bate Building (1883), Traveller's Block (1907), Imperial Dry Goods Block (1899), Confederation Life Building (1912), Pantages Playhouse Theatre (1913), J. H. Ashdown Warehouse (1895), the Donald H. Bain Building (1899), Telegram Building (1882), and Canadian Imperial Bank of Commerce (1910). Also in this historic district are many fine shops, restaurants, clubs, and theaters.

Also in this area are the Centennial Concert Hall, Warehouse Theatre, Manitoba Theatre Centre, and Pantages Playhouse Theatre. Guided walking tours of the district start from the Pantages Playhouse entrance, 180 Market Avenue.

Winnipeg has a rapidly growing **Chinatown,** in the area of King and Princess streets and James and Rupert avenues, where there are restaurants serving savory Cantonese, Szechuan, and Peking dishes; custom tailors; Oriental gift shops; and herb shops.

Aquatic Hall of Fame, Pan-Am Pool Building, 25 Poseidon Road, (204) 284–4031. Open throughout the year. Free. This hall of fame honors Canadians who have distinguished themselves in aquatic sports.

Legislative Building, at Broadway and Osborne; call (204) 945–5813 to arrange a guided tour. Open daily. Free. The architect of Manitoba's Legislative Building was Frank Worthington Symington from Liverpool, England. Gracing the dome of the building is a 240-foot-high heroic statue known as the *Golden Boy,* who holds a torch; it's one of the best-known symbols of the prairie spirit in Manitoba. The building, constructed of Manitoba's Tyndall stone and Italian marble, is considered one of the finest examples of neoclassical architecture in Canada. It stands on the bank of the Assiniboine River. On the beautiful grounds surrounding the capitol are statues of Queen Victoria, Louis Riel, and the great Ukrainian poet Taras Shevchenko. The mansion of the lieutenant governor is also on the grounds, and nearby is Memorial Park, a tranquil place during the summer.

Riel House National Historic Site, 330 River Road, (204) 257–1783. Open mid-May to the end of September. Free. Louis Riel, although tried and hanged for treason, is considered the father of the province of Manitoba (technically, from 1869 to 1870 he was known as the leader of the Provisional Government of Assiniboia and the North West). This house, which belonged to his family, has been restored and furnished to reflect the lives of the Riel and Lagimodiére families, who lived here in the late 1880s. Riel's grave can be found in the churchyard of Saint-Boniface Basilica.

Seven Oaks House, Rupertsland Avenue, (204) 339–7429. Open mid-May to Labour Day. Admission is charged. The oldest habitable home in Manitoba, this is a two-story log house built by John Inkster in 1851, with furnishings from that period.

Oseredok (the Ukrainian Cultural and Educational Centre), 184 Alexander Avenue East, (204) 942–0218. Open Tuesday through Sunday. Free. This ethnic museum has a fine collection of Ukrainian folk costumes, embroidery, weaving, decorated Easter eggs (*pysanky*), wood carving, and ceramics; also coins, stamps, and documents from the Ukrainian National Republic of 1918–21. There are a library of 40,000 volumes, an art gallery, and archives.

Centre Culturel Franco-Manitobain, 340 Boulevard Provencher, (204) 233–8972. Call for performance dates and prices. Home of these performing groups: Cercle Moliére (Canada's oldest continual French theater company); Les Danseurs de la Riviére Rouge (folk dance troupe); Le Cent Nons (young singers and musicians); and L'Alliance Chorale Manitoba, Les Blés au Vent, and Les Intrépides (choral groups).

Royal Canadian Mint, 520 Lagimodiére Boulevard, (204) 257–3359. Open May through September. Tours are offered, and you can see coins being produced for use as Canadian and foreign currency.

Assiniboine Park Zoo, Corydon Avenue West at Shaftsbury, (204) 888–3634. Open throughout the year. A fine zoo, with more than 1,200 animals, including North American species, a Siberian tiger, and a North China leopard. Kinsmen Discovery Centre is a hands-on science and nature display for children.

METRO WINNIPEG

Living Prairie Museum, 2795 Ness Avenue, (204) 832–0167. Open daily July to September. A natural prairie preserve of 200 native plants; tours during July and August.

Dalnavert Museum, 61 Carlton Street, (204) 943–2835. Open daily throughout the year. Free. This Victorian mansion belonged to Sir Hugh John Macdonald, the only surviving son of Canada's first prime minister; it is named after his mother's home in Aviemore, Scotland. Dalnavert has been restored to the beauty it had in 1895 and is open as a museum.

Queen's Own Cameron Highlanders of Canada Museum, 969 St. Matthews Avenue, (204) 786–2205. Open Mondays and Wednesdays. Free. Displays of the history of a famous Manitoba Scottish regiment that fought in World Wars I and II.

Royal Winnipeg Rifles Regimental Museum, 969 St. Matthews Avenue, (204) 783–0880. Open Tuesdays and Thursdays. Free. Weapons, uniforms, pictures, and artifacts of the oldest military unit in Western Canada.

The Tin Lizzie Car Barn, 10 minutes west of Winnipeg on Highway 26, (204) 864–CARS. A two-level barn filled with vintage and classic cars, related memorabilia, a car buff's shop, sweet shop, and diner. Operates year-round.

Western Canadian Aviation Museum, located in Hangar T2 at the airport, 958 Ferry Road, (204) 786–5503. Open throughout the year. Admission is charged. Here is an excellent collection of aircraft: Avro 504K, Vickers Vedette, Canada's first helicopter, Bellanca Aircruiser, Fokker Super Universal, North American Harvard, Vickers Viscount, DeHavilland Tiger Moth, and many others.

Saint-Boniface Museum, on avenue Taché, (204) 237–4500. Open throughout the year. Donations are accepted. This museum of French culture in the Red River Valley is housed in the oldest building in Winnipeg. Erected as a convent for the Grey Nuns in 1846, it later served as the first hospital, girls' school, orphanage, and seniors' home in Western Canada.

Ivan Franko Manor, 200 McGregor Street, (204) 589–4949. Open Monday to Friday. Free. A literary museum dedicated to the memory of the Ukrainian poet Ivan Franko.

Winnipeg Art Gallery, 300 Memorial Boulevard, (204) 786–6641. Open daily throughout the year. Call for hours and fees. An excellent example of contemporary architecture and the pride of the city; the gallery has more than 14,000 works of art in its permanent collection, including the largest display of Inuit (Eskimo) sculpture in the world. It also has a fine restaurant and a gift shop. The gallery was officially opened in 1971 by Princess Margaret.

University of Manitoba, off Pembina Highway on University Crescent; call the information center (204) 474–8346. Visitors are welcome to tour the campus of the oldest university in Western Canada. Bookstores, lectures, and exhibitions are open to the public.

The Forks, located at the junction of the Red and Assiniboine rivers, (204) 943–7752. Free. This historic site has been a meeting place for more than 6,000 years. Now it has shops, restaurants, food kiosks, archaeological-dig site, marina, and river walk.

Manitoba Children's Museum, at The Forks, (204) 956–1888. Admission is charged. Canada's top children's museum, this new facility allows children to create their own television broadcast, put on puppet shows, or make their own video images.

Crystal Casino, located at the historic Hotel Fort Garry in downtown Winnipeg, 222 Broadway, (204) 957–2600. Canada's first European–style luxury casino. "Smart dress" required.

Historic Churches

Saint-Boniface Basilica, 190 avenue de la Cathedrale in Saint-Boniface. The oldest Roman Catholic cathedral in Western Canada, original structure built in 1818. Here is one of the centers for French-Canadian life and culture in Western Canada. In the churchyard is the grave of Louis Riel, a hero of Western Canadian history.

St. James Church, Portage Avenue and Tylehurst Street. The oldest log church in Western Canada (1853).

St. John's Cathedral, 135 Anderson Avenue. The oldest Anglican church in Western Canada; original church structure on this site was built in 1820.

St. Nicholas Ukrainian Catholic Church, Main Street and St. John's Avenue. Byzantine architecture and interior decoration.

St. Paul's Anglican Church, Balderstone Road off Main Street. Built in 1825.

St. Vladimir and Olga Cathedral, 115 McGregor Street. Domed towers and ornate interior are noteworthy aspects of this Ukrainian house of worship.

Ukrainian Greek Orthodox Cathedral, 1175 Main Street. Byzantine domes are a dominant shape on the city's skyline.

St. Andrews, via Highway 9 North to St. Andrews Road. The oldest continuously used Protestant church in Western Canada.

Kildonan Presbyterian Church, Black Avenue and Main Street. The first Presbyterian church in Western Canada, built in 1853, still stands.

Knox United Church, 400 Edmonton Street. An attractive church, built in 1917 of Manitoba stone.

Parks

Assiniboine Park, Corydon Avenue West at Shaftsbury. Playgrounds, picnic sites, English garden, zoo, duck pond, miniature railroad, and Leo Mol Sculpture Garden.

Assiniboine Forest, Shaftsbury Boulevard and Chalfont Avenue. Trails give you access to view wildflowers, deer, and waterfowl.

Fort Whyte Centre for Environmental Education, 1961 McCreary Road, (204) 895–7001. Open throughout the year. Admission is charged. Resident waterfowl, lakes, marshes with floating boardwalks, stands of aspen, self-guiding nature trails, and naturalist-conducted walks.

Stephen Juba Park, west bank of the Red River, between

Alexander Dock and Provencher Bridge. A downtown river park and place where boats depart for tour cruises.

Kildonan Park, 2021 Main Street, on the Red River. Contains some of the largest trees still standing in the province; also has a public swimming pool, an outdoor theater, and a restaurant.

Fun Mountain Waterslide Park, on Murdock Road, east of the city, via the Trans-Canada or the Perimeter Highway, (204) 255–3910. Admission is charged. Features several exciting water slides, inner-tube slide, a giant hot tub holding 150 persons, and much more. A fun place for a young family.

Provincial Parks and Forests Near Winnipeg

Whiteshell Provincial Park, on the Manitoba-Ontario border, via Highways 312 and 44 off the Trans-Canada. Manitoba's first and largest provincial park features a number of hiking and natural history trails, camping facilities, and areas for canoeing, fishing (northern pike, perch, smallmouth bass, walleye, and trout), and hunting. At the Canada goose sanctuary in the park, during May and June, you can get close enough to see hundreds of goslings.

Agassiz Provincial Forest, on the north side of the Trans-Canada, east of Winnipeg. This is mainly a natural preserve, although there are areas where you can picnic.

Sandilands Provincial Forest, on the south side of the Trans-Canada, east of Winnipeg, directly opposite Agassiz Forest. Another forest preserve with picnic sites.

Spruce Woods Provincial Heritage Park and Forest, south of Carberry on the Trans-Canada, west of Winnipeg, has camping and hiking. Spirit Sands is a desertlike island surrounded by a cool stand of spruce trees. It also has lizards and cacti.

Birds Hill Provincial Park, northeast of Winnipeg via Highway 59. There are an aspen fitness trail, several natural history trails, a bike trail, camping facilities, horseback riding, and hiking.

Accommodations

Leading Hotels

The Lombard–CP Hotels, Two Lombard Place, (204) 957–1350; (800) 441–1414. Winnipeg's number-one deluxe hotel. Beautiful rooms with many amenities, fine service, gourmet cuisine in the Velvet Glove dining room, lounges, rooftop indoor swimming pool, and health club. Expensive.

Delta Winnipeg, 288 Portage Avenue, (204) 956–0410; (800) 268–1133. Located in city center and connected by a walkway to the city's largest downtown shopping complex, this Delta offers excellent accommodations with many amenities, as well as dining, entertainment, and an indoor swimming pool with a sun deck and view of the city. Its Signature's dining room offers good food. Moderate.

Crowne Plaza, good downtown location, close to the convention center, (204) 942–0551; (800) 465–4329. Excellent guest rooms with all amenities; fine dining rooms (the Market Grill is superb) and lounges; indoor and outdoor pools and an exercise facility; and many other features. Expensive.

Sheraton Winnipeg, 161 Donald Street, (204) 942–5300; (800) 325–3535. Excellent accommodations located in city center. Many rooms have a balcony and a minibar. Fine restaurants and lounges; twenty-four-hour room service; indoor pool and sauna. Moderate to expensive.

Other Good Places to Stay

All of the following have dining rooms and other amenities:

Best Western Carlton Inn, 220 Carlton Street, (204) 942–0881; (800) 528–1234. Moderate.

Ramada Marlborough, 331 Smith Street, (204) 942–6411; (800) 667–7666. Moderate.

Holiday Inn South, 1330 Pembina Highway 75 South, (204) 452–4747; (800) HOLIDAY. Moderate.

Holiday Inn Fort Richmond, 2935 Pembina Highway, (204) 275–7711. Moderate.

Radisson Suites Hotel, Winnipeg Airport, (204) 783–1700. Ten minutes from city center. Moderate.

Hotel Fort Garry, 222 Broadway, (204) 942–8251. Moderate.

Place Louis Riel All–Suite Hotel, 190 Smith Street, (204) 947–6961. Moderate.

Charterhouse Hotel, 330 York Avenue, (204) 942–0101. Moderate.

Dining

Winnipeg has an eclectic array of restaurants—from the elegant continental with a high-priced tab to match to casual ethnic eateries. The top hotels mentioned earlier also have excellent restaurants. Here's a sampling of what's in town:

Victor's, at the Ramada Marlborough, 331 Smith Street, (204) 947–1526. Elegant and romantic environment; excellent continental cuisine. Expensive.

Old Swiss Inn, 207 Edmonton, near the convention center, (204) 942–7725. Excellent cheese fondues and chocolate fondue; also fondue bourguignonne and *bunderfleisch.* Moderate.

Tiffani's, seventeenth floor, rooftop, at 133 Niakwa, (204) 256–7324. An elegant restaurant serving fine gourmet food, with great views of the city. Expensive.

Merteen's, fourteenth floor, 210 Oakland Avenue, (204) 334–2106. Another top restaurant, with panoramic views of the city. Flambé dishes are a specialty. Expensive.

Alycia's, 559 Cathedral Avenue, (204) 582–8789. Here you can dine like a Cossack on great Ukrainian cuisine for a song. Inexpensive.

La Vieille Gare, 630 rue des Meurons in Saint-Boniface, (204) 237–5015. This is one of Winnipeg's best French restaurants—veal dishes in various preparations, rack of lamb, steak with savory sauces, and *coquille* Saint-Jacques are but a few menu selections for a memorable feast. Expensive.

Oceana, 1910 Pembina Highway, (204) 261–0494. Delicious Chinese renditions of various seafoods; also various other regional Chinese cuisines. Moderate.

Velvet Glove, at the Westin Hotel, (204) 957–1350. An elegant dining room serving gourmet food. One of the best in the city. Expensive.

Red Lantern Steak House, 302 Hamel Street, (204) 233–4841. The name is a misnomer because this is a very special French restaurant in a vintage house. Excellent cuisine; special desserts. Moderate to expensive.

The Rib Room/Charter House, 330 York Avenue, (204) 942–0101. One of the city's favorite beef eateries—steaks, prime rib, and ribs are great here. Moderate.

Entertainment

As the cultural center of the prairies, Winnipeg has entertainment galore, from highbrow to wacky fun. Here are some possibilities:

The Royal Winnipeg Ballet, oldest and most famous ballet company in Canada; for information on performance dates and tickets, call (204) 956–0183. Performances are at the Centennial Concert Hall; during the summer, at Assiniboine Park.

Contemporary Dancers, 109 Pulford Street, (204) 452–0229.

Winnipeg Symphony Orchestra, (204) 949–3999, concerts held in the Centennial Concert Hall.

Westend Cultural Centre, 586 Ellice Avenue, (204) 775–1055; new theater for popular and folk music events.

Manitoba Opera Association, 121–555 Main Street, (204) 942–7479.

Rainbow Stage, (204) 942–2091; outdoor theater in Kildonan Park during July and August.

Manitoba Theatre Centre, 174 Market Avenue, (204) 956–1340.

Gas Station Theatre, 445 River Avenue, (204) 284–2757.

Prairie Theatre Exchange, Portage Place, 393 Portage Avenue, (204) 942–7291.

Le Cercle Moliére, 340 boulevard Provencher in Saint-Boniface, (204) 233–8053, plays in French and some bilingual productions.

Dine-and-dance cruises: Paddlewheel River Rouge Boat Cruises, (204) 942–4500.

Professional Sports

Thoroughbred and harness racing: Assiniboia Downs, twenty minutes east of city center, via Portage Avenue and Highway 101 (Selkirk exit); call (204) 885–3330 for racing schedules.

Professional football: Winnipeg Blue Bombers; call (204) 780–7328 for schedule and ticket information; games played at Winnipeg Stadium, 1430 Maroons Road.

IHL Hockey: Manitoba Moose play at the Arena: call (204) 987–PUCK for schedule and ticket information.

International Basketball Association: Winnipeg Cyclone, Winnipeg Convention Centre, (204) 925–HOOP.

Double-A baseball: The Winnipeg Goldeyes, (204) 982–2273, play at Winnipeg Stadium.

Recreation

The greater Winnipeg area offers horseback riding, golf, tennis, swimming, and many other recreational opportunities. Your hotel concierge or guest relations person will be happy to offer suggestions and make arrangements.

Shopping

Eaton Place, 234 Donald Street, in the heart of city center. More than 110 shops, services, restaurants, and the Cineplex Theatre under one roof. Eaton Place has just about everything you need and offers an attractive environment.

Osborne Village, on the south side of the Osborne Street Bridge near the Legislative Building. Sixty shops, restaurants, galleries, and services in restored buildings. Also here is the Gas Station Theatre.

Crafts Guild of Manitoba, 183 Kennedy Street, (204) 943–1190. Inuit and Indian crafts, handmade quilts, fashions, and jewelry.

Portage Place, three blocks on North Portage Avenue. One of the city's largest shopping places, with many stores and restaurants, as well as a giant-screen IMAX theater.

Global Crafts, 134 Plaza Drive, (204) 261–6381. An outlet for handicrafts from eighteen developing countries.

The Exchange District, in Old Market Square. Shops, restaurants, galleries, handcrafted goods, and nightclubs.

Manitoba's Special Attractions

Churchill on Hudson Bay

Although a prairie province, Manitoba has extensive shoreline on Hudson Bay, that immense inland sea that also touches the borders of Ontario, Quebec, and the Northwest Territories. During the summer, when the ice is out, you can sail from Manitoba to Greenland, Iceland, Ireland, and the British Isles. This is just the way the fur-trading entrepreneurs of the Hudson's Bay Company traveled more than 300 years ago. Prince of Wales Fort was built here in the eighteenth century to enforce the territorial sovereignty of the Hudson's Bay Company, and it still stands for the benefit of interested travelers. A plaque at the fort commemorates Samuel Hearne, who reached the Arctic Ocean through the Coppermine River in 1771.

In 1769 **Churchill,** named after the first Duke of Marlborough, was where the first astronomical observations were made in Canada. The displays of aurora borealis (northern lights) here are magnificent—some say the most intense illumination in the world. A railroad was completed in 1931 to connect Churchill with southern cities so that grain could be shipped more economically to international markets via Hudson Bay–Atlantic Ocean routes. This railroad is now also used by VIA Rail to transport tourists to Churchill. In the 1940s, the U.S. military had a base at Fort Churchill that was used first for air operations during World War II and later as a joint Canadian-American training and experimental facility. The base was closed in 1980.

The best-known Manitoba town on the Hudson Bay coast is Churchill, primarily because of the large number of polar bears that migrate to this area during the fall. *National Geographic* magazine and its television program have featured the polar bears of Churchill, and millions of people have come to know something of this area that way. Churchill was named not for Winston S. but for his equally famous forebear, John Churchill, first Duke of Marlborough. In addition to the polar bears, you can see caribou, beluga whales, four species of seals, Canada and snow geese, and close to 200 other species of birds. Wildlife photo opportunities are everywhere; telephoto lenses are recommended. In the case of polar bears, please heed all safety warnings. Although they look cuddly enough to hug, they've got nasty tempers, sharp teeth and claws, and no hesitation about attacking human beings who venture close to their space.

Some of the points of interest are Bird Cove for bird-watching; Eskimo Museum, with its excellent collection of carvings and artifacts; the Churchill Northern Studies Centre, conducting ecological studies; Cape Merry National Historic Site, a good place from which to see beluga whales; tundra tours on specially designed tracked or rubber-tired vehicles at the junction of three ecological zones—boreal forest, tundra, and taiga; a polar bear denning area, where cubs are born; and Prince of Wales Fort, a stone, star-shaped bastion built in 1731, with walls 40 feet thick. York Factory, an important historic site where Hudson's Bay Company established a post in 1682, is accessible only by air or boat. Artifacts from centuries of human habitation are in this remote region.

Wapusk National Park is Canada's seventh-largest national park, covering an immense lowland area of 11,275 square km south and east of Churchill. Wapusk is the Cree word for white bear, and is home to one of the largest known white bear denning sites.

The best way to get to Churchill and experience everything is to use the services of the appropriate tour companies listed on pages 282–83. There is no highway to Churchill (the highway stops at Thompson), and the only way to get here is by air or VIA Rail. The area is also known for sports fishing and for waterfowl and ptarmigan hunting; there are outfitters here who will take good care of anglers and hunters. In Churchill itself there are a curling rink, a public swimming pool, and a bowling alley; shops where you can purchase Native prints and carvings; restaurants; liquor stores; and churches. While in town, orient yourself to the attractions of the area by visiting Parks Canada at Bayport Plaza, (204) 675–8863.

For more information about Churchill, contact Travel Manitoba, (800) 665–0040, or the Churchill Chamber of Commerce, (204) 675–2022.

Accommodations are all in the moderate price range.

Churchill Motel, (204) 675–8853
Northern Nights Lodge, (204) 675–2403
Polar Inn, (204) 675–8878
Seaport Hotel, (204) 675–8807
Tundra Inn, (204) 675–8831

Western Manitoba

Riding Mountain National Park is located north of the Trans-Canada and the Yellowhead highways, via Highway 10 North, and approximately halfway between the border of Saskatchewan and Lake Manitoba. If you continue through the park on Highway 10, you will come to the town of **Dauphin,** where the famous National Ukrainian Festival is held each summer (see page 283). For more information on the park itself, contact Superintendent, Riding Mountain National Park, Wasagaming, Manitoba ROJ 2HO; (204) 848–7275.

Riding Mountain National Park (3,000 square km/1,150 square mi) has the distinction of being near the geographical center of Canada. The park has three distinct ecological zones: a deciduous forest; aspen and grasslands; and a boreal forest with spruce and fir. Each zone has self-guiding nature trails. Within the park are Lake Katherine, Whirlpool, and Moon Lake campgrounds. A visitor center conducting various interpretive programs is located in the town of **Wasagaming.** A campground and resorts, as well as supplies and services, can be found here. Enjoy golfing, horseback riding, canoeing, swimming, overnight backpacking, fishing, and tennis. Visit the bison herd numbering about thirty animals maintained on a range at Lake Audy.

Experience the rich traditions of the Anishinabe people with Anishinabe Camp at Lake Katherine. Camp in traditional teepees and dine on traditional Anishinabe foods.

Selkirk

Lower Fort Garry National Historic Park is twenty minutes north of the city of Winnipeg on Highway 9, (204) 785–6050 or (800) 442–0600 (in Manitoba). Open from mid-May to Labour Day. Lower Fort Garry was built in the 1830s as a Hudson's Bay Company post. It has been restored to reflect its role in the early days of fur trading and in the development of Manitoba. During your visit, you will see people in period costumes moving about and doing chores—baking scones and oatmeal cookies in outdoor ovens, loading carts with grain and produce, making tallow candles, and shoeing horses. You can poke around the restored buildings, view the historical exhibits, have a satisfying meal at the restaurant, and buy a gift from the prairies for the folks back home. A trip to this fort is a worthwhile excursion back into the early history of the province.

Visit the **Marine Museum of Manitoba,** in Selkirk Park at Eveline and Queen streets, (204) 482–7761. Open from mid-May to September 30. Admission is charged. This museum is dedicated to Manitoba's marine history and the preservation of vessels used on its waterways, such as the SS *Keenora,* a beloved passenger steamship; the CGS *Bradbury,* an icebreaker; and *Peguis II,* a dredge tender. Also in the park is a replica of the Red River ox cart, which helped to develop this part of Canada because it could more easily travel through mud. The replica is 22 feet (6.6 meters) high and 45 feet (13.5 meters) long. Selkirk has a waterfront area in which its fascinating maritime heritage has been preserved with period lighting, walkways, and signs.

Lake Winnipeg Area

From Selkirk you might want to explore some of the lower shoreline of Lake Winnipeg, via highways 8 and 9 on the west side or 59 on the east side. Traveling along the west side of the lake, you will come to **Gimli,** the largest Icelandic community outside the homeland. In Gimli (the name means "the great hall of heaven," from Norse legend) there are an Icelandic heritage museum, a giant statue of a Viking, and the annual Islending a dagurrinn (Icelandic Festival of Manitoba), which is held during the first weekend in August. In **Arnes,** just above Gimli, there's a plaque honoring Vilhjalmur Stefansson, the famous Arctic explorer, who was born here in 1879.

Continuing along Highway 8 will take you to **Hecla Provincial Park** (145 km/90 mi north of Winnipeg), whose islands stretch nearly across the narrows of Lake Winnipeg. This beautiful park features facilities for camping, hiking, tennis, fishing, and sailing. There's a large moose population; thick flocks of waterfowl, bald eagles, great blue herons, and western grebes mass here. The Icelandic influence is expressed in the Gull Harbour Resort and Conference Centre, a luxury accommodation within the park that is open throughout the year. For reservations and more information, call (800) 267–6700. Moderate. Also available are camping, B&B, and cabins.

A drive up the eastern shore of Lake Winnipeg, via Highway 59, will bring you to **Grand Beach Provincial Park.** This park has some of the finest sand beaches in North America. Shifting sand dunes here rise close to 30 ft/9 m in height. A lagoon behind them is a perfect habitat for pelicans, cranes, orioles, and finches. The park features camping, tennis, windsurfing, fishing, lake swimming, and an amphitheater program. Inexpensive accommodations are available in the nearby town of Grand Marais.

Southern Manitoba

In Steinbach, see the **Mennonite Heritage Village (Canada),** which can be reached via the Trans-Canada, east of Winnipeg, and then south on Highway 12, (204) 326–9661. Open from May to the end of September. Admission charged. This village museum is an excellent tribute to the heritage and accomplishments of Mennonite pioneers who settled in the Steinbach area in 1874. The village consists of early Mennonite farm buildings; farming machinery; a pristine, unadorned church for meditation and prayer; an obelisk monument to the early settlers; simple homes with period furnishings; and perhaps the most magnificent shingled windmill in all of Canada. There are demonstrations of farming activities, wagon rides, a barn restaurant that serves traditional Mennonite cooking, and a shop where you can buy souvenirs. A visit here is highly recommended.

South of Steinbach, near the Minnesota border, is Gardenton (reached via highways 59 and 209, south of Winnipeg). Here is **St. Michael's Ukrainian Orthodox Church,** the first Ukrainian Orthodox church built in North America in 1896. There are also a museum and a heritage village in town. Admission charged.

International Peace Garden, a U.S.–Canadian Masonic project near Boissevain, is located along the east boundary of Turtle Mountain Provincial Park (reached via Highway 10 south of Brandon on the Trans-Canada). Open mid-May to mid-September. Admission is charged. The International Peace Garden spans the border between Manitoba and North Dakota in the southwestern region. It honors the longest unfortified border in the world and is a symbol of the strong, warm, and enduring friendship that exists between the peoples of Canada and the United States. Within the park are beautiful flower gardens and extensive landscaped areas; a flower clock (at the entrance); the Peace Chapel; a fountain encircled by stone walls engraved with the writings of famous persons on the theme of peace; the Peace Tower, symbolizing the coming together of people from all parts of the world to form two great nations; and the Errick F. Willis Memorial Centre, which has arts and crafts exhibitions. During the summer the park is the site of the International Music Camp and the Royal Legion Athletic Camp.

CHAPTER 10

Exploring the Yukon and the Northwest Territories

The Yukon: Land of Dreamers

The first people of the Yukon settled here more than 50,000 years ago, perhaps considerably more. The two Amerindian tribes that now live in the Yukon are the Athapaskan and the Inland Tlingit. It is said that the first white person to penetrate the interiors of the Yukon was Robert Campbell, a Hudson's Bay Company fur trader.

In the Yukon Territory are five places that have become ingrained in North American mythology—the Klondike, Chilkoot Pass, White Pass (both passes are partly in Alaska), Dawson, and Whitehorse. In the late 1800s the Yukon was the site of the famous gold strikes, and "gold fever" drew thousands of people here from North America and other parts of the world. George W. Carmack and two Indian friends struck gold at Rabbit "Bonanza" Creek, a tributary of the Klondike River, in 1896. And the dreamers came here in great numbers, about 50,000 of them by 1899, all seeking a great fortune that would turn their lives around and make them as rich as J. P. Morgan. Enough did strike it rich to keep passionate fires burning in the minds of many others who would, after much struggle and hardship, fail. And along with the seekers of wild

dreams came the merchants, the bankers, the dance-hall women, and the preachers. Some stole the dreamers' purses, while others tried to save their souls. To survive in this country you had to be handy with your fists—to make your way through an often-cruel wilderness and to knock the other guy down before he could do it to you. To say that the heritage of the Yukon was wild, rough, and woolly is about as precise as one can get. This was, after all, where Jack London got his inspiration for novels of life and death in the North. But it was also much more. The Yukon was exerting personal courage and vision against all odds and sometimes winning. It was stranger helping stranger to keep going to survive. The traditions of fellowship are so strong here that one can't do better than have Yukon people as friends. It was a pioneering spirit that, when the gold fever finally cooled down, produced stable communities of hardy, creative people who took the long view of things, generation after generation. And so it is right now in the Yukon. Gold is still plucked from here, but heavy earth-moving equipment and sluice boxes have replaced the gold pan of yesteryear. The Yukon's true future lies with dreamers of a different sort, ones better educated and seeing more productive possibilities.

The Yukon, comprising 482,500 square km/186,000 square mi, is essentially a magnificent wilderness with gorgeous mountains, lakes, rivers, forests, and tundra. There is an abundance of wildlife here: bears, mountain goats and sheep, moose, caribou, many species of birds and waterfowl, wolves, and salmon. Sports hunters and anglers from all over the world come to the Yukon for prize trophies and for adventure. For such a vast area, though, there are only 30,000 people residing in the Yukon, mostly in the communities of Whitehorse (the capital), Dawson City, Beaver Creek, Faro, Ross River, Mayo, Watson Lake, Haines Junction, Teslin, and Carcross. They also live in tiny pioneering towns and, in the case of the Gwich'in, in the remote village of Old Crow accessible only by air.

The Yukon borders Alaska to the west and south, the Northwest Territories to the east, and British Columbia to the south along the sixtieth parallel. The Yukon extends north beyond the Arctic Circle and has well over 200 km (120 mi) of shoreline on the Beaufort Sea. Herschel Island in the Beaufort Sea is near the territory's most northerly point. Among the Yukon's many river systems, the Yukon River and the Porcupine River are two of the largest. Mount Logan (5,959 m/19,550 ft)—part of the St. Elias Range and located in Kluane National Park in the southwest corner of the Yukon, close to the

Alaskan border—is Canada's highest mountain and second in height only to Alaska's Mount McKinley, North America's highest peak.

The main highway access into the Yukon is through the town of Watson Lake on the Alaska Highway. Another route is the Inside Passage, delivering passengers to Skagway, Alaska, then on to Carcross, Yukon, and Whitehorse, along the Klondike Highway. Coming south from Fairbanks, Alaska, the town of Beaver Creek, Yukon, is a gateway at the western border. The Alaska and the Klondike are the Yukon's two main highways. Other roads, mostly gravel and with limited services, provide touring into various regions; the Dempster Highway will take you all the way to Fort McPherson in the Northwest Territories and beyond to Arctic Red River and Inuvik, all of which are on the Mackenzie Delta (where Mackenzie, one of Canada's great rivers, empties into the Beaufort Sea). The Yukon has a sophisticated highway system that makes driving easier than it is in Alaska or the Northwest Territories.

Summer days, especially during July, can be quite warm—up to 30°C/86°F (the average is between 10° and 20°C). One of the bonuses of visiting the Yukon during the summer—and for that matter, Alaska and the Northwest Territories—are the long days. Dawson City has almost twenty-four hours of sunlight each day in June and twenty hours in July; Whitehorse has twenty hours of light during June and eighteen hours in July. Unfortunately, the reverse is true during the winter: minimal daylight and temperatures that fall to minus 40°C. The very low humidity, though, makes the winter temperatures more tolerable. If you want a wilderness adventure along with your cross-country skiing, skidooing, dogsledding, or ice fishing, the Yukon is the perfect place for you to test your skills and resolve and have some fun in the process. Rock hounds will find prizes in the Yukon: hematite (from which the Alaska black diamond is made) in Hunker, Dominion, and Haggart creeks; agate (in its various forms) in the Carmack area; azurite, malachite, and chrysocolla (lapidary materials) in the Whitehorse Copper Belt area; garnet in the Von Wilzon Lake region; jasper along the Alaska Highway; and rhyolite in the Wheaton River Valley.

The Yukon: Some Basic Facts

The Yukon River begins near the Pacific Ocean and flows for 2,000 miles to the Bering Sea.

◀ There aren't many boundaries in the Yukon.

In the Yukon above the Arctic Circle, the sun never sets on June 21; it never rises on December 21.

The Yukon is 15 percent larger than the state of California, but it has only one person per 7 square miles (11 square kilometers).

Southwest Yukon has the largest concentration of grizzly bears in North America and the largest number of Dall sheep in the world.

More than $250 million worth of gold has been taken out of the Klondike over the years. (No wonder people got the itch to get there as fast as possible.)

How to Get to the Yukon

By Car

The southern border of the Yukon is 2,200 km/1,367 mi from Vancouver, British Columbia, via the Trans-Canada Highway 1 east to Cache Creek, then Highway 97 to the Alaska Highway. From Edmonton, Alberta, take the Yellowhead Highway 16 west to Highway 43 to Valleyview and Highway 34 to Dawson Creek and then the Alaska Highway—to the Yukon border, a distance of 1,600 km/994 mi. See pages 32–33 for safety and driving tips when taking the Alaska Highway. Much of the highway is paved with asphalt, although there are gravel sections. Other routes of entry into the Yukon are Highway 2 from Skagway, Alaska; Highway 3 from Haines, Alaska; Highway 2 from Fairbanks, Alaska; and the Stewart-Cassiar Highway 37 from southwestern British Columbia (a very scenic route but with few services; see page 180). The highways in this region are well maintained through all seasons, not just for visitors but for the very survival of the people who live here. A number of communities offer full services (fuel, supplies, accommodations) en route to the Yukon and through to Alaska—Siberia it's not. For reports on highway conditions, call Yukon Highways, (867) 667–8215 (twenty-four hours), and British Columbia Highways, (250) 663–4997.

By Plane

Daily jet-plane service is provided to Whitehorse from Vancouver and Edmonton by Canadian Airlines; several regional airlines also provide service in the Yukon and from Alaska. Charters, including Royal Airlines and Canada 3000, have Vancouver–White Horse flights from May to September. Direct flights from Frankfurt, Germany, May through September will start in 1998. Rental cars are available at the Whitehorse Airport.

By Boat

The following regional ferries provide access to the Yukon via Prince Rupert, British Columbia: British Columbia Ferries, (604) 669–1211, and the Alaska Marine Highway, operating out of Juneau, (907) 465–3941. The Alaska Marine Highway ferries stop at Haines, Skagway, and other Alaska ports, and travelers may then continue on to Whitehorse by private vehicle or bus. Costa, Cunard, Exploration, Holland America, Princess, Regency, and Royal Viking are all cruise lines that bring visitors to the Yukon. Check with your travel agent about the itineraries these cruise lines use for the Inside Passage of coastal British Columbia and Alaska.

By Train

The White Pass and Yukon Route provides scenic rail trips from Skagway, Alaska to Fraser, British Columbia, through the historic White Pass. Motor Coach connections are available from Fraser on to Whitehorse. For more information, call (800) 343–7373 or (907) 983–2217.

Tourist Information

For touring and camping information (brochures—especially helpful if you are driving along any of the routes mentioned earlier—and maps), write or call Tourism Yukon, Box 2703, Whitehorse, Yukon Y1A 2C6, (403) 667–5340.

Visitor Reception Centres, open from mid-May to mid-September, are located in Watson Lake, Carcross, Whitehorse, Beaver Creek, Haines Junction, and Dawson City.

Useful Information

Climate: Generally the summers in the Yukon are dry, pleasant, and comfortable.
Area code: 867.
Time zone: Pacific.

Touring Services:
Adventures, Fishing, and Hunting

These companies—Atlas Tours, (867) 668–3161, Gray Line Yukon, (403) 668–3225, and Rainbow Tours, (867) 668–5598—provide comprehensive tours of Whitehorse and Dawson City, the 176-km/110-mi scenic Klondike Highway (Whitehorse to Skagway), exciting Yukon River cruises, Yukon-Alaska cruises, and Pleasure Island salmon barbeques (freshly caught and alder-wood smoked and grilled). Rainbow Tours and Gold City Tours offer charter buses to the Arctic, from Whitehorse and Dawson City to Inuvik on the Mackenzie River Delta in the Northwest Territories north of the Arctic Circle. On this trip you also fly to Tuktoyaktuk, which is a traditional Inuit (Eskimo) community near the Beaufort Sea as well as a marine base for Arctic oil drilling. Atlas, Gray Line, and Rainbow Tours have tours from Whitehorse to Juneau and Fairbanks in Alaska. If you are in Juneau, Fairbanks, or Skagway, you can tour the Yukon from these points using Atlas, Gray Line, and Rainbow.

The following companies provide outdoor adventure expeditions—canoeing, backpacking, mountaineering, fishing, wildlife photography—in the rugged but magnificent Yukon:

Ecosummer Yukon Expeditions, (867) 633–8453
Coyote Adventure Travel, (867) 633–5642
Dalton Trail Lodge, (867) 667–1099
Kluane Adventures, (867) 634–2282
Oldsquaw Lodge, (867) 668–6732
Tatshenshini Expediting, (867) 633–2742
Yukon Mountain and River Expeditions, (867) 668–2513
Wolf Lake Wilderness Camp, (867) 249–4949

The following is a list of fishing lodges; lake trout is the prized catch:

Kluane Wilderness Lodge, (250) 828–1161
Peacock's Yukon Camps, (867) 667–2846

The following are registered hunting outfitters; the species are moose, caribou, Dall sheep, mountain goats, black bears, and grizzlies:

Caeser Lake Outfitters, (867) 536–2174
Dickson Outfitters, (867) 667–7414
Koser Outfitters, (867) 969–2908
Rouge River Outfitters, (867) 633–6286
Teslin Outfitters, (867) 390–2559

David Young Outfitters, (867) 668–4518
Yukon Outfitting, (867) 667–2712
Kusawa Outfitters, (867) 667–2755
Outfitting and guiding is a growing industry in the Yukon. Be sure to ask Yukon Tourism for its list of registered companies.

Government Campgrounds

On the Alaska Highway from Watson Lake to the Alaska border, there are numerous campgrounds. Their location is indicated by the kilometer mark location on the highway heading north from Watson Lake. Most campsites have drinking water, and some have special features, such as beaches and fishing.

Watson Lake, 1,024.9 km (637 mi)
Rancheria, 1,143.4 km (710 mi)
Teslin Lake, 1,309 km (813.1 mi)
Squanga Lake, 1,366 km (850.5 mi)
Marsh Lake, 1,429.6 km (888.4 mi)
Wolf Creek, 1,458.6 km (907 mi)
Takhini River, 1,542.6 km (958.6 mi)
Kusawa Lake, 1,542.6 km (958.6 mi)
Otter Falls, 1,602.2 km (995.6 mi)
Aishihik Lake, 1,602.2 km (995.6 mi)
Pine Lake, 1,628 km (1,013 mi)
Congdon Creek, 1,722.7 km (1,071 mi)
Lake Creek, 1,853.7 km (1,152.1 mi)
Snag Junction, 1,912.8 (1,188.8 mi)

There are also campsites on the Haines Road, Atlin Road 7, Tagish Road 8, the Klondike Highway, the Silver Trail 11, South Canol Road, the Robert Campbell Highway, and the Dempster Highway (contact Tourism Yukon, Box 2703, Whitehorse, Yukon Y1A 2C6, for details).

Special Events

January/February
Annual Yukon Quest Sled Dog Race, Whitehorse to Fairbanks, February.
Frostbite Music Festival, Whitehorse, February.

Yukon Sourdough Rendezvous, Whitehorse, mid-February. If you are in the Yukon this time of year, this event is a good one: dog-team races, Mad Trapper competitions (such as leg and arm wrestling), a Chilkoot climb, snowshoeing, a beard contest, fiddler competitions, cancan dancers, and sourdough-pancake breakfasts.

May
International Gold Show, Dawson City, late May.

June
Commissioner's Ball, Dawson City, early June.
Yukon International Storytelling Festival, late June.

July
Yukon Gold Panning Championships, Dawson City, July 1.
Horse Show, Whitehorse, late July.
International Midnight Dome Race, Dawson City, late July.
Annual Music Festival, Dawson City, late July.

August
Discovery Days, Dawson City, mid-August. Gold was discovered in the Klondike on August 16, 1896, and is worthy of this annual celebration—parades, raft and canoe races, tournaments, dances, and more.
Annual Yukon River Gold Rush Bathtub Race, Whitehorse, mid-August.

September/October
Klondike Trail of '98 Road Relay, Skagway to Whitehorse, early to mid-September. A mixed male and female relay race of 176 km/110 mi between the two cities.
The Great Klondike Outhouse Race, Dawson City, early September.

The Yukon's Special Attractions

Hiking the Chilkoot Trail
If you are the hardy type and are trekking the Yukon, hike the **Chilkoot Trail,** which is actually a slender slice of British Columbia between Alaska and the Yukon. The trail begins a few miles from

Dyea, north of Skagway, a major port of call for Inside Passage ships. If any single place embodies the struggle of hundreds of men trying to reach the gold fields of the Yukon, it is Chilkoot Pass. In old documentary films and photos, you can see hundreds of men trying to push themselves and their supplies up what seems like a wall. Many were injured and some killed in the attempt to cross over. At the summit, the Northwest Mounted Police set up a post where they weighed the supplies of each man. By police decree, each man had to have enough provisions to last one full year (about 2,000 pounds [900 kg]) in order to continue on. Those who were shy of the requirement were sent back down—to go home or start again. Some of these dreamers were so insistent on reaching the Yukon that they tried going over Chilkoot Pass in the dead of winter, with often-disastrous results. Today you can hike this trek in a leisurely manner to enjoy the magnificent scenery and to reflect upon the lives of the dreamers who came this way hungry for gold many decades ago. The trail itself will take you through rain forest, through alpine meadow, over talus rock up the pass, and then to the summit, the scene of so many victories and defeats. Reservations to climb the trail must be made with Heritage Parks Canada (800–661–0486). There is a $35 (Canadian) registration fee.

Kluane National Park

Kluane National Park is located at the junction of Highway 3 and the Alaska Highway 1, in the southwest corner of the territory, bordering British Columbia and Alaska. The key town for the park is Haines Junction, at Highways 1 and 3, 158 km/98 mi (a two-hour drive) west of Whitehorse. For more information, contact Superintendent, Kluane National Park, Haines Junction, Yukon Y0B 1L0, (403) 634–2251.

Kluane National Park is an immense wilderness. It has the highest mountains in Canada; Mount Logan, at 5,959 m (19,550 ft) in the St. Elias Range, is the nation's highest—and the second highest on the North American continent. Mount St. Elias was the first to be climbed—in 1897 by the Duke of Abruzzi. Mount Logan was climbed in 1925. Scientists from different disciplines and top climbers have been attracted for decades by the park's rugged and splendid ecology, and many come here every year to study and experience its natural wonders. The mountains within the park are among North America's youngest and most attractive, with faults averaging a thousand a year. You can see how the earth shifts in this area by watching the seismograph at the visitor center in Haines Junction. This is also a landscape of many glaciers, perhaps as many as 4,000. The snows laid down over thousands of years along the St. Elias Range have made the most extensive ice fields outside of the polar regions. The Kaskawulsh Glacier can be reached by a tough two-day hike. Along the Alaska Highway, from where most people see the park, the Front Range Mountains form a 2,400-m/8,000-ft wall that shields the St. Elias Range and Mount Logan from view. To get into the park and near Mount Logan by trekking takes excellent physical conditioning, much planning, and the right gear (contact the Sierra Club or similar organizations for information on how to take on this adventure so that it's safe and memorable). Another way to see Mount Logan is to fly over it with an air-tour service; some of these services are listed on pages 310–11 and pages 319–20.

Kluane National Park has large populations of grizzly bears, Dall sheep, and other wildlife. If you are camping in the park, keep the grizzlies away from your site by using proper procedures in storing food and garbage (see page 31). There's an Indian village on Klukshu Creek, thought to be the oldest settlement in this part of the territory. Several hiking trails lead off the Alaska Highway: the Rock Glacier Trail, the St. Elias Trail, the Auriol Range Trail, and the Sheep Mountain Trail. Silver City on Kluane Lake is a classic western ghost town, which you should visit. Shells of original buildings remain, as does a sense of the people who long ago put their hearts and souls into ventures that have drifted away with the winds. South of Haines Junction is Kathleen Lake, the park's major campground, open from mid-June to mid-September, with a maximum stay of two weeks. There are a number of other campgrounds along this eastern edge of the park. Motor boating and fishing are allowed on Kathleen Lake; canoeing is discouraged because of the rough water. Mountaineering parties who wish to climb the St. Elias and Icefield ranges must obtain a permit three months in advance from the Warden Service (write to the address given on page 313 for Kluane National Park). The Warden Service will want to know the health, physical condition, and skill of each member of your party; you must provide doctors' certificates and information on supplies and communication support. All precautions are essential because Kluane is the very essence of the Yukon wilderness. North of Haines Junction on the Alaska Highway at Destruction Bay and Burwash Landing is Kluane Lake, the largest lake in the Yukon.

Accommodations in the Haines Junction area (all have dining rooms) are **Mountain View Motor Inn,** (867) 634–2646 (moderate); **Cozy Corner Motel & Restaurant,** (867) 634–2511 (moderate); **Kluane Park Inn,** (867) 634–2261, (moderate); and **MacKintosh Lodge,** (867) 634–2301 (moderate).

All of the following accommodations in Destruction Bay and Burwash Landing have dining rooms:

Talbot Arm Motel, in Destruction Bay, (867) 841–4804. Moderate.

Burwash Landing Resort, (867) 841–4441. Moderate.

Kluane Wilderness Village, near Burwash Landing, (867) 841–4141. Moderate.

Pine Valley Motel, 87 km (54 mi) north of Burwash Landing, (867) 862–7407. Moderate.

Koidern River Fishing Lodge, 114 km (71 mi) north of Burwash Landing, (867) 862–7402. Moderate.

White River Motor Inn, 122 km (76 mi) north of Burwash Landing, (867) 862–7408. Moderate.

Scenic Highways

See page 32–33 for safety and driving tips on driving the gravel roads of the Yukon.

Taking the **Alaska Highway 1** from the southern provinces and states to the Yukon and Alaska is one of North America's great road adventures. Driving across the southwest corner of the Yukon from British Columbia to Alaska (Watson Lake to Beaver Creek) is a distance of 912 km/567 mi, a journey that can take several days if you don't rush but rather take the time to enjoy the natural beauty and heritage of the Yukon. There are plenty of services, accommodations, gas stations, and restaurants along the way. Be sure to visit Kluane National Park and to tour the city of Whitehorse.

The **Klondike Highway 2** from Whitehorse will take you to historic Dawson City, a boomtown in gold rush days. Both Jack London and the poet Robert Service had cabins here. From Dawson City you can take the **Top of the World Highway 9** into Alaska (road open only during the summer), which connects with Alaska Highway 1 and thence to Fairbanks. Carcross is the important town on this scenic highway. Its attractions include the Museum of Yukon Natural History, Frontierland Heritage Park, Carcross Desert, Matthew Watson General Store, and the Visitor Reception Center located in the Old Train Depot.

The **Haines Road Highway 3** goes from Haines, Alaska, the terminus of the Alaskan Marine Highway System, along the eastern edge of Kluane National Park to Haines Junction in the Yukon. From here you can travel the Alaska Highway north or south.

The **Robert Campbell Highway 4** moves in a northwesterly course from Watson Lake on the British Columbia border to the communities of Ross River, Faro, and Carmacks, which are in the south central part of the territory. When you reach Carmacks, you can take the Klondike Highway 2 north to Dawson City or south to Whitehorse.

The **Dempster Highway 5** is a true explorer's road, but you should take it only in the summer. If you follow the Dempster from Dawson City to the literal "end of the road," you will have crossed the Arctic Circle, entered the Northwest Territories, passed through Fort McPherson (the largest community in this part of the world) and over the mighty Mackenzie River, and made it to Inuvik, an Inuit (Eskimo) community where the road does end. From Inuvik you can take a flight to visit the remote Inuit village of Tuktoyaktuk. Between Dawson City and Fort McPherson there is one gas station and hotel, so plan accordingly. Check at the visitor center in Dawson City for suggestions for the trip, or consult your local auto club and environmental society (e.g., Audubon Society or Sierra Club). Finally, the road all the way is gravel, and a reliable, sturdy RV is your best transportation, although any vehicle will do for the trip as long as it is mechanically sound and equipped with at least two spare tires. There are government campgrounds at strategic points. The only commercial lodge facility is at Eagle Plains.

Watson Lake

Watson Lake is the gateway to the Yukon from the provinces and the states. Its major attraction is a forest of posts covered with many signs pointing to cities throughout the world and giving the distance to each one. This tradition was started by a lonely American GI working on the construction of the Alaska Highway (25,000 Americans and Canadians worked on the highway). On the one hand, standing at this signage display, one would think that Watson Lake is the navel of the earth. On the other hand, if you are here, it surely is. Don't leave without having someone take a photo of you by the sign.

Alaska Highway Interpretive Centre, (867) 536–7469. If you are traveling all the way to Fairbanks or on long sections of the highway through the Yukon, this is a good place to get oriented to what's ahead and to learn the history of this tremendous engineering and construction effort.

The new **Northern Lights Center,** (867) 536–7522, is the only planetarium in North America featuring the myth and science of the northern lights.

The following accommodations have dining rooms:

Belvedere Motor Hotel, (867) 536–7712. Moderate.

Gateway Motor Inn, (867) 536–7744. Moderate.

Watson Lake Hotel, (867) 536–7781. Moderate.

Whitehorse

Whitehorse, capital of the Yukon Territory, is located on the Alaska Highway and on the Yukon River, which meanders for 3,185 km/1,980 mi north to the Arctic Ocean. This city owes its birth and initial development to the Klondike gold rush of the late 1800s. Both the river, on which plied steamboats, and a railroad, built from Skagway, made Whitehorse a vital transportation and supply center for the rapidly growing population attracted to the region by visions of getting rich quick. When gold mania subsided, enough people remained to make Whitehorse a permanent settlement, although by 1941 the population fell to fewer than 800 persons. Today the city's population is about 22,000. For a short while, copper mining pumped new life into the local economy, but that also ended. During World War II, Whitehorse became part of the Northwest Staging Route, a chain of airfields that briefly brought in thousands of Canadian and U.S. construction workers. The Alaska Highway, the major land route linking this region with the provinces and states to the south, made Whitehorse a primary transportation center. Whitehorse has fine hotels and restaurants for travelers and a number of interesting attractions. When in town, the folks at the new **Yukon Visitor Reception Center,** 1,475.7 km (917 mi) Alaska Highway, (867) 667–2915, will answer your questions and assist you in whatever way they can.

The official season for most Whitehorse attractions listed below is from mid-May to about mid-September:

Yukon Permanent Art Collection, Yukon Government Administration Building. Northern landscapes and life-styles from promising Canadian artists. Open weekdays, 8:30 A.M. to 5:00 P.M.

Yukon Gardens, off the Alaska Highway, (867) 668–7972. The trees, flowers, and other plants of the Yukon are beautifully displayed. There's also a gift shop.

Whitehorse Heritage Walks, (867) 667–4704. A walking tour will show you many of the historic homes and buildings of the city.

Frantic Follies Vaudeville, (867) 668–2042, in the Westmark Whitehorse Hotel. A Gay Nineties revue with high-kicking cancan dancers, magic shows, Robert Service humor, and wacky skits. This is the best show in town.

MacBride Museum, First Avenue and Wood Street, (867) 667–2709. There are artifacts and photos from the gold rush period, including Sam McGee's cabin (McGee was a local character, celebrated in Robert Service's poem "The Cremation of Sam McGee"), as well as a display of stuffed and mounted Yukon animals.

Old Log Church Museum, Third Avenue and Elliott Street, (867) 668–2555. Opened in 1900, this Anglican church served Whitehorse for sixty years. It now contains artifacts, photos, and documents telling the story of missionary work in the territory and its development.

Sky High Wilderness Ranches, on Fish Lake, (867) 667–4321. Horseback and pony rides; camping by the lake.

SS *Klondike* Sternwheeler National Historic Site, in downtown, (867) 667–4511. Launched in 1929, this restored stern-wheeler was the largest used on the Yukon River. It has been fully fitted and furnished, and it is open for your inspection.

Takhini Hot Springs, located 27.4 km/17 mi from the city on the Klondike Highway 2, (867) 633–2706. This is the place to soothe your aching body in warm mineral waters. Bathing suits can be rented. If you want more aches along with some pleasure, you can go on guided trail rides from Takhini and then come back for a soaking.

Guided Nature Walks, 302 Hawkins Street, (867) 668–5678. The Conservation Society takes visitors on nature hikes in the Whitehorse area.

The new **Beringia Interpretive Center,** on the Alaska Highway, just south of Whitehorse Airport, is a multimedia exposition that features life-size exhibits of animals of the last Ice Age. Interactive CD-ROM kiosks and dioramas depict the unique landscape, flora, and fauna of Beringia. Highlights include a full-size cast of the largest mammoth ever recovered and a reconstruction of the 24,000-year-old Cluefish Caves archaeological site.

All of the following accommodations have dining rooms and other amenities:

Edgewater Hotel, 101 Main Street, (867) 667–2572. Moderate.

Gold Rush Inn, 411 Main Street, (867) 668–4500. Expensive.

Regina Hotel, 102 Wood Street, (867) 667–7801. Moderate.

Westmark Klondike Inn, 2288 Second Avenue, (867) 668–4747. Expensive.

Westmark Whitehorse Hotel, Second Avenue and Wood Street, (867) 668–4700. Expensive.

Yukon Inn Hotel, 4220 Fourth Avenue, (867) 667–2527. Moderate to expensive.

Dining possibilities in Whitehorse are varied:

Cellar Restaurant, at the Edgewater Hotel, 101 Main Street, (867) 667–2572. A gracious dining room in which are served excellent beef, steaks, lobster, and the regional specialty—king crab. Moderate to expensive.

Pandas Fine Dining, 212 Main Street, (867) 667–2632. European cuisine and seafood dishes. Moderate to expensive.

Village Garden Dining Room, at the Westmark Whitehorse Hotel, Second Avenue, (867) 668–4700. Prime rib, salmon, trout, steaks, salad bar. Moderate.

Talisman Café, 2112 Second Avenue, (867) 667–2736. European and North American cuisines. Moderate.

Travel services are available at the following:

Rental Cars

Budget, 4178 Fourth Avenue, (867) 667–6200/6220

Norcan Leasing, mile 917.4 Alaska Highway, (867) 668–2137

Avis, 306 Ray Street, (867) 946–3680

Camper Rentals

Klondike Recreational Rentals, 108 Industrial Road, (867) 668–2200

Ambassador Motorhome & Recreational Services, (867) 667–4130

Norcan Leasing, Mile 917.4, Whitehorse, (867) 668–2137

Whitehorse Motors U-Drive, 4178 Fourth Avenue, (867) 667–7866

CanaDream Campers, 110 Copper Road, (867) 668–3610.

Air Charter Services

This is a good way to experience the territory—Kluane National Park and northern Inuit settlements near the Beaufort Sea—if you're short on time.

Air North, (867) 668–2228

Alkan Air, (867) 668–2107

Peacock Air, (867) 667–2846
Kluane Airways, (867) 667–4070

Dawson City

Dawson City was called the City of Gold, the end of the rainbow for thousands of dreamers who flooded here seeking their fortune in the gold fields near the city. In its heyday, when it was a gold rush boomtown, people who knew the place called Dawson the Paris of North America, meaning that it offered many pleasures (albeit without the beauty and civilization of the real Paris). It was certainly one of the liveliest cities in North America. Among the colorful characters who made Dawson famous were Robert Service, Jack London, Diamond Tooth Gertie, Klondike Kate, and the Northwest Mounted Police. The stereotypical tales of Mounties chasing mad trappers and gold seekers came from here, as did (probably) the slogan "the Mounties always get their man." This was Dawson's exciting, frenetic, crazy, fascinating period. While some dreamers found gold along Bonanza Creek and other gold-rich streams, a large number went bust; but that's the risk dreamers always take, whether in search of gold or Shangri-la.

Today Dawson City is a civilized, proper place of commerce, but with enough gold rush charm to make it a "must" destination for visitors to the Yukon.

For information on things to see and do in Dawson City and on places to stay and dine, stop in at the **Visitor Reception Centre,** Front Street at King, (867) 993–5566.

Midnight Dome, located 8 km/5 mi from town via King Street, is an 884-m/2,900-ft mountain that overlooks Dawson City, the Yukon and Klondike rivers, Bonanza Creek, and many mountain ranges, such as the Ogilvies. This mountain is called the Midnight Dome because at midnight every June 21 the sun shines at the top. (Actually, it does so everywhere in this region, but the thrill is to be at the top of the mountain on June 21 at midnight and still be able to see the surrounding scenery because of the daylight.) The road up Midnight Dome is very steep, and extreme caution should be taken in driving. Your best bet is to use the services of a Yukon tour company.

Dawson City Museum, Fifth Avenue, (867) 993–5291, is the city's heritage museum, featuring exhibits telling the story of the gold mania that took place in this area, the city as a boomtown during this exciting period, and its development thereafter. Call for hours and fees. The museum also has a genealogy service for you to track down dreamers in your family tree—perhaps one who became wealthy beyond dreams.

Diamond Tooth Gertie's Gambling Hall is where you make a quick buck or lose a bundle while being entertained by wildly kicking cancan dancers and honky-tonk music. Open May to September. Call the Klondike Visitors Association, (867) 993–5575, for information. Gertie's is the best show in town and sufficient reason to visit Dawson. Gertie herself was a colorful and now-legendary "woman of the flesh" who was also a savvy business entrepreneur catering to the dreamers' needs for female company, strong drink, and games of chance.

Gaslight Follies, (867) 993–5575, provides an evening of good entertainment. Arizona Charlie Meadows built the Palace Grand Theatre at the turn of the century to provide high-class entertainment to the dreamers and wheeler-dealers of the Yukon. "Olde Tyme" shows are presented nightly, except Tuesday nights.

Bonanza Creek is located 22 km/14 mi away via the Klondike Highway and Bonanza Creek Road. Along here some prospectors found gold. Claims were based on this measurement: 10 BD, meaning "10 claims Below the initial Discovery"; 25 AD was "25 claims Above Discovery." In this area is dredge #4, purported to be the largest gold-recovery dredge in the world.

Visit the **Jack London Cabin,** (867) 993–5575. Call the Klondike Visitors Association for hours. Free. North America's immortal author Jack London had a cabin in the bush on Henderson Creek. It was later relocated to Dawson City, with half of the original structure going to Jack London Square in Oakland, California. London's books told of life in the Yukon and Alaska as a mystical struggle, of individual men and women against an unyielding environment and against their own limitations. Readings of London's works—*Call of the Wild* and others—are presented at the cabin.

Robert Service Cabin, (867) 993–5462, is also open to visitors. Call for hours. The poet Robert Service (1874–1958) is called the "bard of the Yukon." He wrote most of his poetry—"Songs of a Sourdough"—in his cabin, and there are daily recitals of his poetry. As you travel through the Yukon, the images Robert Service wrote about will be seen everywhere you go.

The *Yukon Lou,* Yukon River Cruise, (867) 993–5482, is a miniature stern-wheeler that gives visitors tours on the Yukon River, where the graveyard of old stern-wheelers can be seen. It also offers a cruise to Eagele, Alaska and return, with a salmon barbecue at Pleasure Island.

Harrington's Store, Third Avenue and Princess Street, has a photo exhibit showing early boomtown days in Dawson City.

Stamps can be purchased at the historic **1901 Post Office.** It is a favorite stop for stamp collectors.

Claim #33 Below Discovery is 10 km/6.2 mi up the Bonanza Road, (867) 993–5804. Call for hours and cost. Here you can pan for gold; pans and other gear are supplied, with some gold in every pan.

Early Day Adventures, (867) 993–5423, located 10 km/6.2 mi from town on Bonanza Creek Road, gives an escorted tour of an operating mine.

At **Guggieville,** (867) 993–5008, located 2 km/1.2 mi outside town on Bonanza Creek Road, you can pan for gold at what was Guggenheim's mining camp, which operated in the early 1900s.

Gold City Tours, (867) 993–5175, offers tours of Dawson, Bonanza Creek, and the Midnight Dome.

All of the accommodations listed below have dining rooms and other amenities:

Dawson City Bunkhouse, Princess Street, (867) 993–6164. Newly built, reasonable prices, one block from downtown. All amenities. Moderate.

Downtown Hotel, Second Avenue and Queen Street, (867) 993–5346. Expensive.

Eldorado Hotel, Third and Princess Street, (867) 993–5451. Expensive.

Klondike Kate's, (867) 993–6527. Moderate.

Midnight Sun Hotel, Third and Queen Street, (867) 993–5495. Moderate.

Westmark Inn, (867) 993–5542. Expensive.

Here are restaurants that you may want to sample:

Nancy's, (867) 993–5633. Homemade soups, sandwiches, pastries, ice cream. Also herbal teas and flavored coffees; sourdough-pancake breakfasts. Inexpensive.

Pleasure Island Restaurant, reached by the *Yukon Lou* boat tour, (867) 993–5482. (See page 318.) Salmon barbecues. Moderate.

Beaver Creek

Beaver Creek is the last town of any size on the Alaska Highway at the Yukon-Alaska border. The **Westmark Inn,** (867) 862–7501, has good rooms, a restaurant, dinner theater, RV park, minigolf, store, and a lounge. Expensive.

The Northwest Territories

An Arctic Adventure

The landmass and water areas composing the Northwest Territories are so vast that one could place much of Europe inside with plenty of room left over. The Northwest Territories span the North American continent from the Yukon in the west to Greenland in the east. On the southern border, along the sixtieth parallel, are the provinces of British Columbia, Alberta, Saskatchewan, Manitoba, Ontario, Quebec, and Newfoundland-Labrador. The islands of Hudson Bay are also part of the Northwest Territories. Within the Northwest Territories are Great Slave Lake, Great Bear Lake, the Mackenzie River, Baffin Island, Ellesmere Island, Victoria Island, Prince of Wales Island, Banks Island, the Parry Islands, and the Sverdrup Islands. About half of the region is above the Arctic Circle. The area is the site of the fabled Northwest Passage, from Europe to the Orient. This is the land of the Inuit (Eskimo) and the Déné, a place where countless explorers, from Franklin to Byrd, have sought fame. The Northwest Territories is one of the harshest yet most magnificent regions on earth. Much of it defies extensive land touring because of a lack of roads; however, thanks to aviation, many exceptional natural areas and remote communities are accessible within a few hours of such cities as Edmonton, Winnipeg, Toronto, Ottawa, and Montreal. This part of the chapter describes the western portion of the Northwest Territories.

The western portion of the Northwest Territories borders the Yukon to the west; British Columbia, Alberta, and Saskatchewan to the south; the Beaufort Sea and the Amundsen Gulf to the north; and the Coppermine River and eastern shores of Great Slave Lake to the east. The high Mackenzie Mountains and the Franklin Mountains rise up in the west; a boreal forest makes a swath across the southern zone; the Mackenzie River, including Great Bear and Great Slave lakes, are among the earth's great water systems; and the Beaufort Sea, part of the Arctic Ocean, provides many kilometers/miles of shoreline.

Here is an Arctic climate with long, extremely cold winters. Nonetheless, midsummer days can have temperatures up to 30°C/89°F. Summers tend to be warmer in the Mackenzie River Valley. A tundra environment, during warm weather, does produce mosquitoes. If you are trekking and camping, it is a good idea to

323

wear bug jackets to cover exposed skin areas and use repellent lotions and sprays. Once you overcome this annoyance, you'll love every moment of your stay. July and August are the best months for visiting the Northwest Territories, although many people start coming in mid-May and keep the season going until late September. If you want a real adventure, come here in winter, go dogsledding or snowmobiling, view the spectacular northern lights, or sleep in an igloo you made yourself. When traveling here during the summer, comfortable casual clothes are best, including a sweater or two, a windbreaker, and good hiking or walking shoes with cushioning socks. Cameras with telephoto lenses and binoculars are also important bring-alongs.

There are 64,402 people living in the Northwest Territories, giving the region one of the lowest population densities per square mile on earth. The capital of the Northwest Territories is Yellowknife, located on the north shore of Great Slave Lake, with highway access to British Columbia and Alberta (and thence to all major North American centers). Yellowknife became the capital of the Northwest Territories when the office of federal commissioner was transferred from Ottawa to this city. Its population is now 18,000 persons. Fort Smith, Hay River, Fort Simpson, and Inuvik are western Northwest Territory communities with populations between 2,000 and 3,000 persons. There are only sixty-four communities in all of the Northwest Territories. People make their living here from mining, fishing, tourism, arts and crafts, hunting, and trapping. The native people of this part of the Northwest Territories are famous for such arts and crafts as moose-hair tufting, porcupine-quill work, traditional embroidery and beadwork, fine leathercraft, and fur-garment making.

The Northwest Territories: Some Basic Facts

The Northwest Territories will be split into two northern territories in 1999. Stretching from the Manitoba border to the northern tip of Ellesmere Island, the newly named portion, Nunavut, will be larger than any other province or territory. The land-claim settlement from which the split results gives the Inuit outright ownership to about 18 percent of the land while the remaining 82 percent remain Crown lands. It is the largest and richest native land claim ever in Canada. And, notably, the friendliest and most peaceful division in history.

The current Northwest Territories represent one-third of Canada, or a land area equal to that of the nation of India.

Fort Smith had the highest recorded temperature in the Northwest Territories: 35.4°C/95.7°F; it also had the lowest recorded temperature: minus 53.9°C/minus 65°F.

The Mackenzie River is 1,800 km/1,118 mi long. When considered as including Slave, Peace, and Finlay rivers, it is about 4,216 km/2,635 mi long, the second-longest river in North America.

Great Bear Lake is the ninth-largest lake in the world.

Great Slave Lake is the sixth-deepest lake in the world.

The Northwest Territories entered the Canadian Confederation on July 15, 1870.

The first white explorers were the Vikings, in about A.D. 1000. In 1576, Martin Frobisher was the first of a long stream of explorers who came here searching for the Northwest Passage. Samuel Hearne and Alexander Mackenzie both trekked over much of the uncharted land during the eighteenth century. John Franklin and his expedition in the mid-1800s tried to find the Northwest Passage, but the party disappeared in the Arctic and the search for them was a major cause célèbre for many years. In 1984 the frozen, almost perfectly preserved body of one of Franklin's sailors was discovered in Nunavut. Other nineteenth-century explorers included M'Clure, Amundsen, Sverdrup, and Stefansson.

Tourist Information

For travel information, contact the Northwest Territories Tourism, Box 1320, Yellowknife, Northwest Territory X1A 2L9, or call (800) 661–0788, (867) 873–7200, fax (867) 873–0163.

In Yellowknife you can rent cars from Avis, Budget, Hertz, and Tilden. Call your local rental-car agency for rates and reservations.

Useful Information

Area code: 867
Time zone: Mountain (western Northwest Territories), Central, and Eastern

Nahanni National Park

There is no access by land vehicle into Nahanni National Park, as it is essentially a wilderness park, but you can experience some of the park's natural wonders, such as Virginia Falls, by using the services of an air charter or an adventure tour organization providing canoe or wild-river rafting trips. Wild-river tours on the South Nahanni are considered among the top adventure experiences in North America; some of the companies providing Nahanni trips are listed on pages 310–11 and page 319–20. Fort Simpson is the base of operations for air and many other expeditions into the park, and the town can be reached via Highways 7 or 1. Float-plane tours can also be booked at Watson Lake in the Yukon and Fort Nelson in British Columbia. July and August are the best months in which to visit the park. If you are not an experienced wilderness traveler, it is advisable to explore the Nahanni with a guided tour group. The tour and outfitting services are well versed and supply commentary on the park, its features, and history. For more information on the park, contact Superintendent, Nahanni National Park, Box 300, Fort Simpson, Northwest Territories X0E 0N0, (403) 695–3151.

An exceptional North American wilderness park, Nahanni was the first such area in the world to be designated by UNESCO in 1979 as a natural site of universal importance. One of the wildest waterways in the park is the South Nahanni River, which charges over 322 km (193 mi) before plunging down Virginia Falls, twice the height of Niagara Falls. Downriver from the falls are 8 km (4.9 mi) of turbulent rapids and waves. It is not unusual to see wild orchids blooming next to patches of snow near Virginia Falls. The park also has four great canyons, which are as deep as 1,200 m (3,935 ft). Rabbitkettle Hotsprings and Wildmint Hotsprings are other natural features. The waters gushing up from Rabbitkettle are 20°C/68°F and form a terraced mount of tufa rock that is more than 27 m (88.5 ft) high. The park has thirteen species of fish, such as Arctic grayling and Dolly Varden trout; more than 120 species of birds, including the golden eagle and trumpeter swan; and more than forty species of animals—wolves, grizzly and black bears, caribou, and beaver. Although now a wilderness park, Nahanni during

◀ There is a sense of the eternal about the Inuit living in Nunavut. It seems as if they have always been here and always will be.

327

the gold rush days was combed over by dreamers in search of fortune, mostly to no avail. Their travails gave names to places in the park, such as Deadmen Valley and Headless Creek.

Adventure Touring Services

If you are not planning and executing your own wilderness expedition, the best way to experience this region is through the services of a tour operator in both the NWT and Nunavut who will provide transportation, lodging, meals, outfitters, and knowledgeable commentary. There are both standard packages and those tailored to your interests—hunting and fishing, ski touring, dogsledding, camping, trekking, and so forth. Among the advantages of using professional services is that the guides usually know where such animals as caribou, musk oxen, wolves, buffalo, and bears (including polar bears) can be seen. These guides can take you to remote villages, where you can see something of a way of life existing without major change for thousands of years. They know where to go, how to get there, and what to see. These services maximize your vacation experience in an incredibly rich area that, a few years ago, seemed remote and inaccessible.

Adventure Canada, in Toronto, (800) 363–7566. Canoe or raft adventure trips to Nahanni National Park via the South Nahanni River.

Arctic Tour Company, in Inuvik, (867) 979–4100/summer (800) 661–0721. Mackenzie Delta naturalist tours, festival and cultural tours, town tours, Dempster Highway tours.

Arctic Nature Tours, in Inuvik, (867) 979–3300. Tour packages on Dempster Highway, Mackenzie Highway, Richardson Mountains, Banks and Herschel islands.

Arctic Waterways, in Coquitlam, B.C., (800) 661–6659. Rafting the Nahanni, Horton, Coppermine, and Anderson rivers.

Black Feather Wilderness Adventures of Toronto and Ottawa, (800) 574–8375. Guided canoe trips down the Nahanni, Natla-Keele, and Mountain rivers.

Canoe Arctic, in Fort Smith, Northwest Territories, (867) 872–2308. Fly-in canoe trips and cross-country skiing.

A moose is startled by an approaching canoe. ➤

Great Slave Sledging Company, in Yellowknife, (867) 920–4542. Fishing and camping adventures on the remote western shore of Great Slave Lake. Also offers winter experiences: dogsled trips and skiing expeditions.

Hudson Bay Tour Company, in Rankin Inlet, (867) 645–2618. Variety of tour packages from dog-team trips to fishing expeditions, art to historical.

Northcott Tour Planning & Consulting, in Iqualuit, (867) 979–6261. Custom-designed tours for groups and individuals—dogsledding, kayaking, hiking, fishing, hunting.

Northwinds Arctic Tours, in Iqualuit, (867) 979–0551. Summer and winter package adventures that share the culture and beauty of Baffin Island.

Raven Tours, in Yellowknife, (867) 873–4776. Several day-trip options. "City of Gold" tour, Cameron Falls hike, dog-team rides, fishing, bird–watching, cruises on Great Slave Lake, "flightseeing," caribou viewing, and aurora borealis tours.

Sub-Arctic Wilderness Adventures, in Fort Smith, Northwest Territories, (867) 872–2467. Great Slave circle tour, boating the Slave, trip to Wood Buffalo National Park, dog-team wilderness trip, Tazin highlands, and sub-Arctic spring experience.

Nahanni River Adventures, in Whitehorse, Yukon, (867) 668–3180; (800) 287–6927. Trips on the Nahanni River by canoe.

Yellowknife

On the north shore of Great Slave Lake, with a population of close to 16,000, Yellowknife is the capital of the Northwest Territories. It was founded in 1934 as a result of a minor gold rush. In the area are two operating gold mines. Yellowknife is a good base from which to explore remote areas of the western part of the Northwest Territories. There are adequate accommodations, restaurants, shops, and services in town. Also visit the **Bush Pilot's Monument,** a memorial to the pilots who, in the early days, explored and assisted in the development of the Northwest Territories. For further information on Yellowknife, contact the NWT Tourism Office at (800) 661–0788.

How to Get to Yellowknife

By Car or Recreational Vehicle

Yellowknife is the hub city for visiting the western portion of the Northwest Territories. Most roads and air routes lead to and radiate from Yellowknife. If you are interested in driving to the northwest corner of the region (Fort McPherson, Arctic Red River, and Inuvik), use the Dempster Highway from Dawson City, Yukon (see the description of this route in the Yukon section, page 316).

If you are traveling the Alaska Highway and reach Fort Nelson in British Columbia, you can take Highway 7 North past Nahanni National Park and then to the Mackenzie Highway 1 East, which leads to Highway 3 and then 4 to Yellowknife. If Yellowknife is your primary destination in the north and you are traveling from the east, your best route is the Mackenzie Highway 35 North from Edmonton, Alberta, which connects with Northwest Territories Highways 1, 3, and 4 to the city (see the safe driving tips in chapter 2). Mackenzie Highway is paved to Rae with ongoing construction and paving upgrades during the summer months between Fort Providence and Rae, Northwest Territories.

Road distances to the Northwest Territories border using the Mackenzie Highway are listed below:

Edmonton: 990 km/615 mi
Calgary: 1,276 km/793 mi
Vancouver: 2,330 km/1,448 mi
Winnipeg: 2,357 km/1,465 mi
Toronto: 4,582 km/2,848 mi
Montreal: 4,734 km/2,942 mi
Los Angeles: 3,960 km/2,461 mi
Alberta border: 528 km/316 mi

By Plane

Daily air service to Yellowknife from Edmonton and Calgary is provided by Canadian Airlines and NWT Air. Air service within the Northwest Territories is provided by charter and scheduled airlines, such as Calm Air, Air Providence, First Air, Air Tindi, Buffalo Airways, Northwestern Air Lease, and Ptarmigan Airways. For details, call NWT Tourism's toll-free line (800–661–0788) or your travel agent.

In addition to jet planes, commonly used aircraft in the region are twin-engine Otters, the workhorse of the North; Piper T

1040; F-28; Gulfstream 1; DC-3; Metro II; Navajo Chieftain; Aztec; Cheyenne III; De Havilland Turbo; and Cessna 185. Many of these planes are equipped with floats so that they can land in water in remote areas where there are no airfields. In the winter, skis can be used. Flying in the Northwest Territories can be an adventure in itself, and the pilots here are among the finest in the world.

Special Events in Yellowknife

Midnight Sun Golf Tournament, mid-June

    Raven Mad Daze, celebrating the solstice, mid-June

    Folks on the Rocks, Déné and Inuit folk singers and performers, mid-July

    Commissioner's Cup Race, a sailboat race on Great Slave Lake, September

    Festival of the Midnight Sun, second week in July

Attractions

Prince of Wales Northern Heritage Centre, named in honor of HRH Prince Charles, (867) 873–7551. Open throughout the year. The collection in this museum includes artifacts from Inuit, Déné, and Métis cultures, early mining and aviation history, and other aspects of the ecology and human heritage of the Northwest Territories.

    Bush Pilot's Monument. Atop a solid mass of Precambrian Shield. Follow Ingraham Drive up to the top and then climb the stairs for a spectacular view of Great Slave Lake, the Yellowknife skyline, including Nerco Con Mine, Giant Mine, and Old Town. The monument honors bush pilots who opened the north to industry and exploration.

    Wildcat Café. Opened in 1937 and operated as a café into the 1960s, it then reopened briefly when bush pilots returned to Yellowknife for the dedication of the Bush Pilot's Monument in 1967. Today the café is open only during the summer months.

    Northern Frontier Visitors Centre. Across the causeway from the Prince of Wales Northern Heritage Centre, the new Visitors Centre is full of information on local adventure tours, lodges, and things to do in the city. The building itself has a stylish spiral gallery in which to view photos and read information.

    Yellowknife Courthouse. Just a block away from the Visitors

Centre is the courthouse where, on the second floor, you can view the Sissons-Morrow collection of Inuit carvings depicting cases heard by the NWT's first resident supreme court judge. The collection was given to the people of the north after Judge J. H. Sisson died in 1969.

NWT Legislative Assembly Building. Officially opened in November 1993, the permanent home of the Legislative Assembly is in a natural setting on the shore of Frame Lake, a short walk from the center of Yellowknife. Tours are available at no charge.

Arctic Art Gallery, 5016 Fiftieth Street, (867) 873–5666, displays original paintings and prints from northern artists.

Yellowknife Book Cellar, in Panda II center, (867) 920–2220, specializes in books about the north.

Northern Images, in the YK Center on Franklin Avenue, (867) 873–5944, sells soapstone sculptures, Inuit prints, parkas, and wall hangings.

Accommodations in Yellowknife

Discovery Inn, 4701 Franklin Avenue, (867) 873–4151. Moderate to expensive.

Executive House, 4920 Fifty-fourth Avenue, (867) 920–3999. Completely furnished suites. Moderate to expensive.

Explorer Hotel, Forty-first Street at Forty-ninth Avenue, (867) 873–3531. Moderate to expensive.

Northern Lites Motel, 5115 Fiftieth Street, (867) 873–6023. Moderate to expensive.

Igloo Inn, Franklin Street, (867) 873–8511. Moderate to expensive.

Yellowknife Inn, Fiftieth Street at Fiftieth Avenue, (867) 873–2601. Moderate to expensive.

Yellowknife has several bed-and-breakfast establishments if it's a homey atmosphere that you want.

A&H Great Slave Lake B&B, 87B Morrison Drive, (867) 920–7160. Lakefront house.

Captain Ron's B&B, 8 Lessard Drive, (867) 873–3746. On the shores of Great Slave Lake and near the Wildcat Café.

The Prospector B&B, 3306 Wiley Road, (867) 920–7620. In historic Old Town, across from the Wildcat.

Lodges within the General Yellowknife Area

The following lodges are for anglers and those who want to get away from it all. The accommodations are comfortable, and the food is great. Fishing equipment, guides, and boats are provided as needed. Services and facilities vary; call ahead for full details and reservations.

Blachford Lake Lodge, on Blachford Lake, (867) 873–3303

Frontier Fishing Lodge, on Great Slave Lake, (867) 465–6843

Indian Mountain Fishing Lodge, on Great Slave Lake, (702) 459–8354

MacKay Lodge, on MacKay Lake, (867) 873–8533

Prelude Lake Lodge, (867) 920–4654

Trophy Lodge, on Great Slave Lake, (867) 873–5420

Watta Lake Lodge, (867) 872–5330

Key Communities and Accommodations

All the accommodations cited in this section have dining rooms and other amenities and are priced in the high-moderate to expensive range:

Fort McPherson (reached via Dempster Highway from Dawson City, Yukon) was the northern terminus for Northwest Mounted Police patrols from Dawson City during the early part of this century.

Inuvik means "place of man." Alexander Mackenzie canoed by here in 1789 on his way to the Arctic Ocean. Today the town is the government, commercial, and transportation center for the Western Arctic. It is also a supply base for oil and gas exploration in the Beaufort Sea and headquarters of the Inuvialuit, the first group to receive a land-claim settlement in the Northwest Territories. Accommodations are available at **Eskimo Inn,** (867) 979–2801; **Finto Motor Inn,** (867) 979–2647; and **Mackenzie Hotel,** (867) 979–2861.

Tuktoyaktuk is a remote community on the shores of the Beaufort Sea, only 160 km/99 mi south of the polar ice cap. From here you can see Canada's famous pingos, hills pushed up by heaving permafrost. Visit *Our Lady of Lourdes* mission boat. Alaskan Inupiat descendants and whale-hunting Karngmalit people live the traditional life of hunting, trapping, sealing, fishing, and reindeer herding. **Hotel Tuk Inn,** (867) 977–2381, and **Pingo Park Lodge,** (867) 977–2155, are places to stay here.

Fort Simpson is the center for trips into Nahanni National Park. Established in 1804, it is the oldest continuously occupied community on the Mackenzie River. Pope John Paul II visited the people of Fort Simpson, fulfilling a promise made after a previous stop had to be cancelled because of bad weather. **The Nahanni Inn,** (867) 695–2201, is located here, as is the **Maroda Hotel,** (867) 695–2602.

Fort Smith provides road access to Wood Buffalo National Park (see page 196 for a description). Most of the park is in Alberta, but about one-third is in the Northwest Territories. Fort Smith is located on the eastern border parts, on the Northwest Territories–Alberta border. The town itself was once a part of a chain of fur-trading posts, and Alexander Mackenzie explored this area in his search for the Pacific Ocean. The **Thebacha Campus of Arctic College** is now part of Fort Smith's life. While in Fort Smith, visit the **Northern Life Museum,** (867) 872–2859, and **North of 60 Books,** (867) 872–2606, which has a large selection of books, maps, and charts of the North.

Pinecrest Hotel, (867) 872–2320, also provides accommodations.

Hay River is the southernmost port on the Mackenzie River system. Visit the coast guard headquarters in town. Sandy beaches are on Great Slave Lake, which is good for swimming in the summer, and a golf course is in town. You can drive to Hay River from the South or take a flight from Edmonton, Alberta, on any day of the week. **Hay River Hotel,** (867) 874–6022, and **Ptarmigan Inn,** (867) 874–6781 or (800) 661–0842, provide accommodations.

Index

Abbreviations used in this index

B.C. = British Columbia
N.W.T. = Northwest Territories
Sask. = Saskatchewan
Y.T. = Yukon Territory

Abbotsford, B.C., 61
accommodations, 17, 19
calculating costs, 17
Accordion Festival, International Old-time, B.C., 81
Aero Space Museum of Calgary, 205
Agassiz Provincial Forest, Manitoba, 293
Ainsworth, B.C., 79
Air Canada, 25, 99
airport services, 26
Calgary International, 198
Edmonton International, 232
Regina, 263
Saskatoon, 271
Vancouver International, 99
Victoria International, 146
Whitehorse, 308
Winnipeg International, 286
Air Show
Abbotsford International, B.C., 61
Saskatchewan, 258
Vanderhoof International, B.C., 182
Alaska Highway, 60
safety suggestions, 32–33
Alaska Highway Interpretive Centre, Y.T., 316
Alberni Valley Museum, B.C., 170
Albert, Prince, 184, 251
Alberta, 184–241
attractions, 198–96
climate, 187
economy, 187–88
geography, 187
history, 184–87
map, 186
population, 187
tourism information, 14, 188
Alberta Legislature Building, Edmonton, 235

Alberta Pioneer Railway Museum, Edmonton, 235
alcohol and drug laws, 20
Alert Bay, B.C., 176
Alexander Mackenzie Heritage Trail, B.C., 86
All Fun Waterslide Park, Victoria, 157
Alpine Slide, B.C., 81
Annual Scottish Gathering, B.C., 83
Aquatic Hall of Fame, Winnipeg, 288
Apex Alpine, 89
Art Gallery of Greater Victoria, 155
Art Gallery of the South Okanagan, B.C., 71
Assiniboine Forest, Winnipeg, 292
Assiniboine Park, Winnipeg, 292
Assiniboine Park Zoo, Winnipeg, 289
Athabasca Oil Sands region, Alberta, 195
attractions, calculating costs, 18–19
auto clubs, 30–31
auto insurance identification, 46
automatic teller machines, 49
Aviation Museum, Western Canadian, Winnipeg, 291

Baker, Russ, 182
Bamfield, B.C., 171
Banff, Alberta, 213–24
Banff Festival of the Arts, Alberta, 219
Banff Mount Norquay, 215–16
Banff National Park, Alberta, 213–24
accommodations, 221–22
dining, 223–224
entertainment, 224

museums, 219–20
shopping, 224
special events, 219
sports and recreation, 215–19
tourist information, 221
Banff Springs Hotel, Alberta, 222
Barkerville Historic Park, B.C., 86
Bastion Square, Victoria, 155
Bateman, Robert, 220
Batoche National Historic Park, Sask., 255–56
Battleford, Sask., 254, 261
Battle of Little Bighorn, 9, 197, 251, 253
Bavaria City Mining Railway, B.C., 82
B.C.–Alberta border, 74, 84
B.C. Lions, 137
B.C. Transit, 104
B.C.–Yukon border, 87
Beacon Hill Park, Victoria, 157
bear safety, 31
Beaver Creek, Y.T., 322–323
bed and breakfast
country home/farm vacations, 125
Reservation Services Victoria, 160
Belaney, Archibald Stansfield, 252
Bella Coola, B.C., 85–86
Bennett, R. B., 245
bicycling and tours
Banff, 217
Jasper, 228
Vancouver, 140
Big Foot, 62
Big White Ski Resort, 89–90
Birds Hill Provincial Park, Manitoba, 293
Black Nugget, B.C., 168
Bloedel Conservatory, Vancouver, 119

Blossom Festival, B.C., 79
boat cruises and tours
  Banff, 217–18
  Dawson City, 321
  Jasper, 228
  Manitoba, 282–83
  Regina, 264
  Vancouver, 107–109
  Whitehorse, 318
Bonanza Creek, Dawson
  City, 321
British Columbia, 54–91
  climate, 55
  economy, 56
  geography, 55
  map, 57
  population, 54
  touring, 58
  tourist information, 14,
    56, 58
  winter sports, 89–91
British Columbia Forest
  Museum, B.C., 167
British Columbia Lions,
  137
British Columbia World
  Trade and Conven-
  tion Centre, Van-
  couver, 96
British North America
  Act, 7
Burnaby Village Museum,
  Vancouver, 125
Bush Pilots Monument,
  Yellowknife, 331
business hours in Canada,
  51
Butchart, Jennie, 151
Butchart Gardens,
  Victoria, 150–51
Cache Creek, B.C., 60, 63,
  84
Calaway Park, Calgary, 205
Calgary, Alberta, 196–212
  access, 98, 200
  accommodations, 206–7
  attractions, 203–6
  dining, 207–8
  entertainment, 208–9
  extraspecial events,
    202–3
  history, 197–98
  how to get around in,
    200–201
  map, 201
  professional sports, 210
  recreation, 210, 211
  shopping, 209–210
  touring service, 203

tourist information, 201
useful information, 202
Calgary Cannons, 210
Calgary Centre for Per-
  forming Arts, 208
Calgary Exhibition and
  Stampede, Alberta,
  202–203
Calgary Flames, 210
Calgary Science Centre,
  202
Calgary Stampeders, 210
Calgary Tower, 201, 203
Calgary Zoo, Botanical
  Gardens, and Prehis-
  toric Park, 204
Calona Wines, B.C., 67
Campbell River, B.C., 174
Campbell River Museum
  and Archives, B.C.,
  175
Campbell, Robert, 304
camping, 19
  Banff, 217
  Harrison Hot Springs,
    B.C., 62
  Jasper, 229
  Manitoba, 293
  N.W.T., 328
  safety suggestions, 31
  Sask., 248
  Vancouver, 131
  Victoria/Vancouver
    Island, 167
  Y.T., 310–11
Camrose, Alberta, 193
Canada Customs
  clearing, 40
  passport or visa, 44
  personal exemptions,
    41–44
Canada Olympic Park/
  Olympic Hall of Fame,
  Calgary, 206
Canada 3000, 25
Canadian Airlines, 25
Canadian Confederation,
  55, 244, 262
Canadian Consulate
  General in U.S. cities,
  15–17
Canadian Craft Museum,
  125
Canadian Pacific Rail-
  road, 6, 95, 262
Cape Merry National His-
  toric Site, Manitoba,
  298
Capilano Suspension

Bridge, Vancouver,
  120
Cardston, Alberta, 190
Carillon, Victoria, 157
Carlton Trail, 255
Carr, Emily, 93
Casabello Wines, B.C., 67
Castlegar, B.C., 78
Cathedral Grove, B.C., 170
caving, 175
CBC radio station, 33
Cedar Creek Winery, 67
Centennial Centre, Win-
  nipeg, 287
Centennial Museum,
  Alberta, 193
Centennial Museum, B.C.,
  69
Centennial Square,
  Victoria, 156
Centre Cultural Franco-
  Manitobain,
  Winnipeg, 289
Charles, HRH Prince, 332
Château Lake Louise, Al-
  berta, 222–223
Chemainus, B.C., 168
Cherry Festival, B.C., 77
Children's Zoo,
  Vancouver, 122
Chilkoot Trail, Y.T.,
  312–13
Chinatown
  Vancouver, 113–14
  Victoria, 156
  Winnipeg, 288
Churchill, John, 298
Churchill, Manitoba, 297
Churchill Northern Stud-
  ies Centre, Manitoba,
  298–99
Churchill, Winston, 298
City of Trail Museum,
  B.C., 77
City of Vancouver
  Archives, 123
Claim #33 Below Discov-
  ery, Dawson City, 322
Claremont Estate Winery
  and Vineyards, 67
Cleveland Dam, B.C., 121
climate and weather
  Alberta, 187
  B.C., 55
  Manitoba, 280
  N.T., 323–24
  Saskatchewan, 247
  Vancouver, 92
  Victoria, 142

Y.T., 307
C.O. Card Home and Museum, 190
Cochrane Ranch, Alberta, 193
Comico Gardens, B.C., 82
Comox, B.C., 174
Constitution Act of 1982, 39
Continental Divide, 76
Cook, Captain James, 11, 94, 95, 155, 175
Courtenay, B.C., 174
Cowichan Valley Museum, B.C., 168
Craigdarroch Castle, Victoria, 156
Craigflower Manor Farmhouse, Victoria, 156
Craigflower School, 156
Craig Heritage Park, B.C., 170
Cranbrook, B.C., 80
Cranbrook Railway Museum, B.C., 80
Creston, B.C., 79
Creston Valley Museum, B.C., 79
Creston Valley Wildlife Management Area, B.C., 79
Crowfoot, Chief, 254
Crowsnest Highway, B.C., 60
Crowsnest Pass, Alberta, 90
Crystal Casino, Winnipeg, 291–92
Crystal Garden, Victoria, 154
Cypress Hills Massacre, 253
Cypress Hills Inter–Provincial Park, Sask., 190, 254

Dalnavert Museum, Winnipeg, 290
Dauphin, Manitoba, 299
Dawson, Sir George Mercer, 248
Dawson City, Y.T., 320–22
accommodations, 322
attractions, 320–22
dining, 322
tourist information, 320
tours, 322
Dawson City Museum, 320–21

Deighton, "Gassy Jack," 94
Dempster Highway 5, Y.T., 316
Devon, Alberta, 193
Devonian Botanic Gardens, Alberta, 193
Devonian Gardens, Calgary, 204–5
Dewdney Trail, 62
Diamond Tooth Gertie, 320
Diamond Tooth Gertie's Gambling Hall, Dawson City, 321
Diefenbaker Canada Centre, The, 273
Diefenbaker House, Sask., 252
Diefenbaker, John George, 244
dining, 20
Dinosaur Provincial Park, Alberta, 190–91
District Museum, B.C., 174
Dominion Astrophysical Observatory, Victoria, 156
Dominion Lands Act, 244
Dominion Radio Astrophysical Observatory, B.C., 71
Douglas, James, 143
Douglas, Thomas (Lord Selkirk), 280
Doukhobor Heritage Village, National, Sask., 290–61
Doukhobor Historical Museum, B.C., 78
Drake, Sir Francis, 11
driving
auto clubs, 30–31
auto insurance identification, 46
clearing customs, 39
into Western Canada, 26–27
on gravel roads, 32–33
license, 40
rules of the road, 30
Drumheller, Alberta, 193
Duck Lake Regional Interpretive Center, Sask., 261
Duke of Abruzzi, 313
Dumont, General Gabriel, 256
Duncan, B.C., 167

Dunsmuir, Robert, 156
Early Day Adventures, Dawson City, 322
Edmonton, Alberta, 230–41
access, 232
accommodations, 238
attractions, 234–37
dining, 239
entertainment, 239
history, 230–31
how to get around in, 232
map, 233
population, 231
professional sports, 240
recreation, 241
shopping, 240
special events, 233–34
useful information, 233
Edmonton Art Gallery, 235
Edmonton Eskimos, 240
Edmonton Oilers, 240
Edmonton Police Museum, 235
Edmonton Space Sciences Centre, 236
electricity use, 51
Elizabeth II, Queen, 36, 38
Elk Falls Provincial Park, B.C., 175
Elk Island National Park, Alberta, 195
Emerald Lake Lodge, B.C., 75–76
emergencies, 30
Emily Carr Gallery of the Provincial Archives, Victoria, 155
employment in Canada, regulations, 40
Empress, The, Victoria, 157–58
Erickson, Arthur, 124
Exchange District, Winnipeg, 285
Expo '86, 4, 95

Fable Cottage Estate, Victoria, 156–57
Fairmont Hot Springs Resort, B.C., 82
Fantasy Garden World, Vancouver, 124
Father Pandosy Mission, B.C., 69
ferries to Victoria/Vancouver Island, 145–46

festivals
  Creston blossom, B.C.,
    79
  International Old-time
    Accordion, B.C., 81
  Manitoba, 283
  Okanagan, B.C., 66
  Osoyoos cherry, B.C., 77
  Pysanka, Alberta, 196
  Sask., 248–50
  Vancouver, 105–7
  Victoria, 149
  Y.T., 311–12
Fidler, Peter, 244
fishing
  Banff, 218
  Jasper, 228
  N.W.T., 328–30
  Sask., 247
  Victoria, 164
  Y.T., 310
fishing lodges, Yellow-
  knife, 334
fishing regulations, 35
fishing, salmon
  Campbell River, 174
  Kitimat, B.C., 181
  Port Alberni, B.C., 171
  Vancouver, 139
Fleming, Sir Sanford, 225
Folklorama, Winnipeg,
  284
forest fire safety, 31
Forks, The, Winnipeg, 291
Fort Augustus, 231
Fort Battleford National
  Historic Park, Sask.,
  254–515
Fort Calgary, Calgary, 204
Fort Carlton Historic
  Park, Sask., 261
Fort Churchill, Manitoba,
  298
Fort Edmonton Park, Ed-
  monton, 235
Fort Fraser, B.C., 182
Fort George, B.C., 182
Fort Langley National His-
  toric Park, B.C., 61
Fort Macleod, Alberta, 191
Fort McMurray, Alberta,
  195
Fort McPherson, N.W.T.,
  334
Fort Nelson, B.C., 87
Fort Pitt Provincial His-
  toric Park, Sask., 261
Fort Qu'Appelle Museum,
  Sask., 260

Fort Rodd Hill National
  Historic Park and
  Fisgard Lighthouse,
  Victoria, 157
Fort Rupert, B.C., 176
Fort St. James, B.C., 182
Fort St. John, B.C., 87
Fort Simpson, N.W.T., 335
Fort Smith, N.W.T., 335
Fort Steele Historic Park,
  B.C., 81
Fort Walsh National His-
  toric Park, Sask., 253
Fort Whoop-up, Alberta,
  191
Fort Whyte Centre for
  Environmental Edu-
  cation, Winnipeg, 292
Franklin, Sir John, 244
Franko, Ivan, 291
Frantic Follies Vaudeville,
  Whitehorse, 318
Fraser River Valley, B.C.,
  60
Fraser, Simon, 182
Frenchman Butte Historic
  Site, Sask., 261
Frobisher, Martin, 326
Frog Follies, Manitoba,
  284
Fun Mountain Waterslide
  Park, Winnipeg, 293

Galbraith, John, 81
Galiano Island, B.C., 110
Gaslight Follies, Dawson
  City, 321
gasoline, 35
Gastown, Vancouver, 115
geography of Western
  Canada, 4–6
Ghost River wilderness
  area, Alberta, 194
Gibsons, B.C., 59
Gimli, Manitoba, 301
Glacier National Park,
  B.C., 73
Glass Castle, B.C., 168
Gleichen, Alberta, 194
Glenbow Museum, Cal-
  gary, 203
Golden, B.C., 74
"gold fever," 95
Gold River, B.C., 175
Goldstream Provincial
  Park, 167
golf
  Banff, 218
  Calgary, 210

Edmonton, 241
Jasper, 227
Regina, 269
Vancouver, 138
Victoria, 163
Winnipeg, 297
gondola sightseeing
  Banff, 219
  Jasper, 227
  Whistler Resort Area,
    B.C., 110–11
Goods and Services Tax, 22
Gordon Southam Obser-
  vatory, Vancouver, 122
government, 36–39
Government House,
  Regina, 266
Government House,
  Victoria, 155
Grace Campbell Art
  Gallery, Sask., 252
Grand Beach Provincial
  Park, Manitoba, 301
Grande Cache, Alberta,
  194
Grand Forks, B.C., 77
Grand Trunk Pacific Rail-
  way, 182
Granville Island, Vancou-
  ver, 114–15
Grasslands National Park,
  Sask., 250–51
Gray Monk Estate Cellars,
  B.C., 67
Great Cariboo Ride Soci-
  ety, B.C., 85
Great Divide Waterfall,
  Edmonton, 236
Grey Owl, 252
Grouse Mountain Recre-
  ational Area, Van-
  couver, 89, 120
Guggieville, Dawson City,
  322
Guided Nature Walks, 318
Gulf Islands, B.C., 109

Haines Road, Y.T., 316
Hall of Fame
  Aquatic, Winnipeg, 288
Hanceville, B.C., 85
Hardy, Vice Admiral Sir
  Thomas Masterman,
  176
Harrington's Store, Daw-
  son City, 322
Harrison Hot Springs Re-
  sort Area, B.C., 62
Hay River, N.W.T., 335

"Head Smashed In" Buffalo Jump, Alberta, 192
health insurance, 45–46
Hearne, Samuel, 299
Hecla Provincial Park, Manitoba, 301
Helen Schuler Coulee Centre, Alberta, 191
helicopter skiing/hiking
Banff, 216
B.C., 90
Jasper, 227
Vancouver, 90
Hell's Canyon Airtram, B.C., 63
Helmcken House, Victoria, 152
Hemlock Valley, 89
Henry, G. W., 66
Heritage Park, Calgary, 204
Hind, Henry, 244
history of Western Canada, 6–12
holidays, national and provincial, 46–47
home/farm vacations, 19
Hoodoos, Alberta, 194
Hope, B.C., 60, 62
hostels
Banff, 218
Regina, 268
Hotel Vancouver, 101
hot springs
Ainsworth, B.C., 79
Banff, 219
Fairmont, B.C., 82
Harrison, B.C., 62
Jasper, 227
Nakusp, B.C., 73
Radium, B.C., 83
Takhini, Whitehorse, 318
Hughes, J.W., 67
hunting
regulations, 35
Yukon Territory, 310

Inside Passage, 177
International Air Show, B.C., 61
International Old-time Accordion Festival, 81
International Peace Garden, Manitoba, 302
Inuvik, N.W.T., 334
Invermere, B.C., 82
Islending a dagurinn, 283,
Ivan Franko Museum, Winnipeg, 291

Jack London Cabin, Dawson City, 321
Jasper, Alberta, 228
Jasper National Park, Alberta, 224
accommodations, 229
dining, 229
entertainment, 230
shopping, 230
sports and recreation, 225
Jasper Park Lodge, Alberta, 229
John Janzen Nature Centre, Edmonton, 235
John Paul II, Pope, 335
John Walter Museum, Edmonton, 236

Kamloops, B.C., 60, 63
Kamloops Museum and Archives, B.C., 65
Kamloops Waterslide and R.V. Park, B.C., 65
Kamloops Wildlife Park, B.C., 65
Kaposvar Historic Site Museum, Sask., 260
Kelowna, B.C., 68
Kelsey, Henry, 244
Kenderdine Gallery, Sask., 273
Kicking Horse Pass, B.C., 76
Kildonan Park, Winnipeg, 293
Kildonan Presbyterian Church, Winnipeg, 292
Kimberley, B.C., 81
Kimberley Heritage Museum, B.C., 82
King George VI Provincial Park, B.C., 77
Kinsmen Discovery Centre, Winnipeg, 289
Kipling, Rudyard, 192
Kitimat, B.C., 181
Kitimat Centennial Museum, B.C., 181
Kitwanga, B.C., 181
Klondike Days, Edmonton, 233
Klondike Highway 2, Y.T., 315
Klondike Kate, 322
Kluane National Park, Y.T., 313

accommodations, 315
Knox United Church, Winnipeg, 292
Kootenay Lake, B.C., 79
Kootenay National Park, B.C., 75
'Ksan Village, B.C., 181
Kurelek, William, 273
Kwah, Chief, 182
Kwakiutl Museum, B.C., 175

Lacombe, Father Albert, 195
Ladysmith Arboretum, B.C., 168
Ladysmith, B.C., 168
Lake, John, 270
Lake Louise, Alberta, 213–14, 216
accommodations, 222
ski area, 216
Lake, Sir James Winter, 231
Lakelse Provincial Park, B.C., 181
Lake Okanagan Resort, B.C., 69
Lake Winnipeg, Manitoba, 6, 301
Lanark Place, Sask., 256
La Vérendrye, Pierre Gaultier de Varennes de, 244
Leechtown Gold Rush Site, Victoria, 166
Legislative Assembly Building, Yellowknife, 333
Legislative Building, Regina, 265
Legislative Building, Winnipeg, 288
Lethbridge, Alberta, 191
Lighthouse Park, Vancouver, 119
Little Stone School House, Saskatoon, 272
Living Prairie Museum, Winnipeg, 289
London, Jack, Cabin, Dawson City, 321
Louise, Princess, 214, 263
Lower Fort Garry National Historic Park, Manitoba, 300
Lund, 60
Lynn Canyon Park, B.C., 121

MacBride Museum,
Whitehorse, 318
Macdonald, Sir Hugh
John, 290
Macdonald, Sir John A., 6,
262
Mackenzie, Sir Alexander,
11
Macleod, Colonel, 185
MacMillan Bloedel Place,
Vancouver, 119
MacMillan Planetarium,
Vancouver, 123
MacMillan Provincial
Park, B.C., 170
Maligne Lake (*See also*
Jasper National Park),
224, 224–25
Maltwood Art Museum
and Gallery, Victoria,
157
Manitoba, 278–302
attractions, 287–94
brief history, 280–81
climate, 280
economy, 281
geography, 278
map, 279
population, 281
special attractions,
297–302
special events, 283–84
touring services, 282
tourism, 281–82
useful information, 283
Manitoba Children's
Museum, Winnipeg,
291
Manitoba Moose, 296
Manitou Springs Mineral
Spa, Sask., 258
marina services, 33–34
Marine Drive, Victoria, 151
Marine drives, Vancouver,
107
Marine Museum of Mani-
toba, 300–301
Maritime Museum,
Vancouver, 122
Maritime Museum,
Victoria, 155
Markerville, Alberta, 194
Marmot Basin, Jasper, 225
Martin Mars Water
Bombers, B.C., 171
Massey, Geoffrey, 124
Mayne Island, B.C., 110
McGee, Sam, 318
Meadows, Arizona Char-

lie, 321
Medicine Hat, Alberta, 192
Medicine Hat Museum
and Art Gallery, Al-
berta, 192
Mendel Art Gallery, Saska-
toon, 272
Mendel, Frederick, 272
Mennonite Heritage Vil-
lage, 302
metric system, 33, 47–48
Middleton, General
Frederick, 255
Midnight Dome, Dawson
City, 320
Mile "0," Victoria, 144, 154
Miniature World, Victoria,
154
Mission/Hatzic area, B.C.,
62
money, 48–51
automatic teller
machines, 49–51
Canadian dollar, value
of, 48
conversion of currency
in Canada, 49
credit cards, 51
Moose Jaw, Sask., 258
Morice, Father, 182
Mormon Temple, Alberta,
190
Morris, Edward, 265
Motherwell Homestead
National Historic
Park, Sask., 256
Motherwell, William
Richard, 256
mountaineering
Banff, 217
Jasper, 227
Mount Assiniboine, B.C.,
83
Mounties, 9–11, 184, 197,
255, 264
Mount Logan, Y.T., 313
Mount Norquay, Banff,
216
Mount Pope, B.C., 182
Mount Revelstoke Na-
tional Park, B.C., 73
Mount Robson, B.C.,
64–65
Mount St. Elias, 313
Musée Ukraina Museum,
Sask., 257, 272
Museum of Anthropology,
Vancouver, 121–22
Museum of Archeology

and Ethnology, 124
Museum of Man and Na-
ture, Winnipeg,
277–88
Museum of Northern
British Columbia, 179
Museum of the Regiments
(Lord Strathcona's
House), Calgary, 205
Museum of the Royal
Westminster Regi-
ment, B.C., 61
Muttart Conservatory,
Edmonton, 236
MV *Britannia*, 107
MV *Queen of the North*, 177

Nahanni National Park,
N.W.T., 327
Nakiska, Banff, 215
Nakusp Hot Springs, B.C.,
73
Nanaimo, B.C., 168–69
Nanaimo District
Museum, B.C., 169
National Doukhobor
Heritage Village,
Sask., 260–61
National Exhibition Cen-
tre, West Kootenay, 78
national historic parks
Batoche, Sask., 255
Fort Battleford, Sask.,
254
Fort Langley, B.C., 61
Fort Prince of Wales,
Manitoba, 298
Fort St. James, B.C., 182
Fort Walsh, Sask., 253
Lower Fort Garry,
Manitoba, 300
Motherwell Homestead,
Sask., 256
Rocky Mountain House,
Alberta, 194
national parks
Banff, Alberta, 213
Elk Island, Alberta, 195
Fort Rodd Hill and
Fisgard Lighthouse,
Victoria, 157
Glacier, B.C., 73
Grasslands, Sask., 250–51
Jasper, Alberta, 224–28
Kluane, Y.T., 313
Kootenay, B.C., 75
Mount Revelstoke, B.C.,
73
Nahanni, N.W.T., 327

Pacific Rim, B.C., 172
Prince Albert, Sask., 251–52
Riding Mountain, Manitoba, 299–300
Waterton Lakes National Park, Alberta, 212
Wood Buffalo, Alberta, 196
Yoho, B.C., 74–75
National Ukrainian Festival, Manitoba, 283
Naval Museum of Alberta, 205
Nechako Bird Sanctuary, B.C., 182
New Westminster, B.C., 61
Nickle Arts Museum, Calgary, 205
Nikka Yuko Japanese Gardens, Alberta, 191
1901 Post Office, Dawson City, 322
Nitobe, Inazo, 119
Nitobe Memorial Garden, Vancouver, 119
North Battleford, Sask., 261
Northern Frontier Visitors Centre, Yellowknife, 333
Northern Life Museum, N.W.T., 335
North Pender Island, B.C., 110
North Vancouver Parks, Vancouver, 120
North West Company, 8, 231
Northwest Mounted Police, formation of, 9
Northwest Rebellion, 7–8
Northwest Territorial Days, Sask., 262
Northwest Territories, 323–35
  adventure touring services, 328–30
  basic facts, 324–26
  climate, 323–24
  geography, 323
  national park, 327–28
  population, 324
  useful information, 323
Nunavut, 15, 324–26

Okanagan Game Farm,

B.C., 71
Okanagan/Similkameen region, B.C., 66–72
  festivals, 66
  wineries, 66–67
Okanagan Summer School of the Arts, 70
Okanagan vineyards, 68
O'Keefe Ranch, B.C., 66
Old Log Church Museum, Whitehorse, 318
Old Timer's Museum, Sask., 258
100 Mile House, B.C., 84
Oseredok (the Ukrainian Cultural and Education Centre), Winnipeg, 289
Osoyoos, B.C., 77
Osoyoos Lake, B.C., 77
Osoyoos Museum, B.C., 77
Otter, Colonel William, 254
Our Lady of Assumption Cathedral, Sask., 258

Pacific National Exhibition, Vancouver, 105
Pacific Rim National Park, B.C., 172
Pacific Spirit Regional Park, 123
Pacific Undersea Gardens, Victoria, 154
Palliser, Captain John, 244
Pandosy, Father Charles, 67
Panorama Resort, B.C., 83, 90
Parksville, B.C., 169
Parliament Buildings, Victoria, 151–52
Peachland, B.C., 70
Penticton, B.C., 70–71
Philip, Prince, 96
Phillips, W. J., 220
Point Ellice House, Victoria, 154
Point Grey, 121
Polar Park, Alberta, 194
Pond, Peter, 244
population (Canadian), 38
Port Alberni, B.C., 170
Port Hardy, B.C., 176
Port Hardy Museum and Archives, B.C., 176
Port Renfrew, B.C., 167, 171
postal service (Canadian), 51

Poundmaker, Chief, 254
Powell River, B.C., 59
Prince Albert National Park, Sask., 251–52
Prince Albert, Sask., 252
Prince George Art Gallery, B.C., 183
Prince George, B.C., 182
Prince of Wales Fort, Manitoba, 298
Prince of Wales Northern Heritage Centre, Yellowknife, 332
Prince Rupert, B.C., 178–80
Provincial Museum and Archives, Edmonton, 236
Pysanka Festival, Alberta, 196

Qualicum Falls Provincial Park, B.C., 170
Queen Charlotte Islands, B.C., 179
Queen Charlotte Islands Museum, B.C., 179
Queen Elizabeth Park, Vancouver, 118
Queen's Own Cameron Highlanders of Canada Museum, Winnipeg, 290
Quesnel, B.C., 86

radio stations (Canadian), 33
Radium Hot Springs, B.C., 83
ranch
  O'Keefe, B.C., 68
  Sky High, Whitehorse, 318
  Spruce Meadows Equestrian, Calgary, 205
  Top of the World, B.C., 82
Red Mountain Ski Area, B.C., 77
Red River, 281, 284–85
Red River Settlement, 280
Reg Atkinson Museum, B.C., 71
Regina, Sask., 262–70–67
  access, 263–64
  accommodations, 267–68
  art galleries, 266–67
  attractions, 264–67
  dining, 268–69

entertainment, 269
how to get around in, 264
professional sports, 269
recreation, 269–70
shopping, 270
touring services, 264
Regina Cyclones, 269
Regina Pats, 269
Regina Plains Museum, 266
Remington Alberta Carriage Centre, Alberta, 190
Revelstoke, B.C., 72–73
Revelstoke Art Gallery, 72
Revelstoke, Lord, 72
Revelstoke Museum, 72
restaurants, calculating costs, 18
Reynolds Alberta Museum, 194–95
Richardson, Dr. John, 244
Riding Mountain National Park, Manitoba, 298–300
Riel, Louis, 7–8, 289
Riel House National Historic Site, Winnipeg, 289
Riel Rebellion, 7–8, 255
Rittich, Dr. Eugene, 67
river rafting
Banff, 217
Jasper, 227
N.W.T., 328, 330
Sask., 247
Robert Campbell Highway 4, Y.T., 316
Robert Service Cabin, Dawson City, 321
Robson Square and Robsonstrasse, Vancouver, 115
Rocky Mountain House National Historic Park, Alberta, 194
rodeo
Calgary, 202
Edmonton, 240
Rogers, A. B., 73–74
Rogers Pass, B.C., 73–74
Rogers Pass Information Centre, B.C., 77–78
Rossland, B.C., 76
Royal British Colombia Museum, Victoria, 152
Royal Canadian Mint, Winnipeg, 289

Royal Canadian Mounted Police (RCMP), 9–11, 184, 197, 255, 264
museum, Regina, 264–65
Royal Hudson Steam Train, B.C., 107
Royal London Wax Museum, Victoria, 154
Royal Saskatchewan Museum, 266
Royal Tyrell Museum, Alberta, 193
Royal Winnipeg Ballet, 285, 296
Royal Winnipeg Rifles Regimental Museum, Winnipeg, 290
Rupert, Prince, 280
Rupert's Land, 281
Rutherford, Alexander Cameron, 231
Rutherford House, Edmonton, 236

Saint Albert, Alberta, 195
St. Andrews, Winnipeg, 292
Saint-Boniface Basilica, Winnipeg, 292
Saint-Boniface Museum, Winnipeg, 291
St. George's Anglican Chapel, 176
St. James Church, Winnipeg, 292
St. John's Cathedral, Winnipeg, 292
St. Laurent Shrine, Sask., 261
St. Michael's Ukrainian Orthodox Church, Manitoba, 300
St. Nicholas Ukrainian Catholic Church, Winnipeg, 292
St. Paul's Anglican Church, Winnipeg, 292
St. Thomas More Art Gallery, Saskatoon, 273
St. Victor Petroglyphs Historic Park, Sask., 260
St. Vladimir and Olga Cathedral, 292
sales tax, 22
Saltspring Island, B.C., 110

Samson V Maritime Museum, B.C., 61
Sam Steele Days, B.C., 80
Sandilands Provincial Forest, Manitoba, 293
Saskatchewan, 242–77
climate, 247
economy, 247
geography, 245
map, 243
national historic parks, 253–57
national parks, 250–63
population, 247
special attractions, 257–62
special events, 248–50
tourist information, 14, 247–48
Ukrainian connection, 257
useful information, 248
Saskatchewan Air Show, 258
Saskatchewan Archives, Regina, 266
Saskatchewan Centre of the Arts, Regina, 266
Saskatchewan Roughriders, 269
Saskatchewan Science Centre, Regina, 266
Saskatoon, Sask., 270–77
access, 271
accommodations, 273–74
attractions, 272–73
dining, 274–76
entertainment, 277
how to get around in, 272
shopping, 277
sports and recreation, 277
touring services, 272
Saskatoon Western Development Museum, 273
Sasquatch (Big Foot), 62
Saturna Island, B.C., 110
Sauvé, Jeanne-Methilde, 245
Schaffer, Mary, 225
Science World, 124
Scuba diving
Ucluelet, B.C., 171
Vancouver, 139
Vancouver Island, 173
Sea Festival, Vancouver, 106
Sechelt, B.C., 59

Selkirk, Lord, 280
Selkirk, Manitoba,
    300–301
Service, Robert, Cabin,
    Dawson City, 321
Seven Oaks House, Win-
    nipeg, 289
Shevchenko, Taras,
    statue, 289
Siffleur wilderness area,
    Alberta, 194
Siksika Museum of
    Human History,
    Alberta, 194
Simon Fraser University
    Campus, Vancouver,
    124
Sir Alexander Galt
    Museum, Alberta, 191
Sitting Bull, Chief, 9, 197,
    253
Ski Hall of Fame, 77
skiing, downhill
    Banff, 215–17
    B.C., 89–90
    Jasper, 225
    Vancouver, 138–39
skiing, Nordic and
    cross-country
    Banff, 215
    B.C., 91
    Jasper, 226
    N.W.T., 328
    Vancouver, 110–11
skiing, Snow-Cat, B.C., 91
Sky High Wilderness
    Ranches, Whitehorse,
    318
Smithers, B.C., 181
Snelgrove Art Gallery,
    Gordon, Sask., 273
Sooke, B.C., 166
Sooke Region Museum,
    Victoria, 166
Sport British Columbia,
    137–38
sports, professional
    Calgary, 210
    Edmonton, 240
    Regina, 269
    Vancouver, 137
    Winnipeg, 296–97
Spruce Meadows Eques-
    trian Centre, Calgary,
    205
Spruce Woods Provincial
    Heritage Park and
    Forest, Manitoba, 293
S.S. *Klondike* Sternwheeler

National Historic Site,
    Whitehorse, 318
Standard-bred and
    harness racing, 269
Stanley, Governor-
    General Lord, 116
Stanley Park, Vancouver,
    116–18
Steele, Samuel B., 80
Steele Narrows Provincial
    Historic Park, Sask.,
    261
Steinbach, Manitoba, 302
Steinbach Pioneer Days,
    Manitoba, 284
Stephansson House
    Provincial Historic
    Site, Alberta, 194
Stephansson, Stephan G.,
    194
Stephen Juba Park,
    Winnipeg, 293
Stettler, Alberta, 195
Strathcona Park, B.C.,
    175
Stuart, John, 182
study in Canada, regula-
    tions, 40
Sumac Ridge Estate Win-
    ery, B.C., 67
Sun Peaks Resort, 65
Sunshine Coast, B.C., 58
Sunshine Village, Banff,
    216
Symington, Frank
    Worthington, 288

Takhini Hot Springs,
    Whitehorse, 318
telecommunications, 51
telephone area codes, 23
Terrace, B.C., 180
Terrace Heritage Park,
    B.C., 180–81
Thebacha Campus of Arc-
    tic College, N.W.T.,
    335
Thompson, David, 81, 244
thoroughbred and har-
    ness racing
    Calgary, 210
    Edmonton, 240
    Regina, 269
    Vancouver, 137
    Victoria, 164
    Winnipeg, 296
Thunderbird Park, Victo-
    ria, 151
time zones, 23

tipping, about, 20
Tofino, B.C., 173
Tomison, William, 231
Topham Brown Art
    Gallery, B.C., 68
Top of the World
    Highway 9, Y.T., 315
Top of the World Ranch,
    82
tourism agencies, provin-
    cial and territorial,
    14–15
Tourism Saskatchewan,
    247–48
Trail, B.C., 77
trail rides
    Banff, 218
    Jasper, 227
    Manitoba, 282
Trans-Canada Highway 1,
    B.C., 60, 99
    Mile "0," 144, 154
transportation companies,
    major, 25
travel (*See also* Customs),
    agent, 24
    discount fares, 24
    package tours, cruises,
    vacations, 24–25
Travel Alberta, 188
Travel Manitoba, 281–82
Trickle Creek Golf
    Course, B.C., 81
Tsuu T'ina Culture Mu-
    seum, Calgary,
    205–206
Tuktoyaktuk, N.W.T., 335
Turner, John, 94
Turner Valley, Alberta,
    192–93
Tweedsmuir Park, B.C.,
    85
Tyrrell, Jospeh Burr, 193

Ucluelet, B.C., 171
Ukrainian Canadian
    Archives and Museum
    of Alberta, Edmon-
    ton, 236
Ukrainian connections,
    Sask., 257
Ukrainian Cultural and
    Educational Centre
    (Oseredok), Win-
    nipeg, 289
Ukrainian Cultural Her-
    itage Village, Alberta,
    195–96
Ukrainian Festival, Na-

tional, Manitoba, 283
Ukrainian Greek Ortho-
  dox Cathedral, Win-
  nipeg, 292
Ukrainian Museum of
  Canada (Alberta
  Branch), Edmonton,
  236
Ukrainian Museum of
  Canada, Saskatoon,
  273
U'Mista Cultural Centre,
  B.C., 176
University of British
  Columbia Museums,
  Vancouver, 123
  Anthropology Museum,
    121–22
  Nitobe Memorial
    Gardens, 119
  Pacific Spirit Regional
    Park, 123, 140
University of Lethbridge,
  Alberta, 191
University of Manitoba,
  Winnipeg, 291
U.S. Customs (reentry
  into U.S.A.), 44–45

Valley Zoo, Edmonton,
  236–37
Vancouver, B.C., 92–140
  access, 99–101
  accommodations,
    125–31
  attractions, 121–25
  basic facts, 98–99
  dining, 131–33
  entertainment, 134–36
  history, 94–98
  how to get around in,
    101, 104
  maps, 102–103
  neighborhoods, 116
  parks, gardens, beaches,
    116–21
  professional sports, 137
  recreation, 136–38
  shopping, 136–37
  special events, 105–107
  touring services,
    112–113
  tours outside of city,
    107–112
  useful information, 105
Vancouver Aquarium, 122
Vancouver Art Gallery,
  123
Vancouver Canadians, 137

Vancouver Canucks, 137
Vancouver '86ers, 137
Vancouver, Captain
  George, 11, 95
Vancouver Grizzlies, 137
Vancouver Island, 165–76
  camping at provincial
    parks, 167
Vancouver Millionaires,
  96
Vancouver Museum, 122
Vanderhoof, B.C., 182
Vanderhoof International
  Airshow, B.C., 182
VanDusen Botanical Gar-
  dens, Vancouver, 119
Van Horne, Sir William
  Cornelius, 95
Vernon, B.C., 67–68
Vernon Museum, B.C., 68
VIA Rail, 15, 25, 100, 147
Victoria, 109, 141–83
  access, 144–47
  accommodations,
    157–60
  attractions, 150–57
  basic facts, 144
  dining, 161–62
  entertainment, 163
  history, 143–44
  how to get around in,
    147–48
  map, 150
  shopping, 165
  special events, 149
  sports and recreation,
    163–64
  touring services, 149–50
  useful information, 148
Victoria Heritage Village,
  154
Victoria, Queen, 54, 184,
  214, 281
  statue of, 152, 289

Walsh, James, 253
Wanuskewin Heritage
  Park, Sask., 258,
  272–73
Ware, John, 193
Wasagaming, Manitoba,
  300
Wascana Centre, Regina,
  264
Waskesiu Lake, Sask., 251
water for drinking, 51
Waterton-Glacier Interna-
  tional Peace Park, 212
Waterton Lakes National

Park, Alberta, 212
Watson Lake, Yukon
  Terr., 316
  accommodations, 317
Wayside Garden and Ar-
  boretum, B.C., 79
West Coast Trail, B.C., 171
West Edmonton Mall, 234
Western Aero Center,
  Sask., 271
Western Canada
  geography, 4–6
  great cities, 12–13
  history, 6–12
  map, 2–3
Western Canadian
  Aviation Museum,
  Winnipeg, 291
Western Development
  Museum, Sask., 262
West Kootenay National
  Exhibition Centre,
  B.C., 78
Wetaskiwin, Alberta,
  194–95
Whale Town, B.C., 175
Whaling Station, B.C., 176
Whippletree Junction,
  B.C., 168
Whistler Resort Area,
  B.C., 89, 110–11
White Goat wilderness
  area, Alberta, 194
Whitehorse, Y.T., 317–20
  accommodations,
    318–19
  attractions, 317–18
  dining, 319
  travel services, 319–20
Whitehorse Heritage
  Walks, 318
Whiteshell Provincial
  Park, Manitoba, 293
White Water Trips, 83
Whoop-up Country, 253
Whyte Museum of the
  Canadian Rockies,
  220
Wickaninnish Centre,
  B.C., 172
Williams Lake, B.C., 85
Williams Lake Golf and
  Tennis Club, B.C., 85
Willmore Wilderness
  Park, Alberta, 194
Windermere Valley Pio-
  neer Museum, 82
wineries
  Okanagan/Similka-

meen region, B.C.,
66–67
Winnipeg Art Gallery, 291
Winnipeg Blue Bombers,
296
Winnipeg, Manitoba,
284–97
access, 286–87
accommodations, 294
attractions, 287–92
dining, 295
entertainment, 296
historic churches, 292
how to get around in,
287
map, 290
parks, 292–93
professional sports,
296–97
recreation, 297
shopping, 297
Winnipeg Cyclone, 297
Winnipeg Goldeyes, 297
Wood Buffalo National
Park, Alberta, 196
Wood Mountain Post
Historic Park, Sask.,

260
Wood Mountain
Stampede, Sask., 260
World Heritage Site
Burgess, Yoho National
Park, 74–75
Dinosaur Provincial
Park, Alberta, 190–91
"Head Smashed In"
Buffalo Jump,
Alberta, 191
Writing on Stone
Provincial Park,
Alberta, 193

Yale, B.C., 63
Yellowhead Pass, B.C., 65
Yellowknife Courthouse,
333
Yellowknife, N.W.T.,
330–35
access, 331–32
accommodations,
333–34
attractions, 332–33
dining, 332–33
shopping, 329

special events, 332
Yoho National Park, B.C.,
74–75
Yukon Gardens, White-
horse, 317–18
Yukon Lou Sternwheeler,
Dawson City, 321–22
Yukon Permanent Art
Collection, 317
Yukon Territory, 304–23
access, 308–9
basic facts, 307–8
camping, 311
climate, 307
geography, 306–7
map, 305
population, 306
scenic highways, 315–16
special attractions,
312–23
special events, 311–12
touring services, 310–11
tourist information, 15,
309
useful information, 309